128.3
D575t

ads ord 2·28·85

→The Theory of Will

in

Classical Antiquity

ALBRECHT DIHLE

D0709987

UNIVERSITY OF CALIFORNIA PRESS

Berkeley · Los Angeles · London

67770

c/16 x

University of California Press
Berkeley and Los Angeles, California
University of California Press, Ltd.
London, England
© 1982
The Regents of the University of California
Printed in the United States of America

1 2 3 4 5 6 7 8 9

Library of Congress Cataloging in Publication Data
Dihle, Albrecht.
    The theory of will in classical antiquity.
    (Sather classical lectures; v. 48)
    Bibliography: p.
    Includes index.
    1. Free will and determinism—History. 2. Philosophy, Ancient—
History. I. Title. II. Series.
B187.F7D54   128'.3   81-7424
ISBN 0-520-04059-7   AACR2

SATHER CLASSICAL LECTURES

Volume Forty Eight

The Theory of Will in

Classical Antiquity

CONTENTS

PREFACE

This book contains the text of six lectures which I had the honour of delivering at Berkeley in 1974. They are presented in a version considerably fuller than that which was given originally, although their oral style has been preserved.

I am glad to be given the opportunity to express my profound gratitude to all those who have kindly helped me, directly or indirectly, in producing and publishing the present book. First of all, I wish to thank the members of the Department of Classics of the University of California at Berkeley and their chairman in 1974, Professor T. E. Rosenmeyer. They elected me to serve as a Sather Professor at Berkeley, they extended their warm and generous hospitality to my family, and they made my stay at Berkeley stimulating and rewarding beyond all expectation.

Mr. (now Professor) G. W. Most kindly went through the whole manuscript in order to Anglicize—wherever this was possible—what I had formulated according to the rules of English elementary grammar. Moreover, he added valuable remarks and prevented me from many mistakes. The manuscript was finished in 1978.

The subject of the lectures is large and complex, and inevitably implies problems which are, strictly speaking, outside my competence. So I tried to make clear both in the text and notes whenever I had to depend on previous scholarship. Yet my being indebted to colleagues and friends extends far beyond these documented cases, especially in the field of theological and philosophical studies. In this area I was greatly helped and continuously instructed, over many years and quite independently from the production of this book, by Professor Hans von Campenhausen and Professor Günther Patzig. The errors and mistakes, however, which specialists are likely to discover in various passages of this book, are entirely my own.

I wish to thank Mrs. Karin Harmon for the great pains she took in producing the typescripts of several versions of the book, Miss Waltraut Foss and Dr. William Furley for sharing the tedious task of proof-reading and indexing, and the staff of the University of California Press for their accurate operation.

My wife made greater sacrifices for my scholarly work than anyone else. She also created the conditions under which this book could be produced.

I.
Cosmological Conceptions in the Second Century A.D.

BETWEEN A.D. 170 and 180 the famous physician Galen published, among other works, the treatise, *On the Parts of the Human Body*. In the chapter on the eyes he deals in great detail with the fact that eyelashes are characteristically different in size, number, and quality from any other kind of human hair, and points out that this very fact can be easily explained by the function of eyelashes in the human organism. His argument, therefore, is worked out entirely along the lines of Aristotelian or Stoic teleology.

In this context Galen inserts an interesting digression.[1] The Jews, he says, derive the origin and structure of the universe exclusively from the arbitrary intention of the divine creator.[2] He can transform a lump of earth into a horse or a bird or whatever he pleases. Creation depends solely and entirely on the will of the creator. This opinion, according to Galen, is certainly preferable to the aleatoric conception of Epicurus who attributes everything to chance.[3] But it is quite incompatible with Greek ideas of cosmology and cosmogony as expounded most clearly by Plato and Aristotle. The Greek creator or demiurge brings to reality only what reason evinces as being possible,[4] and from all possibilities he always chooses the best one.[5]

A hundred years earlier, in about A.D. 60 or 70, the Elder Pliny (*nat. hist.* 2.27) had already formulated the very same creed of Greco-Roman intellectuals without any reference to Jewish ideas. "Not even for God are all things possible . . . he cannot bestow eternity on mortals . . . he cannot cause twice ten not to be twenty or do other things along similar lines, and these facts unquestionably demonstrate the power of nature." Seneca (*ep.* 95.49) made a similar statement at nearly the same time, in Stoic terms and with special reference to the relation between God and man: *Errat qui deos putat nocere nolle; non possunt.* "They who believe the gods do not *want* to do harm are mistaken; the gods *cannot*." The nature of the gods makes it impossible for them to do

1

any harm, and even a god is not able to change his nature.[6] Cicero does, in fact, regard the will of the creator as the ultimate cause of man's distinguished position in the universe (*de leg.* 1.27). Yet this will does not mean arbitrary intention or unpredictable exercise of divine power. Every act of divine rule over the universe is but a detail of a comprehensive and perfectly rational programme by which is caused the order, the beauty, and the usefulness of the cosmos.

Theology in the tradition of Greco-Roman philosophy was hardly concerned with the problem of divine power, the most significant difference between man and God according to the fundamental religious experience: ἐπεὶ ἦ πολὺ φέρτεροί εἰσιν (since, in truth, they are mightier by far), to use a Homeric formula. Greek philosophical theology concentrated instead, from the very beginning, on the order, regularity, and beauty that are established and maintained through divine activity. Here Greek philosophy found the most striking, though understandable and almost predictable, manifestation of the divine—in contrast to ideas prevailing in many other religions (cf. Heraclitus B 114). At the end of the dialogue *De divinatione*, Cicero distinguishes between *superstitio* and *religio*: the first depresses the hearts of believers by making them afraid of the power and the unpredictable actions of the gods. The other leads to admiration and understanding of the order and beauty which are brought about by the divine rule (2.148).

This philosophical theology or cosmology rests on a basic presupposition: the human mind has to be capable of perceiving and understanding the rational order of the universe and, consequently, the nature of the divine. Everything that goes on in the universe has been arranged and initiated by the same reason that man has been given, so that he may understand his own position in the universe and act accordingly. There is no need for assuming behind or apart from the entirely rational programming of reality a will of which the impulse or manifestation is unpredictable. The word τὸ θέλον, used by the astrologer Vettius Valens (5.9) in order to denote what is going to happen according to the cosmic order, has not that connotation of will. Nature, cosmos, order of the universe, providence—all these concepts illustrate that everything happens only in consequence of a preconceived and rational arrangement without a separate will spontaneously interfering with the process. That presupposition is not invalidated by the fact that man, in his empirical condition, is not always capable of full appreciation of the cosmic order.[7]

That very conception underlies a great many philosophical theories. For the Stoics, for instance (Cleanthes ap. Sen. *ep.* 41.1, *quaest. nat.* 2.35), the purpose of prayer was only to ascertain the identity between reason as the ruler of the universe and reason as the leading force in the human soul. But even Platonists like Plutarch (*Is. et Os.* 1) or Maximus of Tyre (*or.* 5) who regarded prayer as a dialogue between two partners,[8] explicitly rejected the idea that prayer could influence or change the intention of God. Such a change could only lead to something worse, since God could not possibly improve on his own perfect rationality. Prayer had only to contribute to a fuller cognition of God. It seemed useless to a Platonist to comply with the intention of God without trying to understand it.

The practice of popular religion, in Greece and elsewhere, had always used prayer to influence or change rather than to understand the intention of the divinity involved. So prayer, in the popular sense, referred to the gods' power and benevolence and was not primarily meant to appreciate the immovable order of their government. The notion that divine rule over both cosmic and human affairs is perfect and rational was, after all, a concept resulting from philosophical speculation.[9] It was with regard to the popular notion of prayer that the physician and philosopher Sextus repeatedly contrasted prayer with telling the truth (*adv. math.* 7.401, *hyp.* 3.244 etc.). To pray according to popular practice means, from the philosophical point of view, to disregard the perfect order which the gods have established. Their power, sublimity, goodness—all result from their perfect rationality, according to the belief of Galen and his contemporaries.[10]

This belief, however, which Galen formulated to contest the Biblical concept of creation, was deeply rooted in the philosophical tradition, which had become, in the course of nearly five centuries, one of the main factors of general education. Both conceptions, the Greek and the Biblical, were monotheistic, despite their disagreement in many other respects. Whenever Greek philosophers became involved in theological problems, they ended, with a few exceptions, at the conception of a divine monarch of the universe.[11] Proclus, the Neoplatonist of the fifth century A.D., found this conception fully developed already in Homer (*in remp.* I p. 90.15 Kroll). But this supreme creator and ruler always restricts his activity, according to philosophical doctrine, by laws or rules which the human mind can understand as reasonable, good, and salutary. Such a creator, to be sure, has also the desire to create and to govern the universe. But he does not create *ex nihilo*. He molds what was without shape, he animates what was without life, he brings to reality what was merely a potential. And, above all, he does not transcend the order which embraces himself as well as his creatures.[12] Biblical cosmology,[13] however, was completely different. There is no standard, nor rule applicable to the creator and his creation alike. Creation results from the power and the pleasure or will of Yahveh, and from nothing else.[14] He can create, change, and destroy as He pleases, and it is only because of His benevolence towards His creatures that He has set some rules for the universe. "While the earth remaineth, seed time and harvest, and cold and heat, and summer and winter, and day and night, shall not cease" (Gen. 8:22; cf. Is. 54:9). A promise, however, given by Yahveh to his people, is infinitely more reliable than any rule the human mind can possibly detect in the order of nature (Is. 54:10): for "the mountains shall depart and the hills be removed; but my kindness shall not depart from thee, neither shall the covenant of my peace be removed, saith the Lord that hath mercy on thee."

Man can grasp these rules by his rational understanding and rely on them in his life, not because they are reasonable, but solely because of the promise of Yahveh.[15] According to a legend reported in the Talmud (b Sanh. 9a), the famous Rabbi Gamaliel tried hard to demonstrate to a Roman emperor how everything happens solely because of the will of God and why it does not make any sense to apply the categories of the possible, the reasonable, or the probable to anything that is caused by the will of God. Christian authors, too, treated the topic again and again: Everything comes into being, exists, and passes away—μόνου θεοῦ θελήσαντος (only because God wishes it) as St. Methodius said (*resurr.* 2.20.9).[16] It was not until the eleventh century that Christian theology distinguished between God's *potentia ordinata* and *potentia absoluta*,[17] of which only the former can be understood and evaluated by the human intellect.

Galen was the first Greek author of some intellectual standing who explicitly noted the specific difference between the Biblical and the Greek or philosophical concepts of creation—which is, indeed, astonishingly late. Biblical texts had been known in Greek translation many centuries previously,[18] so that the difference could easily have been discovered. Yet the very interest which some Greek intellectuals took in the Jewish tradition from the time of Alexander onwards led them to the opposite conclusion.

Wherever Greek philosophers or historians, in the Hellenistic and Roman periods, came in touch with elaborate exotic doctrines of cosmology and ethics, they regularly looked for surviving parts of the natural knowledge of the cosmos which all mankind had enjoyed in primeval times. They believed that this primeval philosophy is dimly remembered in the myths, legends, and proverbs of all people, and more distinctly so in the teachings of the priests and sages in foreign, above all Eastern, countries. The view was already held by Aristotle and applied, in the following centuries, to the Brahmans of India, the Magi of Persia, the Druids of Gaul, and of course, to the Mosaic religion, when these successively became known to the Greeks. Thus the doctrines of Greek philosophy could be proved true by their congruity with the old and venerable philosophy of the Barbarians.[19]

In the case of the Jews, even outbursts of strong antijudaic feelings—which became rather frequent, for political and social reasons, in the late Hellenistic and early Imperial periods—did not always affect the attitude of Greek philosophers toward what they called Jewish philosophy. With few exceptions they consistently sought to discover the fundamental agreement between Plato and Moses.[20] As can be seen in the extant fragments of Chaeremon and Apion, antijudaic writings of that period concentrated on denigrating the Jews' historical tradition and denouncing their alleged present crimes rather than on refuting Jewish concepts of God and man.[21]

On the other hand, Jewish authors who gave accounts of their own history and religion in Greek, sometimes even for a Greek public and with the aid of Greek literary patterns, were, for obvious reasons, sincerely interested in demonstrating that Moses and Plato had been teaching the same truth. Philo, for instance, desperately tried to reconcile the Aristotelian doctrine that the universe is preexisting and eternal with the Biblical concept of creation, and for Josephus, who also lived in the first century A.D., the various Jewish sects are schools of philosophers which differ from each other in their cosmology and their moral precepts in exactly the same way as Greek philosophers.

There are, however, passages in Greek texts of Jewish origin which stress the difference between Yahveh and the God of the philosophers. They state that God made the world out of nothing, and that it is blasphemous to apply the categories of reason to the will of God. But those texts which show a certain awareness of essential differences between Plato and the Bible all belong to polemical or apocalyptic literature and were not—or probably not—written for a non-Jewish public. This applies, for instance, to 2 Macc. 7:28 where the difference between Greek cosmology and the Biblical doctrine of creation is explicitly stated: God did not create the universe out of something already existing. Greek had become, after all, the native tongue of a great number of Jewish groups around the Mediterranean, and these were all familiar with Greek ideas about God and the universe.

Still, as late as the middle of the second century A.D., immediately before Galen wrote the passage quoted above, the famous saying according to which Plato is the Moses who speaks Attic (Μωυσῆς ἀτ- τικίζων)[22] was coined by the Platonist Numenius. The same tendency can be observed, at almost the same time, in the writings of Philo of Byblus (*FGH* 790 F 9) and also in the earliest Christian apologies, written by Athenagoras and Justin. The latter, a Samaritan by birth and well trained in both Jewish scholarship and Platonic philosophy, was firmly convinced of the basic congruity between Mosaic law, Greek philosophy, and the preaching of Christ. To him, Abraham and Socrates were Christians before Christ.[23] The divine Logos had spoken through them, as he did through Moses and the prophets, before he took the human body of Christ. Justin even believed that Plato's cosmological doctrine, as set forth in the *Timaeus*, was in full agreement with the first chapters of the Old Testament. God did not make the world out of nothing, Justin said (*apol.* 1.20.41, *dial.* 5); he gave shape and life to the preexisting matter. This view of Justin's is hardly compatible with the text of the Bible. St. Paul had explicitly stated the opposite (Rom. 4:17) a hundred years earlier, as did Philo at the same time (*prov.* 1.8, *div. her.* 160).[24] Yet Justin's view is typical of the syncretistic temper of this time, which embraced religion and philosophy alike.[25]

Galen's treatise, written between 170 and 180, only ten or fifteen years after Justin and Numenius, can therefore be said to indicate a new tendency. In A.D. 178 we find the Platonic philosopher Celsus writing the first detailed refutation of Christian religion. Like Galen, Celsus stressed the difference between the Greek and Biblical views of creation. According to Celsus, the Judaeo-Christian belief that God deals with the universe and mankind simply by His will or pleasure, is both absurd and blasphemous.[26] God does not arbitrarily dispose of anything, since all his activity is perfectly rational. This rationality indeed is the source of divine power, justice, and goodness.[27]

Celsus fervently rejected the Christians' claim that they had been given a special revelation which surpassed any rational understanding of reality.[28] Other religions, Celsus argued, can make the same claim. Once you remove the criteria provided by reason, you might just as well choose between various and even contradictory revelations by a throw of the dice. In fact, he says, there is only one truth, eternal and indivisible. Man can approach it, for he has been given the same reason which provides structure and life to the universe. Philosophy teaches how to use this precious gift, how to attain knowledge. It is only the very last step in the process of cognition leading to the source of being which cannot be taken without the "ineffable power" (ἄρρητος δύναμις). It supplements the rational forces of the soul, provided these have been trained and educated. There is no point in preaching a special truth for the ignorant, as the Christians do, and in circumventing the intellectual endeavor.[29]

In the view of Galen and Celsus, the Judaeo-Christian doctrine is entirely different from the teaching of the Indian Brahmans or Persian Magi, who all corroborated Plato's doctrine and gave testimony to the fact that men were able to recover, by means of philosophy, their primeval or natural knowledge of the cosmic order. Moses ceased to represent the venerable philosophy of the Barbarians,[30] for he does not, as Galen indignantly stated in another treatise of his, offer arguments that appeal to rational understanding. Moses only refers to what God has said or ordered (*On Hippocrat. Anatomy* [arab.] p. 10f Walzer).

How can we explain the fact that the fundamental difference between Plato and Moses, between Greek and Biblical cosmology, was not discovered or at least fully realized by the Greeks until about A.D. 170?[31] Christianity had not yet become, at that time, a serious rival to philosophy, though some men of learning and education were already appearing among Christian theologians. On the other hand, there was absolutely no motive for intensified feelings against Judaism in the second half of the second century. The disaster which had ended the uprising of Bar Kochba in Palestine in A.D. 135 definitively destroyed the basis of the exchange of ideas between Greeks and Jews which had lasted for more than four centuries. But the catastrophe also removed the social and political danger which had repeatedly arisen from Palestine and the Jewish diaspora in the period between Tiberius and Hadrian, and which had provided the background for the well-known antijudaism we find in Horace and Quintilian, Tacitus and Juvenal.[32] The relation between the Jews and Greco-Roman civilization ceased to be a problem for a long time to come.

That is why the discovery of the difference between Plato and Moses which we find, at the same time, in Galen and Celsus alike, is likely to have had its origin within Greek philosophy itself. In order to understand the change of attitude, we have to go back into the past.

Hellenistic civilization as it developed in consequence of Alexander's conquests had its most adequate philosophical expression in the doctrines of the Epicureans and Stoics. Both had much in common. Both were materialists. Both denied the possibility of individual human existence beyond the life of the body. Both tried to show the way towards happiness and moral perfection strictly within the limits of physical and empirical life.

There were, to be sure, longing for immortality, belief in the other world, fear of and hope for divine intervention, among the Greeks of the third and second centuries B.C., as well as in previous and subsequent periods, and there were also cults and creeds to meet these needs. But undoubtedly the rationalistic temper was a typical feature of that particular period, when science and technology attained a level not to be reached again until the nineteenth century, and Stoicism and Epicureanism rather than Platonism reflected the attitude of the educated.

But conditions changed in the first century B.C. From that time onwards, philosophy turned again to the question of whether man was able to attain immortality. Σωτηρία, salvation, a word which means "the preservation of physical integrity" in ordinary Greek, became a synonym of immortality.[33] To reach that goal through philosophy rather than religion was possible only in the steps of Plato. Platonism enjoyed a revival in the first century B.C.[34] and was to become the leading factor in intellectual life for many centuries. Platonic philosophy succeeded in adapting the Aristotelian tradition to its own purposes and in outliving both Stoicism and Epicureanism.

Immortality as a problem of philosophical investigation—not as a hope implied in religious faith—can be dealt with only in the context of the wider question of whether reality is to be found apart from the world as we perceive it by our senses. Such a reality, however, which would transcend empirical vicissitudes, has to be open to intellectual understanding. Immortality, a conception which clearly contradicts our experience, can only be conceived if the true self or the soul of man does, in fact, belong to this intelligible reality, and it is only the intelligible which bestows structure, life, and consciousness on our empirical world.

The answer Plato had given to that question is well known. He and his successors designed a model, according to which our empirical world owes its essence and existence to a higher one. The degree of reality represented by any individual physical or spiritual being can be ascertained or even measured by the human mind according to the standards of immutability, rational order, and eternity. Reality in the fullest sense of the word is to be found in the realm of eternal forms, which man can reach through his intellectual efforts. On the other hand, the material world as experienced by our senses has a very small share in reality, for every detail it includes is permanently changing, perishable, and far from being perfectly structured. The material world entirely depends, with regard to all its elements of structure, life and consciousness, on the inexhaustible creativity of the intelligible, of the divine intellect. Thus the whole realm of being can be compared to a pyramid: every individual being comes to existence through the creative power of a higher one which is more spiritual or less contaminated with matter and has, consequently, a greater share in reality.

But what about the Supreme Being on the top of the pyramid which is the ultimate cause for all other beings, both intelligible and material? Is it ἐπέκεινα τῆς οὐσίας as Plato said (Rep. 509 B), outside the realm of being, not determined from, caused by, or related to anything else? All this undoubtedly meets the definition of the Absolute or of an ultimate cause which is not caused by something else. But once you remove the Absolute from the realm of being, philosophy, based on reason, becomes unable to grasp it. Philosophy, in the Greek sense of the word, entirely depends on the principles that only what is can be thought of or intellectually perceived, and that there only is or exists what the mind can grasp by its intellectual efforts, whereas sensual perception may lead astray. Thinking and being are under the same rule of reason. Parmenides was the first to formulate this axiom, and it had been retained ever since in all dogmatic Greek philosophy.[35] If, then, the Absolute does not belong to the being itself, the intellect cannot possibly be able to grasp it.

Plato and his immediate successors had, in fact, dealt with the problem. But the whole question of the transcendent was largely neglected in the Hellenistic period, to be revived only at the turning point of philosophy in the first century B.C., when Platonism became the leading factor in intellectual life.[36] From that time onwards, no other problem was as intensely discussed for so many centuries as the question of how to perceive the Absolute from which all beings draw their existence. All the Middle Platonic and Neoplatonic system-builders tried hard to describe in detail the peak of the pyramid which represents the whole of reality. Only from this peak far above sensual experience in the realm of the intelligible could one hope to come to a proper understanding of the structure of both reality and human consciousness, and this knowledge was regarded, after all, as the basic presupposition for a moral and happy life. The whole argument of philosophy is about God, says Justin (*dial.* 1), and one of the most distinguished Platonic scholars of our own time briefly states that the system of Plotinus has to be understood as deduced from a number of theological axioms.[37]

Plato's ἐπέκεινα τῆς οὐσίας became the foremost topic in Middle and Late Platonic philosophy. Plato himself had described, in rather vague terms, how the philosopher is taken to this very summit of knowledge by sudden illumination. But this happens only to those who have accomplished all the previous steps of cognition by their own intellectual efforts, by a controlled and methodical use of reason. Revelation, which surpasses rational understanding, has its place only at the very end of a very long road. It is never given to spare a man, in the words of Aristotle (fr. 49 Rose), the slightest part of his intellectual efforts.[38]

Every piece of knowledge that has been acquired through rational understanding can be shared with other rational beings by means of language. What is revealed in that sudden illumination, however, can be spoken of only in the way of negation.[39] Language, reflecting thought, can only point at a being, whereas the Absolute is above any being. It is unlike all beings, *not* limited, *not* necessitated by anything else, *neither* only perceiving *nor* only perceived—and so forth. As Celsus said, it does not participate in being (ἀμέτοχος τῆς οὐσίας)[40] and cannot become, therefore, the substance of direct knowledge. The human mind can only arrive, through inference from the order of the universe, at some sort of indirect knowledge (ἐπίνοια) of the Absolute.

By separating the ultimate cause of being from being itself,[41] the Platonists were able to preserve the unity of being and thought on which Parmenides had based philosophy and firmly established the primacy of reason. Platonic doctrine was, in fact, developing on these lines throughout the Imperial period, regardless of the differences between schools, groups, and individual philosophers.

But the concept remained open to one serious objection. If the Absolute is not determined or necessitated by anything else, if it transcends both being and reason, it must be equally free to interfere with reality at any given level at any given time, simply because of its will or pleasure and regardless of the preestablished, rational order of being. Consequently, the Absolute must also be free to reveal itself to a human being, regardless of his intellectual standing and previous cognitive efforts. If the Absolute is really free, it is also free from the rational order on which both the universe and the human mind rely. Philosophy had to face the desperate twin task of keeping to the unity of thought and being and, at the same time, of grasping something beyond all being.

Many attempts were made in the second century A.D. to find a way out of the dilemma. Hermetics, Gnostics, and the so-called Chaldeans all created elaborate doctrines to show the way to the Absolute, and this exclusively in the context of a soteriological message. All these doctrines were composed of philosophical concepts and worked out by philosophical methods. They appealed, therefore, to a highly sophisticated audience. But at the same time, these doctrines were also proclaimed as coming from suprarational, supernatural, divine revelation. Men had first to accept the message; they had to become converts, regardless of their previous knowledge or their intellectual standing, before they could start to understand by themselves. The very act of acceptance was considered the first and decisive step towards perfect knowledge. But the act itself, though the essential presupposition of any progress on the way leading to salutary knowledge, could hardly be described as an intellectual achievement.[42] It was a turning of the mind, a decision rather than a cognitive effort, although instinct, emotion, or other parts of the lower strata of man's personality were not chiefly concerned. The message was meant to free man's true self, the rational part of his soul, from the bonds of matter and, consequently, from all irrational emotions and desires by which the individual was continuously contaminated with matter. The act of acceptance, therefore, could be adequately described only in terms of a theory of will. But precisely this was conspicuously absent from contemporary philosophy.

The new philosophy as taught by the Hermetics and other sectarians was, in fact, a religion. Its only purpose was to provide direct access to the Absolute which traditional philosophy had failed to offer. It was not meant to curb philosophical investigation. But since the truth had already been revealed in writings of divine authority, philosophical investigation had to expound these texts and deepen human understanding of them rather than to add, by its own intellectual efforts, to the amount of knowledge already available.

Scholarly-minded Platonists of that period had to fight hard against such a transformation of philosophy. The idea, though, that everything of importance had already been said by Plato or Aristotle, and that philosophy, at present, had only to find out, by means of interpretation, the true meaning of their doctrine, was familiar to the main branches of scholarly tradition, too, at least from the first century B.C. onwards, when philosophy turned to dogmatism again. The long series of editors and commentators of both Plato and Aristotle started at that time. But in that scholarly tradition even the essence of what could be called orthodox teaching was never regarded as divinely or supranaturally revealed. Celsus himself and Albinus repeatedly insisted, as Plato and Aristotle had done, that rational thought provided the only way to knowledge. The two types of philosophy are most clearly described in Philostratus' *Life of Apollonius* (5.37), written early in the third century A.D., where the author makes his hero win the case in a long discussion on this particular subject against the old-fashioned, scholarly-minded Stoic Euphrates. In the view of Apollonius one can become a philosopher only after having been given the basic knowledge by divine revelation. You have to turn your mind to the message, you have to accept it, before understanding and intellectual activity can begin.

The controversy had its serious ethical aspect, too. Traditional Greek philosophy had always taught that man, in order to become virtuous and happy, had to adapt himself to nature.[43] The order of nature, however, could be recognized and applied to human life exclusively through intellectual activity.

The new philosophy, in its turn, produced rules of moral conduct which were backed by the authority of suprarational, divine revelation. They had first of all to be complied with, regardless of all ensuing attempts to explain them rationally. Striving for a rational understanding of what had been revealed would certainly contribute to moral perfection. The act of acceptance, however, had to come first and was itself the main personal achievement of man.

It was in the light of these controversies, arising from philosophy itself, that Platonists like Galen or Celsus came to see, for the first time, the basic difference between philosophical and Biblical ideas. They came to realize that the new faith of the Christians and also the traditional Jewish religion jeopardized philosophy more than any of the new pseudophilosophical doctrines, of which, after all, the main ingredients, terms, and concepts were taken from well-known philosophical sources. These doctrines promised, as did philosophy proper, to provide salvation by freeing man's intellectual activity from the bonds of matter, desire, and emotion, by leading to perfect knowledge. So the voluntaristic implications of the new type of philosophy were hidden behind the main body of its teaching, which sounded very traditional according to Greek standards.

In the Biblical texts, even before their content was made explicit in philosophical terms, the voluntaristic approach towards cosmology and ethics came out much more clearly; this was duly noted by Greek intellectuals, once they had become aware of the problem involved. From this point of view the Bible was able to meet the religious needs of the educated in the second or third centuries A.D., and in fact much more effectively so than the Neopythagoreans, Hermetics, or Chaldeans. The importance of the very act of acceptance, which had to be repeated throughout life, and on which all security and all moral standards depended, was spoken of more clearly in the Bible than anywhere in those pseudophilosophical texts.

In the view of the Old Testament, obedience to the commandments of God, compliance with his will, is not only good, right, and salutary, it is also a gift of Yahveh himself, who can, if he pleases, also harden the hearts of people and make them incapable of perceiving his orders. Obedience, moreover, is the presupposition of wisdom.[44] The act of obedience, to be sure, does not result from the rational understanding of a given situation, the plans and arrangements of God, the order of his creation, or the proper insight into one's own capacities. All this understanding comes from obedience rather than leading to it. It is the willingness to listen to God's commandments, the turning of all one's forces and faculties to the divine creator that is required.[45] That is why the act of obedience can never be understood as a performance of the intellect, though to be obedient always turns out to be wise. The kind of wisdom to which a man's obedience testifies has its objects in the past, that is to say in the deeds and promises of Yahveh. As to the future which has to be faced in making a decision, the same wisdom or knowledge is identical with faith or confidence.

The God of the Old Testament is present and perceptible only in his commandments and orders, in the utterances of his will. His thought is far beyond human understanding. "For my thoughts are not your thoughts, neither are your ways my ways. . . . For as the heavens are higher than the earth, so are my ways higher than your ways, and my thoughts than your thoughts" (Isa. 55:8f).[46] Man cannot come to agreement with the intention of Yahveh, that is to say to perfection, through his intellectual efforts.[47] The agreement results entirely from obedience in that special sense of the word. Man has to refrain from upholding his intention against the will of Yahveh, regardless of what he is able to perceive or understand. The life of Abraham, as explained again and again in the Judaeo-Christian tradition, offers the most striking example of that attitude. Abraham is prepared, without the slightest hesitation, to sacrifice his son, the only warrant of Yahveh's promise, for no reason but that because Yahveh has told him to do so. It is not said in Genesis 22 that Abraham even reflected on the sense such an order of Yahveh's could possibly make. His confidence in the results of what Yahveh has initiated does not imply a challenge to his intellect. Rational understanding does not provide any kind of congruity between the intentions of God and man. The prophet Ezekiel is told to convey to his people the words of Yahveh, "whether they will hear or whether they will forebear" (2:7, 3:11). There is no way to give a response to Yahveh's intention apart from hearing and obeying.

Accordingly, in the Old Testament there are many passages, dating from various periods and reflecting different theological approaches, where the universe is praised for its beauty, its magnificence, its order. Yet the universe only bears witness to the power, the mercy, and the will of its Creator.[48] No author of the Old Testament speculates on the question whether the human mind may be vested with the very same reason which gives structure and life to the universe. This does not contradict the extremely high rank man has been given within creation (cf. Ps. 8:5f). But the essential factor is the will of God, which he has to follow in his conduct of life.

Since it is only the will of God which can be ascertained in the relation between God and man, man cannot possibly give his response to God through an act of thinking or perceiving but only by his being obedient or disobedient, that is to say by his will. Any attempt to understand intellectually the motives behind an order given by Yahveh is doomed to fail and even to lead to fatal disobedience. Knowledge can only be expected as a result of obedience, as was shown in the case of Abraham. "The fear of the Lord is the beginning of wisdom"—this maxim is repeated throughout the Old Testament in various contexts, in order to stress the importance of obedience to the commandments of Yahveh (Ps. 111:10; Job 28:28; Prov. 1:7). Obedience is regarded, even in texts of very archaic character, as more important than sacred and well-established rules for the intercourse between God and man. This is pointed out, for example, in the story of Saul's sparing the life of the king of the Amalekites (1 Sam. 15:22).

In the view of the Old Testament, no detail in the relation between God and man can be predicted or calculated by the efforts of the human intellect. The lesson to be learned from history or tradition is only that one must realize that God has always saved his elect beyond all reasonable expectation, and punished those who stood against his will. So the act of obedience to the will of God has to be repeated, collectively and individually, throughout the history of mankind.

The Law of God as given to Moses has to be explained and to be applied to the changing conditions of human and social life, according to the unanimous testimony of Biblical and post-Biblical tradition. This need for permanent interpretation is an infinite challenge for the human intellect, and men acquire wisdom and knowledge by meeting this challenge. But the Law itself can never be questioned, examined, or even fully understood. It has, first and foremost, to be fulfilled through obedience—which again is an act of will and does not result from intellectual activity or emotional disposition.

The picture seems different in the Wisdom Literature, so closely linked with parallel texts from Egypt and Babylonia. Here, vicissitudes and expectations of human life are largely discussed in a completely rationalistic way. The idea of God's interfering with human affairs is barely mentioned, and social life seems to constitute an autonomous area, governed by understandable and calculable rules. So moral conduct becomes a task for man's intellect: one has to know what human life is like, what the consequences of human activity are, and to act accordingly.

A deeper understanding of that part of Biblical literature, as offered by Gerhard von Rad, is likely to make clear the limits of such an intellectualism.[49] The possibility of dealing with social affairs and ethical problems exclusively by means of the human intellect is provided by the conviction that Yahveh, unlike many other gods in the Ancient Near East, has singled out that area of human activity. So man has been freed, by the will of his Creator, to use his wits and to act responsibly, because he is able to know, by his own intellectual efforts, the rules Yahveh has given for the whole field of human interrelationships. Gerhard von Rad has also shown how this kind of intellectualism is more or less tacitly assumed in the early Wisdom Texts, in which ethical speculation is concentrated on the proper use of reason. In the later strata of canonical and post-canonical Wisdom Literature the theological problem involved, that is to say, the will of Yahveh behind the rules and events in human life, becomes predominant, thus destroying the optimistic concept that, in the long run, all questions of moral conduct are to be solved through intellectual efforts. So again and again speculation returned to the problem of how to give the right response to the unpredictable utterances of the will of God.

Later on, the Christians regarded the same obedience, from which true and lasting knowledge originates (Just. *dial.* 61),[50] primarily as the repeated act of acceptance by which the faithful totally delivers himself to the divine grace that has been revealed to him by an equally free act of divine will (e.g. Iren. *adv. haer.* 4.11.5; cf. 2.8.1). This act of acceptance on the side of man is necessary for his salvation, though salvation itself is also a process foreseen in the universal order of creation. But the Gnostics are wrong, in the view of Irenaeus, in restricting salvation to its cosmic dimension, thus disregarding the freedom of both divine and human will.[51]

To give a philosophical explanation of all these ideas, which were present in some way or other throughout the Judaeo-Christian tradition, one needs a clear-cut notion of will and an unmistakable term to denote it.

It is worth noting that the language of the Old Testament provides no possibility of distinguishing, by means of terminology and without information given by the particular context, between human intention resulting from intellectual activity and intention originating from instinct or emotion. No layer of Biblical Hebrew offers psychological terms to denote the difference, though it may be seen from any given text. Human intention in accordance with Yahveh's commandments or orders and human intention against it—this is the only difference that matters—may come from reason as well as emotion.[52] Reason does not provide, as in Greece, the ultimate congruity between the human mind and the divine or cosmic order.

Yahveh's *maḥšᵉbōt* on the other hand—His βουλαί according to the Septuagint—that is to say his thoughts, plans, arrangements, and intentions, are certainly wise, salutary, perfect or—to use a philosophical term—perfectly rational, but they are far beyond the understanding of man. Thus will is the only means man has of responding to God's intention as it is made clear in his orders and commandments. There are very moving passages in Greek literature, especially in Attic tragedy, where the obscurity and inscrutability of divine counsels are spoken of.[53] Yet no hint can be discovered in those passages that man has been given distinct orders by the gods which he simply has to follow for his own benefit even without understanding their meaning and purpose. Unlike the Old Testament concept, Greek tragedy does not foresee the possibility that man can answer the intention of one of the gods by a simple act of obedience without a proper understanding of the given situation. The disobedience towards the divine which the tragic hero sometimes shows testifies to his ignorance and intellectual blindness, which cannot be healed or at least neutralized as to its fatal consequences by an act of obedience.

The will as a faculty of man, by which he can give his response to God quite apart from intellectual understanding, as foreseen in Biblical

anthropology, is much easier to ascertain in cases of conflicting intentions, when obedience and compliance are refused, than in the case of
agreement. The Old Testament frequently uses the verbal root 'bh
where will or obedience is to be denoted and, consequently, something
like the concept of volition underlies the context. But with only two
exceptions in the whole body of the Old Testament the verb occurs always with a negation![54]

The fundamental difference between the Biblical idea of obedience
and the Greek attitude as made explicit in philosophical doctrine comes
out most clearly in a sentence of Seneca: *Non pareo deo sed assentior*. "I do
not obey God; rather, I agree with Him" (*ep.* 96.2). Obedience towards
the divine is, in the view of the Stoic philosopher, far from being an act
of will. It results from or rather is identical with a full and rational
recognition of the divine order of nature, and leads man to agree, freely
and voluntarily, with what nature or God has ordered him to be and to
do. This agreement is reached, without any compulsion from outside
and without any act of submission, through free and uninfluenced intellectual activity on the part of man. *Deo parere libertas est*: "compliance
with God is liberty" (Sen. *vit. beat.* 15.3).[55] This is possible because the
will of God or nature is far from being arbitrary or unpredictable: *Sua
illis* (sc. *deis*) *in lege aeterna voluntas est; statuerunt quae non mutarent* (the
gods' will lies in eternal laws; these they have established to be immutable) (Sen. *de benef.* 6.23.1).[56] There was no need for a term to denote
volition as such in the framework of these ideas about God, the universe, and man. θέλειν, as is pointed out by Epictetus, has to be defined as the correct arrangement (ἐφαρμόζειν) of one's own ideas or aims
and means (προλήψεις). If θέλειν and γίγνεσθαι, the intent of an act
and its result, are in disagreement, the προλήψεις did not come from
the right assessment of what is natural and possible (2.17.14–18). Everything, as can be seen from this doctrine, depends on sound intellectual judgement.

Philosophical terms, so widely used even in very low levels of post-
classical Greek, are absent from Biblical Hebrew. The notion of will has
no corresponding word in either philosophical[57] or non-philosophical
Greek. Consequently, we must not expect to find an unmistakable term
which would make explicit an underlying concept of will where Biblical thought is rendered in Greek, that is to say in Judaeo-Hellenistic
literature.[58] There are only overtones or semantic implications attached

to some words in the vocabulary of both languages which lead the way to such a concept.

The awareness of the problem is, in fact, attested by some minor lexicographical features. It is, for instance, hardly a coincidence that none of the numerous words which denote, rather indiscriminately, intention, desire, purpose, longing, or pleasure in Biblical Hebrew, have been consistently rendered by Greek βούλομαι (βούλησις) in the Septuagint—even where the context clearly speaks of deliberate choice as providing the motive for action. The translators largely preferred θέλω instead. It is true that θέλω steadily gained ground on βούλομαι throughout the post-classical period of Greek (see below, p. 159, n. 2), above all in non-literary language. But θέλω never completely replaced its competitor, and that is why the usage of the Septuagint is surprising. To the translators of Biblical texts intention as such apparently seemed to be more important than the intellectual activity which precedes action.

Yet it still took a very long time to conceive, by the means and methods of Greek philosophy, the clear-cut notion of will which was always implied in the Biblical image of God, man, and the universe, though utterly alien to Greek cosmology and ethics.

II.
The Greek View of
Human Action I

THE WORD "will" and its equivalents in modern languages as applied to the description and evaluation of human action denotes sheer volition, regardless of its origin in either cognition or emotion. Will, considered as separate from its intellectual or non-intellectual context, is explained in many psychological and ethical theories throughout the history of European philosophy and science.[1] Good or ill will as the decisive point of reference in the evaluation of human behavior, for instance, became a favorite topic of ethical speculation. Moreover, the idea of will as a factor separate from both reason and emotion or instinct permeates all layers and periods of European thought. The idea has always been difficult to express distinctly and unmistakably, as can be seen from the usage in many languages, and also from passages where poets deal with the phenomenon of volition.[2]

The Greeks had no word of this kind in their language to denote will or intention as such. Professor Dodds, one of my distinguished predecessors in the series of Sather Lecturers, duly stressed this fact in his first lecture on The Greeks and the Irrational.[3] During the period when the two verbs βούλομαι and (ἐ)θέλω were still different in meaning,[4] the first signified primarily the planning and reflecting which precedes action. The second only meant "to be disposed, to be prepared." θέλει γίγνεσθαι means "it usually happens" (e.g. *Il.* 21.366), οὐκ ἐθέλοισα refers to an act of persuasion which the one to be persuaded is not prepared to undergo (Sapph. 1.24 L.P.).[5] Sometimes preparedness, pointed to by the word ἐθέλω, comes very near to ability. Hesiod reports in the *Works and Days* (134ff), that people in the Silver Age were unable to behave properly toward gods and men: ὕβριν γὰρ ἀτάσθαλον οὐκ ἐδύναντο | ἀλλήλων ἀπέχειν οὐδ' ἀθανάτους θεραπεύειν | ἤθελον. "From outrage and wickedness they were unable to abstain | among themselves; nor towards serving the gods | were they disposed." According to Solon (4.27 W.), the doors of a family's home (αὔλειοι θύραι) cannot

20

(οὐκ ἐθέλουσιν) keep out an evil which has befallen the whole community (δημόσιον κακόν). If men do not plan sensibly (οἰκότα βουλεύεσθαι), God is not prepared (οὐκ ἐθέλει) to support human intentions (ἀνθρωπήιαι γνῶμαι), says Herodotus (8.60γ) in a passage where the difference between preparedness and intention is particularly noteworthy.[6] In Homer we find the juxtaposition of οὐκ ἐθέλω . . . ἀλλὰ βούλομαι (*Od.* 9.96, 18.364) which means that someone is not prepared to do one thing but rather decides on the other.[7] ('E)θέλω does not denote intention unless a word like εἰδώς or γιγνώσκων "knowing" is attached, thereby introducing the concept of intellectual perception which is also implied in the meaning of γνώμη or ἐκ προνοίας "on purpose, deliberately." Hesiod (*op.* 280ff) contrasts perjury and truthful testimony as follows: εἰ γὰρ τίς κ'ἐθέλῃ τὰ δίκαι' ἀγορεῦσαι | γιγνώσκων . . . ὅς δέ κε μαρτυρίῃσιν ἑκὼν ἐπίορκον ὀμόσσας | ψεύσεται. . . (if someone is prepared to utter what is right knowingly . . . but whoever lies in his testimonies having deliberately sworn a false oath). The connotation of intentionality is introduced only by γιγνώσκων and ἑκών.

On the other hand, many words for cognition or thought inevitably imply the semantic element of decision or intention which results from intellectual activity. This applies to γιγνώσκω, διανοέομαι, νοέω, and other words.[8] Προαιρέομαι, which comes very close to our concept of will, clearly refers to the choice which the intellect makes out of several possible objectives of action. Προαίρεσις—literally "predilection" or "preference"—denotes the act of intellectual perception rather than intention itself, the general direction which action takes,[9] or the strength of the impulse towards action. Only the impulse to action which results from emotion, passion, or instinct can be described in words that do not connote, at the same time, the perception of the aim. This also applies to the noun λῆμα, a derivative of the verb λῶ, "I will." The verb occurs only in the Doric vocabulary, where it seems to have corresponded to (ἐ)θέλω. Αἰ λῇς (*Carm. pop.* 24.2 Page; *Epich.* 170.7 Kaibel) can be literally translated by εἰ θέλεις, denoting preparedness and assent rather than intention.[10] Λῆμα does, in fact, point in the general direction in which action leads.[11] But, in any given context, it is always stated whence this intention originates. The word never became a psychological term in the philosophical tradition and occurs mainly in poetical texts.

Another word which even acquired some terminological value in later Platonic philosophy should be mentioned in this context. Τόλμα (τόλμη) not only means risk and the moral attitude required to take a risk (audacity) but also the very act of will by which an individual overcomes his own inhibitions, which might prevent him from acting in a given situation. Every achievement, according to Gorgias (fr. 8 Untersteiner = Clem. Alex. *strom.* 1.51) διττῶν ἀρετῶν δεῖται . . . τόλμης μὲν τὸν κίνδυνον ὑπομεῖναι, σοφίας δὲ τὰ αἴσιμα γνῶναι "[All achievements] need a double virtue . . . on the one hand, the inclination to take risks upon oneself and, on the other hand, wisdom to know what is appropriate."[12] Τόλμα, in this particular meaning, does not denote the impulse towards action that comes from emotional disposition and that can be designated by words like ὀργή or θυμός (see below p. 26). It refers rather to a performance within man's consciousness (ἐνὶ φρεσὶ θυμὸς ἐτόλμα: "the spirit was bold in their breasts", *Il.* 10.232) by which obstacles like fear, reverence, shame and the like are removed and the road to a good or evil deed opened up. Οὐκ ἠθέλησας οὐδ' ἐτόλμησας θανεῖν τοῦ σοῦ πρὸ παιδός (you were neither prepared, nor dared, to die in your son's stead). This is said to old Pheres who was neither prepared nor could bring himself to sacrifice his life for his son (Eur. *Alc.* 644f). So τόλμα, τολμάω in this particular sense always implies a moral judgement, positive or negative according to the moral value of the ensuing action. The drive towards action (λῆμα) which comes from such an act can be called οὐκ ἄτολμον in the language of lyric poetry (Aristoph. *nub.* 457f, *ran.* 898). In a famous passage of the *Antigone* of Sophocles (365ff) the good and bad use is spoken of which man can make of his arts and skills, and it is the τόλμα that prompts the use, rather than the skill itself, which underlies the moral and religious verdict. In this passage, Sophocles clearly stated the fundamental difference between technical and moral knowledge, long before philosophical speculation tried to clarify the problem involved. Τόλμα in this context, however, being itself the decision to initiate an act of moral relevance, seems to depend entirely on moral knowledge or ignorance (620ff).[13] Which τόλμαι and what audacity of thought (φρενῶν θράσος) have led to this deed, Odysseus asks in Sophocles' *Ajax* (46). Notable τόλμα is shown by the great criminal as well as by the hero or the man who sacrifices everything for his neighbor.[14] A man's τόλμα can be judged according to the reasonable, a code of behaviour, or from the general feeling about what should be protected by shame and reverence (αἰδώς).[15] In the passage from Sophocles' *Antigone* quoted above, it is reverence towards the gods which determines the good decision or the τόλμα.

There was a cult of the personified τόλμα at Athens, and the Pythagoreans seem to have speculated on the phenomenon of decision as indicated by the term.[16] Later on, τόλμα, τολμᾶν was gradually restricted to its negative meaning.[17]

The one whose τόλμα is never restricted by any kind of αἰδώς is called αὐθάδης, always pleased with himself. He thinks and acts purely selfishly, and is incapable of seeing the bonds which connect him with the fate of other people. Euripides' Medea offers the classic example of that attitude.[18]

Hesiod and others called αἰδώς one of the essential conditions of social life, and Protagoras, in his theory of the origins of civilization, said it could be attributed to every human being as a part of his moral and political knowledge, whereas laymen and experts can be distinguished according to the extent of their technical knowledge. This is all explicable in terms of knowledge and ignorance. The man who has been given αἰδώς as part of his code of behavior simply knows what rules he has to observe and what restrictions he has to impose on himself. But the struggle between τόλμα, which initiates the drive towards action, and the restricting power of αἰδώς, once made explicit in definite concepts and words, is hard to explain in terms of cognition and knowledge alone.

It has long been disputed whether or not the first half of Phaedra's speech in Euripides' *Hippolytus* directly refers to the plot of the drama.[19] Phaedra says, in the first part, that right action according to correct knowledge is sometimes hindered by lack of energy (ἀργία), pleasure and longing for comfort (ἡδοναί), or αἰδώς. In context, this statement is strange, since what Phaedra is going to do undoubtedly violates both her own moral knowledge of the better and the standards of αἰδώς, which are identical rather than opposed to each other. Thus the meaning of αἰδώς in 384 seems to imply something which normal usage does not always indicate. Αἰδώς can be defined as a collective and prospective conscience which persuades man to apply the moral standards of his society to a situation where he has to act. In this capacity, αἰδώς may turn out, in many cases, to be the principal obstacle for any action whatsoever, since it makes a man aware and, perhaps, afraid of the en-

suing reactions to his deed and of other discomforts that may possibly
result from it. So αἰδώς may prevent him from acting at all, despite his
being obliged to do something, because it can offer appealing excuses
for him to stay inactive and supports the indolence and timidity of
human nature.

According to early and classical Greek thought, then, the function
of αἰδώς can be considered in two ways.[20] Applying current moral standards or creating an awareness of what moral judgement can be expected from other people, αἰδώς contributes valuable pieces of moral
information to the act of deciding involved. Where a man, however, is
simply prevented by αἰδώς from acting spontaneously, a phenomenon of
volition is primarily spoken of.[21] The second aspect comes out much
more clearly if the action prevented by the intercession of αἰδώς was
demanded according to moral standards. In such cases, αἰδώς as the opponent of τόλμα (Eur. Alc. 981) becomes a synonym of indolence, timidity, comfort-mindedness. "It is more comfortable to lie when we are
ashamed of the truth."[22]

We should note again that the element of volition sometimes implied in the meaning of αἰδώς is never expressed separately by that very
word. Where a positive judgement is passed on the behavior of the person involved, αἰδώς, which facilitates the decision to act rightly, always
points to the due knowledge and application of moral standards.
Where αἰδώς prevents somebody from the action required, it is his lack
of energy or his timidity which is spoken of with a clear moral verdict.

This is all well known[23] and does not need to be treated in further
detail, as it does not lead to the medieval or modern concept of will.
However, I should perhaps add one more example: about 300 B.C., the
physician Diocles wrote a largish book on dietetics. One passage is devoted to the problem of determining criteria that indicate an empty
stomach. Among other symptoms he mentions τὸ ὀρεκτικῶς ἔχειν πρὸς
βούλησιν τοῦ φαγεῖν, that is to say "to be instinctively disposed toward
the deliberate decision to take food."[24] Diocles is speaking, in fact, of
two psychological factors: one is the animal instinct of hunger, the
other reasoning on the basis of that appetite which leads to the decision
to eat something. Our term "will" denotes only the resulting intention, leaving out any special reference to thought, instinct, or emotion
as possible sources of that intention. Greek, on the other hand, is able

to express intention only together with one of its causes, but never in its own right.

Diocles did not use a strictly philosophical terminology. But the subdivision of the human soul according to its rational and irrational forces to which he clearly refers was well known to the Greeks long before philosophy started to deal with psychological problems.[25] The language of Homer has many archaic elements. Among these apparently belongs one method of expressing psychological phenomena. Fearing, hoping, reflecting, desiring, and any other mental or emotional activity is often attached to that particular part of the body through which it seems to be produced or performed.[26] So cowardice or fear is located in the legs, because the person in question is running away, and anger in the breast or in the breath, because his respiration is accelerated. The same form of expression can be found in other languages of the archaic type, in Biblical Hebrew for instance, and also, by the way, in modern colloquial expressions. In Hebrew, however, a man can indiscriminately use his heart (*lēb*), his vital power (*nepeš*), his breath (*ruaḥ*) or other parts of his physical self in order to think, to desire, to love, to be angry and so forth. There may be some preferences but certainly no definite and lasting code in the coordination of organs and functions, though the kind of motivation can always be seen from the context, and psychological reflections are sometimes very refined.[27]

The picture looks different in Homeric, that is to say equally archaic, Greek. Perceiving, thinking, planning are usually the business of φρένες (perhaps the midriff) and νόος (mind); emotion and impulses resulting from emotion are produced by the θυμός, which represents, at the same time, the *vis vitalis* of the living individual. Ἦτορ (perhaps the belly),[28] καρδίη (heart), and sometimes στῆθος (breast) are the parts where emotional disposition is located and felt. Psychological functions are very definitely distributed to certain parts of the body, though some confusion is caused by the historical development which is documented, in its successive stages, in the traditional language of Homeric poetry. But in general the psychological vocabulary of early Greek is nearly as precise as the terminology of later philosophy,[29] its terms and ways of expression largely being understandable regardless of context and situation.

This tendency to accuracy led at a very early stage to the distinct classification of rational and irrational factors in the human soul, long before the comprehensive notion of soul as distinct from the body and representing man's moral self was even conceived (in the sixth century B.C.).[30] Man always constituted a psycho-physical unity in the view of Homer.

According to Homeric anthropology, impulses toward action may originate directly from planning or deliberation as well as from emotions like anger, fear, or hatred.[31] They can also result from both reasoning and emotion, as intensified deliberation in a crucial situation affects both the intellectual and the emotional disposition. Achilles desperately tries to find a way out of the shameful position into which he has been manoeuvred by the arrogance of Agamemnon: ταῦθ' ὥρμαινε κατὰ φρένα καὶ κατὰ θυμόν (this he weighed in his heart and mind) (Il. 1.193),[32] and resolves to draw his sword.

The two kinds of motivation, that from reasoning and that from emotion, may reinforce or invalidate each other. Ἑκὼν ἀέκοντί τε θυμῷ (willingly with an unwilling spirit), as Homer formulates it in order to indicate how Zeus has deliberately and intentionally delivered Troy to be destroyed by the anger of Hera, whereas his sympathies told against this measure (Il. 4.43). In a simile, on the other hand, the lion's way of acting is determined by two contradictory yet equally irrational feelings, namely fear and aggressiveness: . . . τάς τε τρεῖ ἐσσύμενός περ (which he fears despite being driven [by hunger]) (Il. 11.554).

Intention itself, whether originating from reasoning or from emotion, can never be named, in the language of Homer, without reference to one or the other of these origins. That is why θυμός, emotion that may or may not lead to action,[33] can rise ἐνὶ φρεσίν, for it comes from information properly perceived by the intellect, as in the case of Odysseus when he had listened to the story of Eumaeus (Od. 15.486f):[34] Εὔμαι', ἦ μάλα δή μοι ἐνὶ φρεσὶ θυμὸν ὄρινας | ταῦτα ἕκαστα λέγων. . . . (Eumaeus, you have stirred the spirit in my φρένες).

In short, the main elements of traditional Greek psychology were already fully developed in Homer, even without the aid of the concept of soul.[35] Within the limits imposed by the divine rule, man is seen to act in accordance with his own rational and irrational forces. In order to cope properly with a given situation he has to perceive it as distinctly as possible and, at the same time, apply the current moral standards, as Odysseus does at Od. 11.402ff.[36] Action that results from such reasoning cannot possibly go astray, unless a god interferes with human planning, as Aphrodite blatantly does in the case of Helen (*Il.* 3.385ff) or Athena in the case of Achilles (*Il.* 1.194f). Yet the actual performance of the act depends largely on the amount of energy drawn from the irrational forces. These can be released and directed by the planning intellect, which produces, in this way, its own θυμός. They can also be mobilized quite spontaneously, but this is always dangerous and may lead to disaster unless the intellect interferes in time. There is no need for an intermediate will, on which the action would directly depend and to which any moral judgement on a man's behavior would ultimately refer. Moral judgement is primarily concerned with the intellectual achievement implied in a man's behavior. That is why Homeric heroes are so often said to know something when their moral attitude is being described.[37] Accordingly, νόος,[38] "planning," can be used, together with or without θυμός, as the noun to denote man's attitude in general: τόνδε νόον καὶ θυμὸν ἐνὶ στήθεσσιν ἔχοντες (having this plan and resolution in their breasts) (*Il.* 4.309) and ἀνθρώπων . . . νόον ἔγνω, "of men . . . he knew the mind" (*Od.* 1.3). Νόος can take this comprehensive meaning because of the leading part played by the intellect in this kind of moral assessment, θυμός because of the actions which are regularly instigated and performed by it and which display the moral quality of the acting person: 'Αλλ' ὁ μὲν ὑμέτερος θυμὸς καὶ ἀεικέα ἔργα | φαίνεται . . . : "Your spirit and unseemly deeds are plainly visible" (*Od.* 4.694f).

The twofold psychology that explains human behavior on the basis of the interaction of rational and irrational forces and has no room for the concept of will prevails throughout the Greek tradition from the time of Homer onwards. This applies, in particular, to Attic drama, where the analysis and description of psychological phenomena became a highly developed art.[39] Emotion and reason are always clearly distinguished and their mutual interaction carefully described when the motives of human action are being discussed, analyzed, or simply mentioned in Greek tragedy and comedy.

A few examples may suffice to illustrate this. Pentheus' activity in Euripides' *Bacchae* is wicked right from the beginning; his attitude during the miraculous epiphany of Dionysus is only the most spectacular instance. His will, as we are inclined to say, was evil, peccable, wicked. Euripides makes the Chorus summarize that impression in the following words (997f): ἀδίκῳ γνώμᾳ παρανόμῳ τ' ὀργᾷ . . . μανείσᾳ πραπίδι παρακόπῳ τε λήματι (with unjust thought and criminal passion, with frenzied mind and misled intent). The second line characterizes Pentheus' drive to action as the result of his being out of his senses, μανεῖσα πραπίς, referring to the loss of his cognitive capacity, παράκοπον λῆμα, his impulse to action being thus misled. The first line gives the moral judgement on this condition: His way of reasoning is ἄδικος (unjust), his striving παράνομος (unlawful). In both statements, reason and emotion are carefully distinguished, yet both stress reduced intellectual capacities as the primary cause of failure and sin.

Sophocles makes Creon reflect on the possibility of ascertaining a man's character (*Ant.* 176): it is impossible to know in every man what his ψυχή, his φρόνημα, and his γνώμη are like before he has been tested in administrative and legal practice.[40] Ψυχή refers to the vital or natural disposition of man,[41] φρόνημα and γνώμη to his moral attitude which is based on intellectual activity.

Euripides' *Medea* offers the most striking illustration of how reason and emotion, both being necessary to bring about any sort of action, can be perverted both separately and in their mutual interaction. Lines 635ff explicitly refer to the perversion of irrational feelings, 1014f describe the perverted use man is able to make of his intellect, whereas 844ff depict, in the context of praise of Athens, the ideal cooperation of emotion and intellect. The same bipartition, by the way, was kept throughout the history of Greek thought inside and outside philosophical speculation. "Every accomplishment is due to two factors, deliberation leading to a decision (βούλησις) and willingness to invest emotional energy (προθυμία)." This is said in a speech in Polybius' Histories (3.107.5).

Aristophanes depicts the contradictory feelings with which personified Athens regards Alcibiades (*ran.* 1425): she longs for him, she hates him—but, in the end, she deliberately wants to have him (ποθεῖ μέν, ἐχθαίρει δέ, βούλεται δ'ἔχειν). Again, volition from emotion, complicated and self-contradictory as it may be, and the final decision which results from reasoning are clearly distinguished.

Γνώμη became a key word in the general vocabulary of moral reflection in the course of the fifth century, not only in tragedy and comedy. Γνώμη and γιγνώσκω mostly have double connotations: adequate perception of and reflection on reality plus a right decision to act according to that insight. Καλῶς ἐγνωσμένα (well conceived) (Eur. *Med.* 779) is the approving comment of Jason when Medea has informed him about her—pretended—change of mind and the resulting intention. We may observe the same thing in 912f:

ἔγνως δὲ τὴν νικῶσαν—ἀλλὰ τῷ χρόνῳ—
βουλήν. γυναικὸς ἔργα ταῦτα σώφρονος.

(You have recognized, although late in the day, the prevailing plan. Such an action befits a decent woman).

Here ἔγνως refers to both cognition and intention. Even γνώμη (maxim, formulated piece of wisdom) implies, at least indirectly, the meaning of volition, for most maxims are coined for parenetic purposes. So it is not always clear whether γνώμη denotes "maxim" or "plan, intention" in a given passage. In Aristoph. *nub.* 896 the γνῶμαι which the Adikos Logos promises to introduce into the discussion have to be taken, in all probability, as maxims. In line 533, where the Chorus is speaking to the audience, γνώμη refers to the favorable attitude the spectators are supposed to foster towards the poet because of their positive judgement on a foregoing play: ἐκ τούτου μοι πιστὰ παρ'ὑμῶν γνώμης ἐσθ' ὅρκια (from this I cherish pledges of your good will). Again, γνώμη includes both intellectual activity and volition, as in Herodotus 3.81.5, where it is said that Otanes in his recommendation of democratic order γνώμης τῆς ἀρίστης ἡμάρτηκε (he falls short of the best judgement).[42]

Γνώμη, γιγνώσκω can refer both to specific judgement plus intention in a given situation[43] and to the general attitude of people.[44] Every action results from γνώμη according to Antiphon (*or.* 5.5): τὸ μὲν γὰρ ῥῆμα τῆς γλώσσης ἁμάρτημά ἐστι, τὸ δὲ ἔργον τῆς γνώμης (the spoken word may be a slip of the tongue, the deed, however, of the mind . . .).

Γνώμη as the motive of action can never be ascribed simply to the nature of a man. It is always due to an intellectual performance. Sometimes nature and γνώμη are in full accordance: καὶ φῦντες καλῶς καὶ γνόντες ὅμοια (born nobly and similarly inclined) (*Lys.* 2.20). In other cases, compulsions from outside or spontaneous and irrational impulses from within are explicitly contrasted with γνώμη as possible forces leading to action. Democritus teaches that all the hardships man imposes on himself originate not from the natural needs of the human body but from the fact that γνώμη does not get hold of the right aim (κακοθιγία τῆς γνώμης Β 223).

There is, however, not only the antagonism of γνώμη and ὀργή, intention based on reasoning and irrational impulse, which sometimes interfere with each other; also fear or hesitation, being irrational factors as well, frequently avert the intellect (νόος) that has to produce γνώμη from its intention (θελήματα), as is pointed out in a fragment of Sophistic literature (Antiph. Β 58). In its quality as the immediate cause of action, γνώμη can be said to produce or to have ὀργή and the like, which is as fatal as uncontrolled emotion if the foregoing intellectual activity has moved the wrong way. Ἄκρατος τῆς γνώμης ὀργή (uncontrolled impulse originating from [mis]judgement), a formulation of Alcidamas to denote that condition, was severely reproached by Aristotle for stylistic reasons (Rhet. 1406a10). Thucydides attributes emotions (τὸ θυμούμενον τῆς γνώμης 7.86; cf. Antiph. or. 2.3) or angry emotions (τὸ ὀργιζόμενον τῆς γνώμης 2.59), inertia or lack of energy (ἐν τῷ ἀνειμένῳ τῆς γνώμης 5.9), alongside intention and suspicion (τὸ βουλόμενον καὶ ὕποπτον τῆς γνώμης 1.90) to human γνώμη. Thus all kinds of impulses, including irrational ones, result from man's intellectual activity. The Sophist Antiphon postulated laws that would prescribe what the νοῦς is not allowed to desire (ἐπιθυμεῖν Β 44 col. III).[45] Consequently, it is not surprising that φρόνημα (purpose), γνώμη (judgement), νοῦς (intellect), διάνοια (notion)[46] to denote moral attitude in general or disposition towards a person can be replaced, occasionally, by ὀργή (impulse), at least in poetic language.[47] Such an expression does not infringe upon the predominance of the human intellect in moral life, because ὀργή may come from γνώμη. But if a man really acts because of spontaneous emotion, this is bound to lead to failure, for his ὀργή is using its own cognitive faculty instead of the right one: this Sophocles called αὐτόγνωτος ὀργά, emotion or drive using its own, that is to say irrational and misleading, cognition (Ant. 875).[48]

A change in one's intention due either to fresh information and second thoughts or to hesitation caused by feelings and emotions is usually spoken of, in both early and later Greek, as a change in one's intellectual activity (μεταγιγνώσκω, μετανοῶ etc.). It is in general not very favorably looked upon (Thuc. 2.61.2f), regardless from which kind of influence it results,[49] for it always implies that one of the two intentions is or was based on error. Acting under the influence of error, however, always means the loss of one's own freedom of choice. Thus Agamemnon's change of mind (μεταγνῶναι), as described by Aeschylus (*Ag.* 221), indicates the loss of his freedom to choose and take the initiative based on reasoning (τὸ παντότολμον φρονεῖν: to intend the all-daring deed), as can be seen from his hesitation. In the case of Xerxes this process is caused by the gods (δολομῆτις ἀπάτα θεοῦ: the treacherous deceit of the god, *Pers.* 93),[50] but this is of secondary importance compared to the negative slant which every case of changed intention usually receives according to Greek moral standards. Someone who has changed his mind for the better because of his suffering and distress is regarded as a fool rather than as a man who has become wise from his own experience of life παθὼν δέ τε νήπιος ἔγνω (a fool learns from suffering) (Hes. *op.* 218).[51] A positive verdict on a man's moral performance can be justified only by a positive intellectual achievement which preceded and determined his intention to act. That is why already in Homer, where the motivation of human activities shifts from wholesale intervention by the gods (e.g. *Il.* 9.188–223) to psychological factors (e.g. *Od.* 6.118–143), attention is focused on the acts of cognition and deliberation rather than on those of volition.[52]

⁜

Late in the seventh century B.C. the Greeks learned for the first time to take into account, in their administration of justice, the difference between intentional and inadvertent killing.[53] The problem of intentionality never ceased to be discussed, from that time onwards, in criminal law, civil law, and legal theory.[54]

Once the difference between intentional and non-intentional offenses had become a common feature in most legal systems of the Greek world, it was usually denoted by the pair of terms ἁμάρτημα and ἀγνόημα,[55] whereby non-intentionality is interpreted as ignorance of the better. Thus intention was assessed, in its legal relevance, according to the amount of knowledge the delinquent had, at the moment of his act, concerning the means and ends of his deed and the legal standards applicable to it. The good or ill will which may have led him in his actions, and which could have been taken into account regardless of the knowledge he had of the given situation with all its implications, is clearly not indicated in that terminology.

Ill will, however, was not unknown in Greek theory of law. A famous fragment from Theophrastus has preserved a lengthy discussion of various Greek laws of sale and their moral and legal content.[56] In some passages Theophrastus gives his interpretation of the purpose of various legal measures. One states that the seller should sell his estate without deceit (ἀδόλως), another, that drunkenness, anger, contentiousness, and insanity should be excluded on both sides (μὴ παρὰ μεθύοντος μηδ' ἐξ ὀργῆς μηδὲ φιλονεικίας, μηδὲ παρανοοῦντος, ἀλλὰ φρονοῦντος), for these factors belong either to occasion (καιρός) or to emotion (πάθος), whereas the legal act should be accomplished intentionally (ἐκ προαιρέσεως). Intention (προαίρεσις), however, entirely and solely depends on intellectual activity (φρονεῖν) as opposed to emotion (πάθος) and conditions prevailing outside the person in question (καιρός). Φιλονεικία was not always defined as a πάθος in ancient theories of ethics and psychology, and ὀργή was often regarded as semirational (see below p. 57f). Yet here, in the context of legal theory, an impulse determined by these factors clearly appears as non rational or emotional, for intention from the legal point of view has to be based on intellectual perception rather than good or ill will. Emotion or passion provides the only psychological alternative to the knowledge of the objective with regard to the ensuing impulse towards action. Good or ill will, though well known in its various appearances such as envy or benevolence, did not become a factor separated from its origin in either intellect or emotion, as the legal and moral evaluation of human activities operated according to the criterion of intentionality.

It is in the framework of this kind of reasoning that Gorgias made a defendant argue in the following way: if I am as intelligent as you all believe me to be, I cannot possibly commit such a crime, but if I have, I am not intelligent (*Pal.* 26). Palamedes, the speaker of these lines, does not discuss the possibility of an inadvertent offense. It is rather the amount of intelligence invested that qualifies the intention leading to the alleged crime. Criminal intention, according to what Palamedes has in mind, corresponds to a low level of intelligence and thus results from ignorance.

This fictitious argument of Gorgias' Palamedes is in full accordance with a number of passages in later texts where, against the normal usage, ἀγνόημα and the like is said of the intentional offense.[57] Where moral accomplishment depends entirely on intellectual performance, lack of intelligence or cognitive abilities (ἀγνωμοσύνη) becomes wickedness.[58] There is no point in introducing the factor of good or ill will as a moral or legal criterion under these circumstances. The Socratic maxim of οὐδεὶς ἑκὼν ἁμαρτάνει, "no one fails on purpose," was deeply rooted in Greek thought.

Knowledge that determines action was of greater importance than the ensuing accomplishment in the entirely moral evaluation of human conduct, although the difference between law and ethics was never explicitly stated by the Greeks. The primacy of intention was increasingly stressed in Greek moral thought from the sixth century onwards, as can be seen in Simonides or Aeschylus.[59] But it was always knowledge or ignorance which determined human intention. Failure and crime were attributed to λόγου τ' ἄνοια: Lack of understanding or reason (Soph. *Ant.* 603). So when the gods decided to destroy or punish a man, they simply disturbed his intellect, making him ignorant of good and evil, as is described by Theognis (402ff). The man who thus becomes a trespasser is justly punished. This cruel mechanism, by which a man is led to intellectual and moral blindness, was labeled by the old term ἄτη, which had a different meaning outside moral and religious speculation.[60] It is referred to again and again in fifth-century literature, particularly in Herodotus. There was no good will in human nature which protected a man from becoming morally bad once his intellectual capacities had been drastically reduced. Words like εὐήθεια became synonyms of ἀβελτερία, in the sense of naive "good-heartedness," and were primarily used in an ironical or even derogatory sense.

All this points to the outstanding importance which the Greeks ascribed to knowledge in any situation where action was required.[61] Accordingly, the moral verdict they passed on a man's conduct always referred to his choice of the means and ends, but never to intention or inclination as such. It has already been said (see above n. 37) that in the language of Homer the man who shows a friendly attitude towards others, who has good will as we put it, "knows friendly things," and people are called fools because of outrages they did quite deliberately. Xenophon (*mem.* 3.11.16) prefers εὐνοϊκῶς φιλεῖν, "being one's friend with moral judgement," το μαλακῶς φιλεῖν, which only refers to emotional sympathy without the control of reason. Εὔνοια, "good will," derives from νοεῖν, νοῦς, which we discussed previously,[62] and the righteous man is εὐθύγνωμος according to Democritus (B 181), that is to say "whose thoughts go straight forward." The intellect is regarded as the origin of volition and desire by the Sophist Antiphon (above, p. 30).

One word in the earliest vocabulary of Greek, however, contradicts the traditional intellectualism. Whenever the Homeric heroes display extraordinary activities, whenever their exploits surpass all expectation, it is due to their μένος. But μένος is something peculiar. Before such extraordinary achievements, before an ἀριστεία, one of the gods usually gives the hero some μένος—in his heart, his θυμός, his στῆθος, or wherever psychological phenomena are normally located according to the ideas of Homer,[63] for μένος does not fit in with the carefully localized faculty-psychology of the Old Epic. Μένος is an additional gift, provided only on a special occasion and not supposed to become a lasting part of the person in question. Its presence can be seen from the outstanding energy displayed, from the irresistible impulse to action.[64] In short, μένος provides will of unusual strength which does not result from the perception of objectives or from any kind of emotion like anger and fury. Yet the meaning of μένος includes the strength of will only and does not refer to its direction.

Moreover, the concept of μένος points to the human will as such, without any attempt to give, at the same time, a moral evaluation of it, as is always implied in the meaning of terms like αὐθάδεια "arrogance, self-willedness," εὐμένεια "benevolence," or καρτερία, "perseverance" or "tenacity." Words of this kind undoubtedly denote human qualities which are usually described, in modern European languages, in terms of will and intention without reference to the intellect. But unlike μένος, they always involve a very distinct judgement on a man's moral attitude and are incapable of denoting intention as such. Only μένος comes indeed very near to the modern notion of will, which is defined by one psychologist of our own time as "energy for acting at the disposal of consciousness" (C. G. Jung). Μένος, however, does not belong to the normal or natural equipment of man according to Homeric psychology.[65] It is something numinous[66] which only appears where the gods unpredictably interfere with human affairs, thus disturbing the calculable sequence of events. And such interference became comfortingly rare after the Trojan War.[67]

The concept of μένος does not go with the usual bipartition into rational and irrational factors which had become the very basis of Greek psychology already in Homer. That is probably why μένος was already losing its original meaning at the time of the Old Epic,[68] and became a word of the poetical vocabulary denoting simply "strong emotion."[69] The word was never used in good prose.[70] The grammarians of Alexandria never came to a proper understanding of the underlying concept in the language of Homer. They took μένος as either physical strength or strong emotion.[71]

The same semantic change from the field of religion or magic to ordinary psychology can also be observed in the derivatives of μένος. Δυσμενής is a well-defined term in Homer. It normally denotes the opponent on the battlefield, that is to say the warrior who has been given μένος against oneself.[72] No reference to his internal or emotional disposition is implied. His hostility is entirely functional and does not need to be explained in terms of psychology. There are only a few late passages in Homer where hostility as an emotional or moral disposition is, perhaps, implied (e.g. *Od.* 6.185).

The opposite is true of εὐμενής, "benevolent," which always refers to somebody's emotional disposition. But it does not occur in the Old Epic at all. It was not coined until the sixth century B.C.,[73] when μένος had already become a word to denote strong emotion, without any magical or numinous overtones. So εὐμενής was said, from the very beginning, of a man who is amicably disposed towards someone else.

Once in the Odyssey (6.184f) we find the form εὐμενέτης. The concord of a married couple gives ἄλγεα δυσμενέεσσι, χάρματα δ' εὐμενέτῃσιν: "pain to their enemies and joy to their friends," says Odysseus to Nausikaa. Clearly the words in question refer to friendly and unfriendly disposition respectively, without any numinous implication.[74]

The archaic concept of μένος was, in fact, the only one through which intention could be grasped independently of both cognition and emotion. Yet it was soon discarded. Only two factors were left to explain and to evaluate human action and its motivation, both belonging, unlike μένος, to the normal or natural equipment of man. Psy-

chology had been reduced to the rational understanding of nature long
before philosophy started.

�֎

Greek philosophy, however, did not draw its origin from reflections
on the human soul or consciousness: it began with an investigation of
the universe. The earliest attempts at philosophical reflection were
made to prove, as Heraclitus said, that the universe is structured and
kept alive according to rules which man applies in his activity of
thought and communication.[75] Parmenides went even further in his
statement that thought and being are identical.

Such an approach seems to be fairly optimistic, as the rationality and
perspicuity of thoughts are taken for granted. But it was, at that time,
far from being an entirely new concept. It is true that the gods of the
Greek cities were certainly regarded not only as the guardians of eternal
laws but even more as powerful allies and protectors whose benevolence
was not predictable and needed to be secured.[76] The theological and
moral concept of ἄτη (see above n. 47) evinces, in a given situation, the
rule of the gods as utterly irrational. Sophocles and Herodotus were
particularly concerned with the overwhelming power of the gods and
the inexplicable way in which they use it. Φιλέει ὁ θεὸς πάντα τὰ ὑπερέχοντα κολούειν: "the god tends to cut short everything that is eminent"
(Hdt. 7.30.2ε). This is clearly not a maxim intended to clarify the humane character of divine rule, and the treatment Ajax receives from
Athena in Sophocles' tragedy is not likely to fortify the faith that the
standards of divine activity are as understandably rational and ethical as
the moral code of honest people.

Yet wherever we find, in early Greek literature, the attempt at a
comprehensive understanding of the divine order rather than reflection
on isolated phenomena in human life, attention is focused on the regularity, perceptibility, and reliability of the divine rule over the world.
Homer explained the events in the Trojan War, extraordinary, complicated, and quickly changing as they were, as resulting from the preconceived plan of Zeus. Hesiod tried to understand the universe, its origin, structure, and life, according to the model of a family or tribe
where everything was ruled and ordered as the accepted law or convention prescribed. Hesiod was the first[77] to make Zeus, unlike earlier
gods, rule the whole world with justice. This idea entails a consider-

able moral stimulus for mankind; it also implies a good deal of confidence in the reliability and perspicuity of nature. This is worth
noting, because we find, at the same time, in Hesiod as well as in
many other texts of the seventh and sixth centuries, the fullest awareness of the weakness, the misery, and, above all, the limited intellectual capacities of man.[78] Nevertheless, the social and cosmic orders remained[79] mutually interpretable. Retaliation and reward provide the
rules for nature and society alike, as was expounded in Solon's poems
and Anaximander's cosmology. According to the historian Ephorus in
the fourth century B.C. (FGH 70 F 31), Apollo founded the Delphic
oracle to convey to mankind the awareness (ἔννοια) of his plans and intentions (τῆς ἑαυτοῦ βουλήσεως). This interpretation of an active religious institution betrays the same belief in the basic congruity between divine rule and human knowledge which we find in early Greek
cosmology.

So when Greek philosophy turned to social and moral problems in
the fifth century B.C., its main task was to find standards of moral conduct that were as rational and generally applicable as the rules of the
cosmic order. If reason was, in fact, the only structuring and animating
factor, if the universe was rational, human action could only be assessed
by standards provided by reason. The same intellect of man had to perceive the order of nature and the objectives of action. Action was morally good if it agreed with the rational order of the universe. Consequently it had to come from rational understanding of the world we
live in. Man was likely to act successfully if he had knowledge of nature. The identity of thought and being applied to cosmology as well as
to ethics.

Even from this extremely abbreviated description of the basis of
Greek moral philosophy, one can easily see that the concept of will has
no place in its ideas. Kant's remark about good will as the only factor
in human life which is unconditionally praiseworthy makes no sense
whatever in Greek ethical thought. All speculation on moral values
which had ever been made in Greece presupposed the view that only
true knowledge leads to right conduct. Different and even contradictory[80] conceptions of reality were put forward in the history of Greek
philosophy, but there was hardly ever disagreement about the principle
that only rational understanding of reality leads to a good life or moral
perfection. And if a man fails in his efforts because the result has been

influenced by forces beyond his control, the rectitude of his moral calculation fully accounts for the moral value of his deed (see above n. 59).

This can be seen in the various attempts the Greeks made to solve a
problem which all medieval and most post-medieval philosophers tried
to handle with the aid of the concept of will.

Experience is likely to teach one that people sometimes do wrong
while knowing the better.[81] They seem to fail on purpose in their moral
performance. The twofold psychology offers an easy explanation which
is already found in archaic Greek poetry: "The man whose intellect is
not stronger than his emotion is always acting in the wrong way and is
always in great distress" (Theogn. 631).[82] This is easy to understand.
The power of passion or emotion prevents such a man from making
proper use, in his actions, of the knowledge that reason has provided.
So he is constantly being pushed towards the irrational, the disorderly,
the evil. His actions are directed against the order of nature in the
given situation, though his intellect is able to perceive and evaluate
that situation with regard to the action required.

This phenomenon was described, in ordinary Greek and later on in
philosophical terminology, by the words ἀκρατής, ἀκράτεια.[83] The underlying idea implies that the intellect has to exercise some sort of rule
over instinct, passion, and emotion when their services are needed in
order to bring about the action in favor of which the intellect has decided.[84] This control has broken down in the case of ἀκράτεια, so that
emotion is acting independently.[85]

A closer examination of the generally accepted concept,[86] however,
leads to considerable difficulties. For if I have come to a proper, rational
understanding of what should be the right thing to do in a given situation, my mind is then in full agreement with reality itself. But it is
hardly conceivable that rational knowledge, which represents the con-
gruence of human mind and nature, can be outdone, in determining
action, by another impulse, since nature or reality includes both emotion and passion as well. Reason, provided it operates rightly and leads
to true knowledge, could on this view be overpowered only by a will
that comes from outside nature and is, consequently, beyond rational understanding. This idea, however, was unknown in Greek philosophy.[87]

Socrates solved the problem of ἀκράτεια, "intemperance," by his famous paradox: nobody fails on purpose. Perhaps Socrates coined the
sentence for parenetic purposes only, as Bruno Snell is inclined to be-

lieve.[88] Plato, however, gave a detailed explanation, chiefly in the *Protagoras*. Each action aims at a true or supposed benefit, even if it is instigated by anger or fear.[89] Nobody aims at something which he regards as an evil at the moment he is going to act. Yet only reason can tell whether or not the object aimed at really has some value. He who fails, who acts against reason because of fear, anger, and the like, does not really do what he wants as a rational being.[90] He only does what he vaguely wishes at this very moment. His knowledge is deficient and weaker than his irrational impulses. So any failure results from lack of knowledge, from inadequate or restricted intellectual activity. That is why nobody fails who really knows the better.

The paradox οὐδεὶς ἑκὼν ἁμαρτάνει is extensively treated, in its various implications, in Plato's dialogues.[91]

The most important passage is *Gorg.* 467Cff.[92] Plato points out that the intention implied in ἑκών is not directed to the action itself but to the objective of action, which is always, in the view of the acting individual, an ἀγαθόν, a good, though sometimes erroneously supposed to be so. If, then, βούλεσθαι always aims at a—real or supposed—good,[93] anyone who fails on purpose does not really act ὡς βούλεται (according to his will), but ὡς αὐτῷ δοκεῖ (according to his pleasure), for he does not act under compulsion from outside. By referring the intellectual judgement according to the categories of good and evil that is implied in the very act of volition to the aim of action rather than to action itself, Plato is able to make proper use of the Socratic analogy of technical and moral knowledge, which has been overdone so blatantly in the *Minor Hippias* (375B–D). Both kinds of knowledge are strictly parallel only with regard to the aims of action. Their specific difference was already noted in the *Protagoras* (323B/C), where a share of moral and political knowledge is attributed to every human being, whereas the difference between experts and laymen is essential in the case of technical skill or knowledge.[94]

The reasoning on οὐδεὶς ἑκὼν ἁμαρτάνει in the *Gorgias* leads to that convincing result only because Plato presupposes a clear distinction between the means and ends of action. This particular problem is not fully discussed in the *Gorgias*. The dialogue offers, however, a theory to explain the way in which freedom of choice is realized in moral life through intellectual activity.[95]

In the *Timaeus*, οὐδεὶς ἑκὼν ἁμαρτάνει is interpreted (81E–87A) according to a strictly deterministic concept of nature: failure in human life is explained by the deficiencies of the material body of man and those of the parts of his soul closely attached to it, which need, but do not always get, a proper training. Volition (βουλή, βούλεσθαι) belongs to the immaterial part of the soul (τὸ λογιστικόν). Despite their being the cause of failure (ἁμαρτάνειν), the irrational forces in the human soul are indispensable for coping with various tasks in moral life (*Leg.* 731C). The definite moral dualism prevailing in the *Republic*, according to which ἁμαρτάνειν can exclusively be attributed to matter interfering with the noetic order, thus to the body as withstanding the soul, is invalidated by the idea that every kind of motion has its origin outside matter. So irregular motion as a cosmic phenomenon is attributed, in the *Timaeus*, to a second soul of the universe, the first being the cause of regular motion, and the drive towards irregularity and evil in human life to the soul of man rather than his body, as in the *Laws*.[96]

The difficult problem of reconciling the maxim οὐδεὶς ἑκὼν ἁμαρτάνει with the separate evaluation of intentional crime and inadvertent offense in criminal law is extensively treated in the ninth book of the *Laws* (860Dff).[97] Here, with reference to legislation and jurisdiction rather than to moral judgement, ἁμαρτάνειν is explained as due either to anger and fear, or pleasure and desire, or hopes and plans which are based on error. This classification, however, if transferred to moral theory, is hardly compatible with the Socratic paradox.[98]

Plato firmly believed that the congruity between the rational intention of a person and the rational order of reality can be verified only in the human consciousness. Only the human mind participates in the intelligible, only the intelligible is entirely real. The world that we experience through our senses is perishable, disorderly, irrational in many respects, unpredictable as to its further development, and has, therefore, only a small share in reality. Knowledge, however, which the intellect acquires, can only refer to reality, to that which is lasting, unchanging, and structured by reason.[99] So knowledge which leads to action cannot be tested by any results this action may cause in the empirical world. Moral quality can only be ascertained by examining the state of mind, the consciousness of the human being who produced the action. Accordingly, the only task in moral life man has to meet is to look after his soul.[100]

Both Epicureans and Stoics essentially differed from each other as well as from Plato in their concept of reality. But on this particular point of moral philosophy they all agree.

According to the Stoics [101] every deed, even the most insignificant detail in everyday life, has been predetermined by nature or fate in the very same way as the cosmic phenomena. Freedom of choice, responsibility, and consequently morality exist only with reference to human consciousness. As a being gifted with reason, man is able to understand this strict and universal determination as perfectly rational and salutary. Such knowledge makes him adapt his own intention freely and willingly to whatever providence has ordained him to do. This very act of free assent causes his moral perfection and his happiness, for nothing of all that may happen to him can change his state of mind once he has achieved this perfect agreement between his consciousness and nature.

According to the Epicurean view, everything owes its existence solely to chance. There is no cosmic order to rely on for moral purposes. Happiness or moral perfection depends completely on man's ability to detach himself from anything which could cause pain or disturb his mental and emotional equilibrium. Being a conglomeration of atoms himself, man cannot possibly escape from being affected by the permanent and unpredictable changes of the universal atomic process. But he can recognize his own position, he can see whether or not something concerns him and, consequently, he can attain the goal of moral perfection or happiness in his own mind. [102]

Thus Platonists, Epicureans, [103] and Stoics alike, despite their completely different concepts of reality, referred the whole problem of moral conduct and moral perfection to the state of the human mind. They firmly established the basis of freedom, morality, and happiness in the consciousness of the individual. They made man independent of anything which might happen to him from the outside world, regardless of whether fate and determination were willingly accepted, their existence simply denied, or considered to be the ontological deficiency of the empirical world.

It was easy to explain under these presuppositions that no man was ever able to do wrong on purpose, for the moral quality of an action could be evaluated only from the state of mind of the acting individual. No action could be morally wrong which resulted from true knowledge, none could be justified which had been motivated by error—regardless of all the consequences in the empirical world. Consequently, there was no will and there was no society either which might set standards of moral conduct apart from the knowledge the individual had acquired of the order of being. In this view, οὐδεὶς ἑκὼν ἁμαρτάνει was not altogether a paradoxical saying. It contained the basic truth that human freedom, that is to say acting according to one's own intention, entirely depends on unrestricted intellectual activity. Being tied down to the needs and necessities of empirical life, man is able to experience his liberty in his consciousness where nothing can hinder his cognitive activity and where he reaches a full agreement between reality and his own striving.

Aristotle gave a somewhat different solution to the problem. We shall discuss it later, after touching upon another question of some interest.

We have already seen that the strictly intellectualistic approach to moral problems was by no means restricted to Platonic, Stoic, or Epicurean philosophy. No doubt, it came from the deep-rooted confidence the Greeks had in the rational order of nature.

Yet we discover in quite a large number of texts a completely different foundation of the same belief that right action only results from right knowledge. This different view is even expressed in some minor branches of the philosophical tradition.[104]

According to this view, the cosmic order may or may not be rational. Man, in any case, is far from being able to come to a full understanding of it by his own intellectual efforts. Yet man does know that his own fate is most certainly ruled by gods or powers or even by mere chance which he cannot control and which his intellect cannot grasp either. So nobody is able to understand properly what is happening to him or what is going to result from his own activity. Too many unpredictable factors interfere with his intention. Blame and praise, therefore, only refer to the question of whether a man has planned well and reasonably under the given circumstances and according to the information available. This is the essence of Isocrates' doctrine of εὐβουλία (sound judgement), which is also referred to in Plato's *Phaedrus* (237 B/C). The moral verdict can only be passed on a man's intellectual achievement, because what he actually performs or produces is due mainly to factors which are beyond his control.

As we can see, the Greeks concentrated their theories of ethics on the part played by human knowledge, even according to contradictory concepts of reality. Knowledge was considered the decisive factor in moral life, regardless of whether or not the human mind was supposed to be able to perceive and understand the order of being. The optimistic view prevailed where human life was examined in close relation to the universe, to nature in general, as in Hesiod, Anaximander, or Plato. But wherever human life became the isolated object of reflection, the pessimistic opinion about man's intellectual capacities inevitably .rose. This pessimism can be seen in Archilochus' fragments,[105] in what is left of Sophistic literature, including the writings of Isocrates,[106] in Herodotus[107] and other historical works, and in the history of philosophical scepticism. Yet already in the Iliad Agamemnon is referred to as the most telling example of the stupidity of men who do not take into account, in their plans and designs, the fact that they are utterly ignorant of what the gods have decided to arrange (2.38).

At a later stage of Greek thought, Thucydides reflected on this particular shortcoming of the human intellect, yet without introducing gods who interfere with human affairs. The freedom to choose, individually and collectively, the means and ends of action by intellectual effort can be drastically restricted in consequence of unfavorable conditions in the outside world such as war, hunger, or pestilence. Once the smooth-running of everyday life is interrupted, men are exposed to various kinds of compulsion which make them adapt their behavior to each other in dealing with the ensuing situation. Under these conditions, human nature tends to forfeit the faculty of free choice, which is a gift given to the intellect. A man who wants to deal politically has to take into account that sensible decisions (ἀμείνονες γνῶμαι) can be expected in times of peace and prosperity only (3.82.2). Again, the freedom to decide on action is entirely regarded as belonging to the intellect. This freedom ceases or suffers grave restrictions if compulsion from outside interferes. Likewise, the evaluation of the ensuing action refers to the preceding intellectual performance. A wise man, however, knows perfectly well that the intellectual mechanism of the human soul is fragile and easily harmed, so that actions are not always determined by sound, rational decisions.

The most illuminating examples of the various attitudes by which man tries to cope with his own intellectual weakness and fallibility can be found in Greek tragedy. Aeschylus' plays are full of events which surpass ordinary understanding. Why does Orestes find himself exposed to two contradictory claims of equally divine authority? Why does Eteocles face disaster in spite of all his righteousness? There seems to be no way to avoid the clash between the planning of Zeus and the well-founded moral standards of man. Yet wherever we can follow the plot of a complete trilogy, the outlook changes. Aeschylus eventually leads his spectator to the proper—that is to say rational—understanding of the universal rule of Zeus. This is possible, because Zeus, according to Aeschylus, brings about his everlasting justice by setting, sometimes rather arbitrarily, fresh standards every time the gap between the knowledge of man and the planning of the gods has become unbridgeable. Thus moral problems which nobody can resolve from their experience of human life become understandable and even soluble in the larger framework of Zeus' universal rule. The power and justice of Zeus can reconcile, in any given situation, divine and human knowledge, though no man involved can foresee how Zeus is going to handle the case.[108] That is why men have to be prudent and modest whatever happens: this prevents them from trusting too much in their own abilities and from additionally blinding themselves in the difficult situations to come.

Sophocles' view was somewhat different. He concentrated on the fate of individual human beings and abstained from speculating on the question whether or not divine planning is perceptible and even understandable *ex eventu*. To him divine and human knowledge remain incongruous, as can be seen in the cases of Ajax and Oedipus. The power and sublimity of the gods prevent man from perceiving or understanding their purposes—except at the very moment of his final demise. So the only thing man can do is to remain aware of his own ignorance and weakness. Consciousness of one's own deficiencies is the essential ingredient of moral knowledge. The claim to any kind of perfection, contentedness or excellence inevitably leads to outrage and, consequently, to divine punishment, because no man is perfect.[109] This is the message of Sophocles' tragedies, Herodotus' histories, and the Delphic tradition alike. Knowledge of oneself, knowledge of one's own shortcomings yields the only way to freedom of moral choice, whereas any pretended perfection prevents a man from dealing freely with the gods and his fellow men.[110]

Both Xenophon and Plato believed that Socrates, "who brought philosophy from heaven and the stars down to the market place," was motivated in all his ethical teaching by the commandment of Apollo, by the γνῶθι σεαυτόν: "Know thyself."[111] To him, moral philosophy was nothing but striving for self-knowledge.

The moral attitude which corresponded to the Delphic commandment was called σωφροσύνη.[112] The concept of σωφροσύνη both corroborates and restricts the essential part which the intellect plays in moral life. Knowledge of one's own ignorance and deficiencies is an intellectual achievement, there is no doubt about that. But it is a peculiar kind of knowledge which one can never describe in general terms. It makes good sense to state one's own ignorance in the field of, say, strategy or architecture. One can speak of and utilize this gap of knowledge as generally and objectively as of any piece of positive knowledge. To state that a man knows his own ignorance, when moral decisions are at stake, however, means something quite different. This kind of knowledge or ignorance can only be spoken of in general terms, with the implication of a moral judgement such as modesty or prudence. But once you try to ascertain the knowledge of your own ignorance in moral life, you have to refer to a given situation where acting is required. On this assumption alone is knowledge of one's own ignorance at the same time knowledge of something definite. This comes out very clearly when Socrates explains, according to Plato's account, that people are afraid of death because they regard death as an evil. He, Socrates, is aware of his own ignorance of whether or not this is true. Consequently he is far from any fear of death (*Apol.* 29A). To know one's own ignorance of the nature of death is relevant only if one wants to be properly prepared to die. This piece of knowledge cannot be tested except in that particular situation. It cannot be treated in the same objective way as a geometric calculation or a piece of historical information. You have to be fully conscious of both your being unable to ascertain adequately and objectively the given situation and your being doomed to act.

The freedom, then, to choose the ends and means of action which human beings seem to enjoy is not primarily, in the Greek view, the freedom to direct one's intention wherever one pleases. Free will does not exist in its own right as it does according to St. Augustine's anthropology. It depends on man's alleged potential ability to reach an adequate understanding of reality by his own intellectual effort. Yet the

free use of one's own intellectual faculties which leads to that free choice
or intention is not only extremely rare in human life. It is also open to
serious risks.

First, man's intellectual activity is often hindered or led astray by
necessities and compulsions from outside, from his own desires, emotions, and passions, or from the interaction of both. Secondly, the given
situation in which an individual has to act may be determined by factors beyond his rational understanding, since any individual possesses
only limited intellectual capacities. As for the result of action, both
kinds of obstacles cannot conceivably be overcome by intellectual
efforts alone, although man is required to take them into account. As
for the moral evaluation of the deed, the concept of σωφροσύνη (which
is, as we have seen, a cognitive achievement) accounts for man's full
responsibility in his intentions to which moral judgement ultimately
refers, at least according to Greek standards from the sixth or fifth century onwards. Man is told to be σώφρων, that is to say to act without
overrating his own capacities and claims. The intellectual effort, additional to the assessment of the ends and means of action, which is implied in the exercise of σωφροσύνη, however, does not altogether prevent the acting individual from moral error. But he can avoid, in this
way, the specific moral blindness which results from a false estimation
of his own capacities and faculties, claims and duties and which falls,
therefore, entirely within his own moral responsibility.

Finally, the full awareness of one's own knowledge and ignorance in
moral life can be reached only by facing and handling the situation in
which the knowledge is needed. This Socrates points out, according to
Plato's *Apology*, in his remarks on the fear of death. The same can
be seen in the final downfall of Oedipus, when he has removed, by his
own intellectual effort, all illusions about his own actions, their consequences, and his own present position. At the end of the drama,
Oedipus has reached, at an extremely high price, the freedom of choice
which the absence of error and illusion provides.

So man has first to become involved in human affairs before he is able
to acquire to its fullest extent the knowledge that leads to right action.
At this point, the intellectualistic approach so consistently followed in
Greek thought fails to provide ultimate standards of moral action.

In a recent study of the modern conception of will,[113] P. W. Strawson
speaks of two types of volition in moral life. He distinguishes between

subjective involvement in other people's affairs and objective dealings with them. It is only the first, according to the author, that invalidates the strict determination of everything that is going on among human beings, and creates the possibility of human freedom.

Our examination of the ideas the Greeks held about human action and their predominantly intellectualistic approach has taken us to the very same point. According to them moral freedom is guaranteed by the free intellectual activity of the human mind, which leads, however, to a proper insight into the immutable laws that determine the whole of reality. On the other hand, awareness of one's own intellectual deficiency as well as of one's inescapable duty towards human affairs seems to be essential in free and responsible human activities. Apparently, man has to rely on the rational order of being and on his intellect, which is supposed to be able to evaluate, according to that order, the means and ends of action. On the other hand, man has to be fully conscious of his own intellectual deficiencies, for he is doomed to become a part of that order through his action despite his inability to perceive the whole of reality. This universal dilemma was particularly strongly felt in Greece.

III.
The Greek View
of Human Action II

THE MAN who behaves according to the command-
ment of Apollo and who is always aware of his own deficiency was
called [a] σώφρων by the Greeks. The primary connotation of
σωφροσύνη, the state of being σώφρων, refers to the human intellect:
"sound thought, sanity, good sense." Various definitions of the concept
of σωφροσύνη which can already be drawn from prephilosophical texts
point in this direction: σωφροσύνη is called knowledge of oneself and
of one's own shortcomings, rational control of desires, temperance,
awareness of one's specific duties, limited as they may be, and the like.[1]
According to Xenophon, Socrates denied any difference between σωφροσύνη and σοφία (*mem.* 3.9.4f), both denoting the moral knowledge
on which virtue entirely and solely depends. You cannot acquire or pos-
sess that knowledge without applying it, and that is why one cannot
distinguish moral knowledge itself from the intention to use it. Virtually the same is said in various passages of Plato,[2] and this echoes a
famous saying of the poet Simonides about a hundred years earlier: he
defines the man who abstains from intentional wrongdoing as someone
"knowing the justice that supports the community"—εἰδώς . . . ὀνησί-
πολιν δίκαν—justice being the consummation of all virtues.[3] Thus the
concept of σωφροσύνη fits particularly well into the picture of early
Greek intellectualism, though on the other hand we are inclined, according to modern standards, to attribute to the human will most of
the modes of behavior which are pointed to by this word.

Yet the text where the equation of virtue and knowledge is questioned more intensely than anywhere else in archaic and classical Greek
literature deals exclusively with the concept of σωφροσύνη. I am speaking of Plato's *Charmides*. The characters of the dialogue repeatedly try
to arrive at a definition of σωφροσύνη, but in vain, since they are restricted in their reasoning by two presuppositions: first, σωφροσύνη has
to be taken as a virtue characteristically distinct from other virtues such

as justice or fortitude, for the generally accepted use of the word pre-supposes such a distinction; second, σωφροσύνη, being a virtue in it-self, has to be a specific kind of knowledge, because every individual virtue results from or is even identical with some sort of knowledge.

The trouble with σωφροσύνη results from the following problem. Any kind of knowledge can usually be ascertained from its object or content. This applies to the know-how and the know-what alike. The joiner knows what a chair is like and how to produce a chair; the just man knows what justice is like and how to act justly. What kind of knowledge is actually added, if the joiner and the just man are also described as possessing σωφροσύνη or being σώφρων? Clearly no better chairs are likely to be produced because of that additional qualification of the joiner, nor do the just man's actions become more just. Other-wise the professional skill of the joiner or justice as the moral knowl-edge of the just man would not suffice to produce good chairs or just actions respectively—which seems hardly admissible. The definition of σωφροσύνη as knowledge of good and evil, however, leads to another difficulty. This applies to any other word which denotes comprehensive righteousness as resulting from knowledge.[4] That is why Socrates, ac-cording to Xenophon, explicitly denied any difference between σοφία and σωφροσύνη.

At this very point of the discussion a new argument starts in Plato's dialogue: σωφροσύνη can be taken as the knowledge of one's own knowledge or ignorance.[5] Socrates explicitly connects this definition with the commandment of the Delphic Apollo (164D): γνῶθι σεαυτόν means "Become aware of your own weakness and ignorance." This gives a clue to the proper understanding of the general intention of the whole dialogue. The discussion is not or not primarily about a problem of epistemology. It is the question of how to act righteously under the prevailing circumstances of human nature and human life that has to be examined. But since the Greek tradition has always taken virtue as an intellectual achievement, any philosophical attempt to describe its na-ture inevitably leads to problems of epistemology. In the *Charmides* Socrates does not refer, as he does in the *Apology* (31D), to his δαιμό-νιον, his inner voice of unknown origin which spontaneously prevents him from taking the wrong course. The nature of the δαιμόνιον cannot be ascertained by mutual and rational understanding between several partners of a dialogue, for it speaks unpredictably and incalculably to

Socrates alone. The goal of the discussion in the *Charmides*, however, is to get at a definition of σωφροσύνη which is both objective and communicable.

Supposing the definition given above is right: the just man is σώφρων at the same time, in so far as he knows that he is just, but not because he knows what justice is like or how to act justly. In that case, σωφροσύνη appears as a kind of secondary or meta-knowledge which, being a knowledge of a knowledge, indirectly refers to the content of the primary knowledge. In addition, σωφροσύνη as a secondary knowledge makes its owner certain of his own primary knowledge or ignorance, but never of that of others (*Charm.* 170D–171E).

Several new problems arise from that conception, however. If you can postulate knowledge of a knowledge, why not knowledge of a knowledge of a knowledge—ad infinitum?[6] But even if you restrict yourself to the secondary knowledge, how can you verify its existence without reference to the content of the primary knowledge? The good architect has professional skill as his primary knowledge, the awareness of the skill as secondary knowledge or σωφροσύνη, and the same is true of the doctor. But how can he be aware of his secondary knowledge, its nature and its limits, without a detailed examination referring to all those pieces of information which form his primary knowledge?[7]

All these problems remain largely unsolved in the *Charmides*, and once again we have to keep in mind that the whole dialogue is about ethics rather than epistemology.[8] It seems obvious that Socrates is trying to get hold of a factor in moral life which would be separate from the knowledge of both the aim and the method of action but at the same time indispensable. It is pointed to but not in the least explained by the traditional concept of σωφροσύνη, and since it is an important factor of moral life determining human action, it must refer to the most valuable part of a man's personality, that is to say to his intellect. Consequently it has to be described as a virtue, a special kind of moral knowledge, characteristically different from other virtues.

In the *Charmides* Plato does not succeed in giving a satisfactory definition of σωφροσύνη. The problem remains unsolved. Later on Plato apparently dismissed the more general definition of σωφροσύνη as knowledge of knowledge, which had turned out to be hard to verify, and returned to its more traditional meaning as modesty or awareness of one's own ignorance, for only the consciousness of one's own deficiency provides the motive for learning and moral progress (*Soph.* 230A). The *Greater Alcibiades* (132D–133C) describes σωφροσύνη as self-cognition in the sense that the human soul uses its most valuable part, its λογιστικόν, as the mirror in which to contemplate itself.[9] But nowhere else did Plato discuss along the same lines the immense difficulties which arise from the identification of knowledge and virtue, so optimistically presupposed in the *Protagoras* or the *Euthydemus*. In these two dialogues, however (344Aff, 278Eff), one point was made quite clear: the knowledge which is called virtue can never be definitively acquired. Moral progress rests on a permanent process of learning[10] which can be interrupted by acts of forgetting. Man is able to deteriorate and to improve many times during his lifetime. This condition can be easily explained in terms of the theory of forms, because the eternal forms have to be constantly approached, though they can never be reached, by the human intellect. The concept of σωφροσύνη denotes the awareness of this particular instability and fallibility of man in a moral context. But the question of the *Charmides*, namely in what respect this knowledge is different from other kinds of knowledge, was left unanswered, at least in the field of ethical speculation. It had been made clear in the *Charmides* that the knowledge called σωφροσύνη did influence moral attitudes apart from the knowledge of the means and ends of action. That is why the Platonic concept of σωφροσύνη, as expounded rather than defined in the *Charmides*, has, in fact, much in common with the theory of will in various branches of Christian moral philosophy. Σωφροσύνη helps to bring about morally right action in a way quite different from that in which all other virtues perform this function. The contribution of σωφροσύνη in that task disregards the intellectual perception and evaluation of the aim of action, which is, after all, the primary concern of the distinction between acting according to virtue and according to vice in any intellectualistic theory of ethics. Σωφροσύνη exclusively refers to the state of mind of the acting individual. The difficulty which Socrates and his interlocutors face in their attempts to define σωφροσύνη results from their intellectualistic approach to the problem. From the basic assumption that any virtue has to be regarded as some kind of knowledge, it is impossible to isolate a moral attitude which is independent of the cognition of the objectives of action. A theory of will is needed to clarify the phenomenon which is pointed to by the term σωφροσύνη in Plato's view.

On the other hand, knowledge remained a problem of its own in philosophical research outside ethical theory. Plato himself treated the problem of whether or not we can conceive of a knowledge of a knowledge in the *Theaetetus* (200Aff). Aristotle dealt extensively with the question of what happens if the intellect turns towards itself instead of perceiving objects outside itself, thus producing a thought of a thought (νόησις τῆς νοήσεως).[11] The Stoics, in their turn, developed the conception of συναίσθησις.[12] The term denotes an act of rational understanding, of which the object is one's own sensual perception together with the thing perceived,[13] and which always accompanies man's sensual activity.[14] Following these lines Plotinus eventually came,[15] for the first time, to a clear distinction between self-cognition and self-consciousness, and even to an adequate understanding of the phenomenon of unconscious or subconscious cognition, as was shown by H. R. Schwyzer.[16]

The above survey is very sketchy. But I am fairly certain that nowhere in the history of that problem is the ethical aspect of Plato's *Charmides* referred to. The question of whether there are different kinds of knowledge had definitively shifted from ethical theory to ontology and epistemology. In addition, the Middle Platonic theory of virtue did not rely on the *Charmides* either. Various definitions of σωφροσύνη which have been preserved in Middle Platonic sources[17] disregard the *Charmides* altogether and betray the influence of Stoic theory instead. According to the prevailing tendency in Hellenistic philosophy, moral criteria were taken from external reality rather than from the analysis of human consciousness, the latter belonging to epistemology or metaphysics.

There is another doctrine in Plato's philosophy which invalidates that rigid intellectualism, so notable in Greek, particularly Socratic, thought. I am speaking of Plato's theory of Eros as illustrated in the *Symposium* and in other dialogues.[18] Through all the levels of the spiritual and sensual world, life depends entirely on the fact that, again and again, one being turns to another to bring about, by such a reunion, what had no existence previously and whose absence was felt as a serious deficiency. Thus all beings in their state of permanent need and imperfection have been given the innate striving for the better, the more perfect, which causes life to unfold and to continue.[19] Intention in that particular sense permeates the whole of reality. It can be seen in sexual desire and the ensuing procreation of organic life, but also in the creative efforts of the artist, the statesman, or the educator.[20] It applies equally to the very act of cognition by which the soul approaches a higher level of reality, thus improving on its own previous condition and moving towards its own perfection. Moral progress, consequently, being identical with growing intellectual knowledge and increasing spiritual life, rests entirely on the ἔρως τῶν καλῶν (love of beautiful things).

The idea of the special character of love among the various types of striving or desire is not restricted to the teaching of Platonic and post-Platonic philosophy. Isocrates inserted an interesting digression on the ἔρως τῶν καλῶν in his *Helen* (55/56). It is pointed out, in that passage, that the desire for all other objects we can possibly want to attain is stilled the moment we reach our aim. This does not happen in the case of the ἔρως τῶν καλῶν. Its power (ῥώμη) is stronger than our own deliberate intention (βούλεσθαι), corresponding to the fact that its objectives are greater than anything we may otherwise wish or desire. Both Isocrates and Plato have forerunners in what they apparently considered the importance of Eros in cosmic and moral life: Hesiod, for instance, and Empedocles. But neither of the latter developed a theory of will on that basis.[21]

Plato apparently abstained from the task of describing by means of a coherent argument this striving for the better, for the more perfect, which comprehends, in all its cosmic and moral dignity, sexual desire as well as intellectual effort. Eros in this particular sense is, in the view of Plato, prior to all factors of moral life that have to be taken into account in a theory of human action. Plato gives his whole argument on this subject in the form of various myths,[22] as he usually does in his attempts to answer ultimate questions. The problem of freedom and determination in human life is also given an answer in one of the myths of the *Republic*, since Plato's creed of man's ultimate responsibility for his moral life is not open to discursive thought.

In the question of the part played by love or will in ethics and psychology, Plato restricted himself to stating that all three parts of the human soul which cause, by their joint activities, man's moral life, have their own special share of volition among their functions (*Rep.* 580Dff; cf. *Tim.* 70A). So volition did not gain, in the context of ethical speculation, the independence that could have enabled it to become the psychological point of reference in ethical evaluation of man's actions. It remained a mere implication of both the act of intellectual cognition and emotional or instinctive drive.

This view was generally held in Peripatetic and later Platonic philosophy. Galen, for instance, mentioned the special ὄρεξις (yearning, desire, instinctive want) of any of the three parts or faculties of the human soul (*de temp.* 2).[23]

Plato's concept of love became additionally important, from a different point of view, at a late stage of Academic philosophy, to be discussed below (cf. ch. V). But since that concept was not transformed into an operable and terminologically fixed theory, neither Plato nor his successors could possibly introduce the isolated factor of intention or volition into their doctrine of human action. In their attempts to set up the psychological frame of moral standards, they always kept to the traditional bipartition of intellect and emotion,[24] rational and irrational forces of the human soul. They concentrated on the problem of how reason, of which the primary achievement is always cognition, could be made and kept the leading factor in moral life, as nature required. It remained more or less tacitly understood that right knowledge always leads to right action.

Yet the bipartite psychology turned out quite inadequate for solving such problems as that of whether, and, if so, why, people do wrong on purpose. The problem was likely to remain unsolved as long as the virtue that leads to right action could only be understood as some sort of intellectual achievement by which reason shows itself, in the field of moral action, superior to instinct and emotion.

A new road to the proper understanding of the interrelation between virtue and knowledge, however, was opened up by Aristotle.[25] He argued against the traditional and Platonic position from three different points of view, without abandoning the traditional bipartite psychology.

1. Already in some Platonic dialogues, such as the *Minor Hippias*, the *Charmides*, and the *Protagoras*, the difference between producing or making on the one hand and acting on the other is duly, though not always consistently, noted.[26] In the first case any judgement can ultimately refer only to the quality of the product: the architect is judged according to the quality of the building he has built. In the second case, however, action itself is subject to judgement, and nothing else. So if both producing and acting are, in fact, directed by knowledge, one has to assume two different kinds of knowledge, whereas Socrates

always argued from the close similarity of technical and moral knowledge. Aristotle stresses the difference, and does so more precisely than Plato.[27]

2. According to traditional wisdom, exercise and practice provide the basis of any achievement. The topic was extensively treated by some Sophists, by Democritus[28] and also by Plato's rival Antisthenes.[29] Plato's own theory of education includes the concept of exercise mainly with regard to the question of how to cultivate the irrational faculties of the soul independently of rational instruction.[30] Aristotle, eventually, put forward the first comprehensive theory of ἔθος (exercise or practice) with reference to all aspects of moral conduct.

3. Finally Aristotle was the first to draw a clear distinction between nature and moral or social life. Everything that results from human action belongs to the realm of what Aristotle calls ἐνδεχόμενα καὶ ἄλλως ἔχειν, things that are capable of becoming real in various ways. The field of human action is not, therefore, knowable and predictable as cosmic or natural events are. Knowledge in the strict sense of the word (ἐπιστήμη) only exists for what is always the same and can be understood according to rules that are generally and permanently applicable. So human action in practical life cannot become the content of knowledge in the same way as a cosmic phenomenon or a technical procedure, and moral rules cannot be directly deduced from the rational understanding of nature, for nature is eternal and unchanging and social life is not. The discovery of a cosmic law is due to an effort of the human intellect which essentially differs from the choice of the objectives for practical action. The intellect cannot make the latter correspond to the knowledge of general principles, because human affairs are in permanent change. There is no science (ἐπιστήμη) of practical life, because general rules may frequently apply to human affairs but not always.

This conception separates practical life where action is required from the realm of natural determination, but it does not devaluate practical life for its lack of rationality. Such a devaluation may cause serious consequences in the field of ethical theory and practice and does, in fact, inhere in the tradition of Platonic philosophy.

This is the basis of Aristotle's theory of ἔθος, by which he avoided the difficulties noted in Plato's *Charmides*, without introducing the notion of will or intention as such.

The traditional understanding of virtue implies the idea that one has first to acquire a virtue in order to use it. This is tacitly presupposed in the Sophistic and Socratic discussions of the problem of whether or not virtue can be taught. Aristotle's view is entirely new and different. He defines virtue neither as δύναμις—that is to say natural gift or faculty—nor as ἐπιστήμη—theoretical knowledge acquired through intellectual activity—but as a disposition of the soul (ἕξις). The disposition results, on the basis of natural faculties, from permanently acting in accordance with the virtue in question. So man does not acquire a justice which enables him to act justly. On the contrary, by practising justice in a chain of individual acts he becomes just. This practice, however, ought not to be a sheer habit. Every act in that process has to be intentional and thus subject to moral judgement. Intention, in its turn, is warranted by the intellect which has to choose, in any given case, the goal of action. In making this choice under the changing conditions of human life, the intellect does not operate in the same way as in its theoretical efforts leading to that kind of knowledge which is lasting, generally applicable, and demonstrably true. Practical and theoretical intelligence are not identical. The latter, called σοφία, provides, in the field of ethics, theoretical knowledge of moral phenomena and standards, but never chooses individual aims of action in practical life. Thus intentionality rests entirely on the practical intelligence (φρόνησις).[31]

This theory of human action, which I have been describing with substantial abbreviations, avoids a great number of difficulties arising from the traditional identification of virtue with knowledge and vice with lack of knowledge. According to this theory, the habitual inclination to act virtuously and to receive correctly the impact of the outside world (πάθη, affections) results from a process of practice. But in every stage of that process the intellect is at work,[32] thus insuring intentionality and moral relevance. Aristotle's conception supersedes the controversy of Plato's *Protagoras* whether or not sensuality and irrational impulses can outdo the moral knowledge which has been acquired through reason. Moral progress, according to Aristotle, does not result from increasing knowledge. Virtue and vice are dispositions affecting the choice which the intellect has to make afresh in any given situation (ἕξεις προαιρετικαί).

This Aristotelian concept of προαίρεσις, deliberate choice of the means and ends according to moral standards and preceding action, greatly contributed towards clarifying traditional Greek ideas on the difference between voluntary and involuntary action which already appear in the Old Epic and in early Greek law.[33] Aristotle's theory of action was extensively used in the art of Greek biography,[34] because the unfolding of a moral character throughout a man's lifetime could be adequately analyzed and described along these lines. Galen's statement (*de opt. med.* 2), that every achievement in human life (κατορθούμενον) is due to capacity (δύναμις) and deliberate decision (βούλησις), is undoubtedly formulated in terms of Aristotelian anthropology, which had been largely integrated into the scholarly Platonism of the period.

One other detail in Aristotle's moral and psychological doctrines could have led to the concept of will as isolated from both instinct and reason. Aristotle rightly observed that anger in a given situation is not a reaction primarily to the action of one's opponent but to his attitude of contempt or disregard (*rhet.* 1378b1ff). So anger seems to originate from man's self-love or self-esteem rather than from the intention to retaliate materially against an offense (ibid. 1371b18ff). Such a peculiarity could have been easily described and analyzed in terms of a theory of will that would provide the point of reference for the moral evaluation of the phenomenon in question. In addition, anger, though undoubtedly an emotion or affection, seems to be brought about with the decisive aid of reasoning, for man becomes angry only on the basis of a preconceived knowledge of what retaliation or just punishment should be like. This kind of knowledge implies the disposition to act spontaneously in the given moment without that thorough intellectual perception of the aim of action which provides, in other cases, the basis of any moral evaluation of the deed (*rhet.* 1370b15, *E.N.* 1149a25ff; cf. Plat. *Rep.* 440A). Sheer desire (ἐπιθυμία) leads to action only if the individual, in addition to his being desirous, has made a rational calculation as to whether or not the desired aim is attainable. From anger spontaneous action can originate because it arises on the basis of an already existing moral or intellectual judgement which applies to the given situation (*E.N.* 1111b23; cf. *rhet.* 1386b8ff).[35]

Thus a closer examination of the affection of anger could, in fact, have led to isolating the volitional factor from both reason and emotion: volition as inherent in previously acquired moral knowledge seems to precede the intellectual perception of the aim of action, thus being independent of the act of cognition of the given situation. Volition can be separated, in that particular case, from the intellectual choice of the objective of action as well as from instinctive drive.

There is no ancient text where this possibility is realized, although the semi-rational character of anger, its affinity to courage and to the sense of justice,[36] caused it to be treated differently from other affections in Hellenistic philosophy,[37] unless it was condemned along with every other type of affection, as in orthodox Stoic doctrine. Thus the possibility of developing a theory of will out of the theory of anger was always present in post-Aristotelian philosophy. Cicero devoted a lengthy section, compiled from various sources, to the problem of why and how the impulse inherent in anger turns out to be necessary in many situations where moral action is required, whereas the affection of anger itself is far from being laudable (*Tusc.* 4.47–55).

The Stoics, however, who defined every affection, including anger, as the impulse towards a morally wrong action which originates solely from an intellectual misjudgement without the contribution of any irrational faculty of the human soul, could not help isolating, to a certain extent, the element of volition in the case of all affection. They spoke of the ῥοπή (inclination), the ὁρμή (impulse), the εἶξις (surrender), the μετάπτωσις (instability) which the whole intellect, but only the intellect, suffers from its own false judgement (e.g. Plut. *virt. mor.* 7.446F = *SVF* 3.459). Here, too, the drive towards acting was named separately, although no Stoic could have agreed with the idea that such a drive could possibly be regarded and morally valued in independence of the foregoing intellectual perception of the aim of action.

Aristotle also loosened, as we have seen, the rigid interconnection between nature and human affairs which is typical of the main stream of Greek ethical thought. Only nature and its lasting order make it possible to know something objectively and to offer rational proof of that knowledge. In moral life objective knowledge can only refer to the nature of man, to the just, and to other entities that never occur as such in empirical life. No man buys a piece of bread in order to perform an act of justice by paying the right price, though he is just in doing so, for he could have stolen the same piece in order to feed himself—which is his principal aim anyway. The intellect can verify, through its theoretical efforts, utility and justice as such as implied in that situation. But it is entirely up to the practical intelligence to come to the decision which coordinates the objectives set by both utility and justice. That is why neither utility nor justice is brought about as such through human action but always in varying combinations and limitations. Human intention, however, underlies moral judgements. These are passed according to the standards of justice as such (αὐτὸ τὸ δίκαιον) which is not identical with the just as appearing in a given action.

Finally, the concept of decision as produced by the practical intellect greatly contributes to the solution of the problem of freedom and determination in moral life. This can be illustrated by an example which was invented by Aristotle and further expounded by his commentator Alexander of Aphrodisias about A.D. 200.[38]

The crew of a ship which runs into a tempest throw the cargo into the sea in order to save their lives. If one tries to understand this event in terms of objective knowledge, one will be led to the conclusion that the act of the crew was non-intentional. No sailor is likely to destroy the one thing for which he is sailing—except when a compulsion from outside turns out to be stronger than his intention. In our case the tempest overpowers the original intention of the crew.

But if you consider the very same event from the point of view of the sailors in the given situation, that is to say as a task for practical intelligence, the result will be the opposite. The crew did on purpose what they did at that moment. They could have postponed the measure, they could have waited until they were drowned or the tempest ended, they could have abandoned ship and so forth. Their action resulted, in the given situation, from their own decision. The decision, however, cannot be grasped, in that view, as an act of will which is independent of the cognition involved. The definition of intentionality refers in both cases to the cognitive achievement of the acting individuals.

The example is intended to show that the problem of freedom and determination concerns the practical intellect only. The theoretical intellect always discovers an uninterrupted chain of causation, unless it falls short in its efforts. But theoretical reasoning does not contribute to the decision which leads to action and which realizes human freedom.

Aristotle's theory supplied the most important contribution Greek philosophy had made to the understanding of human action. He taught that intention should be regarded as belonging to human consciousness and as resulting from intellectual activity. But he did away with the traditional view, according to which the intention of doing the right thing had to be identified with a type of knowledge whose truth can be objectively ascertained.[39] Knowing what is true and deciding what is morally good result from two different activities of the human intellect.[40]

There are some shortcomings in Aristotle's doctrine as well. It is, for instance, hard to explain in his terms whether a spontaneous deed of moral relevance is due to a deep-rooted attitude or rather to a new and unsettled one.[41] But modern philosophy kept closely to the line of Aristotle when it started handling the problem of intention without the concept of will.[42]

Greek philosophy reacted in different ways to Aristotle's conception. Orthodox Stoics[43] and Epicureans[44] alike explicitly returned to the position held by Socrates and insisted on the identity of theoretical and moral knowledge, thus tightening the bonds between the order of nature and human affairs.[45] Consequently they rejected the distinction between practical and theoretical intellect,[46] following the line of some minor Socratics of the fourth century who insisted on the unity of knowledge and virtue.[47] To them, practice or training in moral life only meant repeated meditation and application of the moral knowledge that had been previously acquired through intellectual instruction.[48] This knowledge could entail the information that physical training and the ascetic life were more important for moral progress than erudition and science. But this did not contradict the primacy of moral instruction.

Later on, the term προαίρεσις was used largely to denote the general attitude of a man rather than the moral decision leading to a single action. This applies to later Stoic terminology as well as to normal Hellenistic Greek.[49] Epictetus, for instance, spoke a good deal about προαίρεσις, which he valued higher than learning and knowledge.[50] Προαίρεσις has become, in that usage, the equivalent of Aristotle's ἕξις προαιρετική. Moreover, it seems to entail, in that general meaning, a strong element of sheer volition, especially when opposed to learning or knowledge. This observation is stressed by the fact that, occasionally, the verb θέλειν can go with προαίρεσις: limping is a hindrance of the leg, not of the προαίρεσις, provided the προαίρεσις itself does not wish it (ἐὰν μὴ αὐτὴ θέλῃ Epict. *ench.* 8). Yet θέλειν with reference to personified προαίρεσις does not point so much to the element of volition but rather to a preparedness to recognize correctly the physical deficiency of limping as a factor of no moral relevance (ἀδιάφορον) instead of an evil (κακόν). This was rightly observed by Epictetus' commentator Simplicius in the sixth century A.D. (p. 4.29 Dübner; cf. p. 33.20): it is clear, he observed, that the conception and evaluation of the aim of action (πρόληψις) comes first, and that this is an act of rational cognition (λογικὴ γνῶσις) and appropriate to a human being. At the time of Simplicius, there existed the Neoplatonic definition of θέλησις as "inner motion of the soul" (ψυχῆς ἔνδοθεν κίνησις) which he knew (p. 44.7) but disregarded in the present context, thus underlining the predominance of the intellectualistic element in both προαίρεσις and πρόληψις.[51]

Another notion in the Stoic system of psychology and ethics which seems to fit in with a voluntaristic theory is that of assent (συγκατάθεσις). The intellect, having formed on the basis of sensual perception what may be called an image (φαντασία) of a section of the outside world which mostly entails a motive for action, has to corroborate this motive by passing a special judgement on the target of action involved and thereby automatically setting free the impulse (ὁρμή) towards action. But it would be misleading to interpret the first step (φαντασία) as the intellectual cognition and evaluation of the aim of action, the second (συγκατάθεσις) as the initiating act of volition which continues, as an impulse (ὁρμή), throughout the ensuing action. This clearly was the view of Clement of Alexandria, which is to be discussed later (see below p. 110). Orthodox Stoics, however, again and again insisted on the unity of all faculties and functions of the ruling part (ἡγεμονικόν) of the human soul. Everything that goes on there has to be understood in terms of a rational judgement and of its direct or automatic consequence. The assent, as described previously, is voluntary, yet necessitated in the case of a right decision by the truth of the underlying φαντασία,[52] which entails, in its own right, a judgement on the foregoing sensual perception. All the four basic functions of the ἡγεμονικόν, that is to say perception, imagination, assent, and impulse, are entirely rational in the orthodox Stoic view and can be described or analyzed, therefore, in terms of cognition and judgement.[53] Even the term ἀσθενὴς συγκατάθεσις, "weak assent" (SVF 3.172, 3.548), does not mean the lack of energy in the efforts of the human will. An ἀσθενὴς συγκατάθεσις results from ignorance or rests on insufficient proofs. In the field of human affairs it leads to moral mistakes in the same way as false opinions (μοχθηραὶ δόξαι) do.[54] Again, everything depends on the intellectual performance of the human soul.

The same applies to the Stoic doctrine of the tension (τόνος) of the soul. It was conceived, in the context of Stoic materialism, to explain the coherence of as subtle a substance (SVF 1.563) as the soul was considered to be made of. But in addition, the degree of strength (ἰσχύς) of the soul, as measured by the intellectual and practical activities of man, was identified with the degree of tension.[55] This seems to indicate that τόνος, in Stoic terminology, referred to the energy of volition as displayed in all sorts of human activity. But the notion of τόνος never became closely attached to that of ὁρμή, impulse towards action, for measuring volitional energy. On the contrary: affection (πάθος), according to orthodox Stoic doctrine an excessive drive towards action (πλεονάζουσα ὁρμή) on the basis of, or implied in, a false judgement, sometimes causes a quite extraordinary strength of volition or striving, as no Stoic would have denied. The man motivated by such an affection was compared with the runner who is unable to stop at the end of the course. Yet the ὁρμὴ πλεονάζουσα was explained, in all cases, by the lack of tension.[56] So τόνος appears in the efficiency, rigidity, and infallibility of man's intellectual efforts rather than in the sheer energy of will by which he is driven towards action. Τόνος ψυχῆς does not precisely mean the strength of conviction and the energy displayed in right action which Lucian had in mind when he spoke of the strength of the soul (ἀλκὴ ψυχῆς) and moral attitude (γνώμη) as the decisive factors in the competition between the philosophers of various sects and schools (Eun. 9).

Finally, the use of the term ἐπιβολή, "application," in both Stoic and Epicurean philosophy betrays a certain awareness of the shortcomings caused by the entirely intellectualistic approach to the problems of psychology and ethics. Stoics and Epicureans alike spoke of the ἐπιβολὴ τῆς διανοίας, that is to say the application of the cognitive, planning, and volitional forces of the intellect to the objective of action.[57] Furthermore, the act of ἐπιβολή could also be thought and spoken of with regard to other than cognitive forces and faculties. Thus love was defined as ἐπιβολὴ τῆς φιλοποιΐας.[58] Again the philosophical use of the term was not too different from current usage. Polybius, for instance, used the word very frequently to denote plan, onslaught, or purpose, along with κρίσις, προαίρεσις, γνώμη, or ὁρμή.[59]

Since, in the Stoic view, any impulse towards action (ὁρμή) automatically results from the judgement which the intellect has passed on the chosen objective, the foregoing application of the cognitive, critical, and planning forces to the objective, that is to say the ἐπιβολὴ τῆς διανοίας, can be called an impulse before the impulse (ὁρμὴ πρὸ ὁρμῆς *SVF* 3.173), which comes in fact dangerously near the point where volition might be conceived separately from cognition and judgement. This explains the pointed assertion, even outside the Stoic tradition proper, that any ἐπιβολή has to be understood as a performance of the intellect.[60]

All these details of Stoic and Epicurean doctrine clearly indicate that the problem of will as a factor independent of cognition, in the psychological explanation and the moral evaluation of human action, frequently arose in the course of philosophical discussion. Yet no one in the scholarly tradition of Hellenistic philosophy seems to have been prepared to answer it by a theory of will. The primacy and dignity of reason of which the principal function is undoubtedly cognitive rather than volitional was firmly established throughout that period. For only through the medium of reason could the order of nature and the rules of moral life be brought into harmony with one another.

The intricacies of Epicurean and, above all, Stoic psychology did not substantially improve on Aristotle's theory of human action and its moral evaluation.[61] It was generally accepted, though sometimes slightly modified with the aid of some Stoic concepts, by Platonists from the first century B.C. onwards and, of course, by the Peripatetics. This can be seen from Middle Platonic handbooks such as Albinus' *Introduction*, of the second century A.D., where the part played by practice and exercise in the course of moral progress, the distinction between practical and theoretical intellect,[62] and other topics are reproduced in Aristotelian terms. There was, however, hardly any substantial improvement on his doctrine—perhaps with the sole exception of the interesting theory of human freedom and instability which Posidonius conceived, in the first century B.C., from an entirely Aristotelian point of view.[63]

The first to show, in various minor details, some influence of Po-

sidonius' ethical theory is the Academic Eudorus, a contemporary of
Augustus, whose subdivision of the *pars moralis* of philosophy has been
preserved in Stobaeus' anthology (2 p. 42ff Wachsm.-Hense). Eudorus
replaced the usual bipartition of theory and practice by a tripartition:
θεωρητικόν (theoretical), ὁρμητικόν (volitional), πρακτικόν (practical).
A detailed doctrine περὶ ὁρμῶν (concerning impulses) had already been
developed by the early Stoics (cf. *SVF* 3.169ff), but quite apart from
the question of how theory and practice contribute to moral life.

The orthodox Stoic doctrine[64] of φαντασία/συγκατάθεσις/ὁρμή, as
described above (p. 61), firmly established the predominance of the intellect in all questions of ethics and psychology. Only the intellect, in
the Stoic view, creates the motives for moral action by its cognitive
efforts, from which the impulse towards action automatically follows.

Eudorus, though apparently under the influence of Stoic theory (cf.
Sen. *ep.* 89.14f), does not argue in full accordance with the system of
Stoic psychology as described above. The first, theoretical part of ethics
is about the evaluation of possible aims of action. Without such an
evaluation the following impulse cannot possibly be good and reasonable. The second part deals with the problem of how to direct rightly
the impulse towards what one has premeditated (τὸ τὴν ὁρμὴν τῷ περι-
νοηθέντι καλῶς ἐπιβαλεῖν), and the third is about action itself. Unfortunately, the excerpt of Stobaeus is extremely brief in the further discussion of part two. We are only told that the chapter on ὁρμαί deals
with ὁρμαί proper and affections (πάθη), since affections are, according
to a well-known Stoic definition, excessive impulses (p. 44.3–5) that
lead to false actions. But it seems clear that Eudorus, unlike early
Stoics, but in accordance with the philosopher whose doctrine Seneca
reports in letter 89, must have felt the need for inserting between the
cognition of the aim and the action itself a separate, conscious act of the
acting individual by which the action is definitively directed towards
its aim. There is no indication that Eudorus' ethical system was
adopted or further developed by later Platonists. Yet the same need to
insert a separate act of volition between cognition and action can be
seen from some passages of the pseudo-Platonic *Definitions* which also
date from the Middle Platonic period.

Aristotle defined virtue as neither knowledge (ἐπιστήμη) nor natural
faculty (δύναμις) but rather as ἕξις, that is to say disposition to act
intentionally in a certain way (see above p. 56). The definition was gener-

ally adopted by Peripatetics and Academics and modified by the Stoics who preferred the term διάθεσις instead of ἕξις and did not reject the equation of knowledge and virtue. Accordingly, in the pseudo-Platonic *Definitions*, which betray the considerable influence exercised by Peripatetic and Stoic doctrines on later Platonism, virtue itself (ἀρετή 411D) is not defined as δύναμις. Some individual virtues, however, are called δυνάμεις, besides their being defined as ἕξεις, διαθέσεις, or ἐπιστῆμαι (kinds of knowledge). So φρόνησις, practical intelligence, is called the faculty for producing happiness or perfection (δύναμις ποιητική . . . τῆς ἀνθρώπων εὐδαιμονίας 411D) and εὐσέβεια, piety, "the voluntary faculty for worshipping the gods" (δύναμις θεραπευτικὴ θεῶν ἑκούσιος 412E). These definitions take into account an independent voluntaristic element, since they do not always presuppose, as Plato did (see above p. 48f), that every virtue includes the intention to use it. Ἐπιστήμη, theoretical intelligence, is not defined as a faculty (414B), since there is no action involved which demands the decision to use that particular virtue as in the case of piety or practical intelligence. In its quality as ἐπιστήμη ἀνυπόθετος (absolute knowledge, *i.e.* without content) theoretical intelligence is the only self-fulfilling virtue with no need for application to an object in the world outside the acting individual.

So the gap that is filled by the conception of will in medieval and modern ethical thought seems to have been felt in antiquity as well, particularly during that period of Platonic philosophy when the tradition was far from being voluntaristic.

Yet another detail deserves our attention even more. According to Plato's metaphysics, theory, which leads to the intelligible, has far more dignity than practice, which is inevitably bound to the empirical world. Aristotle, too, believed in the higher rank of theory, as he pointed out in the *Nicomachean Ethics*.[65] But this opinion does not automatically result from Aristotle's own metaphysics and anthropology. According to him, freedom of choice as the basis of morality does not regard the theoretical intellect. It is realized exclusively through the activity of practical intelligence. So Dicaearchus, one of Aristotle's most distinguished pupils, could well give primacy to practice instead of theory without any substantial change in the Peripatetic system.[66]

From the first century B.C. onwards, however, Platonism became the predominant factor in Greek philosophy, and also penetrated non-Pla-

tonic traditions. So the higher rank of theory became firmly established, even in the field of ethical speculation. The wisdom that embraces the ultimate cause of being, beyond all given entities (ἐπιστήμη
ἀνυπόθετος),[67] that is to say knowledge resulting from pure thought
without reference to the sensual world, was regarded as the highest
achievement of both intellectual and moral progress. It became generally agreed that man enjoys the gift of freedom only when his activity is
entirely intellectual or spiritual and thereby disentangles him from the
ties of matter.[68] Every act of practice, on the other hand, subjects him
to the law of matter and its inescapable determination. There is hardly
any doubt about the dignity of theory in relation to practice in post-
Hellenistic philosophy. Platonic ontology provides only one answer to
that question.

But once the superiority of theory and spiritual life has been firmly
established in ethical thought, practical action comes dangerously near
the point where it loses moral relevance altogether. If human perfection
can be achieved through theoretical or non-empirical knowledge only,
action as such, and also the intellectual activity which leads to deciding
about action, are likely to become disturbing factors rather than a
means of moral progress. On the basis of the strict ontological distinction between spirit and matter it became increasingly difficult to prove
that the highest part of the human soul is concerned with action as well
as with theory. The problem did not arise in Stoic or Epicurean philosophy, which denied any difference between matter and spirit, and, accordingly, between theoretical and practical knowledge.[69] The problem
was tolerable and even soluble in Aristotle's view of reality. He did not
deny the difference between spirit and matter, but he did not admit
that reality could rest upon only one of them. The problem, however,
became crucial in post-Hellenistic Platonism.

From the second century A.D. onwards representatives of the scholarly tradition of Platonic philosophy such as Albinus or Plotinus had to
oppose sectarians who regarded themselves as followers of Plato and
other sages of the past and who tried to contest the importance of any
kind of action in moral life. Their argument was largely based on a
radical reinterpretation of the Platonic dualism, by which matter became inextricably attached to evil and spirit to good.[70] The scholarly-
minded Platonists made extended use of Stoic and Aristotelian concepts in order to prove the need for practice in moral life, regardless of

the superior rank of theory. Plotinus, in the third century, made the most noteworthy attempt in this direction; we shall discuss it later. But they did not develop a notion of will, which could have been a useful tool for handling the crucial questions arising from such debates: can we grasp intention as such in order to pass our moral judgement? Can we evaluate an action according to moral standards regardless of the amount of knowledge to which it testifies?

IV.
St. Paul
and Philo

IN THE TWO preceding chapters we came to understand why the Greeks, in their attempts to analyze and to evaluate human action, never developed a distinct concept of will. All the questions implied in that problem, however, were to be dealt with, through the many centuries of medieval and post-medieval philosophy,[1] predominantly with the aid of such a concept, which also made a lasting impact on all European languages.[2] Yet the disregard which the Greeks had for this possibility of explaining human action and moral responsibility is apparently in agreement with some recent attempts to handle the problem philosophically,[3] whereas various schools of modern psychology still seem to need the concept.[4]

One topic which has been extensively treated, in medieval and post-medieval philosophy, with the aid of the notion of will, is the question of human freedom. It belongs to metaphysics, moral theory, and psychology, and is usually referred to, in modern scholarship, by the term Free Will.[5]

The freedom to decide for a certain way of acting in a given situation, which every human being is likely to experience in his life, mostly in a quite trivial way, becomes debatable once reasoning starts from the question to what extent the outcome has been determined by the very act of decision. Such a reflection may reveal that the outcome has largely been determined by the realistic assessment of the objective aimed at which preceded the action and which was achieved by the intellectual forces of the acting individual. Reflection can also teach, in a given situation, that this intellectual activity was hindered or distorted by error or emotion, or its cognitive results rendered inappropriate by compulsion exercised from outside. A register of these factors, carefully composed for a given situation, could provide, at least in theory, an exhaustive explanation for every human action as to the extent of its being caused by a free decision of the deliberative intellect. Clearly this condition applies to acting individuals and groups alike; hence it can also provide a guideline for historiography, as was pointed out, for instance, by Max Weber with reference to Thucydides.[6] If human action is guided by the rational perception and evaluation of aims (which intellectual act can be restricted by the factors mentioned above), the historian has to elucidate, as thoroughly as possible, the planning of the acting individuals and the interfering factors. Thus he may be able to show in his narrative how and to what extent historical events were caused by the free decisions of acting individuals.

All this makes good sense, provided intention in social and moral life solely results from rational perception of the means and ends on the one hand, and error, emotion, and compulsion on the other.[7] But once a good or ill will can be identified behind or apart from these factors, the situation changes. Now, human freedom is no longer evaluated exclusively according to the free choice of the means and ends of action which the intellect has made, and according to the degree to which error, emotion, or compulsion have interfered with the choice.

The concept of choice (προαίρεσις) is based on the assumption that intention, psychologically as well as with regard to moral judgement, depends on the knowledge of something definite. This knowledge draws its reliability and its moral relevance from the way in which a part of subsisting reality has been assessed in the very act of intention. Intention, however, determines the moral verdict upon the ensuing action. Thus intention, being prospective in its leading to action, is closely bound to knowledge which directly refers only to what actually is or exists. Whatever belongs to the future is not open to direct cognition. In the field of human action, the future can be assessed only because of the knowledge which has been acquired, by the intellect, of something already brought to reality, already existing. Hence this assessment can never be adequate.

That is one reason why the concept of choice does not admit the existence of a will separate from the intellectual cognition and evaluation of means and ends. It only admits intention as an intellectual phenomenon and striving as the result of instinct or emotion or a combination of both. Will as separate from both emotion and cognition can be thought and spoken of in metaphysics or ontology, ethics, and psychology—and even in the current usage of modern European languages—without regard to any chosen goal of action and, consequently, as independent of the intellectual assessment of a given situation.[8] Good or ill will, with regard to its moral value, is not necessarily bound up with the adequate cognition of a definite part of the existing world in which the action is going to take place. It can be grasped separately from the intellectual achievement which precedes action in any given case. Yet, in this quality of being defined separately from the choice of means and ends, the notion of will seems to offer a way of dealing with the problem which arises from the fact that both intention and action refer to the future rather than the present time. This aspect of human life is difficult to investigate if the moral assessment of intention has been linked too closely with the question of knowledge. We have seen how Aristotle tried to handle the problem involved, by strictly separating the knowledge of the means and ends of action from the habitual disposition to act in a certain way, yet without the concept of will.

Men are likely to find by experience that action is, at the same time, urgently required and open to a later religious or moral judgement, although the acting persons are unable to perceive, fully and directly, a future event, fact, or condition in human life. This experience is usually neutralized, in more or less intellectualistic theories of human action, by prudential precepts rather than theoretical arguments: one has to be cautious in all attempts and to realize one's own intellectual deficiency. We dealt with the notion of σωφροσύνη in the preceding chapter.

But wherever the contrast between the ignorance of the future and the responsibility for one's decisions becomes the basis of ethical, psychological, or ontological reasoning, knowledge of the aim of action cannot possibly become the decisive factor to which all moral judgements ultimately refer. Intention that leads to right action has to be determined by a good will rather than true knowledge. Good will, as distinct from the right cognition of the given case, can be measured according to accepted standards without special reference to the aim of action and its adequate perception. It can be identified without an object to which it is directed. This argument can be corroborated by the following consideration.

If people try to act according to moral standards exclusively on the basis of their own rational cognition of the aim, they dispose, in the very act of intention, of future facts or objects as if they belonged to the present time. They disregard the fact that they have to face the future, which cannot become, in the usual sense of the word, the content of knowledge.

Acting solely according to one's own intellectual judgement can even be considered, regardless of the outcome, as a fatal failure in itself, when only divine powers are believed to have the privilege of disposing of the future.[9] This belief is strongly expressed in the Old Testament, where people are frequently praised for having decided according to the order of Yahveh without attempting to perceive, by their own intellectual effort, the end of their action. Their action, then, can be classified in the religious category of obedience. The philosophical equivalent could only be will. But the standards according to which obedience or will respectively can be assessed are attributed to the laws and commandments of the same God who freely disposes of the future. They can be observed rather than understood.

Consequently, freedom realized in the free choice of the means and ends in human activity, as the Greeks put it, considerably differs from the Christian concept of Free Will which already underlies, without being made explicit, the anthropology of the Old Testament. In the Greek view, freedom is brought about when the human intellect has chosen the aim of action according to the true order of being, and has not been hindered in its efforts by error, emotion, or compulsion. So human freedom only exists as good and salutary intention, whereas ill intention results from restrictions imposed, for whatever reason, on man's intellectual activity. The concept of Free Will opens a different view on human freedom. It entails the belief in man's ability to decide and to act both ways, regardless of the intellectual effort spent on the intellectual assessment of the aim. Although the wrong decision is bound to predetermine further decisions and actions, thus encroaching upon the free use of the will, the primary act of decision is always free, regardless of whether intention has been directed the right way or not.

Both concepts, that of choice and that of will, cannot be understood satisfactorily in terms of ethics and anthropology. There are corresponding ideas in the field of cosmology. Proheretic choice goes with an image of reality showing that everything comes to being, exists, and passes away according to everlasting rules. Man is able to understand these rules, to rely on them, and to act accordingly, because he has been given the same reason that provides structure and life to the universe. The concept of Free Will results from a completely different view. The world as experienced in human life owes its existence to a creator who is free to interfere, at any given time, with what is going on in his creation. It is only due to his benevolence that he also has given some regularity to the cosmic process. So man is to experience, first of all, the will of the creator. He becomes conscious of his own intention through continuous acts of obedience or disobedience—that is to say through acts of will—by which he freely reacts to the utterances of the divine will.[10] He also may improve on his knowledge of the divine will in consequence of these acts of obedience, since the outcomes of the ensuing actions are likely to teach him. But he does not become conscious of his intentions through continuous acts of cognition by which he comes to acknowledge that the lasting order of the universe also applies to his own life, and that acting according to such a knowledge automatically produces happiness. We described in the first chapter how Greek intellectuals fervently criticized, in the second century A.D., the belief that God creates and rules the universe solely according to His will or pleasure. Once man was no longer believed to understand, by his own intellectual efforts, the plans of God, and, consequently, the order of the universe, reason ceased to be the decisive factor in moral life. Although acting in accordance with reason would continue to provide success in human life, the standards of moral conduct could only be derived from the commandment by which God conveyed his will to man. The commandment of God could be obeyed or disobeyed[11] but never proved or disproved by the same reason which caused, in the words of Pliny, "twice ten to be twenty." "For my thoughts are not your thoughts, saith the Lord" (Isa. 55:8).[12]

The idea, however, that the intention rather than the ensuing action itself should be judged according to religious and moral standards is well known in Jewish thought, too.[13] But intentionality, in its legal, moral, or religious relevance, refers to the question of whether or not the individual acts in accordance with the commandment of God rather than on the basis of his own intellectual perception and assessment of a given situation.

Obedience to God that has become habitual is called faithfulness, fidelity, firmness (Hebr. *'amunāh*).[14] The term can apply to the personal relation between God and man, as in the case of Abraham (Gen. 15:6), but also to man's trusting in the divine Law which becomes, in that way, the immediate object of faith (*Sir.* 35[32].24, Jos. *ant.* 20.48). 'Amān, 'amunah* is rendered by πιστεύω, πίστις, in Greek. Thus πίστις, faith, instead of knowledge—quite contrary to the Greek tradition, where belief was always valued far below knowledge gained through rational understanding [15]—becomes the point of reference for the moral assessment of intentional action in the thought and language of Jews and early Christians. [16]

Faith can be called a disposition of will which need not be realized through the choice of an aim for action, though every chosen aim can be valued only according to it. Yet to choose your goal of action and to value it according to God's commandment does not coincide with the distinction between *honestum* and *utile* as foreseen in Greco-Roman philosophy, from whose point of view these turn out to be identical, once a man has come, by his own intellectual effort, to a proper understanding of what nature itself wants him to do. In the Biblical view, a man cannot possibly avoid, by his own intellectual efforts, the clash between his intention and the will of God as set forth in his commandments and orders. Man cannot come to a rational understanding of anything behind the will of God. He can give his response to God's commandment only through an act of obedience or disobedience, that is to say by his will. Thus the will of man as a phenomenon of religious or moral relevance and subject to evaluation according to the standards of good and evil comes to existence in consequence of the commandment of God. It is only the very act of will that determines the moral value of the ensuing action. Man is able to make his will a good one, if he complies with the commandment of God. His will is bound to be ill, if he upholds his own intention by an act of disobedience. [17]

The commandment of God, according to the Biblical tradition, also challenges the human intellect, because it may be difficult to understand properly. If it has been laid down in a lasting code, it has to be interpreted and applied to the varying conditions of life. Consequently the Torah, which contains the will of God, is the source of all wisdom in Israel. [18]

Moreover, it always seems wise and prudent to acknowledge, by an act of obedience, the overwhelming power of God. [19] This is different from, though comparable with, the idea of σωφροσύνη, so notable in Greek thought of the classical period. In the view of Sophocles, Herodotus, and others, man has to remember, in all his thoughts, words, and deeds, the limits set him by the gods, although he can never know where precisely they have been drawn. He should simply be aware of his own ignorance and imperfection and act accordingly. Otherwise he is likely to neglect or even to offend, quite inadvertently in most cases, the privileges of the gods and to provoke their cruel, sometimes outrageous punishment. Σωφροσύνη, in such a context, means prudence, modesty, abstention from extravagance and outrage, a sense of the utter instability of one's own position, awareness of one's own weakness and fallibility even in the time of good luck. Men can never be absolutely certain of what they actually ought to do.

Yahveh's orders, on the other hand, usually are quite explicit, whereas his way of acting remains inexplicable according to human standards and sometimes even seems to be unjust or cruel.[20] Abraham, for instance, is told very precisely what he has to do and what is going to happen to him, although he cannot possibly make much sense of that information by his own insight. The people of Israel have been given the Law that teaches them what to do in order to meet the requirements which result from their being, quite incomprehensibly, the elect of God.[21] This is different from the attitude of prudence, modesty, and self-containment that comes from a general awareness of one's own weakness and ignorance, and that is called σωφροσύνη by the Greeks.

Σωφροσύνη, in that particular sense, motivates abstention from action much more than action itself, whereas obedience to the orders and commandments of Yahveh immediately leads to definite actions or ways of acting, without intellectual reflection interfering with the decision to act.[22]

Obedience, above all, if it has become habitual, thus testifying to a man's fidelity or faithfulness ('amunāh), fear of God (yir'āh), confidence (mibṭāḥ), also provides the solid basis of both intellectual and moral progress.[23] Knowledge and wisdom result from the repeated attempt to arrive at a better understanding of the will of God and presuppose the initial act of obedience, acceptance, or confidence.[24]

That human knowledge or wisdom thus depends on the previous activity of the will, which has to turn towards God and to give an initial response to a very definite divine order, is a well-known idea throughout Biblical and post-Biblical tradition, even where it has been formulated in Greek. The polyptoton in Isaiah "if you have no confidence (ta'amenu), you have no firm stand (ta'aminu)" is mistranslated by "if you have no faith (πιστεύειν), you cannot get knowledge (συνιέναι)" in the Septuagint (Isa. 7:9).

Where Hellenistic influence became predominant, such ideas could be interpreted in the light of the Platonic doctrine of Eros. Yet the Platonic Eros continuously impels towards fuller cognition through intellectual activity, without asking for any initial act of obedience, acceptance, faith, or even compliance, for it belongs to human nature. The apocryphal *Wisdom of Solomon* teaches that the divine wisdom comes (φθάνειν) and is visible (θεωρεῖσθαι) only to those who look for (ζητεῖν), desire (ἐπιθυμεῖν), and love (ἀγαπᾶν) it.[25]

Voluntaristic ideas underlie many stories, sayings, and reflections in the Old Testament. It suffices to recall what is related about Abraham[26] in Jewish and early Christian literature.[27] Faith, in the Biblical view, is not primarily seen as knowledge or the cognitive effort leading to such a knowledge and caused by mere persuasion.[28] It appears, wherever the relation between God and man is concerned, as the way to acknowledge the will of God and, above all, to act accordingly. Faith is thus described as a phenomenon of will to which decisive achievements in religious and moral life are to be ascribed.[29]

The Old Testament is far from supplying a coherent theory of human action and its moral assessment comparable to what Greek philosophers would have conceived on the basis of such ideas. That is why Biblical Hebrew does not yield an unmistakable term to denote the concept of will and why obedience and disobedience are not attributed to either intellect or emotion.[30] Both complying with and opposing the intention of God result from the whole of the human personality. It is, therefore, of little importance which faculty of the soul is chiefly responsible for the will of man, alone subject to moral judgement (cf. Gen. 2:21, 6:5). Such judgement, however, can be passed solely according to standards which are far beyond human understanding, since they have been set by the orders and commands of God.

This comes out most clearly also in those passages of the Old Testament and post-Biblical literature where the phenomenon of "stiffheartedness" is referred to.[31] Man has been given the freedom to ignore or even reject the information and the commandment that God conveys to him, thus blinding himself and going astray. Sometimes God himself encourages or corroborates such an attitude in a man whom he wants to destroy because of his initial disobedience, very much as the gods acted

against Xerxes according to Herodotus.[32] The Greek historian, however, concentrates on Xerxes' deception by the gods. He becomes intellectually incapable of going the right way. Yahveh, on the other hand,
renders the heart of Pharaoh "heavy" or "hard." So he repeatedly refuses
to be obedient, although he realizes perfectly well, from the miracles
performed and signs given, both the power and the will of Yahveh. The
narrative of Exod. 7ff clearly interprets the behavior of Pharaoh in terms
of volition rather than cognition.

The Manual of Discipline of the Qumran sect[33] defines stiffheartedness ($\check{s}^{e}rirūt$) as rejection of the salutary knowledge which could cause
people to convert and go the right way.

Again and again the knowledge of the words and commandments of
God is described as depending on an initial act of acceptance and obedience that precedes every kind of religious or moral cognition.[34] Man,
however, is capable of refusing and performing this act, which is the
basis of his religious and moral responsibility.[35] Even the righteous man
can turn away from his righteousness in that way, but also the wicked
can become righteous.[36] The voluntaristic element in this idea of turning oneself is quite notable throughout the Biblical and post-Biblical
tradition.[37] It acquired such an importance because the idea that the
human intellect, operating freely and autonomously, could discover the
ultimate congruity of the plans of God, the order of the universe, and
the needs and purposes of men, was never conceived. The intellect does
not automatically lead the right way when it has done away with irrational desire or emotions.[38] The sovereignty of God[39] which is beyond
human understanding and cannot be assessed by the standards of the
reasonable or the probable demands, on the part of man, an act of will,
that is to say obedience or disobedience, acceptance or refusal. Such an
act of will is prior to all intellectual efforts and achievements, and it is
often produced, not unlike the hardening of the heart, by divine intervention.[40] The belief in both human responsibility as resulting from
free decision and predestination as caused by divine omniscience and
omnipotence is always present in the Old Testament. The antagonism
of the two principles, however, became the object of theological reflection only in post-Biblical literature.[41] The historian Josephus classified
the Jewish sects of his time according to their attitude toward fate and
freedom. The problem involved was discussed in terms of divine or hu-

man will rather than deliberation. The members of the Qumran congregation called themselves "those who are willing" (1 Q.S. 5.8), their statutes "the rule for the will" (C.D. 14.3), and they tried "to choose the Law" or "what pleases the Lord" rather than "the will of their own spirit" (C.D. 3.3, 2.15; cf. 8.8). Good will according to this conception is not preceded by intellectual activity. The grace of God is first to strengthen the volitional faculty of man in order to render him righteous and pious in his planning (1 Q.S. 4.4f).

The important function attributed to the will of man, though convincingly described in many ways in Biblical and post-Biblical literature, never found a coherent and concise terminology in Hebrew comparable to the psychological vocabulary of classical and post-classical Greek. Yet we find one interesting attempt to make explicit, in a coherent theory or imagery and quite independently of the *interpretatio Graeca* of the Bible, this very idea of human action. It occurs, for the first time, in some parts of post-Biblical literature such as the Testament of Twelve Patriarchs and the Manual of Discipline from Qumran, and became of great importance in later Rabbinic orthodoxy.

Man finds himself placed between two spirits, a good and an evil one. These are spoken of either as faculties and inhabitants of the human soul or as cosmic powers. They are called instinct, impulse, spirit, intention, angel and the like.[42] In each of his actions man turns his mind or intellect towards one of them. The turning is referred to in this doctrine separately from the intellectual act by which the immediate goal of action is being chosen. The human intellect chooses—namely the objective of action—and turns itself—namely to one of the two angels or spirits.[43] Thus the voluntaristic and the intellectualistic aspects of human intention are separated in this imagery, and only to the voluntaristic one has moral relevance been attributed, for it is the spirit or angel that determines the moral or religious value of the ensuing action. By separating the intellectualistic from the voluntaristic aspect the doctrine of the two spirits distinguishes itself from the image of the two ways which is well known in Greek, Jewish, and early Christian parenetic literature from the time of Hesiod onwards,[44] and which was referred to by the letter Y in the Pythagorean school: man always finds himself at the crossroad and has to decide for himself the right way. Here no distinction between what a man is actually about to do and the intellectual decision can be ascertained from the image. The right choice of the immediate goal implies the moral evaluation of the ensuing action. Both depend on one and the same act of intellectual activity. There is no will to distinguish from the knowledge of what to do.

We need not deal with the further development of the doctrine of the two spirits, especially in later Rabbinic theology,[45] nor trace the close and distant parallels in Greek literature and philosophy.[46] Another detail of that influential doctrine, however, is worth mentioning in our context.

Whether the mind turned towards the good or the bad spirit can be assessed only according to the Torah[47] and not through the free use of the human intellect.

Only because of the Torah is man able to react, consciously and responsibly though never by a purely intellectual effort, to the will of God, despite his utter inability to grasp the plans or thoughts of his Creator. He can and he must reconsider the means and ends of his action, as chosen by his reason, in their relation to the commandment of God. That is why the just man, according to the first psalm, "in his law . . . doth . . . meditate day and night."[48] Good will, that is to say obedience to the commandment of God, necessarily leads to such a meditation. Yet, as the response to the commandment of God, good will is independent of the amount of wisdom which the individual has spent on the preceding choice of the objective of action. So all striving after moral perfection and happiness has to concentrate on the will of man. This comes out most clearly in a saying of Rabbi Gamaliel in the first century A.D. (Ab. 2.4a): "Render your will His will so that He can render His will your will."

The word *raṣōn*, used in the above saying and in comparable texts to denote the will of God and man, can have many connotations in Biblical and post-Biblical Hebrew, such as desire, pleasure, purpose, intention, benevolence. A similar variety of meanings is typical of many words in the ethical and psychological vocabulary of Hebrew such as *ruaḥ* or *nepeš* which are both also used to denote volition (see above p. 25). In the present context, however, the concept of Free Will is unmistakably pointed to by the word *raṣōn*: man is supposed to be capable of directing and shaping his own will. The problem of free will, too, is spoken of or referred to in a variety of terms and expressions in Jewish literature. The verb *'bh*, for instance, used almost exclusively with a negation in the Old Testament, clearly refers to the free act of negative decision which can be performed by God and man.[49] The enigmatic, though necessary, existence of the free will of man beside divine providence is denoted, in a saying of Rabbi Akiba,[50] by the word *r^ešut* which means "permission" or "allowance." The same problem is of some importance in the Psalms of Solomon, where the terms ἐκλογὴ καὶ ἐξουσία τῆς ψυχῆς (the selection and power of the soul) appear,[51] and Israel's decision to attach themselves to Yahveh is described by the word *n^edabāh*.[52] The use of these and other words shows that neither volition as such nor the idea of free will, though frequently spoken of in both Biblical and post-Biblical literature, was described in a fixed terminology of which the elements can be understood regardless of the context. That is why the reader is almost always told whose will is being spoken of, and under which circumstances.

Yet in some passages of Jewish and early Christian literature *raṣōn*[53] and its Greek equivalents[54] εὐδοκία, θέλημα occur without such additions. They are used as technical terms, in the strict sense of the word, to denote the will of God. The development of terminology mirrors the belief that the will of man presupposes the will of God, as do the saying of Rabbi Gamaliel (above p. 78) and the prayer at Gethsemane: πλὴν οὐχ ὡς ἐγὼ θέλω ἀλλ' ὡς σύ: "however, not as I wish but as you wish." Jesus' human will, which had been opposed to the preconceived intention of God, comes to agree, in a free act of volition, with the divine will.[55] H. von Campenhausen has shown in a recent contribution[56] that antagonism and agreement between two kinds of volition are unheard of in St. John's conception of Christ, which foreshadows monophysite doctrine. So human will as distinct from cognition and as answering the order of God is made more explicit in the synoptic narrative of the life of Jesus, although a concept of will is not absent from the fourth gospel.

Εὐδοκία is used, in well-known passages of the New Testament such as Luke 2:14[57] and Rom. 2:18, to denote God's benevolence towards those he has elected according to his free and incomprehensible choice.

In the passage from the Epistle to the Romans mentioned above, St. Paul deals with the problem of whether and according to which standards God's final judgement will be passed upon Jews and gentiles alike. The Jews, he says, know what God wants them to do, since they have been given the Torah. (This was common ground with contemporary

Jewish theology.)[58] So they shall not have any excuse in their trial. On the other hand, there will be gentiles who have fulfilled the Law although it was never revealed to them. That is why the gentiles, or at least some of them, will have, on doomsday, three advocates or witnesses: the work of the Law inscribed in their heart, their conscience (συνείδησις), and their thoughts (λογισμοί)[59] that accuse and excuse one another (Rom. 2:14/15).

"The work of the Law written in the heart" (v. 15) does not refer to what one may call the inborn or natural knowledge of the law.[60] This idea, important as it may be in Greek ethical speculation where right action is always explained as the result of right knowledge, is of little weight even in the preceding verse.[61] St. Paul only stresses the fact that the gentiles in question did fulfill the Law, but he does not give much consideration to the problem of how they possibly could be aware, in some way or other, of its content. This problem, however, is of outstanding importance from the point of view of Greek or modern ethical thought. To St. Paul, every factual fulfilment of the Law is primarily an act of obedience, appropriate in every creature towards the Creator. It can be performed, as St. Paul observes, with and without the explicit knowledge of the divine commandment, and it is only the act itself that really matters (v. 13). So the ἔργα τοῦ νόμου (the work of the Law) testify to the will rather than the intellect of the fulfiller—which is, however, difficult to express unequivocally in first-century Greek.

The most telling parallel can be found in the Testament of the Twelve Patriarchs (Jud. 20): the deeds man has performed in his lifetime are inscribed on his breastbone to bear witness in the presence of the divine judge. The author of this text was only thinking of Jews who had to know the Torah. St. Paul, however, was speaking of Greeks or gentiles of whom at least some have spontaneously fulfilled the Torah without knowing it and who can, therefore, rely on the testimony of their heart where their life in accordance with the Law is recorded.

The second witness these gentiles can produce is offered by their conscience. Conscience, according to St. Paul, does not originate from the intellect, which has thoroughly examined what the individual has done or is about to do. This, however, is the meaning of συνείδησις wherever it occurs in Greek philosophical texts—which happens very seldom, anyway.[62] St. Paul refers to this type of self-examination under the third heading, when he is speaking of thoughts which accuse and excuse one another.[63]

Conscience, in the view of St. Paul and those authors who betray his influence, spontaneously and distinctly indicates to its owner whether or not a doing of his has been or will be in accordance with the will of God. That is why conscience can bear witness on many occasions,[64] its testimony being irrefutable, for nobody, even if his knowledge be far superior in all respects, is able either to prove or disprove the conscience of someone else. This particularly applies to those cases where conscience is, in fact, weak or leads astray.[65] The advanced Christian whose knowledge of the Law and its new interpretation is nearer to perfection has to accept and to respect the hesitations and fears of his weaker brethren, when they are acting according to their conscience but against the deeper understanding of the divine message. No one is entitled to outdo the conscience of somebody else by his own, superior knowledge; no individual conscience can be silenced simply by instruction from those wiser. To acknowledge that your neighbor has to be guided by his conscience, even if you cannot approve of his actions, is, in the view of St. Paul, one of the main achievements of the mutual love and mutual responsibility on which the congregation is founded. Through his conscience everybody, including gentiles, is able to become certain of God's having spoken to him, even if he does not fully understand the message. Accordingly, St. Paul recommends loyalty to the political government διὰ τὴν συνείδησιν, according to conscience (Rom. 13:5).[66] Conscience, being the means of direct communication between God and man, can also convey an awareness, however dim, of the fact that all secular rule represents, to some degree, the divine government of the world and is backed, therefore, by divine authority (Rom. 13:1). To interfere with the conscience of someone else is an assault on his freedom (ἐλευθερία) resulting from his direct and unhindered relation to God (1 Cor. 10:29).

It becomes clear from these and similar passages in early Christian literature[67] why conscience, to a certain extent and in special cases, can replace the knowledge of the Law, at least in the view of St. Paul and his followers. Through his conscience man may become aware of what God wants him to do and, accordingly, the judgement God is going to pass on his conduct. This awareness determines his moral actions, but

it is independent of the degree to which he has come to the right understanding of the divine Law and its new interpretation as laid down in
the Scripture and as communicated through preaching. The Law and
its interpretation, however, is the basis of congregational life and enables everybody to communicate with his neighbor about the standards
of moral conduct. In this context the question of progress in knowledge
is of outstanding importance. Yet by testifying to the will of God, conscience can create the motivation for action in the individual. It brings
about, regardless of the intellectual standing of the man in question,
an act of will that, being the immediate response to the will of God,
cannot be invalidated or corroborated from outside, even by arguments
which are based on the communicable interpretation of the Law, let
alone by reasoning. This kind of human will or intention seems to be
completely detached from any intellectual achievement, yet it can become the essential cause of a person's religious and moral responsibility.
By acting against his conscience man is likely to forfeit his final salvation, since, according to St. Paul, the testimony of his conscience can
save a man, even if he was never explicitly told by the Law what the
will of his Creator wanted him to do. The ἔργα τοῦ νόμου written in his
heart testify, so to speak, objectively to his being elected, whereas conscience offers the same proof subjectively and spontaneously. One's
λογισμοί, ratiocinations in their turn, corroborate the awareness of one's
own achievement by means of reflection.[68]

But this is, after all, a doctrine specific to St. Paul. The righteous
who find themselves justified on doomsday according to St. Matthew
(25:31ff) seem to be very surprised that the word of the law has been
written in their hearts. They do not realize that they have, in fact, fulfilled the will of God by their actions of compassion and benevolence,
when they were visiting prisoners and feeding the hungry. Obviously,
their conscience does not bear witness for them. We have to admit that
conscience was by no means a concept of primary importance in Jewish
or early Christian thought, though of some importance in the theology
of St. Paul. In general, Jews and Christians were firmly convinced that
God had uttered His commandments quite plainly to mankind. The
standards of moral behavior were open to the understanding of everybody willing to listen and to obey, according to this tradition,[69] and no
one in the community had to rely on his inner voice alone. St. Paul's
doctrine of conscience sounds rather surprising in that environment,

and the impact it made on Christian theology in the following two or three centuries was not too heavy.[70]

St. Paul enumerates, as we have seen, three sources of moral knowledge which exist outside the Torah and which are accessible to any human being. This is very noteworthy. To my knowledge, no Jewish text of the period provides close parallels. We do find, in post-Biblical Jewish literature, the opinion that the Patriarchs were fulfilling the will of God before the Torah was given to Moses or that all nations and tribes were offered the Law and only Israel accepted it, so that everybody can be expected to know the will of God.[71] But for the present, attention focused on the question of how God was going to judge those who had been given the Law. Not until the message of God's final judgement was preached to Jews and gentiles alike did the question of how the will of God could be fulfilled without any knowledge of the Torah become really important.

St. Paul would be easier to understand in this chapter of his doctrine, had he introduced an unmistakable term to denote the will of man; for it is, in his view, a will, as distinguished from all intellectual achievements—even with regard to the knowledge of the divine Law— as well as from all unconscious and spontaneous emotions, which responds to the commandment of God. Thus the will of man, in fact, determines human action and is, therefore, subject to divine and consequently moral judgement.

There is no such term in the language of St. Paul and his contemporaries. Even the will of God, which provides the ultimate cause for the human will to emerge, and which has to be detached, in the language of man, from God's thoughts and plans—the latter being, unlike the utterances of the divine will, inexplicable to the human mind—has no definite term. θέλησις, θέλημα, βουλή, βούλησις, βούλημα, εὐδοκία, γνώμη are used almost as synonyms with reference to the will of God in the earliest writings of Christian literature.

The underlying concept, however, is quite clear and can be gathered from many passages in St. Paul and elsewhere. It can be seen behind his doctrine of conscience, above all in what he says about the relationship between conscience and love (1 Cor. 8); it is also to be found in his teaching about humility, obedience to the commandment of God, and abstention from striving for one's own righteousness. Yet the concept of good and ill will remains without its own term. In the famous passage where he deals, from the specifically Christian point of view, with the old problem of why man is able to do wrong though knowing the better, St. Paul uses θέλω and γινώσκω indiscriminately[72] to denote intention. Yet he is far from solving the problem by the identification of knowledge and virtue.

The answer to this crucial question,[73] already raised by Euripides, Socrates, and Plato, is completely different from every attempt to solve the problem which we know from the Greek tradition. No emotions or instincts overpower the intellect, which ought to be, by its very nature, capable of an adequate perception of nature and thus of the standards of right action. Reason by itself, according to St. Paul, does not enable man to fulfill the orders of his Creator. Thus the Greeks—and, of course, their philosophers—have not been led, by their rational understanding of nature, to a proper knowledge of what their Creator wanted them to do: they utterly failed in their moral conduct (Rom. 1:19–24).

Man's incapacity to act rightly is due to the fact that he leads his life κατὰ σάρκα, according to the flesh. This important term in the terminology of St. Paul does not, or at least not primarily, point to the dualism of matter and spirit, sensual and intellectual life.[74] Σάρξ (flesh), as opposed to πνεῦμα (spirit), denotes rather the empirical condition of man, in which all his activity, including his religious, intellectual, and moral endeavor, finds its ultimate goal in himself. Pride and self-assuredness, for instance, characterize the fleshly existence. The proud man has forgotten that he is a creature of God whose life and salvation depend entirely on the grace of the Creator. He attributes to, and expects from, his own activity the main achievements in his life, instead of hoping for the Creator to meet his needs and instead of turning to his neighbor in order to use rightly what has been given to him. The main factor of the life κατὰ σάρκα can be seen in man's strong feeling of independence by which he separates himself from his Creator.

The most notable result of that separation comes out in man's striving for "his own righteousness"[75] or justification. By reasoning and acting according to the flesh, man tries to bring about his own perfection and salvation, his own justice according to the standards of the divine Law. He is constantly trying to fulfill the commandment of God through his own performance. In doing so, he turns the salutary Law, which has been given to reveal the will of God, to make men aware of their short-

comings, and to enable them to take refuge in the mercy of their Creator, into a means for his own attempts to acquire salvation without the
aid and mercy of God.

I need not go into further details of St. Paul's doctrine of σάρξ and
πνεῦμα, since the topic has been extensively dealt with in modern New
Testament studies. Yet it is worth mentioning that σάρξ comprehensively denotes the whole of man's personality. So all kinds of intellectual activity, knowledge, wisdom, and the like, provided they share
man's being restricted to himself, belong to the realm of flesh. There is
no difference between intellect and emotion from the point of view of
man's salvation from that fleshly existence.

Once a man has decided or become accustomed to lead the fleshly
existence, he loses his freedom altogether.[76] He is pinned down to his
own needs and purposes, he has to rely on his own faculties instead of
trusting in the mercy of God by which all his deficiencies may easily be
overcome, and he is incapable of love, that is to say unable to think, to
speak, and to act with regard not for himself but only for the sake of his
brother. Thus sin, ἁμαρτία, being the result of his separation from God,
enslaves man. Only the mercy of God, as revealed and operating through
Christ, can free him again.[77] The grace of God conveys to him the divine πνεῦμα which restores his freedom, renews his nature, and brings
back to him the ability to love.

It is in this context that St. Paul treats the problem of deliberate
wrongdoing in Rom. 7:7ff. A man who leads a fleshly life under the
rule of sin is bound to realize, again and again, that he has intentionally acted against what he knows to be the will and order of God. Yet
this knowledge cannot protect him from doing wrong, from offending
the Law of God, because sin in the sense explained above has already
predetermined his intention and has turned, almost automatically, his
activity toward himself instead of toward God or his neighbor. So his
intention, regardless of whether it originates, in a given situation, from
reason or emotion, is bound to produce a wrong action. Knowledge as a
purely intellectual achievement cannot possibly divert intention from
its predetermined course. This can only be caused by the divine πνεῦμα,
which is bestowed on man solely by the salutary act of divine grace.
Thus both right intention and performance are due to God's own guidance: man can but anxiously and humbly hope for his salvation, his
only contribution being humility,[78] awareness of his utter deficiency

that leads him to expect everything solely from divine mercy. Thus weakness, both physical and intellectual, becomes the very basis for man's religious and moral perfection, for only an intention that is in accordance with the weakness of man can possibly point in the right direction and meet the commandments of God.[79]

St. Paul's whole argument is about human intention, whether or not it is in accordance with the will of God. In his view, no intellectual cognition, no moral effort can restore and preserve the freedom of man, which is the faculty of invariably producing intentions toward action that are provoked by the needs of one's neighbor and the unshaken confidence in the will of one's Creator rather than by the attempt to gain or preserve one's own independence.

Surprisingly enough, St. Paul never coined a term to denote the pivotal concept of will in the context of his soteriology and anthropology. Intention as such is called by a great variety of words, regardless of its being described as determined by either sin or grace, σάρξ or selfishness, let alone sensuality or spirituality, emotion or intellect. To denote volition he indiscriminately uses βούλομαι, θέλημα (θέλειν), φρόνημα, νοῦς, νόημα, διάνοια, γινώσκω, ἐπιθυμεῖν, and other terms taken from the semantic field of cognition and emotion.[80] Sometimes even πνεῦμα is used to denote intention itself rather than the divine gift of renewal from which it comes (Gal. 4:6), and frequently the heart of man is spoken of as the origin of intention.[81]

As already stated above (p. 84) the distinction between intellectual activity and emotion is far from being stressed in the search for the origin of human intention, although St. Paul fully shared the Platonic temper of his period and was inclined to believe that man's sensuality did, in fact, constitute an area where sin could establish its rule.[82] But terms like sin and grace, σάρξ and πνεῦμα, are used to apply to the whole of man's life and personality. Thus νοῦς, νόημα, νοεῖν, that is to say words taken from the semantic field of intellectual life, are also often applied to man's fleshly condition. Men can deliberate, plan, and act κατὰ σάρκα, without much emotion or sensuality being involved, they can even be wise according to the flesh.[83] On the other hand, ἐπιθυμεῖν, a word traditionally restricted to the meaning of sensual and emotional desire, can denote the conscious intention of man according to both his fleshly and his spiritual condition.[84]

Therefore, the conflict which is spoken of in Rom. 7:7ff cannot be

taken as one of a deliberate intention contradicted or thwarted by an
unconscious impulse, as Bultmann is inclined to believe, with reference
to Rom. 13 : 3 and Gal. 6 : 12.[85] The two ways of life—this seems important for their moral relevance—are always present in the consciousness of man. Man does learn what he is supposed to do from his conscience, from the Law, and eventually from the message of Christ. Thus
both kinds of intention, κατὰ σάρκα and κατὰ πνεῦμα, come to being in
the full light of human consciousness, though independently of the intellectual achievement of the individual in question (see above p. 84).
Consequently, both have a bearing on the question of responsibility.

St. Paul has made very explicit in various contexts that, for the time
being, even the Christian who has set all his hope on the mercy of God
as revealed through Christ is still subject to the conditions of the fleshly
existence.[86] Thus he has to suffer from contradictory intentions which
he constantly produces, very much like the man who has not accepted
the salutary message but knows, from conscience or Law, what God expects him to do. Yet the conflict becomes bearable for the Christian,[87]
since he has already been given, by the very act of accepting grace without trusting in any of his own achievements, the pneumatic life, which
will be revealed, however, in all its clarity only at the end of time.[88]
Accordingly, the progress in knowledge that has been inaugurated by
the initial act of will, namely the acceptance of God's mercy[89] and love of
one's neighbor, will also come to its end at that point.[90] In the meantime,
σάρξ and πνεῦμα in Christian life can be ascertained only from the sort of
intention which men produce towards God and fellow creature.

The same voluntaristic approach to the problems of moral life that
results from his soteriology can also be seen in other topics of St. Paul's
doctrine. It may suffice to recall his description of what were later called
the Christian or spiritual virtues,[91] especially of love, which he regarded
as the most important among the three.

Ἀγάπη (love), πίστις (faith), and ἐλπίς (hope) certainly imply, in the
view of St. Paul, some kind of knowledge or awareness. They cannot be
reduced to a mere emotional disposition. The knowledge in question
refers to the fact that God's mercy has been revealed in Christ,[92] that
the whole of creation will be judged and redeemed,[93] and that the love
of one's neighbor according to the example of Christ is the only way to
meet God's commandment.[94] Yet this kind of knowledge is different
from all other kinds. Its content will be open to a full understanding

only in the future,[95] when the conflict between σάρξ and πνεῦμα will have come to an end. At present, it is neither calculable nor fully comprehensible, nor can it be treated like any other piece of knowledge.[96] It becomes visible and real only through intention, through love of one's neighbor.[97] So it does, in fact, exist only as intention. Again and again St. Paul tries to show the difference between this kind of knowledge and wisdom or knowledge κατὰ σάρκα, which can be disposed of, which is calculable, and which causes disastrous results in moral life, for it "inflates" man[98] by corroborating his pride, self-assuredness, and sense of independence, which prevent him from turning toward his neighbor. Pneumatic knowledge, on the other hand, is realized in human life as sheer love, which is the most sublime kind of intention and leads to increasing cognition of God and man.[99]

The voluntaristic approach of St. Paul fully agrees with the Old Testament and Jewish thought. He succeeded in giving a more precise and succinct description of that particular detail of Biblical and post-Biblical anthropology than most contemporary and later Jewish authors. Yet St. Paul's theology by no means results from the *interpretatio Graeca* of the Bible, despite its being formulated in Greek, even with the use of some philosophical terms that were incorporated into contemporary Greek. The voluntaristic approach which he shared with the religious and moral tradition of his people led to an image of God and man and their mutual relation which substantially differs from any system of Greek anthropology and cosmology, as we tried to point out in the first chapter.

It is an open question whether St. Paul abstained from coining an unequivocal term to denote the notion of will, so important in his theology and anthropology, simply because he could not, for obvious reasons, take it over from contemporary Greek. St. Paul's language is most vigorous and expressive, yet he was not a trained philosopher, and that is why his use of technical terms lacks the consistency that characterizes philosophical language from the time of Aristotle onwards. St. Paul did, in fact, use some terms to denote specific concepts of his doctrine, such as καταλλαγή (reconciliation), οἰκοδομή (building-up of the congregation), and above all πνεῦμα and σάρξ. Both latter, however, are also used non-terminologically in his epistles. Their meaning as coined terms has fewer and less complicated implications than a term for the notion of will would have in the context of St. Paul's doctrine.

This difficulty about a term for will, so badly needed in St. Paul's entirely voluntaristic interpretation of man's life and salvation, results from its very nature: the notion, although not the term, of will occurs, with substantial changes and variations in function and meaning, in the discussion of theological, soteriological, and ethical questions. It is not restricted, as comparable concepts and terms in Greek philosophy undoubtedly are, to the theory of human action with its psychological and ethical implications. Thus intention of man in its importance for his being saved or condemned by his Creator certainly has its psychological aspect, too, once the attempt is made to ascertain its nature and its operation from the facts of practical and moral life. In such a context the questions automatically emerge whether or not right knowledge necessarily precedes right intention, whether or not the moral evaluation of an action rests on that knowledge, and what the nature of such knowledge could possibly be—which were, after all, the fundamental problems in Greek ethical thought.

Yet human intention, in the view of both St. Paul and the Old Testament, comes to existence only in response to the will of the Creator, an experience that cannot be adequately described or explained in terms of psychological investigation and theory. This kind of reasoning only covers the results of human intention in moral life, but it does not reach intention's very origin, where the salvation of man is at stake. Human intention becomes important and recognizable at various levels of reality. Accordingly, it has to be approached through various modes of cognition, and spoken of, in theological doctrine and religious precepts, in varying terms.

Perhaps it is the great variety of different aspects under which the phenomenon of intention and will is considered that prevented St. Paul from inventing a definite term. Each of these aspects could have demanded a separate set of terms to denote the results of speculation. St. Paul's theological reflection embraced his own and his people's religious experience as well as the needs and purposes of practical, above all congregational, life. So comprehensive a doctrine, which included the results of strict and sober reasoning and conveyed, at the same time, details of profound religious experience, was hard to render in a coherent terminology. Perhaps this is also one reason why Christian theologians failed to understand, for more than three centuries, essential ideas in his epistles.[100] Most of them were, in addition, much too well trained in Greek philosophy.

Now let us turn to Philo of Alexandria. St. Jerome[101] reported an ironical saying about Philo which had been coined and circulated by Greek philosophers of his time: "Either Philo is speaking like Plato or Plato like Philo." We can easily find some lexicographical evidence in support of this opinion. Perhaps the reader recalls a detail mentioned in the first chapter.[102] For reasons we tried to fathom, the words βούλησις or βούλημα, which denote the intellectual activity preceding action, are largely absent from the Greek translation of the Old Testament, where θέλησις or θέλημα are mostly used instead. Philo, in his turn, exclusively used βούλημα and βούλησις with reference to the intention of both God and man. In doing so he joined the philosophical authors of the imperial period.[103]

Philo had to use the word βούλησις with reference to the intention of the divine Creator, because he was eager to find in Yahveh's rule the same perfect reason which Greek philosophy had always attributed to the Supreme Being. "God has the power (δύναμις) to produce good and evil, but his intention is directed (βούλεται) only to the good." This[104] is well known from Plato's *Gorgias*, in that the use of βούλομαι is restricted to the meaning of the βούλησις τοῦ ἀγαθοῦ (decision for the good) (see above p. 39). Yet, by taking this argument from Platonic and Stoic tradition, Philo did not want to restrict the boundless power of his God. So he opposed Aristotle's doctrine that everything which has been made or created is bound to pass away. The will—βούλησις— of God, he argued, is free to bestow eternity even on the lowest of his creatures. The problem involved was keenly discussed in the Academy. Plato made his Demiurge address the minor gods, saying that they, being created or "joined" by him, are not immortal by nature. But since their "joining" has been perfectly accomplished, the Demiurge, because he is entirely good, cannot conceivably be prepared (θέλειν) to dissolve so perfect a structure. Thus the minor gods are immortal or continuously held together by the intention (βούλησις) of the Supreme Creator. The passage was much debated in the Platonic school, as can be seen from Proclus' commentary.[105] The opinion, held by Atticus and others,[106] that God's will could change the nature of a being and bestow immortality on what is mortal by nature, was strongly opposed by orthodox Platonists such as Proclus himself. They insisted on the identity of the intention of God and nature. What has been joined impeccably by the divine creator is destined for longevity though not eternal by its own nature, since it has its beginning in time. But its duration, its becoming imperishable, is far from being against nature. The will or intention of God (βούλησις), his power or potential (δύναμις), and the order of being cannot possibly disagree with each other. Apparently, Philo was already familiar with the divergent interpretations of that passage, to which he repeatedly referred. He, however, stresses the grace, care, and benevolence of God,[107] who sometimes bestows immortality on some of his mortal creatures. Thus, for Philo, the will of God acquires a different quality from that in the philosophical tradition.[108] The whole universe, in his view, owes its existence solely to the grace of God.[109]

Philo also says that Yahveh could never destroy his creation, for replacing order by chaos would contradict his own perfect rationality. This is an entirely philosophical doctrine,[110] since it presupposes the same reason in God and the human mind. But the statement is also in agreement with the Bible, at least in one respect. Indeed many passages in the Old Testament refer to the order and regularity of the universe, saying that man can rely on it in all his life.[111] But the salutary rules of nature are due to the mercy, fidelity, and benevolence of God rather than to the entirely rational order of his creation. In the Biblical view, the human mind is not able to understand fully and adequately the duration and structure which God has given to his world. Man can only trust in God's promise to maintain that order. To say that God cannot possibly contradict his own perfect rationality points in quite a different direction.

Philo was very fond of the idea, so generally accepted in Greek philosophy, that reason provides the common ground where divine activity and human understanding meet. Thus he adopted and used the well-known argument that the human intellect can assess God's perfect rationality by inference from the rational order of his creation.[112] Cognition of God, however, which is based on the rational perception of the universe, is deficient in comparison with cognition from revelation and faith which is, in the end, cognition of God's incomprehensibility.[113]

All these examples indicate that Philo tried, in his exegesis of the Biblical texts, to reconcile wherever he could the philosophical concept of the Supreme Being with the creed of his people. Yet he did not overlook the deficiencies of that method by which Yahveh was identified with reason itself, since Yahveh was spoken of, in nearly all the texts of the Old Testament, as merciful, zealous, revengeful, imperious—that is to say distinguished by qualities of will—and, above all, powerful beyond any human understanding. Philo tried to bridge the gap between the two concepts by his doctrine of δύναμις.

A great variety of connotations was attached, in post-classical Greek, to the word δύναμις. They range from "faculty, ability, and strength or potency" in colloquial Greek, to "potentiality" as opposed to actuality in philosophical language, to what is multiplied by itself in mathematics, and to numinous power in the terminology of cult, magic, and religion.

Philo's use of the word was equally multifarious. He called δυνάμεις, without any differentiation, all the qualities of God such as mercy, wisdom, goodness, forgiveness, because they denote the means through which God carries out his rule.[114] Even the universe can be called δυνάμεις, according to Philo, since it is a means of divine rule and testifies to the goodness of God.[115] Philo also identifies the Platonic ideas with the δυνάμεις of God.[116] This doctrine has two aspects. One is entirely philosophical: the archetypes of everything in the world are to be found in the divine mind, as the potential from which each individual being is brought to reality. The second also accounts for religious experience: by his ability to grasp, through intellectual effort, these ideas or archetypes, man finds himself exposed to the power of God rather than performing an act of cognition of God himself.[117]

One more point in Philo's doctrine about the δυνάμεις of God is of particular interest. He argues that God makes use of his entire power only if he turns all his activity, which is purely spiritual, towards himself. None of his creatures could possibly endure such a confrontation. That is why God, when dealing with his creatures, always uses his reduced power.[118] This doctrine of Philo's, however, was easy to understand in terms of contemporary Greek metaphysics with its combination of Platonic and Aristotelian concepts.

In the realm of the intelligible—where reality itself alone can be grasped—any being of superior standing includes, in his potential, several inferior ones. Consequently, such a being brings to reality a lower being by using only a part of its intellectual activity and a part of its potential. Correspondingly, the lower being is able to communicate only with a part of the superior one. The Supreme Being, however, represents the whole of reality. It includes in its potential and creates or brings to existence by its intellectual activity all the other beings which, in their turn, have a share in reality only in so far as they communicate with the Supreme Being. Only the latter is perfectly real in the sense that everything it enacts, performs, or creates is brought about through intellectual activity. Thus reality ultimately depends on the identity of thought, action, and existence in the Supreme Being.

Philo was, in fact, familiar with this doctrine, and he made extended use of it in his exegesis of the Old Testament.[119] Yet in his specific doctrine of God dealing with his creatures by means of reduced power only, he argues differently. He refers exclusively to God's mercy. God, he says, willingly forfeits the unity of thought and action, from perfect rationality, whenever he deals with his creatures, because he is aware of their weakness.[120] Even the Law which he gave does not primarily result from his omniscience, by which he can predict all the future needs of mankind and their limited capacities.[121] He has given the Law because of his sheer mercy and friendliness.[122] He simply wanted to communicate with His people. It is also entirely due to the mercy of God, if some people come nearer to Him than others.[123] He "goes to meet them," yet only to those whom He wants.[124] Thus the will of God, which appears in His mercy, His friendliness, His turning to His people, is inexplicable in terms of philosophical theology and cosmology, which try to interpret the perfect rationality of the universe and its Creator. Philo describes the will of God in great detail and, moreover, in basic accordance with the religious tradition of his people, but without the use of a specific and unmistakable term. Such a term did not exist in philosophical Greek of that time, yet Philo had to use this conceptual tool. Consequently, he spoke of the "will of nature,"[125] which points to the creed that every impulse that is in accordance with the order of being can necessarily be perceived and understood by the human mind. Philosophical cosmology did not have recourse to the inexplorable thoughts of the divine Creator.

The same applies to Philo's anthropology and ethics. He considers, like most of the Greek philosophers, right action basically as resulting from right knowledge, and explains sin or wrongdoing in terms of the well-known theory of πάθος or affection:[126] reason, which has to establish the agreement between moral conduct and the order of nature, succumbs to emotion. The human intellect, in its permanent striving for cognition, has to make use of man's sensuality, yet without losing its leading function.[127] Man also must stay aware of his dependence, in all his intel-

lectual activity, upon the grace of his Creator: To know one's nature
means to be aware of one's own having been created[128] and thus being
subject to the will of the Creator. Thus sin, being an affection by which
man attaches himself to his material body rather than to his spiritual self,
is against the rational order of nature—as in Greek ethical thought—
and, at the same time, is an act of disobedience against the will of the
Creator.[129] Consequently, intelligence (φρόνησις), being the best condition of the human intellect, stands for the consummation of all virtues,
and is, at the same time, the basis of human freedom. This opinion is
in full accordance with Socratic, Platonic, and Stoic tradition.[130]

Yet, according to the Old Testament, man does not attain his moral
knowledge by his own free intellectual activity. He is simply instructed
by the commandment of God, whose thoughts and plans are beyond
human understanding. Philo bridges this gap between Bible and philosophy by his theory of revelation.[131] God supplements the defective
knowledge which the "normal" human intellect can attain by revealing
some of his plans and ends, and by conveying his supranatural intellect
(λόγος) to man. The additional knowledge which man acquires through
divine revelation is infallible, incontestable, not open to rational dis-
pute, and applicable to all kinds of moral action. Every human being,
regardless of his erudition, can receive it. Yet in order to be able to
receive the supranatural intellect man has to train his normal one by
detaching himself from his body and by imitating those who have already attained the divine knowledge.[132] In the case of prophets and saints
God goes even further. He replaces, according to Philo, the rational
part of their soul by His divine spirit (πνεῦμα).[133] So the psychological
mechanism, as foreseen in philosophical theory, remains unchanged.
But now it is the divine spirit and no longer human reason that controls
affections and emotions. Perfection in human life can be brought about
by the supranatural gift of the divine Logos or Nous that provides the
superior knowledge and restores man's nature as the image of God.[134]
Man, however, does not become divine in consequence of that gift. Philo
does not altogether reject the Platonic formula of ὁμοίωσις θεῷ to describe the ultimate goal of moral progress.[135] But in the more detailed
discussions, Philo depicts human perfection as resulting from the un-
swaying knowledge, granted by revelation or the divine spirit, that God
is imperceptible to the human intellect. Yet the human intellect fully
realizes, in the state of perfection, that God is the source of everything

that is good in the universe and that man can perceive.[136] The awareness of God's imperceptibility, power, and goodness implies insight into man's own baseness. Moses offers the outstanding example of that kind of human perfection. He, like other human beings, was never admitted to a direct contemplation and cognition of God. Yet since the whole of his life was determined by the desire to achieve such a contemplation, to reach what is unattainable for man, he came, with the aid of the divine Logos, to the complete and perfect understanding of both God's incomprehensibility and his own nothingness[137]—which transcends the limits of rational thought.[138] The miracle of human perfection as described by Philo has two aspects: first of all, perfection is identical with knowledge that has no foundation in sense perception or other pieces of empirical information. Secondly, to get at that knowledge man has permanently to learn it with the supranatural aid of his divine teacher and illuminator, yet without giving up his own free intention or decision and, consequently, his responsibility. This is pointed out in Philo's exegesis of Gen. 17:22, where God is said to have terminated, at a certain point, his speaking to Abraham.[139] The voluntaristic implication of this particular notion of supranatural knowledge seems obvious. Knowledge of this kind transforms man's behavior so that he is inclined and prepared to fulfil the orders of God, though being unable to grasp, by his natural or normal understanding, the author of that commandment, to whose power and sovereignty he feels exposed.[140]

There are many shortcomings in this doctrine with its strong voluntaristic implications, indicated by the conception of two kinds of intellect, the desire for divine knowledge, the importance attributed to supranatural revelation and, correspondingly, to faith and obedience to the will of God.[141] Furthermore, how can one explain the repeated change from the better to the worse—and vice versa—in a man's moral career? How can a man fail again once he has been given the supranatural knowledge which cannot be invalidated by his own reasoning or by emotion? How can he lose such a supranatural knowledge, which must happen when he fails afresh? And has God, in fact, bestowed upon him that precious knowledge for a second, third or tenth time, if his action becomes right again? Obviously, the problems involved in these questions cannot adequately be treated in terms of traditional Greek intellectualism, that is to say by examining the gains and losses in moral knowledge. That is why we find Philo repeatedly concerned with the problem of τροπή, of how man turns his intention from evil to good, from him-self to God [142] and vice versa [143]—a turning which cannot adequately be described in terms of intellect and emotion.

Repentance offers a special case of such a turning. [144] Repentance had never been highly valued in Greek ethics, where it was merely regarded as the inevitable consequence of every action which had not been initi-ated by a sound, rational judgement, and thus, on many occasions, as indispensable for moral progress. [145] The Stoic sage is always without regret or repentance. [146] To Philo, however, repentance was the turning of human intention, which only God's mercy can bring about. [147] Again, there is no term to denote human will or human intention as such, though that seems necessary to make explicit so voluntaristic a concept.

A term denoting will is also most notably absent, though badly needed, in Philo's elaborate theory of conscience. [148]

Neither in Greek philosophy nor in the Old Testament can we find a distinct and generally accepted notion of conscience, although phe-nomena which we usually explain by the concept of conscience are fre-quently described in many of these texts. [149] This is far from surprising. According to both traditions the human mind does not need to internal-ize the standards of moral conduct. They exist, objectively and invari-ably fixed, outside man's consciousness, either in the divine Law or in the order of nature; man has only to take notice of them. This opinion, however, turned out to be too simple once St. Paul came to take seriously the fact that some gentiles fulfilled the will of God without knowing His Law. Philo, in his turn, tried to show, by mutual interpretation of Bibli-cal and philosophical texts, that Moses and Plato pointed to the same truth, regardless of all their differences in knowledge and approach. [150] Once you admit that somebody else is able, by his intentional actions, to meet your own standards without knowing them, you have to as-sume a guide in his soul that is not identical with his normal intel-ligence, but that has to be considered the ultimate and metarational factor in his moral decisions.

There was, in fact, an old belief, in Greece and elsewhere, that men are guided through life by divine teachers and protectors. [151] Yet as early as the fifth century, Greek philosophers applied this idea to the part which reason was supposed to play in moral life. It is reason that guides man through the vicissitudes of life. [152] By his own intellectual activity man can meet the two fundamental requirements of moral life, namely, the proper choice of the individual means and ends of action and the moral assessment of what he has done, what he is doing and what he is going to do. Insight into one's own action results from intellectual activity and is called conscience, *conscientia*, συνείδησις. To the Greeks, this knowledge which accompanies human action is attained in the very same way as any other kind of knowledge and is by no means due to any special faculty of the human soul.[153] That is why the Greeks never coined the term to denote conscience as a very special kind of knowledge.

Philo, in his turn, frequently and approvingly refers to the philosophical conception according to which man has been given reason to be his divine guide throughout his lifetime.[154] Yet, at the same time, he repeatedly speaks of the conscience, the examiner, the holy priest as dwelling in the soul quite apart from the intellectual faculties.[155] This inner voice is called, in various contexts, accuser, judge, teacher, admonisher. It cannot be silenced by rational arguments.[156] It is a gift given by God's mercy through which man comes to a sudden insight into what is right and wrong,[157] thus revealing what the nature of man should be.[158] It prevents the human intellect from turning to the worse. When it has left the soul, man is bound to do wrong on purpose, that is to say by the choice which he makes through his intellect.[159] For Philo, as can be seen from this description, conscience and its function in moral life do not result from the normal use of reason. Conscience owes its existence to God's direct interference with the life of man. That is why we should pray for so precious a gift.[160] It does not draw its origin from the normal or natural equipment of the soul. Philo speaks of conscience as an addition to every soul but also mentions the possibility of its leaving the soul.[161] The extent, therefore, to which conscience determines human action, in any given case, is not as predictable or calculable as is the influence of either reason or emotion. Conscience, though, has to be considered as the very last instance on which every moral decision ultimately depends. Thus no factor in moral life is of greater importance with regard to the origin of human intention. Intention, which originates from conscience, cannot be invalidated by reason or emotion, because it entails the response to a divine commandment. Yet a divine order, according to the Biblical tradition which Philo wanted to make explicit, can only be obeyed or disobeyed. Once Philo introduced the concept of conscience in order to explain this act of obedience, no possibility was left for assessing the value of any action only with respect to

its moral calculability. Will, intention as such, became the decisive factor in moral life, even if there was no term to denote it.

This concept of will inheres in Philo's doctrine of conscience as it
does in St. Paul's teaching. But neither one came to choose a definite
term to denote the concept. Both of them had to rely on the vocabulary
of contemporary Greek which had been shaped, to a large extent and
over a long period of time, by philosophical doctrines. Philo, though
fully aware of essential differences between the two traditions, definitely tried to show that Plato and Moses did not contradict each other.
His exegesis of the Bible replaced, to a large extent, Hebrew concepts
and ways of thought by Greek ones. St. Paul did not make the attempt
to give the *interpretatio Graeca* of the tradition of his people and the new
message. He seems to have been firmly convinced that both traditions
were in fundamental disagreement, above all in the way they provided
standards for assessing man's religious and moral responsibility and for
guiding his life. But both St. Paul and Philo had to use contemporary
Greek, and this very fact prevented them from coining the unmistakable
term to denote the concept of will to which both of them were led in their
speculation, regardless of the difference of approach in their quest.

V.
Philosophy and Religion in Late Antiquity

A CRUCIAL PROBLEM was transmitted to the early Christians together with the Biblical tradition, once they began to feel the need for theological explanation of their faith:[1] how is one to reconcile the belief in the goodness of the Creator who governs everything according to his omniscience and omnipotence, with the consciousness of sin and distress, with the existence of both moral and physical evil? Jewish as well as Christian faith collapses without either divine predestination or human responsibility, and both are stressed with changing emphasis in all extant texts. As can be seen from many religions in the history of mankind, the belief in divine or natural predestination, especially the consciousness of being divinely and inevitably elect, is far from paralysing human initiative, which rests on the feeling of being free to act in various ways. The ἀργὸς λόγος (the indolent argument) which was directed against Chrysippus' doctrine of fate turned out to be a very weak argument (Cic. *de fat.* 31).[2] In religious and moral life confidence in the all-embracing rule of God or Nature and a feeling of one's own responsibility are likely to reinforce rather than contradict each other. This applies particularly to the Biblical tradition, where this confidence is defined as obedience to the unfathomable plans and orders of God. St. Paul's doctrine of grace and predestination, as pointed out in Rom. 9–11,[3] and many of his sayings about the will of man being produced by his Creator, were not meant to contradict the presupposition that man is free and responsible in his moral conduct. St. Paul's theory of grace and predestination was properly evaluated only from the fourth century onwards. Yet the belief that both divine predetermination and human responsibility have to be accepted is common ground in the writings of the apostolic period.

Theology, however, had to offer rational interpretation of Christian faith in a civilization dyed with philosophy, and to solve the contradiction described above. This was done, for the first time and very elaborately, in the Gnostic systems of the second century.

Regardless of considerable differences amongst themselves, the various schools and sects of the Gnostic movement[4] basically agreed in their answer to the question raised above. The world that we experience by our senses as imperfect and changing came to existence only by the regrettable intermingling of some beings or particles of the really existing realm of Light or Spirit with shapeless and inert matter. That is why such particles now are imprisoned in some human souls and bodies, but all individuals who have been endowed with that precious gift have completely forgotten their true self. Yet the Supreme Being, because of his boundless goodness, has sent a messenger from his realm who conveys to all those who belong to him the knowledge of their origin. So they become able to return to their home, to be saved and reunited with their Father.

Thus the fall and salvation of the individual soul are strictly determined in a cosmic process of which the decisive events have already taken place in the immaterial world of Light. For the individual, salvation is performed through an act or a series of acts of cognition. Cognition disentangles man from evil and from the necessities of the material world, and restores the freedom of an entirely spiritual existence.[5] Whether or not a given human being can be saved entirely depends on his previous possession of the pneumatic particle. Men without that endowment are incapable of receiving the salutary message.

The cosmology and anthropology which underlie such a concept of man's salvation have to stress two factors: the free, creative, animating activity of the spirit both in God and man, and the irrational, destructive impulse originating from the fatal mixture of spirit and matter to which our present world owes its existence. The first cannot be displayed by man or any other being on earth in his empirical condition, where he has lost his freedom. Thus his salvation must have been planned and brought about solely by the Supreme Being, and his own decision to accept the message has been conditioned by his nature.[6]

Gnostic doctrine usually depicts the unfolding of the universe and the implied fall and return of man in an endless chain of mythical characters and events. So the will and intention of the Supreme Being to create or produce is spoken of in various Gnostic systems and with reference to various levels of reality as a separate hypostasis called θέλησις or βούλησις.[7] Will, however, is usually described as the explicit result of an act of cognition,[8] and nowhere do we find that it can be thought of separately from that preceding act. Matter or sensuality, on the other hand, can produce their harmful impulses only because of the absence of knowledge. That is why sin or fall or guilt is always spoken of in terms of ignorance, error, forgetfulness. No human being, no cosmic power is thought to do wrong on purpose because of his ill will, though knowing the better. Irrational impulses that lead to evil not only presuppose the absence of knowledge, they additionally blind the intellect.[9]

There are only a few neuralgic points in the Gnostic image of world and man and fate; though everything seems so well ordered and predetermined, man's salvation can indeed be expected, but only from the knowledge of a divinely revealed truth. Some decisive steps in the cosmic drama, however, cannot possibly be understood as inadequate or poor performances of the intellect.

When one of the first spiritual beings left its proper area for the first time to be mixed, in some way or other, with matter, it did so because of its imprudence, its preparedness to take a risk or its desire to act independently of the Supreme Being.[10] This initiating cosmic event is clearly depicted as an act of pure volition rather than will caused by inappropriate cognition. It was only in consequence of this act that the being in question became forgetful, ignorant, involved in matter, and the primary cause of evil. On the other hand, the decision of the Supreme Being to send his messenger and to save the enslaved members of his kingdom does not result from a special act of cognition: it stems from His boundless goodness and sovereignty[11] and could be spoken of easily in terms of pure volition. Finally, those men who are bound to be saved because of their pneumatic nature are described as being eager to be taught and to acquire the salutary knowledge, though they are still in the state of ignorance.[12] Again, their longing, which is neither the result of an act of cognition nor an irrational affective impulse, can be understood only as a phenomenon of sheer volition apart from knowledge.

None of these three conceptions contradicts the strict determination which rules the universe and the destiny of man. They do, in fact, impair the idea, never abandoned in any branch of Gnostic doctrine, that fall and salvation are caused exclusively through error and knowledge.[13] Yet the imprudence of the first divine being in becoming tainted by matter, and the grace of the Supreme Being which initiated man's salvation, are distant events. They are separated from man's individual destiny by many providential acts and events which form the content of the salutary knowledge and which can be grasped in their logical consequence. The longing for salvation, however, which testifies to the quality of those who will be saved can be fulfilled, very much like the Platonic Eros, by means of cognition only. It shows, nevertheless, the limits of the entirely intellectualistic approach as proposed by the Gnostics.

In the Biblical view the election of those who are going to be saved or become the people of God has been made by an initial act of divine will which appeared in an historical event. The same will, inexplicable and unfathomable as it might be, continuously interferes with the life of man by acts and orders and promises. Both elect and non-elect have to cope with the unpredictable manifestations and the unrestricted sovereignty of the divine will throughout the history of mankind. The Gnostics transposed the interaction of God and man from history with all its vicissitudes into the unchanging order of being which they could find only in the realm of pure spirituality. This inevitably led them to a strictly deterministic and intellectualistic approach to the question of fall and salvation. The free decision of man, though never completely disregarded in Gnostic thought, especially in the moral admonition of the saved to preserve their privilege by constant moral efforts, could not possibly become the decisive topic in Gnostic soteriology.

Philosophy in the Hellenistic and Roman periods was regarded as the *ars vitae* leading to εὐδαιμονία. The latter concept traditionally meant the happy life in agreement with nature. Some schools, however, included man's salvation (σωτηρία) even beyond the limits of time and space, a view which was regarded as increasingly important from the first century B.C. onwards.[14]

The relation between freedom of choice and the predetermined order of nature was extensively discussed in all branches of philosophy: the former seemed to be the basis of any moral judgement, the latter had to be acknowledged because nature was supposed to provide a rational order of being. Only the Epicureans simply denied such an order and attributed everything to chance. Consequently, no natural or divine predestination could possibly interfere with man's free decision to act.

Various theories to explain the relation between the two factors were current in the first centuries of our era. The Stoics still held the doctrine that nature links everything, including the minor actions of men, into a coherent chain of causation. Everything is prearranged and predetermined by Fate (Heimarmene) according to a perfectly rational order.[15]

Human freedom has but two aspects in the Stoic view. Firstly, man has been endowed with the same reason that governs the universe and is, therefore, able to ascertain the salutary and perfect order of nature. This leads him to identify unchangeable Heimarmene and benevolent Providence. That is why the wise man will choose freely, consciously, and willingly, what Heimarmene orders or even forces him to do, for he knows that this is at the same time necessary, salutary for himself and the universe, and perfectly rational. *Volentem fata ducunt, nolentem trahunt*, as Seneca puts it.[16] "Fate leads the willing, and drags the unwilling." To meet the objection that this doctrine destroyed rather than established human freedom, Chrysippus conceived the theory of the two modes of causation:[17] every action in human life is initiated by a cause outside the acting individual and controlled solely by Fate. This primary cause (αἰτία προκατάρχουσα), however, does not suffice to bring about the action in a particular way that can be valued according to moral standards. This entirely depends on the condition of the acting individual which thus becomes a cause for action in its own right (αἰτία αὐτοτελής). A cylinder has to be pushed to start rolling downhill. But only because of its shape is it able to perform this particular kind of motion all the way down. Similarly the moral condition of the acting individual is the secondary, but more important cause of action. The nature and condition of the acting individual, in its turn, has been caused by Heimarmene, very much like the initiating cause of the action.

The Stoic concept of all-embracing Fate corresponds to a monist and materialist interpretation of reality. According to the Platonic tradition there are several layers of reality. Consequently, Platonic Heimarmene operates differently at the various levels of being. The most elaborate doctrine on this topic is to be found in pseudo-Plutarch's treatise on fate,[18] where a distinction is made between πρώτη πρόνοια (first providence) for the uppermost level of reality without the impact of matter, cosmic πρόνοια as executed and indicated by the stars,[19] and προμήθεια in human life supervised by lower divine beings. At the uppermost level of reality no conceivable conflict between freedom of choice and rational determination can happen, since pure reason with its perfect rational order always chooses what is good and perfectly ordered. The gift of choice owned by all rational beings can be used for the better or the worse only in the realm where spirit and matter intermingle. This applies to man. Being endowed with reason he is always able to choose freely, unlike animals who are guided by their senses and instincts, and gods that are incapable of choosing the worse. But the consequences of his choice are predetermined and inevitable as to whether he has chosen in the right or wrong way.[20] The wrong decision may be due to irrational affections and emotions to which he is exposed in his physical existence, or simply to error and ignorance. Thus Fate not only operates with varying degrees of strictness; it also offers a twofold aspect of man in his present condition, since it enslaves him in consequence of his own sin or mistake and frees him once he has made the proper choice.

Different again is the Peripatetic view of the problem. Aristotle had classified very carefully and under various headings the various types of causes, the difference between what is caused by nature and what by human activities, the essential and the circumstantial ingredients of any act or event, and the different types of motivation in human life. The opinion on free choice and natural predetermination current in his school during the imperial period has been concisely expounded in the first six chapters of the treatise On Fate, which Alexander of Aphrodisias directed against the Stoic doctrine of Heimarmene in around A.D. 200.[21]

Alexander speaks of three independent factors that contribute to causation. Many things happen according to the order of nature, and since everything that happens in this way is strictly regulated and open to rational understanding, even to the degree of being predictable, we may well speak of Heimarmene in this context.[22] Yet not everything that happens by nature also happens necessarily. Both the deliberate decision of man and mere chance can divert the course of events, so that something which is going to happen κατὰ φύσιν (according to nature) comes out as an act παρὰ φύσιν (contrary to nature). Nature made Socrates a man of strong sensuality. But since he deliberately acted all his life according to strict moral standards, he became a paragon of self-restraint. The same relation also subsists between chance and deliberate decision: a farmer starts digging his garden and finds a treasure.

Chance has substituted, in this case, for the deliberately chosen aim a different one, thus converting an action initiated κατὰ τέχνην καὶ προαίρεσιν (according to technical or moral purposes) into one ἀπὸ τύχης καὶ αὐτομάτου (by chance and without external agency). The three determining factors can reinforce or counteract each other, and two of them, namely chance and nature, drastically restrict the area within which human action takes place, and deeply influence or even overturn its outcome.[23] Yet they do not impair man's freedom to plan and decide reasonably and, consequently, his moral responsibility, which he satisfies only in his intentions. Man is even free to create his own moral character by reasoning and deciding, through all his lifetime, according to moral standards.

These theories, different as they may be, all agree in two essential details. They all provide a framework of predetermination for human activities which is set, in varying degrees of stringency, by the order of nature. This opinion results from the common creed of Greek philosophy that nature is strictly ordered by reason and does not admit exceptions to its rules. These are open to the intellectual understanding of rational beings such as gods and men. On the other hand, they all insist on freedom of choice as the very basis of human morality. Because of their deep-rooted "naturalism," man's freedom is taken as the consequence of his being endowed with reason rather than as a gift to be separated from the cognitive faculties, through which man can bring about the congruity of his own consciousness with the order of being. Thus the obvious fact that people sometimes do choose the worse needs a special explanation, since reason is to be taken as the unique cause of order and goodness in man as well as in the universe. The explanation is given in various ways: weakness of the intellect, involvement in matter, irrational impulses originating from the body or the lower strata of the soul, difficulties in handling a situation which is caused by chance, lack of discipline, self-indulgence, and the like. All these obstacles, which prevent the intellect from making its right choice, can be overcome by intellectual efforts and systematic exercise. There is no need for a good will which would operate independently of the intellect. Exercise can restrict the fallibility of the human intellect and form the habit of choosing rightly.[24] But it can replace neither the act of cognition in each individual case nor the knowledge of what is good and evil.

Thus the solution philosophy gave to the problem was derived from a concept of restricted predetermination which allowed an important area to human freedom, as well as from a strict intellectualism. Neither the philosophic nor the Gnostic approach led to a distinct notion of human will. But again, some neuralgic points are easy to discover. They come out most clearly where the soteriological function of philosophy becomes predominant.

If a philosophy claims to bring about the definitive salvation of man's proper self beyond the limits of space, time, and empirical life by means of positive doctrines, it has to offer basic assumptions or insights that are not open to doubt or discussion. Only where philosophy is supposed to provide merely the way to salvation rather than its attainment can even its basic assumptions become the subject of sceptical investigation. These two opinions of what philosophy really is about are distinctly expounded in a discussion between Apollonius of Tyana and the old-fashioned, scholarly-minded Stoic Euphrates which Philostratus has inserted into the biography of his hero.[25]

Official Platonism throughout the imperial period always insisted on a scholarly attitude towards the means and ends of philosophy. But Platonic tradition contained many specific details that were particularly well suited to becoming the basis of religious doctrine rather than theories for philosophical investigation. These include the complete separateness of the Supreme Being ἐπέκεινα τῆς οὐσίας (outside the realm of being), the dualism of spirit and matter with all its ontological and anthropological implications, the belief that everything has been definitively said in Plato's writings, which have to be properly understood and expounded rather than discussed and questioned. Thus at the fringes of scholarly Platonism, but sometimes even within its official tradition, we discover coherent doctrines, composed from philosophic, predominantly but not exclusively Platonic, elements and proclaimed as the divinely revealed truth about God and man. The so-called Chaldean Oracles written in the second half of the second century represent this type of text. Their fragments have much in common with those of Numenius of Apamea, who was a Platonist with strong Pythagorean sympathies at about the same time.[26] His example is designed to show that the tendency to transform philosophy into religion, which did not pass unnoticed at the time, was by no means restricted to authors outside the philosophical tradition proper.[27]

In this area the neuralgic points mentioned above came out most clearly: if, then, the Supreme Being is beyond the grasp of the human intellect, separate from everything that comes into being and passes away, and yet the ultimate cause of existence, life, consciousness, and order in everything, the first and decisive step in the unfolding of the universe must be due to an act of sheer volition rather than cognition on the part of the Supreme Being. There is no reason open to intellectual understanding for this initial act of the Supreme Being. The Chaldean Oracles describe this condition by means of a trinitarian doctrine:[28] the Father, that is to say pure, immovable, noetic existence, produces Dynamis, that is to say random motion, life, will. Together, because they can be taken as the male and female principle,[29] they become the origin of the Second Nous which gives limit, aim, and consciousness to the undefined motion, thus being the creator of the ordered universe. We need not go into further details[30] of that cosmology, for we have already seen that will has become, in the context of such a doctrine, an ontological entity in its own right instead of a byproduct of cognition. The inexplicability of the First Cause of the rational order of being led to this concept.

Doctrines like that of the Chaldean Oracles have to be accepted before the convert can try to understand them by his own intellectual efforts. The first step on the road towards knowledge and salvation comes from an act of volition that does not result from any kind of cognition.[31] But speculation did not concentrate on the problem of human will with the same intensity as on its cosmological aspect. Communication with the divine and, consequently, perfection in human life are brought about exclusively through intellectual activity, through knowledge: this was common ground for philosophers, Gnostics, Hermetics, and "Chaldeans" alike.

The intellectualistic approach also prevails in the Chaldean doctrine on Fate and Free Choice as can be seen in fragment 215. The solution given to the problem is predominantly deterministic. There is no indication that the conception of, or term for, will occurred in this chapter of Chaldean teaching, despite the fact that it had an important place in Chaldean ontology. Moral theory in the Greek world was reluctant to accept such a conception.

❖

The refutation of Gnostic determinism became one of the most important tasks of Christian theology in the second and third centuries.[32] Most of the arguments by which man's free decision was corroborated were taken from philosophical doctrines. So, for example, both Justin and Irenaeus derive the faculty of free choice from man's endowment with reason, that is to say from his intellectual forces. Reason, however, is the basis of his being or becoming the image of God in both the philosophic and the Christian view.[33] Clement of Alexandria, too, follows the philosophical tradition in attributing free decision on which moral responsibility rests to man's intellectual perception and judgement (προαίρεσις) which leads to the view that human action is the consequence of cognition.[34]

Many attempts were made to harmonize human freedom with divine predestination, for both concepts were indispensable to Christian orthodoxy. Two of them deserve a closer examination.

About A.D. 200 Bar Daiṣān of Edessa conceived his doctrine on fate which has been preserved in the *Dialogue on the Laws of Countries*, written in Syriac.[35]

The nature of man, created by God, determines his physical existence with regard to his being born, getting old, and the like. But it also includes his faculty of free decision, which is attached to his true self. Only men and angels have been given full freedom of choice, the other beings of creation only to a lesser extent. Hence everyone will be judged by the Creator at the end of the world, but only for actions caused by free decision. Nature as created by God is entirely good. So man feels content if he has made his choice for the better, that is to say according to nature and the intention of the Creator. The will of God is easy to ascertain: the so-called Golden Rule covers all orders and commandments. There is no need for special knowledge or revelation. God's commandments for a life according to nature can be equally fulfilled by the poor and the rich, the weak and the strong, the wise and the unwise, since one needs neither wisdom nor health to be charitable or sincere; this depends entirely on one's free decision. And it is only in this respect that man will be subject to the final judgement of God. Undoubtedly, man's life is deeply influenced by factors outside his power such as good health and illness, poverty and wealth. All this is distributed by Fate, which Bar Daiṣān understands in terms of astrology. The stars, having been created as an instrument of divine rule, have become a factor in disturbing the perfect order of nature, in so far as they use their freedom against the will of God. Man is exposed to their influence because of his having a soul and a body attached to his pneumatic self. But this does not impair his ability to make his moral decisions in accordance with nature and the commandments of God. So both moral evil and salvation depend entirely on man's free decision.

Bar Daiṣān opposed the Stoic, Gnostic, and astrological concept of a comprehensive Fate, as well as the Epicurean concept of chance.[36] He also avoided Platonic doctrines such as that of the several levels of determination, and the opinion that man's decision is always free, though its consequences are determined by fate. Bar Daiṣān conceived his theory after the model of Peripatetic doctrine, which introduced three independent factors, namely nature, chance, and human decision,[37] which interact at the same level, nature being superior only insofar as it has set the frame of possibility. The influence of the stars was thought of by the Peripatetics as a less important part of natural determination. Bar Daiṣān, in his turn, replaced chance in the Peripatetic system by the stars. Thus the astral powers became, at the same time, more important as an independent factor and less valuable as being separated from the entirely good order of nature or creation,[38] which Bar Daiṣān stressed against his Gnostic, above all Marcionite, adversaries.[39]

His doctrine does not seem specifically Christian, since neither the grace of God nor Christ's death and resurrection are of any importance for the salvation of man. Yet Bar Daiṣān regarded himself as a Christian, and there are, in fact, some elements of his doctrine that point in that direction. First of all, Bar Daiṣān restricts his modified Peripatetic system of threefold causation to the present age of the world with all its imperfection. It is only due to the grace of God, who can directly interfere with everything on earth, that man has been given, in the period of time before doomsday, the freedom to choose the means and ends of his actions.

So, unlike the philosophers, Bar Daiṣān tries to explain a preliminary rather than a lasting and unchangeable order of the world.

Secondly, Bar Daiṣān does not share the philosophical creed that moral perfection comes from or rather is identical with perfect knowledge. God's commandments can be perceived and obeyed by everyone who has been given the faculty of free decision. There is no need for special knowledge to become virtuous, since human nature agrees with the will of God and can tell whether someone has chosen the right way. Here we find, for the first time, that Biblical voluntarism has been formulated, however imperfectly, in terms of philosophical anthropology.

Unlike Philo, Justin, Irenaeus,[40] and many others, our author no longer describes, in the footsteps of Greek philosophy, man's freedom and responsibility as resulting exclusively from his cognitive potential.

Clement of Alexandria offers an interesting parallel. In his *Protrepticus* (12.118.4), he discusses the fact that simple Christians often surpass educated ones in their moral conduct.[41] Clement describes their firmness to decide for the better by the term συγκατάθεσις, which he sometimes also uses to denote the Christian faith.[42] Apparently Clement wants to contrast superior knowledge to firmness of moral purpose, of which the latter seems to be more valuable in Christian life, though the perfect Christian is always the "wise" or "gnostic" in his view. The term συγκατάθεσις has been taken from the Stoic theory of cognition and action.[43] An idea formed in the mind mostly implies a possible goal of action, but has to be given assent (συγκατάθεσις) by the intellect in order to create the drive (ὁρμή) towards action. Clement has transposed the term from the entirely intellectualistic[44] conception which the Stoics had of human action into a context where the sheer, but voluntary, decision for the better is rated higher than superior knowledge of the means and ends of action.[45]

A different picture of the relation between human freedom and divine rule was given by Origen,[46] some decades after Bar Daiṣān and probably quite independently. Origen is concerned with the story of the Pharaoh (Exod. 4:21ff), whose heart was hardened by God's direct intervention. So he disobeyed the divine orders and was severely punished together with the people of Egypt. Origen flatly denies that God's intervention could be taken as the reason for Pharaoh's sin and the subsequent evil. The boundless and unsurpassed goodness of God does not admit such an interpretation of the Biblical account. Origen offers two alternative explanations instead.

God hardens the hearts, as is repeatedly stated in the Bible, only of those whom he knows already to have an evil intention either habitually or occasionally. So the hardening only brings to light an already existing vice or, in other words, the hardening is the initiating and external cause of the evil in question, the nature or condition of man being the real and efficient cause (αἰτία αὐτοτελής). This is, as we have seen, the Stoic doctrine applied to the Biblical text in order to show that in spite of divine intervention human responsibility remains undiminished.

The second explanation has a similar tendency. God hardens the heart of the trespasser in order to involve him deeper in sin and guilt, because only by feeling the whole burden of sin can man become capable of self-cognition and lasting repentance. God acts like the physician who reinforces the power of illness in order to bring about the salutary crisis in the process of healing.

Both explanations are drawn from Stoic philosophy, which distinguishes between initial and essential causes (see above, p. 103) and explains the existence of evil as a means of providential education of man.[47] Another argument which Origen uses in these chapters is taken from Platonic sources. Since the human soul is preexistent and immortal, punishment and reward, education and purification, cannot be realized within the period of just one of its incarnations. Thus evil which unexpectedly befalls a man may have been caused by his sins in a previous physical existence.

On the basis of these Platonic ideas Origen is even able to cope with St. Paul's doctrine of predestination as expounded in Rom. 9–11. The "vessels of wrath fitted for destruction" may either be turned into "vessels of mercy" because of their own endeavor, as Origen interprets 2 Tim. 2:20f, or be punished because of their sins in a previous life.

Finally, Origen has to deal with St. Paul's general statements about human intention and performance being brought about by God's intervention.[48] He points out that St. Paul only wants to give prudential and parenetic precepts. No one can reasonably deny that a steersman, who has guided his vessel through a storm with all his skill and courage, acted freely and responsibly. Yet the aid of God was of far greater importance for all those who got home safely. By attributing even our intention to God's activity the Apostle merely wants to dissuade us from becoming proud of our moral standing. He wants us to be humble and trusting in God's help—without diminishing our freedom and responsibility.[49]

Origen's reasoning on this particular problem completely agrees with the philosophical tradition. He insists on the rational character of God's rule, even with regard to the enigmatic hardening of the heart,[50] and, consequently, on the full congruity between intellectual and moral perfection in human life. According to him, the will of man proceeds from his reason without becoming separated from it (*princ.* 1.2.6). Neither obedience and disobedience on the side of man nor the phenomenon of Pharaoh's divinely hardened heart is explained in terms of will as independent from knowledge and error. Man's free decision can be led astray or impaired by error, sensuality, or evil demons, that is to say by all kinds of influences originating from inert matter. Agreement between human conduct and the divine order of being can only be established, in the view of both Plato and Origen, through intellectual activity. There is no will to be taken as an independent faculty on either side to which human freedom refers. Perfect freedom depends on and is, in fact, identical with unhindered intellectual activity.[51]

The picture does not look too different in the numerous passages where Irenaeus defends human freedom against Gnostic determinism.[52] For him as for Clement, Origen, or Justin, the freedom of man, his having been made after the likeness of the Creator, can only be found in the gift of reason.[53] Faith is described as the free assent given to God's commandment.[54] Because of his being created man is able to attain life and perfection only through voluntary and unrestricted obedience to his Creator. This, however, depends, as does every proper use of one's freedom, on the cognition of truth. Intention of moral or religious value is based on rational cognition (νοῦς ὀρεκτικός, ὄρεξις νοητική).[55] It is only with regard to the intention of God that Irenaeus discards the traditional belief that cognition always precedes intention. God is almighty, omniscient, and not subject to affections that impair His entirely spiritual activity.[56] Thus He enjoys, in contrast to the condition of man, boundless freedom and sovereignty, and that is why His intention is, at the same time, cognition and action.[57] This can be seen from the *creatio ex nihilo*[58] and the resurrection of Christ.[59] Predestination in nature and history as imposed by God is to be considered as the law He gave to His creation rather than the rule of necessity to restrict Himself or the freedom of man.[60]

It seems fair to say that Christian theology succeeded, in the course of the second and third centuries, in defending the Biblical conception of man's responsibility against Gnostic determinism without abandoning the belief in God's omniscience and omnipotence. Yet the terms and concepts used in this controversy had to be taken without exception from various philosophical doctrines, all of which had come to agree on one essential point: it is only through intellectual activity that man can harmonize his own conduct with the order of nature. The Biblical idea of man being exposed to the inexplicable commandments and promises of God and supposed to respond by his obedience could not possibly be made explicit in terms of philosophical anthropology without drastic changes in its system of reference. That is why we can discover only weak attempts to introduce the distinct notion of will in the Christian texts mentioned above.[61] The will of God, however, was to become one of the main topics of theological investigation during the fourth century. The problems involved were solved with the aid of some new ontological concepts of the Platonic school.

Plotinus, though far from wanting to be an innovator in the Platonic tradition, nevertheless designed a completely new model of the uppermost layer of reality whence everything draws existence, life, and structure.[62] The unmoved One (῞Εν) embraces everything, even the two entities presupposed in any kind of intellectual activity, that is to say the perceiving and the perceived.[63] From its inexhaustible wealth and without being diminished in any way, the One produces, in an eternally continuing act of creation or emanation, the Intellect (Νοῦς), thus inaugurating activity, cognition, and the division of perceiving and perceived. The Intellect, in its turn, produces the Soul (Ψυχή) by which the mere potential of unstructured and, consequently, non-existent matter becomes open to the various degrees of structure, life, and consciousness. Thus the progression of the Spirit that originates from the One permanently creates, shapes, and animates the universe.[64]

Yet this ontic process does not develop in only one direction, that is to say from the top to the bottom. Every individual being, regardless of its standing in the universal hierarchy, is connected, however indirectly, with the One and strives, therefore, to leave the area of change and imperfection, to return to its origin, and to share the unchangeable perfection of the One. Thus the infinite progression (πρόοδος) is always being counterbalanced by the return (ἐπιστροφή) of everything.

Evil, both physical and moral, is not to be ascribed to an independent cosmic power. It is a byproduct rather of the unfolding reality: every individual being originates from the intellectual activity of a higher one and is, therefore, less real than its antecedent. The degree of structure, life, and consciousness of every individual being is inversely proportional to its distance from the One, the source of all beings. Correspondingly, evil as the absence of structure, life, and consciousness is identical with non-being. That is why the creative πρόοδος, to which the universe owes its existence, implies at the same time the permanent turning towards non-being instead of being, multiplicity instead of unity, which innumerable beings constantly perform. In doing so, they make use of their freedom (ἐξουσία) to exist and to act independently (δι' ἑαυτῶν εἶναι), instead of reuniting themselves with the One. This concept, which has far-reaching consequences in the theory of ethics, is called τόλμα by Plotinus, a term already used in Gnosticism and earlier Platonism (see above p. 22) and has important voluntaristic implications. Yet Plotinus took great pains to prove,[65] especially in his anti-Gnostic polemics,[66] that the descent of the spirit into matter is not only the cause of evil, but primarily the origin of the ordered, animated, and beautiful universe.

Plotinus' model of reality seems dominated by a vertical structure: reality was explained in terms of descent and ascent, and later Neoplatonists followed this line by adding one or the other hypostasis above the One.[67] However, Porphyry, Plotinus' most eminent pupil, supplemented his master's doctrine by the concept of what one may call the horizontal unfolding of reality.[68]

By means of an extensive interpretation of the trinitarian theology of the Chaldean Oracles (see above p. 107), Porphyry put forward his own ontology. Unchangeable and pure Existence (Ὕπαρξις) causes, because of its own perfection, boundless and permanent Life, Power, or Will (Ζωή), of which the infinite motion has to be limited, structured, and brought to consciousness by the reflecting Intellect (Νοῦς). The Intellect, therefore, is Demiurge or Creator and the immediate cause of the structured and animated universe. In every individual being all three modes are present, though one of them always predominates. They are connected, all three, in terms of causation rather than time, and each of them, because of their togetherness, represents the whole of reality. What man experiences as reality through his intellect is constantly being brought about by their interaction, both in the universe and in the human mind.

According to the conceptions of both Plotinus and Porphyry, perfect reality is to be found in the Intelligible, far from the disturbing influences of the sensible world, and open only to intellectual understanding. Both doctrines account for the rational order, goodness, and perceptibility of the existing universe, in which inert matter is constantly being shaped and animated by the spirit. Both provide the basis of a theory of ethics, according to which progressive cognition of the order of being leads, at the same time, to moral perfection, since the human intellect, by its cognitive performance, disentangles itself from the bounds of matter and, consequently, of moral imperfection.[69] The state of perfection, both ontologically and morally, can be understood as perfect union of the individual being and the ultimate source of being. It is to be brought about by a chain of intellectual acts.[70]

Up to this point everything in Plotinus' and Porphyry's doctrine seems to agree with traditional Greek, especially Platonic, intellectualism, the notion of will being quite superfluous in such a context.[71] There are, however, some details which, from an intellectualistic point of view, seem to be unduly stressed.[72]

On the side of Plotinus,[73] the permanent overflow from the One down through all the subordinate hypostases into the minutest details of the empirical world cannot be explained in terms of subtraction and addition. Though realized in a chain of intellectual acts, it is set in motion by an inexplicable longing to be creative, which pervades the whole of reality but is concentrated in, and proceeds from, the One. Accordingly, the return of every individual being to the perfect and all-embracing One is again realized in a chain of cognitive acts. Yet the individual act neither precedes nor follows, but is rather identical with the ἐπιστροφή (return), since every being has been conditioned for this return. The metaphysical will of unfolding and returning which determines the existence of the spiritual and empirical world is thought of as prior to and independent of its rational and, consequently, perceptible structure. Finally, the negative aspect of the unfolding of reality, namely the insolence (τόλμα) of the individual being that turns away from its origin and tries to become independent, can only be described in terms of volition, though the act of turning is undoubtedly realized as a poor intellectual performance of the being in question.[74]

Porphyry even made will a separate mode of being: reality as experienced by the human mind includes the elements of existence, motion or change, and structure or limit. None of these can be perceived either individually or in combination with only one of the two others. Reality presupposes something like will as a metaphysical factor. Accordingly, Porphyry's ethical theory, especially his doctrine of moral progress, has some important voluntaristic details.[75]

The metaphysics of both Plotinus and Porphyry had new and, according to traditional Greek standards, unusual voluntaristic implications.[76] But from this innovation neither of them drew radical consequences with regard to their ethical doctrines.[77] Both of them insisted on freedom of choice in human life against all deterministic doctrines. However, they derived this gift, which enables man to become similar to God, from his being endowed with intellect, rather than introducing the anthropological category of will to make explicit the concept of freedom.[78]

Yet both Plotinus and Porphyry were extensively referred to by the Fathers of the fourth century, who were obliged to form a clear conception of the will of God in consequence of the Christological controversies then current.

Origen had taught, apparently without many afterthoughts, that the Son proceeded from the will of the Father.[79] This formulation was designed only to explain that God saved mankind quite voluntarily because of his mercy rather than because of any kind of predetermination.[80] But it became unacceptable, from the orthodox point of view, since the will of the Father had always been considered mainly as the cause of creation, the Son thus being created and separated from the Father, like any other creature, by the hypostasis of the divine will—which indeed was the opinion of Arius who stressed the subordination of the Son more than the orthodox tradition could admit. Athanasius, instead, identified the Son with the will of the Father.[81] This agreed with the creed that Christ was not created but came from his Father's substance (οὐσία) and also with widespread and old speculations about God's own Sophia or Logos having been the mediator in the work of creation. As the will of His Father, Christ was not subordinate as was the second hypostasis in relation to the One in the system of Plotinus.

Yet a new difficulty arose from Athanasius' definition. It was common ground in Platonic and Peripatetic philosophy that the result of a free choice (προαίρεσις), which always implies the possibility of the opposite, is, from the ontological point of view, inferior in dignity to what is necessitated by the order of being.[82] Plotinus, however, had used the term προαίρεσις, in contrast to the Aristotelian and Platonic tradition of his time, only to denote the free, conscious, and habitual choice of the better.[83] This of course the Platonists had always valued more highly than anything inevitably caused by nature. On the basis of the Plotinian notion of προαίρεσις Gregory of Nazianzus opposed

Athanasius' formulation that God had generated the Son by necessity and not voluntarily (ἀνάγκῃ καὶ μὴ θέλων).[84] Since God's intention is always qualified in the sense of the Plotinian προαίρεσις, He must have had the will to generate the Son. Likewise, Gregory refuted the use of the image of well and water, by which Plotinus had illustrated the overflow from the One,[85] and Athanasius and other orthodox theologians the relation between Father and Son and their unity in substance and time. The image did not correspond to the idea of God's salutary intention to generate His Son in order to save mankind. Gregory solved the problem of the will of God by introducing a new distinction. As the cause of creation the will of God became a hypostasis called θέλησις, separate from its origin and thus perceptible by the human mind. When God generated His Son, His intention or will was certainly at work, but remained a quality attached inseparably to the substance of its owner. That is why the voluntary generation of the Son is not open to human understanding, whereas man can ascertain the order of creation separately from the imperceptible substance of the Creator. This distinction enabled Gregory to maintain the unity of Father and Son and to restrict the subordination of the latter to His being caused by the Father, very much like the relation between Existence, Life, and Intellect in Porphyry's metaphysics.[86]

The opinion that will or intention cannot become a hypostasis on its own had already been put forward by Origen.[87] He had said that will always originates from the intellect without separating itself from its origin. This is clearly the non-hypostatic will which Gregory assumed as the cause of the generation of the Son. The divine will, however, that the human intellect can ascertain in the structure of creation, has been separated from its origin and is identical with the will of God, which is present and open to human perception and understanding in God's orders, promises, and commandments.

The most coherent theory of the divine will was propounded in the Trinitarian doctrine of Marius Victorinus. As was most convincingly shown by P. Hadot,[88] he adapted the ontology of Porphyry to the orthodox view of the Trinity. Porphyry's trinity of Existence/Life/Intellect was still reminiscent of the ancient, semi-Oriental belief that the universe is governed by the trinity Father/Mother/Son, the first representing primarily divine rule, the second the principle of life, the third the order and structure of creation. *Ruaḥ*, the animating breath, is feminine in all Semitic languages, and so was the second hypostasis in some Gnostic systems.[89] The female character of the second item in Porphyry's trinity can still be seen in later texts where his doctrine is reproduced by pagan Platonists.[90]

Marius Victorinus did not hesitate to identify the second person of Porphyry's trinity with the Son: Christ is *voluntas et potentia Dei*.[91] The principle of predominance in Porphyry's metaphysics facilitated this change.[92] Since every mode of being represented the whole of reality and only predominantly one of the three aspects, no complete separation or distinction between them was permissible. This detail became important in the attempts to strengthen the orthodox doctrine of consubstantiality.

Above all, Marius Victorinus' adaptation of Porphyry's metaphysical concept contributed to preserving the idea of the unity of will and intellect in God's nature. This was an old topic which had already been stressed, for instance, by Irenaeus and Origen. Yet in specifically attributing will as the moving and animating power to the second person of a consubstantial triad which altogether belonged to the realm of the intelligible, Victorinus preserved, at the same time, the priority of the intellect. Will, though defined as a metaphysical entity on its own, remained the offspring of intellectual activity. This doctrine was in full agreement with the general tradition of Greek philosophy. The belief in the creating and ruling God of the Old Testament was thus expressed in terms of Platonic ontology, according to which reality could be created and perceived only by intellectual activity. Plotinus' detailed description of how thought and will, energy and substance coincide in the One enabled the Fathers of the fourth century to speak in adequate terms of the will of God.

Victorinus did not develop in his theological writings a comprehensive anthropology and soteriology. His main interest was concentrated upon the Christological debate. But it seems safe to assume that a concept of anthropology and soteriology that corresponded to his Trinitarian doctrine would hardly have needed a human will as a factor, conceived and defined separately from emotion and intellect, which would give the decisive response in man's reaction to God's promise and commandment. Human will and human freedom could still be regarded, in the view of Victorinus, as a function or result of primarily intellectual activity, since he kept his concept of God and reality within the limits of Platonic and Neoplatonic ontology.

Man's voluntary turning towards his creator could be understood, according to this ontology, only as an act of man's spiritual self which connects itself with the structure of reality, consciously and willingly, by means of cognition alone.[93]

We have seen from these examples and episodes that the Christological debate of the fourth century led to a clear-cut notion of the divine will. Christian theological speculation did not come, at the same time, to an equally distinct notion of the will of man. This very condition comes out most clearly in the anthropological doctrine of Gregory of Nyssa, perhaps the most learned and penetrating scholar of the fourth-century Fathers.

Freedom of choice (τὸ αὐτεξούσιον) is the most precious gift of human nature and indeed constitutes the similarity between God and man. It enables man to govern his own life and to shape his moral character, thus becoming "his own father."[94] Yet this freedom, taken separately, is only the faculty to choose and to act arbitrarily.[95] It becomes a will (προαίρεσις), which underlies moral or religious evaluation, in consequence of its being governed by the cognition of good and evil. "Thoughts are the fathers of the will."[96] The choice of the worse results from ignorance, affections, or demons,[97] that is to say exclusively from factors which impede the activity of reason. Accordingly, Gregory interprets the old Jewish doctrine of the two spirits (see above p. 77) in terms of the battle between reason and affection, and Pharaoh had his heart hardened by Yahveh because his intention had already been evil before.[98] The faith of the Christians is perfectly rational:[99] the divine grace primarily operates by strengthening and illuminating the human intellect and repelling the irrational influences from affections and demons, so that the believer is able to make his choice according to knowledge rather than ignorance.[100] Logos, the Good Shepherd, guides his sheep to reasonable intentions.[101]

This is all in full agreement with philosophical, especially Platonic, anthropology. Will as an independent factor in human life as implied in the Biblical tradition does not appear. Gregory does not even use a concept which was first introduced by Tertullian, in order to harmonize the voluntaristic approach of the Bible with the traditional intellectualism of Greek ethical thought. According to Tertullian and others the divinely revealed knowledge, which alone enables man to choose rightly, differs in quality from every other piece of conceivable knowledge. That is why complete ignorance in all other fields may well go with the salutary, divinely revealed knowledge in any individual soul.[102] This doctrine, however, was difficult to reconcile with Gregory's (and others') belief in man's gradual ascension to religious and moral perfection.

There is one point, first identified by Ekkehardt Mühlenberg,[103] where Gregory transcends the traditional intellectualism of Greek ethics. Conforming with Plato and his school Gregory ascribes an innate striving for the cognition of God to human nature. This striving has to be realized, in the course of a man's lifetime, by an uninterrupted chain of intellectual acts. Following the doctrine of the Seventh Letter, the Platonists believed in—some of them even testified to—the possibility that the human mind achieves, through sudden illumination and in some rare cases, the full cognition of and unification with the Supreme Being. This, however, can happen only after one has passed through all grades of scientific, controlled, and communicable speculation. Only the result of the final act of illumination is no longer communicable between two beings endowed with reason, since it implies man's unification with the One which embraces the perceiving and the perceived. In the view of Gregory the ultimate goal of intellectual, moral, and religious progress is simply not attainable. The highest step on the scale to perfection as reached by exemplary saints or prophets like Moses only leads to the full recognition of God's imperceptibility. So even those who have attained perfection according to human standards are bound to continue their search, and even the beatitude of those who have been saved beyond the limits of time and space is but the infinite progress towards the cognition of God.[104]

This seems to be a specific doctrine of Gregory's without a convincing parallel in either Jewish or Christian texts. Some Gnostics were known to have interpreted Matt. 7:7 in a comparable way: the pneumatic man, who has been given the salutary knowledge, has to conduct his life as a permanent search for further cognition.[105] Otherwise he runs the risk of forfeiting his election by falling back into deadly ignorance. This admonition, however, is meant for the time being, while the pneumatic has to preserve his distinctive quality in the present life under the rule of the Archons of the created world of evil. The need for permanent search results not from the imperceptibility of the ultimate goal of cognition but from the elect's being particularly exposed to dangers under the present conditions of the world. His returning into the world of Light implies full cognition of himself as well as of the Source of Being. There is no unbridgeable gap between Creator and creation, which prevents man from attaining the full cognition of God, as is foreseen, entirely conforming with the Biblical view of man, in the doctrine of Gregory.

Gregory's doctrine of moral and religious progress seems to be peculiar in the way it combines intellectualism and voluntarism. Following the lines of the Platonic tradition he defines the goal of progress in terms of an ultimate cognition.[106] This knowledge entails perfection and final happiness, since man's true self is regarded as essentially spiritual and intellectual. Yet, by taking over the Biblical idea that no man or creature is capable of the full cognition of God, Gregory is led to describe the way towards the goal in voluntaristic terms. Man has to fulfil his proper task in religious and moral life by permanent striving in a certain direction rather than by reaching the goal of his activity. The Socratic heritage within Platonic tradition had already opened up the possibility of considering the way towards the goal as more important in moral life than the goal itself. But such a revaluing of the way towards knowledge was motivated by modesty and insight into one's own limitations rather than by the basic belief that the order of nature is, in the last instance, inaccessible to the human mind. On the contrary, the unshaken confidence that the human intellect and the order of being strictly correspond to each other remained the main incentive of philosophical research in general, and ethical theory in particular, throughout the history of Greek philosophy. That is why at least the possibility of perfect cognition was never flatly denied, except by a few sceptics and agnostics. Both the Stoic sage and the Platonic mystic stood for that ultimate possibility and, consequently, for the priority of cognition in relation to any kind of will or intention in the moral life of man.

The element which Gregory of Nyssa introduced, for the first time, into the traditional conception that moral and religious progress was the way to final and perfect cognition, radically changed its content. If man was told to proceed, in the moral and religious conduct of his life, towards the cognition of something which was imperceptible by its very nature, the admonition had to be made explicit with the aid of an anthropological notion of will. The creation of such a notion was overdue by the end of the fourth century.[107]

VI.
St. Augustine and
His Concept of Will

IT IS GENERALLY ACCEPTED in the study of the history
of philosophy that the notion of will, as it is used as a tool of analysis
and description in many philosophical doctrines from the early Scholas-
tics to Schopenhauer and Nietzsche,[1] was invented by St. Augustine.

As was shown in the preceding chapter, Marius Victorinus had already arrived at a clear-cut concept of the divine will in consequence of
his and other orthodox theologians' attempt to make explicit, in terms
of Neoplatonic philosophy, the consubstantiality of the three divine
persons of the Christian creed. He applied, with slight modifications,[2]
Porphyry's interpretation of the Chaldean triad to the Trinity of the
Christians. Christ, the second person, thus became the equivalent
of Life or Will in the process of unfolding reality from the boundless
potential of God to the structured multitude of spiritual beings. For
reality itself could only be immaterial and intelligible in the view of a
fourth-century philosopher or theologian.

Two presuppositions were held in common by Platonism and Christian theology at that time: that reality is immaterial, and that God is
primarily the Supreme Being or Divine Substance (οὐσία), thus being
perceptible or describable, however imperfectly, only in terms of ontology rather than from the experience of divine power. These fundamental assumptions precluded the transference of the notion of will, which
had been invented to attain an adequate description of the unfolding of
reality, from theology and ontology to the field of Biblical anthropology, ethics, and soteriology.

Two arguments were almost irrefutable on such premises. First, in
the predominantly ontological view of both Neoplatonists and Christians, man partakes of divine nature or reality by his intellect alone.[3]
The firm belief in many similarities between God and the human soul[4]
motivated a good deal of psychological investigation throughout the
history of Platonism.[5] But the goal of human life, under this presup-

position, was assimilation to God by intellectual activity. God and man were located at different places in a well-ordered system of being according to that view of reality, and no human will was able to circumvent the need for comprehensive understanding of the whole order and to establish communication with God.

Thus the will of the One or God, as described by Plotinus, Porphyry, Marius Victorinus, and others in ontological terms, could not simply serve as the model or counterpart of the human will. Moreover, the divine will defined ontologically appealed to man's intellectual understanding rather than provoking his spontaneous intention to obey or to disobey, as divine utterances are supposed to do according to Biblical tradition.

Secondly, reality, because it is entirely spiritual, has to be identical with or created by intellectual activity.[6] Intellectual activity, in its turn, is always primarily cognitive, will only being either the mode of its application (ἐμβολή) or the byproduct of cognition. Thus the primacy of thought over will was undisputed also for Marius Victorinus (*in ep. ad Eph.* 1.1).[7] Again, will, as the only factor in human life through which man is able to communicate with God (who is by definition beyond human cognition), cannot be grasped in terms of such an ontology.

St. Augustine was entirely familiar with the philosophical approach of Marius Victorinus and his sources. He knew the Chaldean triad and its Porphyrian interpretation and noticed its inconsistencies with the Christian conception of the divine Trinity.[8] He also knew the difference between Plotinus' and Porphyry's conceptions of how to explain the unfolding of reality,[9] and he agreed with Marius Victorinus in taking the Porphyrian triad *esse/vivere/intellegere* as an adequate model of the order of being.[10] But unlike Marius Victorinus he did not use the Porphyrian triad, however modified, in order to explain the Trinitarian creed of his church,[11] although he did make extended use of many details of Neoplatonic doctrine in other contexts of his theology.

St. Augustine approached the problem of will in various ways, but always on the basis of the Biblical belief that man was created according to the image and likeness of the Creator. That the similarity of God and man could only be ascertained in the human soul was the obvious interpretation of Genesis 1:27 for a Roman or Greek intellectual about A.D. 400. But St. Augustine's attempt to verify the similarity by discovering the points of direct reference on both sides was quite against the philosophical tradition. He attempted to apply what he had perceived by means of introspection and self-analysis to the image of the Trinity. So Trinitarian theology and human psychology became directly related to each other rather than integrated into a comprehensive doctrine of the order of being.

It is not necessary to go into all the details of St. Augustine's Trinitarian doctrine, since the topic has been extensively treated in recent scholarship.[12] It may suffice in this context to illustrate his method and to point out the new part he attributed to the will of both God and man.

In the traditional view of Greek philosophy intention appeared either as the result or byproduct of cognition,[13] as the mode of its application, or as its potential.[14] St. Augustine separated will from both potential and achieved cognition. Arguing strictly psychologically, he explained the act of vision as a result of the following process: the faculty of seeing is joined with the object of visual perception by the will of the perceiving individual.[15] The same relation subsists, according to St. Augustine, in the case of thought, i.e. purely intellectual cognition, with the only difference being that the object of cognition is presented by the perceiver's own memory rather than from the outside world.[16] That is why the triad *memoria, intelligentia, voluntas* accounts for the whole of the human self (*mens*), which is, in the view of St. Augustine, entirely spiritual. The three factors or faculties are inseparably linked and cannot work independently of each other. Intellectual activity would be impossible without the potential of objects of cognition offered by the memory, without the faculty of reasoning, and without the moving force of will. St. Augustine's approach to the problem of intellectual life was completely different from what Stoic and Platonic psychology had worked out in this field. All Greek theories about sense perception and intellectual cognition tried to establish a firm relation between the individual and the order of being as it was supposed to exist, objectively and independently, outside the perceiving subject. St. Augustine's psychology, as set out in *De trinitate*, seems to be self-sustaining, at least with regard to man's intellectual activity. One need not understand any attached or underlying conception of the order of being to appreciate his ideas about the intellectual life of man. Both the raw material of cognition and the drive towards understanding can be found in the soul without an indispensable point of reference in the outside world.[17] It is perhaps not unfair to say that Greek theories of cognition try to explain which part or aspect of reality is being perceived by the human intellect. St. Augustine, on the other hand, concentrated on the problem of what is going on in the human mind during the act of cognition. This particular difference also applies to the role of volition on both sides. In Stoic and Platonic psychology the element of will occurs before and after the very act of intellectual perception: man applies his cognitive power to an object of the outside world (ἐπιβολὴ τῆς διανοίας), before the act of cognition begins, and an impulse towards action, originating either from the intellect or from the non-intellectual potential of soul, may result from the intellectual perception and evaluation of such an object. In the view of St. Augustine, will indeed partakes in the very act of cognition and is by no means restricted to preliminary and subsequent activities.[18]

St. Augustine applied the concept described above to his doctrine on the Trinity. The consubstantiality of the three persons, as required by the orthodox creed of his days, he explained solely by the term *mens* (νοῦς [the mind]): the substance of the Supreme Being is purely spiritual, as is the dominant part of the human soul. This corresponds to the fundamental beliefs of both Pagans and Christians in the fourth or fifth century. The three functions of that spiritual substance, that is to say memory, intellect, will, are individually attributed to Father, Logos, Spirit.[19] Everything which comes into being in the universe, both immaterial and material, owes its origin and preservation to the intellectual activity of God, who has no need, in his threefold existence, of anything outside Himself. Creation and salvation are only the result of His boundless and inexplicable goodness. God's perfect autonomy has its analogy in the self-sufficient activity of the human intellect as described above.

St. Augustine's theory differs considerably from that of Marius Victorinus (see above p. 117f), particularly in one respect: Victorinus explained the generation of the Son in ontological terms. From the boundless potential of Being or pure Existence, as represented by the Father, Life comes to actuality in an act of spontaneous and non-determined motion. The basic concepts of Aristotelian ontology, δύναμις (potentiality) and ἐνέργεια (actuality), can easily be recognized behind this theory. For St. Augustine, generation is but a term for the continuously existing relation between Father and Logos. The latter does not stand, in St. Augustine's theology, for the principle of Life,[20] Motion, or Will, but for the divine creativity—which corresponds to the traditional belief in the Logos as the mediator of the divine creation of the structured universe. Motion or Will that brings about creation is represented by the Spirit. Unlike in Victorinus the triad *esse/vivere/intellegere* has not been aligned with the hypostatic subdivision of the Trinity, since attention is focused on psychological rather than ontological analogies.[21] The principle of predominance, which enabled Victorinus to coordinate the triad *esse/vivere/intellegere* both collectively and individually with the three persons of the Trinity, is absent from St. Augustine's Trinitarian theology: again, the reason for this difference is to be seen in the fact that St. Augustine conceived his theory from the psychological point of view.

The key role attributed to will (*voluntas*)[22] in St. Augustine's corresponding systems of psychology and theology results mainly from self-examination. It is not derived from earlier doctrines in the field of philosophical psychology or anthropology, and seems to mark a turning point in the history of theological reasoning. For the first time, the same notion of will could be applied in both theological and anthropological contexts. This exactly corresponded to the indistinct but persistent voluntarism that permeates the Biblical tradition (see above ch. I). From St. Augustine's reflections emerged the concept of a human will, prior to and independent of the act of intellectual cognition, yet fundamentally different from sensual and irrational emotion, by which man can give his reply to the inexplicable utterances of the divine will.

The *Confessions* abundantly testify to the intensity of St. Augustine's introspection, and many famous passages from this book on will, memory, sense of time, sensuality, cognition, emotions, and other psychological topics have been extensively commented on in modern scholarship.[23] It is mainly through this entirely new concept of his own self that St. Augustine superseded the conceptual system of Greco-Roman culture.[24]

St. Augustine used the new notion of will in various chapters of his teaching. Will became the point of reference in the doctrines of intellect and sensual life, freedom and determination, moral evaluation of purpose and action, and, above all, in that of fall and redemption. We can restrict ourselves to some examples.

Sensuality, in its moral importance, was no longer the only counter-part of the intellect, though St. Augustine shared the dualistic temper of his contemporaries. He advocated an ascetic life in order to attain freedom from the bonds of matter and regarded man's self (*mens*) as spiritual. But the affections to which human nature is exposed because of its share in the material world were no longer regarded as an evil in themselves. It is the will of man, which yields to the sensual affections instead of turning to the higher level of reality, which alone is the cause of sin or moral evil.[25] This can be seen in the case of sexuality: in the primordial state of man, sexual desire was controlled by the will, very much like the movements of hands and feet.[26] It is only due to the fall of Adam and to the ensuing perversion of the human will,[27] that man in his present condition is exposed to sexual affections: they are volun-tary because of the assent of the will and, consequently, sinful, but he cannot avoid them because of his perverted will. Sensuality itself is by no means the cause of evil,[28] as the Manicheans believed. It was present already in the original, undistorted condition of man, but firmly con-trolled by his undistorted will. Everything depends on whether the will of man is directed to spirit (*spiritus*) or flesh (*caro*), i.e. to the more or less valuable.[29]

The same applies to the doctrine of *cupiditas triplex*[30] which St. Au-gustine conceived according to Plato's tripartition of the soul after the model of Neoplatonic ethical theory. *Cupiditas* or *libido* (ἐπιθυμία), *am-bitio* or *superbia* (φιλαρχία, φιλοτιμία), and *curiositas* (φαντασία) do not result, as the Neoplatonists believed,[31] from a misconception of reality but from the perverted will (*mala voluntas*). The Neoplatonic idea of the separation of an individual being from the order of being (ἰδίωσις)[32] was explained in terms of will.[33] Evil as the mere *privatio boni*, the absence of good,—a concept of the Platonic tradition which had been largely accepted in Christian theology[34]—was replaced by ill will[35] without, however, attributing substance to evil, as the Manicheans did.

Even in intellectual life, every moral or religious evaluation of human activity refers to the will.[36]

St. Augustine interpreted freedom of choice, traditionally attributed to all rational beings, as the freedom of will. This can be seen from his doctrine of angels and demons.[37] The will of the fallen angels has been perverted by their attempt to be and to act independently of their Crea-tor, whereas the good angels never changed the direction of their will.[38]

The direction of the will, however, is thought and spoken of as being independent of the cognition of the better and the worse. This indeed supersedes the famous Socratic problem of οὐδεὶς ἑκὼν ἁμαρτάνει, no one does wrong on purpose.[39]

It is not surprising that everything, in the view of St. Augustine, depends on *voluntas* in religious and moral life.[40] Faith (*fides*), for instance, is closely attached to will. The reply to the call of God precedes, as a decision of will,[41] all kinds of reasoning and indeed leads to intellectual cognition,[42] since it is a performance of rational beings.[43] St. Augustine also describes the life of the faithful as a condition of will. Whereas man in his natural condition can direct his will (*attentio*) to either the future or the past by means of *exspectatio* and *memoria*, the faithful exist only with regard to the future (*intentio*).[44]

St. Augustine even speaks of the collective will of a social group, very much as Rousseau does of *volonté générale*.[45] But he did not integrate his concept of conscience into the theory of will. Instead he explained conscience as the innate knowledge of good and evil which every human being possesses. It precedes, therefore, any cognition resulting from the intentional activity of the intellect and cannot be refuted by rational arguments.[46]

Yet the most important topic of St. Augustine's theology in which the new concept of will became prominent was his doctrine of freedom, grace, and salvation. There had been no comprehensive and coherent theory of the grace of God in Christian theology before St. Augustine, as has recently been shown by Alfred Schindler.[47] Words like χάρις and *gratia* were used to express the fact that God had not only given the Law to save his people, but also gifts like baptism or individual conversion and renewal. Χάρις can designate God's forgiveness of the sinner as well as the special gifts of prophets, bishops, or teachers.[48] The word can denote the rebirth of the saved resulting from the divine πνεῦμα which enters the human soul,[49] but it can equally well refer to the widening of man's intellectual capacity because of divine revelation.[50]

The fundamental belief behind these varying statements about God's grace can be described as unreflected synergism. In the practical life of Christian congregations before Constantine, that is to say in an alien or even hostile environment, both the consciousness of being elected, guided, and saved solely by the inexplicable grace of God, and that of being responsible for an appropriate Christian conduct of life must have been present without much awareness of the theoretical contradiction implied.[51] The synergistic attitude was strengthened in Christian theology, which made extended use of the ontological and anthropological concepts of Greek philosophy: man's individual salvation could be set in relation to God's objectively existing plan of creation and salvation of the world and also to the freedom and responsibility of man as a being endowed with reason. Both factors seemed to be indispensable in the process of salvation.[52] The concept of will, however, was not necessary in such a synergistic context, since good and evil in human life could be ascertained by the revealed plan of divine government and by the rational rules for moral action.

Things changed radically when Christian religion was officially recognized and soon became the dominant factor in public life. Conduct according to Christian norms ceased to be a distinctive feature in the changed social environment. Such a distinction was restricted to the monastic communities which rapidly grew in the fourth century for this very reason. The Pelagian controversy resulted from this situation. For parenetic reasons, Pelagius understandably exaggerated the importance of man's own efforts and, in the course of his struggle with St. Augustine, he came to attribute to the grace of God only the gifts of reason and free choice. Being endowed in such a way, man is fully able to understand God's message, to obey His commandments and, eventually, to be saved. It all depends on his own efforts. Divine grace, insofar as it precedes human activity, only provides the natural faculty of free choice in every situation of life.[53]

St. Augustine radically opposed Pelagius' doctrine: man has indeed been created with the ability to distinguish between good and evil and to decide for the better. Yet the fall of Adam, resulting from his disobedience to God's commandment and from his attempt to be independent of his Creator, has perverted the will, the most important factor of human nature.[54] In its present condition, the will of man is bound to choose the worse, regardless of whether or not its owner knows the better. Even man's virtuous deeds are worthless, since they only contribute to his becoming virtuous without regard to the needs of his neighbor. They are a means to acquire status and reputation, they support man's continuous attempts to forget that he is entirely dependent on the mercy of God, and they are not performed for the sake of someone else, either God or the neighbor who represents God in moral life.[55] The will of man has been transformed, in consequence of the fall of Adam, from love into concupiscence, i.e. self-centeredness, from *humilitas* into *superbia*. Cognition, knowledge, exercise, or any other kind of human activity is of no use, since every effort is necessarily directed towards evil because of the perverted will. This belief is the background of St. Augustine's famous paradox that sin or vice combined with humility are far better than virtue together with pride. Accordingly, humility is the root of all virtues, as is pride of all vices.[56]

Only the grace of God can renew the human will and restore its original freedom of choice. But the intervention of divine grace has to precede all intellectual, moral, or practical efforts of man. For the will has to be healed, and God has to change the present nature of man, before he can even want to act according to virtue and God's commandment,[57] as he knows he is supposed to do,[58] and, eventually, to pass the final judgement and be saved.

The intervention of the divine grace which virtuous life and salvation presuppose is, however, unpredictable, inexplicable, and not to be provoked or influenced by human activity. It is merely due to God's sheer love, out of which he has elected a number of human beings to be saved. (In that context St. Augustine rediscovered St. Paul's doctrine of predestination as set out in Rom. 9–11.) God's love has been revealed in the life and death of Christ, which becomes the model[59] of the renewed will of the elect. St. Augustine's famous precept for the Christian conduct of life becomes clear from this doctrine: *Dilige et quid vis fac*! "Love, and do what you will."[60] An action which is exclusively motivated by love for God or one's neighbor can only be virtuous and in accordance with God's commandment.

The will of man after the final restoration of human nature, which will be brought about on doomsday, is expected to become superior to the will of primeval man: Adam was able to choose between good and evil, whereas his restored freedom will lead his intention exclusively towards the better.[61]

We need not go into further details of St. Augustine's doctrine of freedom and grace;[62] this would be outside our scope and competence. Nor shall we discuss the reasons for which Christian orthodoxy soon discarded the more radical opinions of both Pelagius and St. Augustine. The official doctrine of the Church returned to the synergistic position of the previous period, which turned out to be well-suited for the purposes of religious practice, regardless of its inconsistency from the point of view of pure theory.

Another point in the story, however, is important in our context. Both Pelagius and St. Augustine extensively used the term will, *voluntas*. But it seems to be clear without further explanation that a notion of will, as distinct from both irrational impulse or decision on the basis of knowledge, was indispensable in the theory of St. Augustine, but hardly in that of Pelagius. Pelagius' position can be understood and evaluated without the notion of will and within the limits of the traditional intellectualism of Greek and early Patristic philosophy. On the other hand, St. Augustine would have been led in his doctrine of grace and election to the Gnostic concept of φύσει σῴζεσθαι, salvation because of privileged nature (see below appendix II),[63] if he had not found a new point of reference in the notion of will. The traditional concept of human intention as a byproduct of cognition could only have led him to an ontological assessment of divine predestination, for cognition always refers to what exists objectively and independently of the perceiving subject. Pelagius' doctrine of free choice can be understood, as can Victorinus' doctrine of the Trinity, from the point of view of Greek ontology. St. Augustine's doctrine of grace, very much like his Trinitarian theology, can only be properly understood on the basis of the fundamental belief that the direct relation between God and the human soul is prior to and independent of any objectively existing order of being and can be ascertained in the will of both.

So St. Augustine's essential contribution to the development of the medieval and modern notion of will has to be seen in the wider context of the change from the ontological to a psychological approach to religion and ethics which he initiated.

Yet the question remains whether one can adequately understand the rise of the notion of will only in terms of the history of ideas, or whether St. Augustine as a Western theologian was additionally conditioned by Latin, his native language, to develop such a tool of theological and anthropological analysis.

❖

In a letter to his friend Atticus, written[64] a short time after the assassination of Caesar, Cicero reports a saying of the victim about the murderer: *non magni refert ille quid velit, sed quidquid volet valde volet* "what he wants is no great matter, but what he wants, he wants with a will." The statement clearly refers to Brutus' energy and firmness, regardless of whether this results from the conclusiveness of his rational planning or whether such stubbornness belongs to the irrational part of his personality. Plutarch gives the Greek version of the saying: πᾶν δ' ὃ βούλεται σφόδρα βούλεται. This is not idiomatic Greek. Βούλομαι always has—at least in classical and classicistic Greek—the connotation of planning which precedes the decision to act. It often goes with an adverbial expression of preference (μᾶλλον, ἤ, etc.), but hardly with an adverb denoting intensity alone (μάλα, σφόδρα), as is common with those verbs which point to irrational impulses (ἐπιθυμῶ, ὀρέγομαι, etc.). Plutarch explicitly says that Brutus had a mature personality at a very early age. So he had to attach his firmness to βούλησις (plan) rather than mere ὄρεξις (desire).

Unlike classical and post-classical Greek, the Latin language had a group of words to denote impulse or intention to act regardless of whether they originated from rational or from irrational factors in the human soul. This can be seen from many passages in Latin literature, dating from different periods. Perhaps it is due to a lack of psychological refinement in the Latin vocabulary rather than to what has been called "römische Willenshaltung" in previous scholarship.[65] But the indiscriminate use of *velle* and *voluntas* for various kinds of impulse and intention undeniably contributed to the voluntaristic potential in Roman thought.[66]

When Cicero translated the ethical and psychological terminology of Greek philosophy, he mostly used *velle* and *voluntas* to express conscious, deliberate intention in contrast to irrational impulse, instinctive drive, or compulsion from outside. *Voluntas*—defined as *quae quis cum ratione desiderat* (one's faculty, or exercise, of rationally-determined desire)[67] is the correct translation of the Middle Platonic definition of βούλησις (purpose) as εὔλογος ὄρεξις (well-reasoned desire). Cicero renders the Peripatetic theory of causation by the statement that everything is set in motion *aut natura aut vi aut voluntate* (either by nature, or by compulsion, or by intention),[68] and in his doctrine of fate he contrasts *fatum* (εἱμαρμένη) and *voluntas* (προαίρεσις).[69] There is no indication whatsoever that Cicero came to reflect on the "voluntaristic" connotation by which *voluntas* in general Latin usage differed from Greek words like προαίρεσις, διάνοια, βούλησις, γνώμη. So it is useless to speculate whether Greek theories of human action sounded more "voluntaristic" to Cicero's contemporaries in Latin translation than in their original language.[70]

Cicero, however, used the word *voluntas* not only to denote what was called προαίρεσις or βούλησις in Greek. Sometimes, even in philosophical texts, *voluntas* means desire or spontaneous wish rather than deliberate intention,[71] and in other passages the impulse itself (ὁρμή), which comes from deliberation or from conscious moral attitude, is called *voluntas*.[72] The large semantic area which is apparently attached to the word in Cicero's philosophical vocabulary corresponds to the general usage of his time. So he does not seem to have seen any difficulty in the identification of "intellectualistic" βούλησις and "voluntaristic" *voluntas*, since he presupposed their identity even outside philosophical discussions.[73] The fact that προαίρεσις had already become the term to denote the general moral attitude of an individual[74] apparently facilitated its being rendered by *voluntas*, especially where moral practice and its foundation were set in contrast with erudition in moral theory.[75]

The picture looks somewhat different in the late writings of Seneca, who apparently became aware of the voluntaristic implications of the meaning of *voluntas*. Some peculiarities in Seneca's usage of *velle/voluntas* were first noted and explained by Max Pohlenz.[76] Seneca's description of *sapientia* as the continuity of will rather than knowledge,[77] the identification of virtue and *bona voluntas*,[78] and the moral preference given to *voluntas* instead of to action[79] can be understood in terms of traditional Greek philosophy, if one is prepared to take *voluntas* as the simple equivalent of προαίρεσις. But precisely this was not Seneca's opinion, for he says: *velle non discitur*,[80] i.e., *voluntas* is not an instructed, or disciplined, faculty. Προαίρεσις, however, comes into being through both instruction and exercise according to traditional Stoic doctrine.[81] On the other hand, Seneca is far from attributing virtuous action to spontaneous, irrational impulses. This can be seen from a passage[82] where he starts from traditional Stoic intellectualism: he who is guided by reason is also able to act freely and correctly, because he is not pushed or pulled by the objects of the outside world. But in the following sentence, Seneca attributes the impulse towards action to an independent act of will rather than to reason itself, and he explicitly refuses an explanation of this phenomenon. Seneca did realize that will should be grasped independently of both cognition and irrational impulse. But he did not proceed to a clear notion of will. So he treated the topic of progress in philosophy or in life[83] along the traditional lines of Stoic philosophy and without the aid of a notion of will:[84] Man is supposed to acquire and to internalize the teaching of philosophy, which provides an answer to every question in practical life (*ep.* 16.5f). The impulse toward action automatically results from this knowledge (16.6), but one has to protect the impulses from becoming weak by learning and training throughout life. The tendency to act virtuously has to become a lasting attitude.[85]

Seneca's vague voluntarism[86] was never systematized into a clear concept of will, either by himself or by later Roman authors. Roman philosophy, mainly because it depended entirely on the Greek tradition, did not develop the distinct notion of will before St. Augustine. So the impact which philosophy made on the Latin language throughout the imperial period could only weaken rather than reinforce voluntaristic elements in Roman thought. On the other hand, the use of the words *velle/voluntas* in both philosophical and non-philosophical texts seems to indicate that the idea of pure volition as separate from both cognition and emotion was inherent, however indistinctly, in the Roman vocabulary. So one comes to ask whether this phenomenon is to be explained in the context of the many archaic features of Latin, or whether a notion of will which could influence the general usage was perhaps developed apart from the philosophical tradition in the Latin-speaking world.

Voluntas in a strictly terminological sense was undoubtedly used for many centuries in the language of Roman law. A theory of will became increasingly important in the interpretation of civil law from the second or first century B.C. onwards. This led to a notion of will which characteristically differed from the concept of intentionality (ἑκούσιον, πρόνοια) in Greek law.[87]

In 93 B.C. the distinguished orator L. Licinius Crassus defeated the equally distinguished lawyer Q. Mucius Scaevola in a famous case, the *causa Curiana*.[88] A testament could not be executed according to its text, because the foreseen first heir had died before the testator. The written law prescribed for such a case that the testament be disregarded and the legal hereditary succession followed instead—which was also the opinion of Scaevola. Formulas and ritualized actions were the decisive constituents of any legal procedure according to the tradition of

Roman civil law. His opponent argued that the chosen after-heir should get the inheritance according to the intention of the testator, even against the wording of the law in question. The will (*voluntas*) which could be ascertained in a written text should be valued higher, in its legal relevance, than the text itself (*verba*).

The first speech of the Athenian orator Isaeus offers an interesting counterpart to the above case, the *causa Curiana*. A certain Cleonymus had willed in his testament his two nephews to become his only heirs. Later on, he disinherited them, not because he had anything against them, but because of a quarrel which he had with their guardian. He did not want this man to dispose of the property. So he replaced his nephews by three distant relatives. Shortly after this had happened, the guardian died, and Cleonymus took his nephews into his house to educate them. But he forgot to adapt the testament to the altered situation. Only on his deathbed did he send for an official in order to change the text, but the man was turned away at the door by one of the distant relatives. Now a lawsuit began between these and one of the nephews, for whom Isaeus wrote the extant speech. It contains two main arguments:[89] either the deceased called for the official in order to change the text of the testament, or he was insane in unjustly and immorally disinheriting his closest relatives, whom he did not dislike. In both cases the testament as presented by the opponents has to be cancelled by the court. Isaeus did not simply contrast *verba* and *voluntas*, as a Roman advocate would have done; he looked rather for objective reasons to have the testament annulled by the judges. The subjective intention of the testator is frequently spoken of.[90] Yet it is morally assessed to obtain objective reasons for invalidating the testament. Furthermore, this intention is not assessed separately, but is taken into consideration only together with the alleged insanity. There is no definite concept of will behind the argument.

Crassus took his argument in the *causa Curiana* from Greek ideas of equity, fairness, benevolence (ἐπιείκεια). The strict application of the written law to individual cases in human life may lead to utter injustice. The ἀκριβοδίκαιον (strict construction of the law), in the words of Aristotle, has to be permanently corrected by the ἐπιεικές (equity);[91] justice according to the law (νομικὸν δίκαιον) never is identical, once and for all, with justice itself. These ideas were incorporated into the doctrines of justice in all philosophical schools,[92] but they had been at work long before, when, above all in criminal law, intention was taken into account in the administration of justice, e.g. in distinguishing between murder and non-intentional killing.[93] Both kinds were usually conflated in those archaic codifications which tried to provide rules for handling the fact alone. The connection between the rules of criminal law and the accepted standards of moral life in general has always been particularly close, for obvious reasons, as a criminal case usually interferes very deeply with the life of the persons involved. So we may infer from conditions in criminal law to prevailing ideas in moral thought far more easily than from those in civil law, as can be seen, for instance, from Aristotle's discussion of ethical problems.[94]

In Hellenistic times, however, the ideas of fairness or equity as distinct from strict justice were current above all in the rhetorical tradition. There were no professional lawyers in the Greek world: the Greeks always had an astonishing and somewhat naive confidence in the social efficiency of legislation, which is, after all, a predominantly political or, at best, philosophical task. Lawgivers were considered the outstanding experts in the field of social and human activity. The actual administration of justice, on the other hand, was done exclusively through lawcourts composed of laymen. These had to be influenced by advocates or conflicting parties through moral rather than legal argumentation. The future advocate had to learn in his rhetorical training how to appeal to the moral standards of a jury in favor of his client. The methods of interpretation which developed under these conditions were all designed to find in the wording of the written law or legal document (ῥητόν) a meaning (διάνοια) which was at the same time favorable for one party *and* persuasive, because of its general equity, to the judges.

A speech of Hyperides offers a good example of this task. The increasing use of written documents in commercial life had caused much trouble to the Athenian lawcourts because of their total lack of expertise or professional training. So a law was passed whereby no written contract whatsoever should be open to contestation in a lawsuit, regardless of its content. Hyperides' client wanted to break a written contract. So he made him argue that such a law could not conceivably apply only to contracts of which the content was illegal or immoral![95]

The need for moral argumentation in the attempt to establish the intention or will of the author behind a written text of legal importance did not lead to a distinct concept of will in either criminal or civil law.

Will or intention, as shown above, was a predominantly intellectualistic concept of Greek ethical thought. Thus any moral evaluation of will
with special regard to its juridical relevance inevitably referred to the
knowledge or cognition from which it originated.[96] That is why in
Greek legal theory will itself never became a possible object of interpretation.[97] Inquiring into the will of a person only meant raising the
question of whether somebody had acted or formulated knowingly.[98]
Consequently, if one had to find—with regard to a given case and by
means of moral argumentation—an intention different from what was
plainly said in a written text or official statement, the problem could be
solved only in terms of rule and exception. Applying moral standards
to the case in question led the way to the true and justifiable intention
which only seemed to contradict the wording under consideration, but
in fact corresponded to it in the special situation. This method is well
attested in the fragments of Hermagoras of Temnos, who was the most
distinguished teacher of the theory of juridical oratory among the rhe-
toricians of the Hellenistic period.[99]

The idea of equity or fairness modifying the strict application of the
law was imported to Rome together with rhetorical theory in general,
and was soon applied to legal practice. The famous *causa Curiana* offers an early example of this process, and it is no mere chance that the
orator Crassus upheld the standards of equity against the lawyer Scaevola. Yet Roman jurisprudence was increasingly influenced by the ideas
of Greek popular ethics as formulated and transmitted in the rhetorical
tradition. The opinion that the whole administration of justice, especially the interpretation of the written law and the choice between
several solutions offered by its text, should always be guided by equity
(*aequitas*) and benevolence (*benignitas*)[100] became firmly rooted in Roman jurisprudence.

Conditions of Roman criminal law were comparable to those in the
Greek world during the Hellenistic period. Roman civil law, however,
totally differed from its Eastern counterpart. Thus the application of
Greek ideas about equity, as exemplified by the *causa Curiana* in 93
B.C., led to new and characteristic concepts in Roman civil law.[101]

Civil law was codified for the first time—under Greek influence, by
the way[102]—in the early days of the Roman republic, that is to say under fairly primitive conditions in economic and political life. The law
code of the XII Tables was never altered or replaced between the fifth

and first centuries B.C., and was supplemented only by some minor acts of public legislation, regardless of the immense changes in Roman society and economy during that period. Unlike the Greeks, the Romans had no great confidence in legislation. They preferred to rely on interpretation and reinterpretation of a few laws and legal formulas or fixed procedures, and they entrusted this permanent task to persons backed by a distinguished social group and the authority of a state office. The permanent adaptation of unchanged laws to the quickly changing conditions of social and economic life by means of authoritative interpretation on the basis of experience rather than of theoretical reasoning had been practiced long before Greek philosophy and rhetoric were introduced to Rome. The authority needed for such a use of existing laws was provided by the unrestricted legal power (*imperium*) of the praetor. During his year in office he was entitled to make use of nearly every application, interpretation, or suspension of existing legal prescripts, and his decisions were likely to be adopted by his successor, if they had turned out to be useful and practicable. The *ius honorarium*, which thus developed beside the *ius civile*, and the complicated and permanently changing interrelation between these, became the special province of a lawyer or expert in law (*iuris consultus*).[103]

One example may suffice to illustrate the consequences which such an administration of justice could have in public opinion and consciousness.

A significant feature of traditional Roman law is the *patria potestas*, the unlimited power of the head of a family, which even extended to adult and married sons. As late as in the age of Cicero, a father was legally entitled to inflict capital punishment upon his disobedient son —but this hardly ever happened at that time, because the generally accepted moral standards would have been deeply offended by such an act. A father could also sell his son as a slave. Freed by his purchaser, the son automatically fell back into full dependence (*manus*) upon his father. His manumission became effective only if he had been sold for the third time (*Leg. XII* tab. 5.2). These legal prescripts were invented and formulated under archaic conditions of social life. They presupposed the predominance of large, self-sustaining families in an entirely agrarian society without much commercial intercourse. The economic, social, and moral claims of the family were regarded as superior to those of both the individual and the political community. Yet the *patria potestas* as defined in the prescripts mentioned above became an obstacle rather than a useful social institution in the highly developed economy of the second or first century B.C. When rationalized and large-scale production in both agriculture and industry, far-reaching trade around the Mediterranean, credit and banking, and land ownership in distant regions had become significant patterns in economic life, it could hardly contribute to the prosperity of a family if a forty-year-old son was legally prevented from acting in his own right, only because his father was still alive. The Roman banker whose agencies were located in Alexandria or Delos had to emancipate his adult son in order to keep his business running, as did the land owner because of his plantations in Sicily or Spain. It became customary, therefore, as an officially recognized legal procedure to sell one's son three times to a friend in the presence of the praetor for a nominal price but by means of the archaic legal formula. The friend was supposed to free his slave immediately after each purchase, also with the solemn words, and when the legal act had been repeated three times in one session, the intended emancipation became effective at no cost whatsoever. Thus archaic legal prescripts for the purchase and manumission of a slave and for the maintenance of *patria potestas* were used to emancipate an adult son in accordance with the economic needs and the moral standards of the given society.

This is, as has been said before, just one among innumerable examples of how the Romans managed to retain their completely atavistic set of codified laws in drastically changed and further changing social conditions. It also illustrates the fact that the Romans became accustomed to the idea that laws, actions, formulas, and statements as a means of legal intercourse always need interpretation in order to clarify the intentions of the persons involved—the lawgiver included—and to solve the given problem in accordance with their needs and purposes. Finally, this example helps us understand the task of the expert in civil law who was asked for advice by a client or even by the praetor himself: he had to have comprehensive knowledge of all the prescripts, formulas, and procedures of the existing law (*verba*); he had to know what was just and equitable according to the accepted moral standards (*iustum et aequum*); and he had to attain a precise conception and evaluation of what the persons involved really wished or intended (*voluntas*).

This catalogue was formulated by Quintilian late in the first century

A.D.[104] At that time, the mere expertise of the *iuris consultus* had already long been transformed into jurisprudence as a discipline in its own right. In the field of civil law the introduction of Greek rhetoric and philosophy created awareness of the need for theoretical concepts. What had been the empirical technique of application and interpretation thus became a legal theory with distinct notions and a corresponding terminology. It is in this historical context that one has to understand the origin of the juristic notion of will.

When Crassus insisted, for reasons of fairness and equity, on the will of the testator in contrast to the unequivocal precept of the written law, he perhaps did so in the tradition of Greek popular ethics, according to which τὸ ἐπιεικές was valued higher than τὸ ἀκριβοδίκαιον. But once such an argument was incorporated into the existing method of pleading and jurisdiction in Roman civil law, will or intention rather than facts or statements became the point of reference to which the letter of the law had to be applied in any individual case. Likewise, the standards of a given law rather than its formulations, that is to say the will of the lawgiver, had to be taken into account by the judge or advocate.[105] There are many passages in juristic literature where preference is given to *voluntas* instead of *verba*,[106] and only words under consideration which are absolutely unmistakable in their meaning and intention supersede the search for and evaluation of the *voluntas*.[107]

Quintilian's statement on *voluntas* as one of the primary topics of legal science is easy to understand on this basis. The lawyer or judge has to ascertain the will of the persons involved in the case, including that of the lawgiver, before he can apply the written law and its formulations to words, facts, or claims. This concept of will was indeed unknown to Greek legal theory, which never became independent of the doctrines of ethics and politics. It belonged to Roman jurisprudence as a discipline in its own right.

Will as a term of jurisprudence had no ethical or psychological connotations: the underlying notion was only a tool of juristic analysis. Only where the concept of will had to be defined rather than applied was the psychological factor duly taken into account. Children and idiots have no will in the legal sense of the word because of their deficient rational capacity.[108] But apart from such definitions no juristic text speculates on the problem of whether will originates from reason or from emotion. The abstraction which led to the juristic concept of will effectively discarded such implications. They would have been useless in the practice of legal argumentation, once the concept had become a recognized tool of the business.

Roman thought of all periods was very much preoccupied with legal practice and theory, jurisprudence being the only science which the Romans developed almost independently of Greek models. The fact that the Latin language of all periods and layers is dyed with juristic terminology is the result of this strong preoccupation. This also applies, of course, to the language of the early Christians.[109] So *voluntas* must have had some terminological value, even outside legal usage proper.[110] Yet in this particular meaning *voluntas* signified mere volition, regardless of its originating from either cognition or emotion. Individuals who spoke Latin had, in fact, a means to render a voluntaristic concept, although Greek intellectualism dominated for many centuries in the field of psychological and ethical speculation among the Romans too. This can be ascertained in the case of Seneca, as pointed out above.

In the fourth century, Christian theology felt with increasing urgency the need to render explicit the voluntaristic ideas inherent in the Biblical tradition. The task was fulfilled, fairly successfully, in the course of the Arian controversy, but only with regard to the will of God. Neoplatonic ontology provided the notions and terms, since the difference between volition and intellectual cognition could be disregarded altogether in the case of the Supreme Being, according to the ideas of both Neoplatonists and Christians. In their view, the activity and, above all, the creativity of God were purely intellectual with no intention that could be separated from cognition. Yet this particular difference was essential in any Christian doctrine of ethics and soteriology. According to Biblical belief, man was not only conditioned by his sensuality, which Greek philosophy regarded as the cause of error, blindness, or emotional impulses. He was additionally separated from his Creator by the unbridgeable gap of sin which made all his intentions contravene the divine commandments, regardless of whether they resulted from cognition or from emotion. Thus the term denoting the rational and salutary intention of God could not apply without considerable qualifications being added, to the human will. The difference between both kinds of intention could not simply be pointed out, according to the philosophical tradition, in terms of greater and smaller shares in reality or intellect and sensuality.

The Greeks had no word which could become the philosophical term for the notion of pure will, since words like βούλησις or προαίρεσις had important intellectualistic connotations, especially in philosophical or scientific terminology. Roman jurisprudence, on the other hand, could offer an unmistakable term to denote the idea of pure volition with special regard to man. Moreover the word *voluntas* was likely to have some terminological value even in the general usage of Latin as pointed out above. This again could lead to its terminological use in other fields of speculation without its being deliberately fixed as a new technical term. *Voluntas* had already been used to render the Greek words which denote the will of God in Greek theology of the third and fourth centuries. St. Augustine adopted it as an unmistakable term for a new notion in the field of anthropology, ethics, and soteriology, where it was to play an important part for many centuries of medieval and post-medieval philosophy.

There is no doubt about the fact that *voluntas* denotes an anthropological concept in St. Augustine's theology and philosophy. The idea of sheer volition had to be expressed in his specific doctrine about man's life, thought, and salvation. Yet the juristic term *voluntas* designated a hermeneutic rather than an anthropological concept. It was invented to grasp the intention which underlies words or formalized actions, but it was far from giving the psychological explanation or moral evaluation of human action. For this very reason, *voluntas* in legal usage did not explicitly refer to the origin of will in either cognition or emotion or in both. The legal relevance of human *voluntas* in a given case could always be ascertained objectively, but only on the basis of the judge's or advocate's interpretation of the words or deeds in question, in which alone that *voluntas* was present. The absence of any psychological implication from this concept of will turned out to be particularly useful for its application to Christian doctrines of ethics and soteriology.

Thus the new notion of the pure will of man which St. Augustine invented and introduced into the theological discussion of ethical and soteriological problems seems to have resulted not entirely from its inventor's introspection and self-analysis, nor did it simply derive from Neoplatonic ontology. The word *voluntas* designated a hermeneutical rather than an anthropological concept in Roman jurisprudence and, we may suspect, sometimes also in general Latin usage. St. Augustine transferred this concept to the field of psychology,[111] thus creating a tool for interpreting and classifying psychological observations independently of the traditional patterns of philosophical psychology. He was able to attach his own psychological insights to the word *voluntas*, since the psychological connotations had been absent from its previous terminological usage. Together with its new psychological connotations the word for the new concept could easily be applied to soteriology, ethics, and gnoseology in order to describe precisely the voluntarism which underlies the Biblical tradition.

St. Augustine was, in fact, the inventor of our modern notion of will, which he conceived for the needs and purposes of his specific theology and in continuation of the attempts of Greek theologians, who developed their doctrine of the Trinity in terms of Neoplatonic ontology. He took the decisive step towards the concept of human will by reinterpreting a hermeneutical term as an anthropological one.[112] This eventually led him to an adequate philosophical description of what the Biblical tradition taught about man's fall, salvation, and moral conduct. But in doing so, he was greatly helped and tacitly guided by the Latin vocabulary[113] of his time.

Appendix I

ALBERT WIFSTRAND showed as early as 1942 (*Eranos* 40.16–26) that (ἐ)θέλω and βούλομαι—which had been characteristically different from each other both semantically and idiomatically in Archaic and Classical Greek (e.g. Plat. *Rep.* 437B or *FGH* 140 F8)— became synonymous in the course of the Hellenistic and Roman period. Βούλομαι was used, because of its predominance in late classical Attic, in literary texts, θέλω in those which were nearer to the spoken language. Thus Βούλομαι occurs more frequently—occasionally many times more often than θέλω—in Polybius and Aristeas, Philo of Alexandria and Plutarch, Dio Chrysostom and Lucian, whereas θέλω dominates in Epictetus and Marcus. Some authors, though, prefer θέλω, either because of affected simplicity in their narrative (e.g. Charito, Longus), or in imitation of early Attic and Ionic (Arrian) where (ἐ)θέλω had covered a much larger semantic area. In grammatical texts both verbs are used indiscriminately, when their specific use is not the point under discussion (e.g. Schol. Dion. Thr. p. 400.5 Uhlig). The expanding use of θέλω in the spoken language is well attested in non-literary papyri.

Fifty-nine private letters dating from the last three centuries B.C. which Witkowski selected for his edition offer θέλω 10 times and βούλομαι 11 times. There is no indication in these texts that the two words were regarded as being different in meaning. Sixty-four private letters of the first to fifth centuries A.D. which have been edited by Hunt and Edgar as no. 105–169 of their collection of non-literary papyri represent, with regard to differences in style and erudition, a comparable set of texts. They offer 24 instances of θέλω and 9 of βούλομαι. The latter only occurs in a few pieces of the third and fourth centuries which attest comparatively high standards of language and avoid θέλω altogether. There is hardly any indication that a semantic difference between βούλομαι and θέλω was felt on this level. The applicant of Pap. Colon. 52.6 (third century A.D.) uses the formula βούλομαι ἑκουσίως to denote his willingness to take over a job. Βούλομαι, according to the strict use of the word in the philosophical language, always implies that a decision comes from deliberation and is, therefore, voluntary. The writer of Pap. Colon. 52 apparently has no such feelings about βού-λομαι. It seemed to him simply more apt than θέλω, and he adds a special expression of his willingness. The archive of Petaus (ed. Youtie-Hagedorn, Köln 1972), which includes 127 official documents dating from a few years of the late second century A.D., has only 4 instances of θέλω against 22 of βούλομαι. In the public documents published as in-scriptions from Hellenistic and Roman times that are assembled in Dit-tenberger's collections the average proportion of θέλω and βούλομαι is 1:3.5, with no considerable variation either in meaning or date of the documents. Βούλομαι was preferred, for stylistic reasons, both in litera-ture and in public use throughout the Hellenistic and Roman periods. The technical term to denote the last will was βούλημα, never θέλημα. Θελημάτιον, in the same meaning as βουλημάτιον (will, testament), does not appear in the Greek papyri until the sixth century A.D.

Many passages in literary texts, too, particularly from the Roman period, testify to the fact that the two verbs are largely identical in meaning and are chosen for stylistic reasons only (Cass. Dio 43.15; Herodian *hist.* 3.14.2; Clem. *protr.* 4.4=*GCS* 1.48.18; Numen. fr. 24.15 Des Places; Sext. Emp. *hyp.* 2.167; Origen *in Matt. comm.* 14.3=*GCS* 10.278 and 18–21; Athan. *c. Ar.* 35.15=*PG* 25.308; Greg. Naz. *or. theol.* 3.6=*PG* 36.80–82).

This can be seen from a detail. Throughout the post-classical period, and sometimes even before, we occasionally find βούλομαι denoting ar-bitrary rather than deliberate choice. The anonymous sophist whose treatise has been preserved in a fourth-century B.C. speech, falsely at-tributed to Demosthenes (*or.* 25.26), contrasts legal order (νόμος) and individual arbitrariness (βούλησις). In the lengthy discussion about whether words (and their inflections) originate from coining at random and the hazards of social convention or according to the rational order of nature (W. Spoerri, *Spälhellenistische Berichte über Welt, Kultur und Götter* [Basel 1959] 134ff) words like βούλομαι, θέλω, *voluntas* appear in a well-established terminology which describes the process of arbi-trary giving of names (Ammon. *in Aristot. de interpret.* p. 35.15 Busse; Varro, *ling. Lat.* 8.21). According to the account of Agatharchides, the tribe of Fish-eaters on the east coast of Africa ate οὐ πρὸς μέτρον καὶ σταθμόν, ἀλλὰ πρὸς τὴν ἑκάστου βούλησιν καὶ χάριν—that is to say quite unreasonably and without much deliberation (Phot. *Bibl.* p. 449b29f).

Still, there are some indications that the semantic difference which existed in some way or other between (ἐ)θέλω and βούλομαι in the early language did not entirely disappear, even apart from the archaistic— and sometimes mistaken—use of θέλω in classicistic literature.

Scholarly philosophy, as can be seen from its regular terminology, had always been aware of the intellectualistic implications of the meaning of βούλομαι, which denotes, in its traditional use, deliberation plus decision rather than volition: πᾶσα βούλησις ἐν λογιστικῷ: all βούλησις is to be located in man's rational faculty (Arist. *top.* 126a13; *de an.* 432b5; *M.M.* 1187b35; cf. Plat. *Gorg.* 467C ff; 509A ff). This concept was kept throughout the philosophical tradition. Stoics and Platonists defined βούλησις as εὔλογος (reasonable) (Stob. 2.87.14 W.H.; ps-Plat. *def.* 413C), and the pseudo-Stoic definition of θέλησις as βούλησις (Stob. 2.87.15) makes no sense in that terminology. It seems to have been propounded only for reasons of completeness, because θέλησις never enjoyed terminological status in Hellenistic philosophy, and was even condemned by the Atticists (Poll. 5.165). Βούλομαι, βούλησις, alongside προαίρεσις, προαιρεῖσθαι, always pointed, in the language of ethical theory, to a voluntary, deliberate decision in the field of moral conduct, fundamentally different from any instinctive or natural way of behavior. Philosophy never adopted (ἐ)θέλειν in that sense.

This philosophical use of βούλομαι, which persisted during the whole post-classical period, derived from classical usage, both Attic and non-Attic. In Euripides' *Helena* Theonoe describes herself saying ἐγὼ πέφυκά τ' εὐσεβεῖν καὶ βούλομαι: "I am pious by nature and I wish to be (pious)" (998). (Leontius *vit. Iohann.* p. 76 Gelzer, some one thousand years later, formulates this somewhat more crudely: πῶς ἐγένου ἐλεήμων; ἐκ φύσεως ἢ ἑαυτὸν βιασάμενος; "How did you become merciful? From nature or did you force yourself?") Lysias praises those who have been killed in action calling them men φῦντες καλῶς καὶ γνόντες ὁμοίως: "nobly born and similarly minded" (*or.* 2.20); Andocides attacks his opponent (1.95): ὁ πάντων πονηρότατος καὶ βουλόμενος εἶναι τοιοῦτος: "of all men the basest, and wishing to be such." Similarly, βούλησις, διάνοια or προαίρεσις are used as comprehensive terms to speak of the moral conduct of life (Isocr. *antid.* 7, 69, etc.), and in literary theory the same words are used to distinguish the conscious and deliberate use of a certain literary style from a natural gift or talent (Cic. *de or.* 2.92/93; Dion. Hal. *de Dem.* 3).

The philosophical and technical use of βούλομαι in post-classical Greek drew its origin, as we have seen, from the ordinary usage in classical Greek which no longer persisted, with its specific relationship to (ἐ)θέλω, in Hellenistic and Roman times. Yet Ammonius, whose classifications apply to non-philosophical, though literary, language of about A.D. 100, prescribed the use of βούλομαι only with reference to ζῷα λογικά, reasoning animals, i.e. men and gods, whereas (ἐ)θέλω could be said of both ἄλογα καὶ λογικὰ ζῷα, creatures without and with reason (*diff. verb.* 110 Nickau). Hellenistic grammarians repeatedly noted that βούλομαι and (ἐ)θέλω were synonyms in Homer (Hesych. *Lex.* B 930, E 653, Θ 223 Latte; all these glosses derive from commentaries on Homer). This is true by and large, though sometimes βούλομαι, together with ἤ, πολύ or μᾶλλον, has the precise meaning of "to prefer on the basis of preceding deliberation" (e.g. *Od.* 3.232 c. schol.; *Il.* 16.387 and 11.319), which is never attested with equal clarity in the much more extended Homeric usage of (ἐ)θέλω. Sometimes οὐκ ἐθέλω, "I am not prepared," is explicitly combined with ἀλλὰ βούλομαι, "but I prefer" (*Od.* 9.96 and 15.364). Βούλομαι is extremely rare in extant lyric poetry (cf. Rutherford, *Phrynichus* 189 and 415f), so that the ancient grammarians were likely to become aware of differences in meaning which existed between βούλομαι and θέλω in poetical and classical Greek, in contrast to their own, contemporary language. This is also attested by the attempt to revive the literary use of (ἐ)θέλω in the Atticistic movement. (For the persistence of ἐθέλω in post-classical Greek, see L. Rydbeck, *Fachprosa, vermeintliche Volkssprache und Neues Testament* [Uppsala 1967] 172.)

So we may assume from this evidence in grammatical and philosophical texts, that there was a certain awareness among the educated of the specific meaning of both θέλω and βούλομαι, apart from their different stylistic value and regardless of their alternative usage in contemporary language. The anonymous author of the earliest extant version of the novel of Alexander (ps.-Callisth. 2.37 Kroll), whose text represents rather low standards of literary Greek in the second or third century A.D., narrates that Alexander deliberately rejected (οὐκ ἠβουλήθη) a counsel because of his desire (θέλων) to see the ends of the world.

To return to our point of departure, the use of βούλομαι in the context of Galen's polemics against the Biblical concept of creation is surprising, for Galen was a well-trained Platonist. Did he react to the usage he found in Jewish or Christian texts? The Septuagint fundamentally differs from the literary usage of post-classical Greek. It offers 162 instances of (ἐ)θέλω and only 132 of βούλομαι. The canonical books of the New Testament have an even greater proportion of θέλω with the sole exception of the Acts of the Apostles (see G. Schrenk, *Th.W.N.T.* 3.43–63). Goodspeed lists 115 entries of θέλω and 36 of βούλομαι taken from Christian literature between the New Testament and the middle of the second century. The apologists in the second half of the second century, however, offer θέλω 49 times and βούλομαι 127 times, which corresponds to the literary usage of post-classical Greek as represented in Polybius, Philo of Alexandria, or Plutarch. In the third and fourth centuries, eventually, the Christian use of the two verbs came to show no significant differences from that of non-Christian authors, as can be seen, for instance, from the writings of Clement, Origen, or Athanasius.

It is hard to decide whether the predilection for θέλω in the Septuagint and in the earliest texts of Christian literature simply betrays the influence of spoken Greek, or whether θέλω was deliberately chosen to render various Semitic words denoting volition, in order to avoid the intellectualistic connotation of βούλομαι. At any rate, the earliest Christian texts simply continue, with regard to this detail, the usage of the Septuagint and foreshadow the further expansion of θέλω in the spoken language from Roman to Byzantine times which led to the conditions in spoken Modern Greek. This can be seen from early Byzantine hagiography. Theodorus' *Laudatio* of St. Theodosius (ed. Usener) from the early sixth century has 3 examples of βούλομαι and 8 of θέλω, Leontius' *Lives* of St. Tycho (ed. Usener), St. Symeon (ed. Rydén), and St. John the Almsgiver (ed. Gelzer), all dating from the early seventh century, 42 of βούλομαι and 82 of θέλω. (Wifstrand p. 35 wrongly attributes conditions prevailing in the theological literature to early hagiography.) In all these texts, of which only the prologues and epilogues were written in a somewhat elevated style, θέλω absolutely dominates in direct speech with its vulgar vocabulary, and can be found in a great number of idioms such as θέλετε ποιῶ (Do you want me to do . . . ?); or θέλω ἵνα (I want to . . .). But there is no definite difference in meaning between θέλω and βούλομαι.

Appendix II

SOME SCHOLARS have recently objected to the opinion, so widely presupposed in the anti-Gnostic literature of the Platonists and early Christians, that Gnostic doctrine of all sorts and kinds announced salvation only to those whose predetermined nature was capable of receiving it, independently of their own endeavor. L. Schottroff (*ZNW* Beih. 37 [1969] 63ff), E. H. Pagels (*VChr* 26 [1972] 241ff), E. Mühlenberg (*ZNW* 66 [1975] 172ff), Barbara Aland (*Nag Hammadi Studies* VIII [Leiden 1977] 148ff), K. Koschorke (*Wort und Dienst* 14 [1977] 51), and others strongly reject the view of R. Bultmann and his school, according to which in Jewish-Christian thought as opposed to Gnostic determinism the concept of *Entscheidungsdualismus* can be taken as a distinctive feature. They argue that the formula φύσει σῴζεσθαι (salvation through one's nature), though well attested in Valentinian Gnosticism (*Exc. Theod.* 56 and 61), cannot fairly account for the Gnostic concept of salvation in general, since many Gnostics regarded man's free and conscious decision to accept the message as the decisive step in the process of salvation.

Undoubtedly many Gnostic texts, especially those from Nag Hammadi, which testify to Gnostic beliefs directly rather than through the medium of anti-Gnostic polemics, exhort the pneumatic man, who has already received the salutary message, to strive for further knowledge and to maintain the ascetic conduct of life in a permanent chain of voluntary acts. Otherwise he may lose his distinctive quality (e.g. Ev. Thom. log. 1 [Nag Ham. Cod. II]; Test. Ver. p. 41.4 and 43.5ff [Nag Ham. Cod. IX]; cf. K. Koschorke, *ZNW* 69 [1978] 91ff; Ev. Phil. p. 64.29 [Nag Ham. Cod. II]). But the strong appeal to man's moral responsibility after he has accepted the salutary knowledge does not necessarily imply that salvation itself entirely depends on his decision and is, therefore, offered to everybody regardless of his previous ontological standing. On the contrary, freedom of decision presupposes the accep-

150

tance of the salutary revealed knowledge (Test. Ver. p. 43.5–10 [Nag Ham. Cod. IX]).

On this particular problem, the evidence of our texts, both polemical and non-polemical, is hard to evaluate. First, it is not always clear whether a Gnostic myth points to a cosmic event that may determine the nature of a given individual, or whether it refers to something that goes on in the human mind. The Apocryphon Johannis (p. 13.16ff [Nag Ham. Cod. III]; cf. C. Colpe, *JbAC* 19 [1976] 123) attributes the origin of πνευματικοί and ψυχικοί (pneumatic and psychic characters, respectively) to different cosmogonic acts. This corresponds to the neat subdivision of the various classes of men according to their capacity for being quickly saved, saved with some complications, or not saved at all (Apocr. Joh. p. 62.20ff and 67.14ff; Pap. Berol. 8502 Apocr. Joh. p. 32.3ff [Nag Ham. Cod. III]; Apc. Ad. P. 67.14 [Nag Ham. Cod. II]; Test. Ver. p. 31.7–10 [Nag Ham. Cod. IX]). It is hard to believe that this difference exclusively derives from the act of decision which the individual performs in accepting the message, since nowhere do we find in Gnostic literature a statement comparable to 2 Cor. 5:15 or Tit. 2:11, that the message has been offered to everybody. Ev. Ver. 30/31, the most important Valentinian text, seems to indicate the opposite, and according to *Corp. Herm.* 1.26 only those will be told the message who deserve it. That the salutary knowledge is given by the sheer grace of God does not necessarily imply that everybody is by nature able to receive the gift (Ep. Petr. p. 140 [Nag Ham. Cod. VIII]).

Secondly, statements about faith and love leading to salvation (*Exc. Theod.* 67.2; Carpocrates ap. Iren. *haer.* 1.25.5) can fit into a deterministic or non-deterministic context equally well, since faith may well be explained in terms of decision and, as can be seen in several Gnostic texts (*Exc. Theod.* 56.3; Basilid. ap. Clem. Alex. *strom.* 5.3.2), in terms of a cognition to be performed by the pneumatic nature of the privileged. Moreover, most Gnostics, especially in a Christian environment, explicitly taught the elect to respect the religious and moral standards of the Biblical tradition (Koschorke, *ZThK* 74 [1977] 323ff), regardless of their being the élite of the faithful. (This may have been different in the case of the pagan Hermetics: cf. *Corp. Herm.* 12.5–8.) So it does not seem fair to suppose that Clement of Alexandria put forward his argument in *strom.* 2.10.1–2,11.2 either *mala fide* or grossly mistaken about the intention of his Gnostic adversaries. He says that Valentinus and Basilides alike did away with προαίρεσις (choice, free decision), as they attributed salvation to the privileged nature of the pneumatics. Similarly, Origen (*princ.* 3.1.8) opposes those who destroy man's αὐτεξούσιον (self-determination and freedom) in their ethical and soteriological theories by introducing different classes of human nature in their exegesis of St. Paul's doctrine of predestination (Rom. 9:18). Incidentally, both the conception of mankind being subdivided according to endowment with divine substance and that of a particle of Light residing, along with body and soul, in every human being is attested in Gnostic texts (e.g. *Exc. Theod.* 56f; *Corp. Herm.* 1.26 and 9.3f; *Asclep.* 29). No one should underrate the diversification of Gnostic teaching in pagan, Jewish, and Christian environments. But it cannot possibly be due to mere chance that all orthodox and heterodox Christians—together with their colleagues of the schools of philosophy— who wrote against the Gnostics of various denominations unanimously opposed their opponents' deterministic doctrines on salvation and stressed the importance of man's free decision and the intended salvation of everybody instead.

E. Mühlenberg and Barbara Aland have argued that Heracleo the Valentinian in his interpretation of John 8:44 derives man's salvation or his attachment to evil from his deeds rather than from his nature. They regard Origen's assertion that Heracleo attributed faith and salvation to man's φυσικὴ κατασκευή (natural constitution) (*in Joh. comm.*, *GCS* p. 235) as being as mistaken as the testimony of Clement quoted above. Aland even understands the terms οὐσία and φύσις (substance and nature, respectively) in Heracleo's description of the classes of πνευματικοί, ψυχικοί, χοϊκοί (pneumatic, psychic, earthly characters) as referring to changing moral condition rather than unchanging nature or substance. It is hard to believe that Heracleo, who was an educated man very much like his teacher Valentinus, could have used such terms in a philosophical discussion quite against their meaning, unless he was deliberately trying to mislead his non-Gnostic readers—successfully in the case of Origen—which is highly unlikely.

The crucial text in this respect seems to be fr. 46 Völker, which has been preserved from Heracleo's commentary on the Gospel of St. John and contains six more or less specific details of his doctrine. (1) ᾿Εκ τοῦ πατρὸς τοῦ διαβόλου (from your father, the devil) in John 8:44 denotes ἐκ τῆς οὐσίας τοῦ διαβόλου (from the substance of the devil) and refers to the χοϊκοί. (2) Τὰς ἐπιθυμίας τοῦ πατρὸς θέλετε ποιεῖν (you choose to carry out your father's desires) in the same verse indicates that the devil, being a μὴ ὄν (non-being) and, consequently, restricted to negation and destruction, has no θελήματα. (The Platonic view of evil as μὴ ὄν and of θέλημα or βούλημα as intention originating from the cognition of the better was shared by orthodox Christians; cf. Adamant. *dial.* 3.2; Athan. *incarn.* 4 = *PG* 25.104.) (3) Those who like and fulfill the wishes of the devil are different from the χοϊκοί, who are called φύσει τοῦ διαβόλου υἱοί (sons of the devil by nature). They have to be understood as the ψυχικοί who become the adopted (θέσει) children of Satan because of their behavior according to the wishes of their master. Some of them, however, can be called υἱοὶ θεοῦ καὶ φύσει καὶ θέσει (sons of God by nature and adoption), which implies that some of the ψυχικοί will be saved because of both their nature and their moral and voluntary performance. (4) Those who love and fulfill the wishes of the devil become his children without being so by nature, which again points to the natural predisposition for salvation of the ψυχικοί. (5) Three meanings can be attached to the word son (υἱός): φύσει υἱοί (sons by nature) have been generated by their father, γνώμῃ υἱοί (sons by purpose) have become sons from ποιεῖν τὸ θέλημα τοῦ πατρός (doing the will of the Father), and ἀξίᾳ υἱοί (sons by rank or worth) are those who are called sons of darkness, sons of injustice and the like in the Scriptures. (6) Sons of darkness have not been generated by the devil, since his power is restricted to destroying. They become sons of darkness from their doing the works of darkness.

The content of that fragment does not seem as enigmatic as some scholars have rendered it by their interpretation. First of all, statement (5) certainly does not point to the three classes of πνευματικοί, ψυχικοί, χοϊκοί; it merely describes three *façons de parler*. According to (3), the χοϊκοί are attached to evil by nature, and the word ἀξία denotes "standing, dignity, worth" rather than "merit." So the group of ἀξίᾳ υἱοί (sons by rank or worth) could have been easily exemplified by the πνευματικοί as well, as is the case in Dial. Sot. p. 143.14 (Nag Ham. Cod. III), where this class is called "Sons of Truth." Ἀξίᾳ υἱός (son by worth) only means, in the view of Heracleo, that the religious or moral standing of an individual can be described by that metaphorical expression.

Fragment 46 does not say anything about the pneumatics, whose sal-

vation comes from their insight into the causes of their sins, whereas
the psychics only attain the simple knowledge or consciousness of their
sins, which, however, suffices to save them (frr. 20 and 40). In fr. 46
the interest clearly is concentrated upon the psychics, who are capable
of becoming good or evil. Statement (3) on the choïcs, whose substance
is wholly earthly, and who are explicitly called φύσει τοῦ διαβόλου υἱοί
(sons of the devil by nature) apparently contradicts the Platonizing doctrine of the sterility of evil put forward in (6). The physical attachment
to evil of this group cannot be adequately described in terms of generation. But if the χοϊκοί do not participate, in some way or other, in the
divine substance of Light, they are, in fact, as non-existent as their "father," thus really sharing his οὐσία or φύσις (substance or nature, respectively) without being generated by him.

Heracleo's doctrine corresponds exactly to the classification of men
according to their being saved immediately and without hindrance
(πνευματικοί, pneumatics), saved with some complications and not in
every individual case (ψυχικοί, psychics), and not saved at all (χοϊκοί,
earthly men) (see above p. 99f). The divine knowledge, whose revelation
brings about salvation, can be accepted only by those who are pre-
disposed for cognition, according to Valentinian theory (Ev. Ver. 11).
It is of no essential importance whether one attributes this quality to
divine election or creation. Determinism can be founded on the belief
in creation or nature as well as on that of divine election. But it seems
clear that in the view of Heracleo the ψυχικός (the psychic man), apparently the representative of average human nature, has the natural
faculty of being saved, but must also contribute to his salvation by
means of his own προαίρεσις.

In the Apocryphon Johannis even the χοϊκοί or σαρκικοί (of the earth
or of the flesh) will—eventually—be saved. But the strong deterministic tendency prevailing also in this piece of Gnostic literature has
caused the author to add, quite against the usual Gnostic tripartition, a
fourth group of those who can by no means receive the salutary knowledge (pp. 35.2ff [Nag Ham. Cod. III] cf. C. Colpe, *JbAC* 19 [1976]
124).

The deterministic view which Christians and Platonists (e.g. Tert.
adv. Marc. 2.5–9, *de an.* 21.6; Plot. 2.9.14; Simplic. *in Epict. ench.* p.
70 Dübner) attributed to Gnosticism in general did not pervade all
Gnostic schools and currents in the same way. Apparently, there were

tendencies to restrict the deterministic approach and to strengthen the idea of man's freedom and responsibility in soteriology and ethics. But the attempt to explain fall and salvation in terms of myth and ontology rather than referring these essentials of religious experience to the documented history of man, which was made again and again in the Gnostic movement, inevitably led to deterministic conceptions of man's destiny—and this was duly noted in the early Church. The attachment to philosophical ontology, however, became predominant in the Gnostic systems of the second century.

The philosophical background of these Gnostic systems does not seem compatible with the theory of E. H. Pagels. She rejects the alternatives freedom of choice/determination in her reconstruction of Gnostic, especially Valentinian, anthropology: the pneumatics have been elected for salvation by the will of God, the psychics are qualified for salvation and said to deserve it by their own endeavor, but not elected, whereas the choïcs have been elected for damnation. This conception, according to Pagels, was developed from the exegesis of St. Paul's Epistle to the Romans and cannot be adequately described in terms of philosophical anthropology, since it testifies to the predominantly religious experience of election.

This interpretation of Valentinianism does not account for the neat tripartition of man which is alien to St. Paul and comfortingly weakens his doctrine of predestination. It is, in fact, hardly possible to explain this conception of Rom. 9 in terms of an acceptable and coherent ontological or anthropological theory. No one can distinguish the elect from the non-elect, as foreseen in St. Paul's doctrine, by a convincing philosophical argument. St. Paul's teaching appeals to faith rather than philosophical understanding. Yet by the careful tripartition which the Valentinians and other Gnostics introduced into the interpretation of the Epistle to the Romans, they succeeded in adapting the harsh and alarming doctrine of predestination to the requirements of philosophical anthropology. The ψυχικοί exactly meet the standards of average that is to say predominantly Platonic—anthropology in the second century. Man is capable of moral progress and even perfection because of his natural endowment as a rational being, but he has to reach the goal through his voluntary moral conduct (προαίρεσις). Strict and inexplicable determination which inevitably results from the attempt to understand divine grace in terms of an ontological system, has been

restricted, in the field of anthropology, to the two marginal or exceptional groups of men, pneumatics and choïcs, respectively. The traditional standards and values of philosophical ethics work perfectly well
in ordinary social life, despite the supra-rational content of the salutary
knowledge which has to be accepted, with all its deterministic implications, by an act of fundamental assent.

Origen mentions only choïcs and pneumatics in his refutation of
those who destroy the freedom (αὐτεξούσιον) of man by introducing
different kinds of human nature destined either for salvation or damnation (*princ.* 2.5.2, 3.1.8; cf. 2.9.5, where the distinction between different natures of men is simply attributed to Marcio, Valentinus, and
Basilides without further specification). Perhaps Origen was aware of
the Valentinian doctrine of the psychics as pointed out by Heracleo.

St. Paul's concept of predestination as set forth in Rom. 9–11 is of
the utmost austerity and acceptable only for those whose religious zeal
and consciousness of being the elect outweigh the longing to find the
standards of human justice in the rule of God. Origen as well as the
Valentinians circumvent the stumbling block of so offensive a doctrine
in different ways, but without refuting the apostle. They open up a
large field where human activity can be performed and morally evaluated according to exclusively rational standards. Divine grace, inexplicable as it may be, provides the basis of human existence, lends help
in all adversities and difficulties of life, secures the future beyond the
limits of time and space, but directly operates in exceptional cases only.

The same need for an area of calculability and predictability in
human life appears in an entirely different doctrine, which was developed in medieval Scholastic philosophy.

The will of God is free, his power unlimited, his plans unfathomable. Consequently, everybody has to be prepared, at any time, to meet
with God's unpredictable interference and with the inexplicable utterance of His will. This apparently goes beyond the faculties of man as a
rational and moral being. Only faith can endure the idea of being exposed to God's unlimited power. That is why God has created and
structured the universe according to rules that are open to human understanding. In dealing with his creatures God only uses His *potentia
ordinata* (His power expressed within and through the order of the universe). Philo had already introduced this difference; see above p. 92.
Thus man is able to rely on his reason in the conduct of his physical and

moral life, whereas his salvation depends on the grace of God, which is but one aspect of his *potentia absoluta*. Again, overwhelming religious experience has been harmonized with confidence in the human intellect as the guide in social life.

(Dr. K. Koschorke kindly gave me most valuable help in my dealing with the intricacies of Gnostic tradition.)

NOTES

Full references to authors and abbreviated titles cited will be found in the Bibliography.

CHAPTER I

1. Gal. *de part.* 11.14 p. 158.2 Helmreich. The passage is thoroughly discussed by Walzer, *RAC* 8 (1972) 780ff.

2. Galen used the verb βούλομαι to describe, in this context, the unlimited power and arbitrariness which the Jews attributed to the divine Creator: We, the Greeks, οὐ τὸν μὲν (sc. God) βουληθῆναι λέγομεν, τὰς δὲ (sc. the eyelashes) εὐθὺς γεγονέναι· μὴ γὰρ ἄν, μηδ' εἰ μυριάκις βουληθείη, γενέσθαι ποτ' ἂν τοιαύτας ἐκ δέρματος μαλακοῦ πεφυκυίας. (We do not say that God determined and eyelashes came to be directly; for they would not, not even if he wished a thousand times, have grown thus from soft skin.) A few lines below, though, he refers to the same quality of the God of the Jews by the verb θέλω: πάντα λὰρ εἶναι νομίζει (sc. ὁ Μωυσῆς) τῷ θεῷ δυνατά, κἂν εἰ τὴν τέφραν ἵππον ἢ βοῦν ἐθέλοι ποιεῖν. (For Moses thinks that all things are in God's power, even if He wished to make a horse or cow from dust.) This lexicographical detail is worth noting (see Appendix I).

3. The Jews fervently opposed Epicurus because he denied divine providence (Jos. *ant.* 10.11.7 §§ 277–281; cf. W. C. van Unnik, *Romanitas et Christianitas* [1973] 341–355). So Galen might have known of that particular point of disagreement between Epicureans and Jews; the latter sided, in that respect, with Stoics and Academics. The same applies to the early Christians. To deny divine providence must have been regarded by them as much worse than the certain lack of respectability (cf. Schmid, *RAC* 5 [1962] 779f and 792f) the Epicureans had in the view of many educated people in the first and second centuries A.D. (cf. ps.-Clem. *recogn.* 8.1ff and 10ff, *hom.* 20 and 21). Epicureanism opposed the rest of Greek philosophy in that it did not consider the universe as structured and ruled by reason. That is why perfection in moral life, according to Epicurus, resulted not from any kind of congruity between the intention of the individual and the cosmic order, but solely from the congruity between the intention of man and his own, individual nature. This difference was duly noted by the Christians: Didym. *in Eccl.* 7.13 Kramer-Krebber (*PapTextuAbh* 16 [1972] 42–44).

4. According to Plato's *Timaeus*, the most influential cosmology of the Greek philosophical tradition, the universe as created by the Demiurge represents a perfect rational order. The same conception prevailed also in later Pla-

tonism (e.g. Cels. ap. Orig. *c. Cels.* 7.68). It is only in the permanent existence of the universe that its creator's will comes in: the universe is bound to
last, because the Demiurge does not want to destroy it (Plat. *Tim.* 41A/B).

5. A century later Alexander of Lycopolis in Egypt, presumably a Platonic
philosopher, argued against Manichean cosmology, which attributed the emer-
gence of the universe and its further destiny to a First and Second Will (βούλημα), along the very same lines. "What sense can it possibly make to attribute
to God something that cannot even reasonably be attributed to man? For the
term βούλεσθαι, used in such a context, implies that something (logically) impossible is being spoken of and, furthermore, one should not use the word
βούλεσθαι (with reference to God) too easily, even if something possible is
being dealt with" (Alex. Lyc. *adv. Man.* 26 p. 39 Brinkmann):

> τίς ὁ λόγος θεῷ ἀναθεῖναι
> πράγματα ἃ οὐκ ἐπ' ἀνθρώπων
> καλῶς ἔχει ὑπονοεῖν; τὸ γὰρ
> ἀδύνατον πρόσεστι τῷ βούλεσθαι
> ἐπὶ τῶν τοιούτων, πρὸς τὸ μηδὲ
> τὸ βούλεσθαι κἂν δυνατὸν ᾖ
> προχείρως χρῆναι λέγειν.

It has to be remembered that βούλομαι denotes, in the Platonic tradition (cf.
Plat. *Gorg.* 467E), intention based on the knowledge of what is really good
and reasonable.

Manichean cosmology further developed the Gnostic conception. Expound-
ing their dualistic doctrine, the Gnostics made extended use of the Platonic
devaluation of the sensible world. However, they applied the devaluation to
the whole of creation. According to a recently edited text from Nag Hammadi
(Cod. XIII p. 39.27; cf. *Muséon* 87 [1974] 368f) the Archon Jaldebaoth
(called also Saklas and Samael) is stupid enough to regard himself as the Supreme Being and to create for this reason the present universe by his arbitrary
decision. It goes without saying that this sort of universe does not convey,
through its order and structure, any knowledge of the true Supreme Being,
nor can the human intellect, which is bound to use its power within the limits
of the existing universe, arrive at the true knowledge without divine and supranatural inspiration or revelation.

6. According to Epicurus and his followers, nature is more powerful than
the gods, who do not care for the destiny of either the universe or man. But
Lucretius seems to formulate that opinion even without special regard to Epicurean theology (5.309f): *nec sanctum numen fati protollere finis / posse neque adver-
sus naturae foedera niti.*

7. E.g. Aristot. *phys.* 195b31–198a13 with the commentary of H.
Wagner, *Aristoteles Physik* (1967) 466ff and Alex. Aphrod. *de an.* p. 179.6f
Bruns.

8. Among the Platonists, Porphyry formulated the most coherent theory of
prayer. The ultimate goal of prayer is the union of the human mind with the

divine (*ad Marc.* 11, *abstin.* 2.45f; cf. Plat. *Tim.* 90C; Aristot. fr. 49 Rose; Plot. 5.1.6). Unifying one's mind with the divine is an act of cognition which causes both purification and salvation. But since no man can attain, through his own intellectual effort, perfect and direct cognition of God, prayer, being an attempt at cognition, implies the element of confidence in God's perfect, immutable rationality which can be gathered from observation of the rational order of nature (*abstin.* 3.11; Sall. *de deis* 14.3). Reason, though perhaps partly transcending the potential of the human mind, provides the common ground where God and man can meet and communicate, even according to Neo-platonic speculation which strives to get in touch with the suprarational One. (Where philosophy, however, was regarded as a means to make explicit and to deepen the understanding of divinely, supranaturally revealed truth, as in Hermetism, in the tradition about Apollonius of Tyana, and also in some branches of the late Neoplatonic school, prayer could, in fact, divert the course of events as foreseen by nature [cf. Damasc. *vit. Isid.* pp. 96–98 Zintzen].) The creed underlying the main stream of Greek philosophy does not differ too much from the opinion attributed to Themistocles by Herodotus (8.60 γ): if man, in his planning, fails to keep to the reasonable (οἰκότα), God is not willing (οὐκ ἐθέλει) to support his intention (γνώμη). Herodotus' saying is prudential rather than speculative. Still, the basic belief that the divine order is immutable and that, consequently, the gods cannot possibly change their mind (for this could only restrict their perfection) is as firmly established in Herodotus' Histories as in Platonic philosophy. Even the gods' inclination to curb everything that is prominent (φιλέει γὰρ ὁ θεὸς τὰ ὑπερέχοντα κολούειν 2.41), which leads them to acts of outrageous injustice according to human standards, does not result from whims and freaks, but is intended to preserve the cosmic order in which no individual man is allowed to trespass over the boundaries set to all mankind. Xerxes is prepared to revise his first decision, by which he has offended against the divine law. But the gods do not allow him to follow the right course he has, in the end, deliberately chosen. They force him, by means of a deceptive dream, back to his first step, in order to arrange the catastrophe and to show by way of example the full punishment of his initial mistake. These gods are not free to act solely according to their will. They watch over a cosmic order that embraces themselves. So prayer and sacrifice performed before decisive battles and the like were supposed to ascertain existing conditions rather than to influence the intention of the gods. This can be clearly seen from Herodotus' account of the battle of Plataea (9.61/62).

Yahveh, on the other hand, drastically changed the punishment which had been solemnly pronounced because of King Ahab's repentance (1 Kings 21:29), and an extended bargain with Abraham leads him to repeated modifications of his plans (Gen. 18:22–32). Yahveh is even willing to answer an oracular question (Judg. 6:37–40) or to announce his interference with human affairs by the laws of his own creation (Josh. 10:12/13). There is no rule, either cosmic or moral, that cannot be upset, without losing its further validity, by an act of will of Yahveh. That is why prayer means something different in the Biblical tradition and in Greek literature and philosophy (cf. Severus, *RAC* 8 [1972] 1134–1258).

9. Plato, in particular, stressed the idea that cosmic or divine order can only be perfectly rational. This is pointed out in connection with the proof of the existence of the gods, which is, in Plato's view (cf. also Aristot. fr. 11 Rose), the essential presupposition of social and moral standards (*Leg.* 888D ff; cf. H. Görgemanns, *Beiträge z. Platons Nomoi* [1960] 193ff with further references). According to this doctrine, both cosmic and moral life as they unfold under the divine rule constitute an uninterrupted chain of deed and recompense. Man, though intellectually incapable of ascertaining its full extent, should firmly believe that everything that has been done is going to be compensated in due proportion (*Leg.* 898D–899D). There is no Supreme Will at work which could possibly modify or even interrupt the sequence of deed and recompense by disregarding, in some way or other, the prearranged and strictly rational order of being. Thus man can rely on universal justice. Motion without order, which points to the existence of an animating though non-rational factor (*Leg.* 896C ff, *Epin.* 988C), precedes the activity of the Demiurge, who has animated and structured matter by reason, thus creating the universe as an image of his own, perfect rationality (*Tim.* 30A ff), which is both beautiful and just.

St. Augustine, on the other hand, rejects the idea that anything caused by the sheer will of God could possibly be explained in terms of reasoning. This applies, for instance, to the Final Judgement, where the many are going to be condemned and the few saved. This cannot be understood in terms of logical calculation, according to the principle of deed and recompense, nor can the sufferings of Job or the election of St. Paul be explained in that way (*civ. D.* 21.15).

In these and similar passages St. Augustine gave a very adequate interpretation of the Biblical ideas about creation and the destiny of man. Greek philosophy, except for the Sceptics and Epicureans, consistently sought to corroborate the archaic belief that social order and moral standards had their roots in the order of nature as established and maintained by the gods. That is why Plato tried to understand social and political order as the magnified model of the human soul which, in its turn, represented the perceptible aspect of the universal order of being. The Stoics, arguing in a different way but facing the same problem, derived all moral and social standards from the gift of sociability which man has been given by nature. Thus philosophy could easily interpret, in its own terms and concepts, the close interconnection or even identification of natural and social order which people had always tried to establish by means of myth and cult, especially by the cult of the rulers in the Hellenistic and Roman periods. This can be seen from the many treatises περὶ βασιλείας (concerning kingship) which were written at that time (ps.-Ecphantus, *Corpus Hermeticum* XVIII, Dio of Prusa and many others). They all try to demonstrate that the monarchical system of political rule, and all the moral and social values for which it stands, are deeply rooted in the divine or cosmic order, which man can perceive and explain by his intellectual efforts, for it is perfectly rational.

The Biblical approach is quite different. The social community of the people of Israel does not result from the natural sociability of men. It has been created by an act of divine will which can be ascertained in the commandments of God (e.g. Exod. 19:3–8; Ezek. 2:21f and 4:1). The special relationship between God and his people, according to the Biblical understanding, does not primarily guarantee, as in most archaic cultures, the accordance between a human society and its natural environment. The Israelites have to obey the orders of their God, that is all they can do (cf. G. v. Rad, *Theologie d. AT* 1[6] [1969] 267–273). Even rituals do not constitute, according to their theological interpretation in many passages of the Old Testament, some sort of communication between man and God, but rather establish the community of men on the order of God (Deut. 12:7; cf. W. Eichrodt, *Theologie d. AT* I[7] [1962] 93ff).

Virtually the same applies to the Christians. They are not *membra unius corporis*, limbs of a single body, because they realize, as do the Stoics (Sen. *ep.* 95.52), the natural brotherhood of men. Their sociability is not provided by nature. It results solely from their being reconciled with God through an incomprehensible act of divine will or grace. That is why their primary relationship connects them with their redeemer. They are limbs of the body of Christ, and by no means limbs of the cosmic body (Rom. 15:26f; 2 Cor. 1:4 and 9:13; Eph. 2:11–22; 1 John 1:3 and 6f; Heb. 2:14). So moral standards cannot be derived, in the Christian view, from the structure of the universe and its perfectly rational order. They emanate from the will of God through His orders and commandments and have to be met, accordingly, by repeated acts of human will.

10. The Stoics offered a proof for the existence of God drawn from the rational order of the universe, which can be perceived and evaluated by the human intellect (e.g. Cic. *nat. deor.* 3.27). This doctrine was attributed to Socrates too (Sext. *adv. math.* 9.98–102; cf. Xen. *Mem.* 1.4.5), perhaps rightly, because it was held by Plato and his followers (e.g. *Phileb.* 30A ff; *Leg.* 897B ff) and virtually shared by all schools and sects of Greek philosophy, except Epicureans and Sceptics. The incomprehensibility of God, as spoken of in the Old Testament (e.g. Wisd. of Sol. 9:13 τίς γὰρ ἄνθρωπος γνώσεται βουλὴν θεοῦ, ἢ τίς ἐνθυμήσεται τί θέλει ὁ κύριος [For what man will know the plan of God or what man will ponder what the Lord wants?]) prevented men from drawing the inference from the nature of creation to its creator, nor could the state of moral or religious perfection, that is to say existence in accordance with God, be understood as resulting from knowledge in the Greek or philosophical sense of the term. Philo tried to bridge the gap between the two concepts by his doctrine of revelation: the human mind is widened and illuminated by divine revelation, so that it can attain some kind of direct cognition of God and dissolve what seems to be contradictory, in the order of being and

in God's activity, to natural understanding (cf. U. Früchtel, *Kosmolog. Vorstellungen bei Philon* [1968] 164–171). Virtually the same is taught by Justin a hundred years later (*dial.* 4.1): the human intellect, in its natural condition, is incapable of achieving direct cognition of God, unless it has been supranaturally equipped with divine πνεῦμα (spirit). Consequently moral perfection, living in accordance with God, can be defined, by such an *interpretatio Graeca* of Biblical ideas, as the result of knowledge (e.g. *leg. alleg.* 3.113; cf. *RAC* 6 [1966] 698f). The Biblical concept of sin, though, did not fit in with that syncretistic anthropology and had to be described, quite against the Greek or philosophical understanding of nature, as an essential part of human nature (e.g. *vit. Mos.* 2.147; cf. Z. Knuth, *Sündenbegriff bei Philon* [1934]).

The problem of whether the perfectly rational order of nature, which the human intellect can ascertain by its own efforts, has any bearing on the cognition of God, who is, according to the Biblical tradition, incomprehensible and whose orders have to be obeyed rather than understood, was continually discussed throughout the history of the early Church (cf. St. John Chrysostom, *L'incompréhensibilité de Dieu*, ed. Cavallera-Daniélou [1951] Introduction p. 16ff with further references).

11. The monotheistic tradition of Greek philosophy goes back as far as Xenophanes (B 23–26 D.K.) and was maintained throughout the classical and post-classical periods (e.g. Plat. *Tim.* 28A ff and Cleanthes *SVF* 1.537). Antisthenes (fr. 29 Decleva-Caizzi) taught that there are many gods κατὰ νόμον (according to law or custom), but only one κατὰ φύσιν (according to nature). It was this monotheistic conception which Greek intellectuals discovered in the Old Testament (cf. Ps.-Aristeas 132; Philo, *de opif. mundi* 170–172).

12. That is why the close interconnection of the cosmic order and justice among men, both being warranted by divine rule, was an old topic of philosophical speculation: Vlastos, *CPh* 41 (1947) 106ff.

13. We disregard, in the present context, the changes in Hebrew thought as documented in the different layers of Biblical tradition, for no Greek intellectual or Christian theologian who had to deal with the Old Testament was thinking of such a historical development.

14. I could not obtain J. L. Glisson, "The Will of God as Reflected in Greek Words" (diss., 1951).

15. God's power and faithfulness are spoken of as the reason for the creation and maintenance of the universe and its regularity in Ps. 33:4–10.

16. Priscillian (*tract.* 5 p. 63f; cf. H. Chadwick, *Priscillian* [1976] 76) refuted philosophic doctrines on the eternity of the universe and its cyclic changes on the basis of the simple argument that the cosmos entirely depends on the unpredictable will of its creator. See also C. M. Edsman, *Mélanges Pedersen* (1946) 11–44.

17. The topic is treated by K. Bannach, *Doppelte Macht Gottes bei Wilhelm von Ockham* (1975).

18. "Pagan authors of Hellenistic and Roman imperial times knew more

about Moses than one might commonly expect": J. C. Gager, *Moses in Greco-Roman Paganism* (1972) 102. The material has been collected by M. Stern, *Greek and Latin Authors on Judaism I* (1974).

19. The topic of φιλοσοφία βάρβαρος (Barbarian philosophy) which was very important throughout the history of Greek thought, has not been adequately treated so far. For some material see A. M. Malingrey, *Philosophia* (1961); Waszink, *EntrFondHardt* 3 (1955) 139–182; H. Dörrie, *Romanitas et Christianitas* (1973) 99–118; id., *Antike u. Universalgeschichte* (1972) 146–175; Gager (above n. 18), 36.

Megasthenes' statement (*FGH* 715 F 3) that no cosmological doctrine of the Greeks had not been previously formulated by the Indian Brahmans or the Jews is repeatedly quoted by Christian authors such as Clement and Eusebius.

20. The anonymous author of the treatise *On the Sublime* interpreted, about a century before Galen, the wording of Genesis 1:3 (εἶπεν ὁ θεὸς γενέσθω—καὶ ἐγένετο [God said let there be (light)—and there was (light)]) as the most appropriate description of divine δύναμις (power). He did not refer to God's free decision to create whatever He likes (9.9). Cf. Gager, 42ff.

21. This can be seen, for instance, from the part played by the notorious *sacramentum infanticidii* (ritual eating of children) in antijudaic, later on also antichristian, polemics (Jos. *c. Ap.* 2.91ff; Democritus *FGH* 730 F 1; Justin *dial.* 10.2; Athenag. *suppl.* 3). For the social and political motives that underlie the antijudaism of the early imperial period see Braunert in *Gesch. in Wiss. u. Unterr.* (1975) 521–547 and below n. 32.

22. Cf. Whittaker, *Phoenix* 21 (1967) 196–201.

23. Socrates and the Stoics, however, were inspired only κατὰ σπερματικοῦ λόγου μέρος, οὐ κατὰ παντὸς λόγου γνῶσιν καὶ θεωρίαν as Justin writes (*apol.* 2.7/8). Complete knowledge of the divine will became possible only in consequence of the incarnation of Christ. That is why all the titles and epithets of Christ derive ἔκ τε τοῦ ὑπηρετεῖν τῷ πατρικῷ βουλήματι καὶ ἐκ τοῦ ἀπὸ τοῦ πατρὸς θελήσει γεγεννῆσθαι (*dial.* 61). Again, the will of God can be ascertained by the human mind only because of the example of perfect obedience that has been given in the life of Christ.

24. It was generally agreed among Christian theologians, once cosmology had been integrated into a system of Christian theology, that God's βούλησις suffices for the creation of the universe, and that the creator has no need for any kind of raw material (e.g. Orig. *princ.* 35.5; Aug. *c. Prisc.* 3). That is why it had to be held against Arius that the Logos could not possibly draw his origin from the will of the Father but rather, being no creature, only from his οὐσία (essence) (e.g. Athan. *c. Ar.* 3.60). On the other hand, even as religious-minded a Platonist as Numenius in the second century A.D. was firmly convinced that God needs matter as the potentiality out of which he creates the universe (fr. 52 des Places = *Calc. in Tim.* p. 295 Waszink). The same view was held by his Christian contemporary Justin. But conditions changed, not only on the Christian side. The emperor Julian, in the middle of the fourth century, blamed Moses for having taught a cosmology according to which God

created the universe simply by shaping preexisting matter (*c. Gal.* 49E Neumann; cf. Gager, *HebrUnCollAnn* 44 [1973] 99). Obviously such a doctrine, though well-founded in the philosophical tradition, is by no means compatible, in the view of Julian, with the dignity of a Supreme Being. According to this view, God as the ultimate cause of being has to precede the differentiation into matter and intellect, as does the One of the Neoplatonists and their predecessors.

25. Regardless of all attempts, above all in the fourth century A.D., to reconcile the philosophical concept of nature and the Biblical idea of creation, most Christian theologians were perfectly aware of the difference. Hippolytus, for instance, stressed his belief that God Himself is not limited in His activity by any law He has given to His creation (*in Dan.* 1.8.2.4; cf. Aug. *civ. D.* 21.8). Ambrose reminds one of his addressees of the unbridgeable gap between God and His creation which is usually overlooked by the Greek philosophers (*ep.* 44.1; cf. *in Hex.* 6.2.7). Basil replaces the σπερματικὸς λόγος (seminal reason) of Stoic cosmology, which provides rational order, life, and creativity all over the world, by the will of God. God is free to interfere with the regular cosmic process wherever He pleases, as can be seen from the fact that the plains of Egypt are not flooded, although they are below the level of the Red Sea (Basil, *in Hex.* 4.3; cf. Aristot. *meteor.* 352b20). Another problem arising from this debate can be seen, for instance, in Prudentius (*c. Symm.* 1.305–330): Greek philosophy had always taken its main argument in proof of the divine character of cosmic order from the regular, mathematically describable, and predictable motion of the heavenly bodies. The Stoics had even justified the practice of astrology by that particular argument. Prudentius reversed the argument: the stars reveal, by the strict regularity of their motion, that they are subject to a powerful will that has given them laws and is, consequently, free to interfere with the cosmic process. The faithful, having a direct link with the owner of that powerful will, is free from being determined by the cosmic order. Astrology and its prophecies do not apply to him. This was an important issue throughout the history of the early Church (Just. *apol.* 1.61.10; Tat. *or. adv. Graec.* 9.2; Hieron. *ep.* 96.16.2; cf. Gundel, *RAC* 1 [1950] 825–830). Similarly, Irenaeus' main objection against Gnostic cosmology and its determinism, which identifies necessity and reality, is based on the firm belief that the divine will does not admit any bounds to its freedom (cf. Meijering, *Nederl'TheolTijdschr* 21 [1973] 26–33).

On the other hand, the Christians adopted very eagerly the philosophical argument according to which the existence of a supreme Creator and ruler of the universe can be gathered from its perfectly rational structure (Xen. *mem.* 1.4.8; Plat. *Phileb.* 30A; Sext. *adv. math.* 9.98–101; Cic. *nat. deor.* 3.27). The argument is already repeated and adapted to the use of the Christians in the first epistle of Clement (53)—interestingly enough, together with the well-known apologetic topos according to which Judaeo-Christian and pagan examples of perfect virtue can be measured by the same standard (cf. H. Lietzmann, *Handbuch zum NT* 3.1 [1919] 39f ad *Rom.* 2:14–16). Justin offers the same cosmological doctrine about fifty years later (*apol.* 1.20). The term βούλημα, used of the intention of the Creator (8.5), seems to point, in such a context, to God's perfect and comprehensive planning rather than to His freedom in deciding whatever He pleases. Βούλησις, the will of the Creator and Ruler of the universe, could always be interpreted along the lines of Plat. *Tim.* 41A–B: the intention of the Creator is perfectly rational, so that this very intention causes the rational structure and regular motion which matter enjoys in the cosmic order; but this contradicts the uniqueness and unpredictability of God's action in bringing about salvation (cf. Meijering, *VChr* 28 [1974] 15–28). There is no need for a concept of will in such a cosmology. Even the Creator's desire to extend his own perfect rationality by permanently creating other beings that partake in the cosmic order is implied in the concept of universal reason. This aspect of Platonic cosmology became particularly popular in late antiquity, even outside the scholarly tradition of Platonic philosophy (*Cat. cod. astrol.* 9.1 p. 113.22).

There were, however, some essential constituents of the Christian faith which were hard to explain in a coherent doctrine along these lines. One was the idea of a *creatio ex nihilo*, so deeply rooted in the Biblical tradition. This concept was always retained, with a few exceptions (see G. May, *Schöpfung aus dem Nichts* [1978]) by the Christians (Rom. 4:17; Herm. *vis.* 1.1.6 and *mand.* 1.1; 2 Clem. 1.8) and was kept alive, in the early Church, in liturgical texts as well (*const. Apost.* 8.12.7). It contradicted philosophical cosmology of the traditional type, in which reason was primarily regarded as the animating and structuring factor in the universe, creation being mainly considered an act of organizing, shaping, and vivifying. Accordingly, something unstructured and unanimated had to underlie and, consequently, to precede in time the activity of the Creator or Demiurge. The coming to being of this something, mostly defined as matter, could not possibly be ascribed to the Creator, who had established a perfectly rational order of the universe. Aristotle's doctrine of potentiality and actuality removed the problem, for he kept everything that is not yet structured or animated by reason outside the realm of being proper. Along these lines Philo could even interpret the Biblical idea of *creatio ex nihilo*: matter itself, being dead and unorganized, is, in fact, a μὴ ὄν (non-being) before the beginning of creation (*prov.* 1.8, *div. her.* 160), which can be said, therefore, to be a creation out of nothing. Even time has been created together with the cosmos, for time results from motion (*opif.* 8–10, perhaps taken from Eudorus).

Yet, strictly speaking, this sort of reasoning did not agree with the Biblical account of the creation. If everything, including matter or potential which is not yet structured by reason or brought to reality, had to be created by an initial, though perhaps repeated, act of divine will, the perfect rationality of creation could not be maintained. If, on the other hand, stress was laid, according to the philosophical tradition, on the perfect rationality of the cosmos, even the Biblical account had to be interpreted as reporting how the divine Creator shaped and animated the preexisting matter, as Justin taught against the Biblical tradition (*apol.* 1.20 and 41, *dial.* 5). The solution offered by the Gnostics, who ascribed the existing world to a divine creator of minor dignity or even evil intention, thus limiting the activity of the Supreme God to the realm of the intelligible, could not serve as the basis of a lasting social order and of its set of ethical values. Finally, in the fourth century, Gregory of Nyssa explicitly ascribed the creation of an infinite potential to the Biblical Creator. But at the same time, he holds that the perfectly rational order of the present universe and all its further unfolding has already been prearranged in that potential. Creation began when God made the inexhaustible potential and all its possibilities, which meet the requirements of perfect rationality. Creation has been continuing ever since, for reality is always unfolding according to that infinite potential. Thus the sharp contrast between the condition of matter before and after the act of creation, as expounded in the *Timaeus*, was considerably softened, as was the Biblical concept of creation out of nothing initiated and executed by the incomprehensible will of God, who does not limit his activity by any rules or laws which the human intellect can, at least partly, ascertain. This idea of creation had never been admitted in philosophical cosmology (Plat. *Tim.* 30A; Aristot. *cael.* 279b32; Xenocr. fr. 54 Heinze). Gregory did not introduce the notion of a divine will, freely and unpredictably interfering with the cosmic process, in order to describe the incomprehensibility of the act of creation. In this particular detail we note a remarkable difference between his cosmology and his brother's. The incomprehensibility of God's activity is merely an aspect of the infinite potential represented by His creation which is, in itself, perfectly rational (Basil, *Homélies sur l'hexaéméron*, ed. S. Giet [Paris 1949], Introduction pp. 30f with further references).

Another essential detail of Christian belief which was incompatible with philosophical cosmology referred to the resurrection of Christ and its soteriological interpretation. Here even Justin freely admitted that no explanation in terms of philosophical doctrine was available (*apol.* 1.19), and simply quoted Luke 18:27: "The things which are impossible with men are possible with God."

26. Orig. *c. Cels.* 6.53ff, cf. 5.14.

27. Heraclides Ponticus (fr. 49/50 Wehrli), however, argued the other way: divine power can be seen from the fact that God is able to produce miracles against the rules of His own creation and without abolishing them for the future. This doctrine was quite unusual in fourth-century philosophy. Cf. F. Wehrli, *Schule des Aristoteles* 10 (1959) 112.

28. Orig. *c. Cels.* 4.23 and 7.45; cf. 3.44, 55, and 59.

29. Dörrie, *NAWG* 2 (1967) 23–55, esp. 36–41. The concept of ἄρρητος δύναμις (ineffable power; i.e., incomprehensible to reason and therefore not necessarily expressing the perceived natural order) clearly points to the limitations of an entirely intellectualistic approach to both ontological and ethical problems.

30. Orig. *c. Cels.* 6.78f. This remained an important point in polemical and apologetic theology. St. Ambrose, for instance, insists on the fundamental

congruity between the Christian doctrine and the *philosophia barbarorum* (*ep.* 37.34 36).

31. It is hardly mere coincidence that the first Christian to attack Greek philosophy in a way similar to Galen's and Celsus' opposition to the Judaeo-Christian tradition belongs to exactly the same period, that is to say the seventies of the second century. Unlike his teacher Justin, Tatian insisted on the incompatibility between Plato and Moses and tried to demonstrate, in his *Oratio ad Graecos*, that the Greek philosophers surreptitiously took some pieces of wisdom from the writings of Moses who had lived, after all, no less than 400 years before the Trojan War (ad. Graec 31). On the exact date of Tatian, see Clarke, *HThR* 60 (1967) 123.

32. Diodorus (34.1.3), Horace (*sat.* 1.4.143, 5.100, 9.70), Quintilian (*inst.* 3.7.21), Tacitus (*hist.* 5.4f), Juvenal (*sat.* 14.103ff), and of course, many passages in Philo and Josephus testify to a widespread antijudaism of educated people in the early imperial period. Its main justification was the alleged misanthropy and xenophobia of the Jews. Hostility and distrust towards the Jews is referred to as a normal attitude, quite incidentally, in a private letter dating from A.D. 41 (*BGU* 1079).

33. Cf. Dörrie (above n. 29) 24. In the language of Plato, however, σωτηρία (salvation) in that spiritual sense demands an explanatory addition (σωτηρία τῆς ψυχῆς: salvation of the soul, *Leg.* 909A). Σωτηρία in the sense of physical health, maintenance of physical integrity, did not disappear from either spoken or written language during the imperial period, as can be seen, for instance, from private letters: *CPh* 22 (1927) 243 (2nd century A.D.), *BGU* 423 (2nd century A.D.), P. Ox. 939 (4th century A.D.).

34. Cf. H. Dörrie in *Le néoplatonisme* (1969) 17ff.

35. Cf. Verdenius, *Phronesis* 12 (1967) 91–97.

36. It is still an open question when the problem of the transcendence of the Supreme Being started to be systematically investigated again in scholarly or professional philosophy and, above all, when the method of "negative theology," first attested in Albinus' *Didascalicus* (10), was developed. See below n. 36.

The problem which Plato denoted by the formula ἐπέκεινα τῆς οὐσίας (*Rep.* 508B / 509A) was extensively treated in the Early Academy by Speusippus, Xenocrates, and others, in connection with supposedly Pythagorean doctrines. I need not enter into the much vexed question of whether and to what extent Plato's own "unwritten doctrine," especially his lecture περὶ τἀγαθοῦ (On the Good), had already given a detailed treatment, as the partisans of Plato's *Ungeschriebene Lehre* try to demonstrate (cf. the useful collection of testimonies given by K. Gaiser, *Platos ungeschr. Lehre* [1963] 446–556). Harold Cherniss' prudent analysis of Aristot. *met.* 987a29ff still offers the best guidance towards a possible distinction between Plato and his immediate successors on the basis of Aristotle's testimony (*Aristotle's Criticism of Plato*[2] [1946] esp. 170–198). The outcome of this intensive speculation, however, can be described, regardless of all differences between individual philosophers, sects, and groups, along the following lines: the source or, to use a different metaphor, the summit of reality is the One, which unites and thus transcends every kind of relativity and all sorts of contrast the human mind can grasp either by evaluating sense perception or by using its own speculative abilities. The One also precedes the split between perceiving and perceived by which intellectual cognition is conditioned. Consequently, the One is not open to full rational understanding. It cannot become the content of knowledge. The human mind can only get in touch with the One, by becoming aware, through its own effort, of the first step of differentiation that causes the unfolding of reality. Aristotle was fully aware of the possibility that the Supreme Being is beyond any kind of intellectual perception. Ὁ θεὸς ἢ νοῦς ἐστιν (god is either mind)—and consequently, open to intellectual cognition—ἢ ἐπέκεινά τι τοῦ νοῦ (or something beyond the realm of the mind), he wrote in his lost treatise *On Prayer* (fr. 49 Rose). Later on, in Neoplatonic ontology, ἐπέκεινα τοῦ νοῦ (beyond the realm of the mind) became a standard predication of the One (Plot. 5.3.13; Porph. *sent*. 25; Iul. *or*. 11.3 Lacombrade). But Aristotle's own ontology, which was being worked out with permanent and special regard to the doctrine of the early Academy and its Pythagorean elements, superseded the problem of transcendence as formulated and discussed, on the basis of Plato's Theory of Forms, in the Academy. Chiefly with the aid of his elaborate concept of potentiality and his theory of the nature and origin of motion, Aristotle succeeded in designing a model of reality of which even the summit was open to a full rational understanding. In doing so he created, to a large extent, the basis for the materialistic systems of the great Hellenistic schools, though remaining, in his doctrine of spirit and matter, a loyal Platonist. Still, according to the Aristotelian concept of reality, ideas such as indirect knowledge of the Supreme Being, intellectual contact with the One as distinguished from its intellectual cognition, the turning of one's mind towards the unattainable summit of being, did not make much sense. But all these ideas indicate neuralgic points where either the ultimate cause of being or the ultimate goal of human life can no longer be spoken of in terms of intellectual activity. The notion of will, however, had not yet been invented at that time. Negative theology, as expounded by Albinus and later Platonists, is only one of the methods to circumvent the concept of will in the field of ontology.

   The question of the transcendent, as posed by the early Academy and superseded by Aristotle, seems to have been present throughout the Hellenistic period in a lower stratum of philosophical speculation. Pseudo-Archytas (Stob. 1 p. 279 W.H. = ps.-Pythag. p. 19 Thesleff) holds that the One, as the ultimate cause of everything, transcends both Being and Thought. Therefore it cannot be grasped by the human intellect nor defined, in its creative power, as Supreme Intellect. (Supreme Will would have been the adequate term to speak of what the author had in mind, but the term was not available.) All attempts to assess the exact period to which the extant pieces of pseudo-Pythagorean literature belong have failed so far (cf. *EntrFondHardt* 18 [1971] 23–102). But the early first century A.D. does not seem too unlikely for the treatise in question (T. A. Szlezák, *Pseudo-Archytas* [1972]), and there can hardly be any doubt that this sort of literature was also being produced before the revival of Platonic dogmatism in the first century B.C.

In the scholarly or "official" tradition of Platonic philosophy the problem of transcendence or at least some of its aspects reappear, for the first time to our knowledge, in a fragment of the Alexandrian Platonist Eudorus, that is to say in the last decades of the first century B.C. (Simplic. *in Arist. Phys.* p. 181.10 Diels; cf. Dodds, *CQ* 22 [1928] 129ff). He taught that the pair of μονάς and ἀόριστος δυάς (monad and undefined duality, respectively), which provides the basis of being and perception, draws its existence from the One (ἕν), which, consequently, is beyond both being and perceiving.

Eudorus, however, gives no hint of the system of negative theology so prominent in Albinus and later Platonists. On the other hand, Philo of Alexandria makes extended use of that method in trying to show that Yahveh cannot be adequately spoken of in terms of human language nor become the content of human knowledge (*somn.* 1.67, *deus imm.* 11, *rer. div. her.* 187, etc.). It has been held that Philo invented the method of negative theology in order to make explicit, in terms of philosophical investigation, his belief in the God of his people. But it seems highly unlikely that official Platonism as represented by people like Albinus took over any important detail from Philo or any other Jewish theologian (cf. Dillon, "The Transcendence of God in Philo," Colloquium, Berkeley 1974). Presumably the concept of negative theology had already been systematized, in the Platonic school, before Philo's lifetime. The few pieces of information about Eudorus' metaphysical doctrine do not contradict the hypothesis that it was, in fact, Eudorus who introduced negative theology into the programme of Academic teaching.

37. Dörrie, *Der kl. Pauly* 4.942.

38. Cf. Wolfson, *HCSPh* 56/57 (1947) 233–249.

39. Cf. Whittaker, *SO* 44 (1969) 109–124.

40. Orig. *c. Cels.* 6.64. Perhaps Origen did not render the formulation of Celsus quite correctly, since God is not without any contact with being in the view of contemporary Platonic theology. Cf. Dörrie, *NAWG* 2 (1967) 46. Yet the congruity of thought and being is drastically restricted in consequence of the underlying concept, at least with regard to God.

41. Cf. Whittaker, *VChr* 23 (1969) 91–104, and H. Dörrie, *Gregor von Nyssa* (1976) 21ff. For the Platonic origin of that idea (*Rep.* 501B) see Krämer, *AGPh* 59 (1969) 1ff.

42. A. J. Festugière, *Hermès Trismégiste* III (1953) 109ff, has brilliantly shown the importance of the voluntaristic component in the Hermetic doctrine. First and foremost, man has to become a convert (μετανοεῖν *Corp. Herm.* 1.28) and to turn his attention to the divine message (4.4). The human soul, though still lost in the darkness of ignorance, is able to perform this turning to the message (4.4f), above all if supported by ascetic practice (9.10 and 11.21). Thus the act of will precedes the acquisition of knowledge on which salvation depends (μαθεῖν θέλω, ἀκοῦσαι βούλομαι, ποθῶ ἀκοῦσαι 1.7; βαπ-

τισθῆναι βούλομαι 4.6; θέλω ἀκοῦσαι καὶ βούλομαι νοῆσαι 13.1;15 [I want to learn, I wish to hear, I long to hear, I wish to be baptised, I want to hear and I wish to know]). The way towards salvation or immortality is described as τὸ δὲ δύνασθαι γνῶναι καὶ θελῆσαι καὶ ἐλπίσαι ὁδός ἐστιν εὐθεῖα (the ability to know and to wish and to hope is a straight road 9.21). Salvation itself depends on knowledge, but cognition that leads to knowledge is initiated by an act of will which is unmistakably pointed to by the aorist forms. Sometimes that act of will is answered by the intervention of the divine Nous, so that the faithful may even gain his salutary knowledge by sudden illumination (1.22.12/14). That is why faith is spoken of so frequently in Hermetic preaching (1.32, 4.4, 11.1 etc.). The act of will, so badly needed in order to set foot on the path that leads to full knowledge, which is, after all, the only possibility for salvation, presupposes faith. It has to be performed by the human soul when it is still intellectually blind and unable to perceive the object of its confidence (4.9).

In spite of the vital importance of will in this context, no Hermetic teacher ever worked out a coherent theory of will with an appropriate terminology. Concepts, notions, and terms used in that philosophy originate from the Platonic tradition, where such a theory did not make any sense. The sovereignty of the Supreme Being in the cosmic hierarchy (νοῦς τῆς αὐθεντίας 1.2) is not pointed out, in the Hermetic corpus, in terms of a theory of will either. In this respect, Hermetism sticks to the intellectualistic tradition of Greek thought.

According to a curious doctrine of the Hermetics, God wants to save every soul, and every soul is, by its nature, capable of being saved. Yet only a few men turn out to be worth receiving the salutary revelation. Of course, everybody is considered lost and ignorant in his empirical condition (*Corp. Herm.* 1.26; Ascl. 29; cf. Iambl. *vit. Pyth.* 17.72). Again, no attempt is made to clarify this religious belief in the election of the few by a theory of will.

43. A. J. Festugière, *Personal Religion* (1954) 109.

44. Catanzaro, *CanadJournTheol* 9 (1963) 166–173; Moran, *CatholBibl-Quart.* 25 (1963) 77–87; Kuyper, *Interpretation* 1 (1947) 490ff.

45. Botterweck, *"Gott erkennen" im AT*, Bonn. Bibl. Beitr. 2 (1951).

46. "Thoughts" in this passage corresponds to Hebrew maḥšᵉbōt, which has the connotation of both cognition or deliberation and volition, very much like βούλησις or βουλήματα in Greek. The term is rendered by βουλαί in the Septuagint.

47. This idea is repeatedly referred to in the Old Testament (e.g. Isa. 13:19; Wisd. of Sol. 1:3 and 9:17). Wisd. of Sol. 24:29 the plans of Yahveh are said to come from a deep abyss. The same image occurs, however, in Aeschyl. (Suppl. 1057f) who also speaks of the "dusky ways of Zeus" (Suppl. 87f). For further parallels see Wartelle, *BAG* 13 (1967) 373–383.

48. Gen. 1:31 and 8 passim; Ps. 8:4, 19 passim and 46:9; Isa. 42:5; Dan. 4:32; Wisd. of Sol. 13:3.

49. G. v. Rad, *Weisheit in Israel* (1970).

50. In the language of Christian piety the difference between the two kinds of knowledge was continuously made explicit. Knowledge from revelation is

different from wisdom acquired by man's own cognitive effort. The origin of the former is described in Eph. 1:9: γνωρίσας (sc. ὁ θεὸς) ἡμῖν τὸ μυστήριον τοῦ θελήματος αὐτοῦ (God makes known to us the mystery of his will). This knowledge, however, has been bestowed on the believers as a divine gift and is, therefore, "full" or "complete" (Eph. 1:7 κατὰ τὸ πλοῦτος τῆς χάριτος αὐτοῦ ἧς ἐπερίσσευεν εἰς ἡμᾶς ἐν πάσῃ σοφίᾳ καὶ φρονήσει: according to the wealth of his grace which he lavishes on us in all wisdom and knowledge), whereas human knowledge is deficient (1 Cor. 1:25 and 13:9; Col. 2:3). That is why Leontius (*vit. Sym.* p. 152 Rydén) disqualified γνῶσις καὶ σοφία (knowledge and wisdom) which the great Origen, though a heretic, undoubtedly possessed, as οὐκ ἐκ θεοῦ ἀλλὰ φυσικὸν πλεονέκτημα (an advantage not from God but from nature). On the other hand, σοφία ἐκ θεοῦ, wisdom from God, can be bestowed on a man simply by the very fact of his formally entering monastic life (σοφίζεσθαι p. 134.28). An apparently formulaic prayer which has been inserted in the narrative of the same *Life* calls the same knowledge by the term ἐπίγνωσις . . . τῆς ἁγίας . . . τριάδος, knowledge of the Holy Trinity, which already occurs in the Septuagint (Prov. 1:5), and was continuously used in Christian language, from the first century A.D. onwards, to denote the direct, supranatural cognition of God and His will (Rom. 10:2; 1 Clem. 59.2; Tat. *or.* 13; Diogn. 10.1; Sim. Mag. *ap.* Hippol. *ref.* 6.19, etc.). In ordinary Greek, especially in the terminology of science and philosophy, words like ἐπίγνωσις and ἐπίνοια usually refer to some sort of indirect and indistinct knowledge that has been acquired by means of inference from sense perception and may even belong to the natural equipment of the human soul in its empirical condition. Aristotle, for instance, ascribed the early ἐπίνοια of the gods, which is now present in every human soul, to those who first realized the order and magnificence of the universe. Drawing a conclusion from their being overwhelmed, they came to an indistinct knowledge of the existence of the divine (fr. 11 Rose). According to orthodox Stoic doctrine, ἐπίνοια, though some sort of knowledge at man's disposal, never results entirely from intellectual activity. It depends on direct sense perception (περίπτωσις *SVF* 2.88). In Plotinus, ἐπίγνωσις denotes the indistinct feeling of affinity to the intelligible which every soul has been given and which precedes and stimulates intellectual activity (3.5.1.18). The same can be called ἐπίνοια, which also means some sort of secondary knowledge that derives from the primary or direct one (5.8.7.42) which results from direct intellectual perception.

The difference between Christian and non-Christian usage seems to me very noteworthy in this particular detail.

51. Meijering, *NederlArchvKerkGesch* 53 (1973) 147.

52. H. W. Wolff, *Anthropologie des AT*,[2] (1974) 68–95, esp. 87ff.

53. E.g. Aesch. *Suppl.* 93ff and Soph. *Trach.* 1275ff.

54. Isa. 1:19: obedience of Israel to the commandments of God; Job 39:9: obedience of animals to man.

55. The same idea occurs also in earlier Stoicism (Chrysippus ap. Epict. *diss.* 2.6.9 = *SVF* 3.191).

56. Cf. Sen. *nat. quaest.* 2.24.2 and 7.27.6; M. Ant. 10.24. Thus the voluntary motion (κίνησις προαιρετική) of the heavenly bodies is not arbitrary but regular and predictable (Cleom. *de mot. circ.* p. 150.24 Ziegler).

57. Characteristically enough, Gregory of Nyssa, the most learned Platonist among the Fathers, stresses the rational aspect of God's plans and arrangements (οἰκονομία) for leading mankind through history to salvation. In his view the will of God has to be perfectly rational. His incomprehensibility is not due to a lack of rationality but only to the weakness of the human intellect (*de anim.* 11–16=*PG* 46.105A; *in cant. cant.* p. 144f Langerbeck).

58. For this problem in general see D. Hill, *Greek Words and Hebrew Meanings* (1967). He concentrates, however, on soteriological terms.

CHAPTER II

1. The indispensability of a distinct concept of will in modern philosophical thought has been convincingly demonstrated by Hardie, *Philos. Quart.* 21 (1971) 194–206.

2. E.g. Shakespeare, *Troilus and Cressida* II 61ff

> I take to-day a wife, and my election
> Is led on in the conduct of my will;
> My will enkindled by mine eyes and ears,
> Two traded pilots 'twixt the dangerous shores
> Of will and judgement. How may I avoid,
> Although my will distaste what I elected,
> The wife I chose?

Or *Romeo and Juliet* II 27f

> Two such opposed foes encamp them still
> In man as well as herbs, grace and rude will.

Or Goethe, *Hermann und Dorothea* 1.85f

> Denn was Verstand und Vernunft nicht immer vermögen,
> vermag oft
> Solch' ein glücklicher Hang, der unwiderstehlich uns
> leitet

Thomas Rosenmeyer drew my attention to the first quotation.

3. E. R. Dodds, *Greeks and the Irrational*[3] (1959) 6 and 105. For the early Greeks see H. Fränkel, *Dichtung u. Phil. d. fr. Griechentums* (1962) 87f and 446. The absence of the concept of will in Greek moral philosophy is also discussed by Franz Dirlmeier in his commentary on Aristotle's *Nicomachean Ethics* (1956) 327f.

4. See above Chapter I, n. 2 with App. I and Joüon, *RecSR* 30 (1940) 227–238. At *Il.* 6.522 Hector blames Paris for his conduct: you are a qualified warrior (ἄλκιμος), but you shrink from the fight voluntarily (ἑκὼν μεθιεῖς) and you are not prepared (οὐκ ἐθέλεις) to enter the battle. The contrast

of θέλω and βούλομαι comes out most clearly in Eur. *Alc.* 281 λέξαι θέλω σοι πρὶν θανεῖν ἃ βούλομαι, "I am willing to tell you before I die what I wish."

5. Cf. *Il.* 20.250; Hes. *op.* 721; *Alc.* 341 L.P.; Eur. *Med.* 600, 614, etc. Later on there was no difference in meaning between θέλω and βούλομαι, cf. Epict. *diss.* 2.14.7.

6. See also Hdt. 1.32.1 or Heraclit. B 32. In the language of cult and religion, θέλω, without further specification, can describe the suitable attitude of God and man (Aesch. *Suppl.* 144f):

θέλουσα δ᾽ αὖ θέλουσαν ἁγνά
μ᾽ ἐπιδέτω Διὸς κόρα

(Let Zeus' holy daughter look affectionately on my devotion.)

The graciousness and benevolence of the goddess and the devotion of the praying woman are pointed to by the same term. In a similar way, χάρις can denote the right attitude of both the giver and the receiver of a gift.

7. Cf. Coulon, *RhM* 103 (1960) 116. The difference between various verbs of volition in classical Attic can be ascertained most clearly in Plato's *Protagoras* (341D) where Socrates says: I am prepared (ἐθέλειν) to explain what Simonides wants (διανοεῖσθαι) to convey in his poem, if you have decided (βούλεσθαι) to test my ability to handle ancient poetry. Διανοεῖσθαι is the intention of the author as seen from the content and the meaning of his work, ἐθέλειν the willingness of a man who has no objections against the intentions of others, and βούλεσθαι refers to both decision and foregoing deliberation.

8. Snell, *Phil. Untersuchungen* 29 (1924); Fritz, *CPh* 38 (1943) 79ff, 40 (1945) 223ff, 41 (1946) 12ff; Zucker, in *Studies to Robinson* (1949) 1064ff. G. Jäger, *Nus* (1967) gives an extensive survey of the prephilosophical use of νοεῖν, νοῦς and διάνοια. He argues that Plato kept the traditional unity of cognition and intention in his theory of moral action, especially in the *Gorgias*. Yet, in the view of Plato, cognition which leads to right action refers to the eternal forms rather than to the details of the given situation in practical life (172f). For words of basically intellectualistic meaning used to denote intention in archaic and classical Greek see, e.g., *Il.* 4.361 (εἰδέναι), Pind. *Nem.* 5.18 (νοεῖν), Inscription of Darius I, dated 494 B.C., *SIG*[3] 22 (νοῦς), Hipp. *de aer.* 16 and Isaeus 1.7 (γνώμη), Eur. *Alc.* 1080 (γιγνώσκειν).

9. This even applies to the metaphorical usage of προαίρεσις in the sense of "literary style," for the underlying idea is that of a deliberate choice of stylistic means. That is why προαίρεσις, in this sense, is used as a synonym of βούλησις. (E.g. Dion.Hal. *de Dem.* 3.) The contrast between deliberate choice and unaffected speaking is referred to in Dion.Hal. *de Isocr.* 3: πέφυκεν ἡ Λυσίου λέξις ἔχειν τὸ χαρίεν, ἡ δὲ Ἰσοκράτους βούλεται, "Lysias' discourse naturally contains the pleasant element, but Isocrates consciously cultivates this element." The same distinction can be made in the description of human behavior: Ἐγὼ πέφυκά τ᾽ εὐσεβεῖν καὶ βούλομαι, "I am by nature and deliberation pious," says Theonoe in Euripides' *Helen* (998).

10. Λῶ in the language of Doric laws has, in fact, the implication not only of willingness but also of intention (e.g. *Leg.Gort.* 2.35 and 3.18). The same, however, applies to θέλω in the legal usage of other dialects, as can be seen from the inscription in Schwyzer, *Exempla* no. 619 (Mytilene) where θέλων corresponds to Attic ἐκ προνοίας. But even apart from legal usage θέλω sometimes has a strong connotation of volition in non-Attic dialects. Heraclitus, for instance, uses this word to refer to the totality of emotional striving: θυμῷ μάχεσθαι χαλεπόν· ὅ τι γὰρ ἂν θέλῃ, ψυχῆς ὠνεῖται: "It is difficult to war with the spirit, for whatever it wishes it buys at the expense of life" (B 85).

11. Γενναῖον λῆμα (Pind. *Pyth.* 8.45); εὐπόλεμον λῆμα ψυχῆς (Simonid. fr. 140 P.); οὐκ ἄτολμον λῆμα (Ar. *nub.* 457 lyr.); λῆμα θούριον (Aristoph. *equ.* 756f lyr.); λήματος πλέος (Hdt. 5.111); λήματι τῶν αὐχεῖ Θεσπιὰς εὐρύχορος (Epigram on the Thespians who were killed at Thermopylae: *Griech. Versinschriften* 5 Peek) "courage"; λήματος κάκη (Soph. *El.* 1427; Aesch. *Sept.* 616) or κακὸν λῆμα (Eur. *Alc.* 723) "cowardice"; ὠμὸν λῆμα (Soph. *Ant.* 471) "harshness"; ἔσχε . . . μεγάλαν ἀνάταν . . . λῆμα Κορωνίδος (Pind. *Pyth.* 3.25) "desire"; θυμέ . . . , κάτισχε λῆμα καὶ σθένος θεοστυγές (*Neophr. Tr. G. F.* 15 F 2.4) "fury"; ἀπότομον λῆμα (Eur. *Alc.* 981) "recklessness."

12. I prefer Bernays' τὰ αἴσιμα to Diels' τὸ πλίγμα for τὸ αἴνιγμα of the manuscript tradition.

13. The same applies to the use of τλῆναι in Attic tragedy and elsewhere. Cassandra has freely and knowingly decided to die (Aesch. *Ag.* 1246) πράξω, τλήσομαι τὸ καὶ θανεῖν, "I shall do it, I shall have the courage even to die," and Medea (Eur. *Med.* 796) calls the deliberate murder she is going to τλῆναι . . . ἔργον ἀνοσιώτατον, dare an utterly unholy deed.

14. Τοσόν δ' ἔχεις τόλμης πρόσωπον, "you show so great a façade of daring" (Soph. *O.T.* 533; cf. Aesch. *Choeph.* 585ff) against τὰ μέγιστ' ἀέθλων ἕλη τόλμα τε καὶ σθένει: he wins the greatest of prizes by his daring and strength (Pind. *Pyth.* 10.24; Pindar never uses τόλμα in a bad sense).

15. Τόλμη ἀλόγιστος: irrational daring (Thuc. 3.82); τόλμη ἄφρων: mindless daring (Plat. *Lach.* 193D); τόλμη καὶ ἀναίδεια: ruthless daring (Antiph. 3.3.5); τόλμης ἔργα καὶ ἀναισχυντίας: deeds of shameless daring (Ar. *Thesm.* 702). Cf. also Aesch. *Choeph.* 594ff.

16. Schol. Aesch. *Pers.* 12; Scipio is said to have sacrificed to Τόλμα (App. *Lib.* 21); cf. Pythag. ap. Plut. *Is. et Osir.* 381E/F.

17. E.g. Luc. *Men.* 14, where τὰ τετολμημένα, deeds dared, is synonymous with τὰ ἁμαρτήματα, errors. See below p. 100f. on τόλμα in Gnostic terminology.

18. Cf. D. L. Page ad Eur. *Med.* 1028.

19. Cf. Wilamowitz and Barrett *ad loc.*; Willink, *CQ* 62 (1968) 11ff. I have learned much in dealing with the problem from a paper given by Dr. Manuwald (Saarbrücken).

20. Erffa, Αἰδώς, *Philologus* Suppl. 30 (1937). Hesiod seems to have been the first to distinguish between the two aspects of αἰδώς (*op.* 317–319).

21. Solmsen, *Hermes* 101 (1973) 420–425 where Eur. *Hipp.* 372 is illustrated with parallels from Thucydides.

22. Cf. Wilamowitz *ad* Eur. *Hipp.* 384.

23. Much material has been collected by R. B. Onians, *Origins of European Thought* (1951).

24. Cf. U.v. Wilamowitz, *Gr. Lesebuch* II² 282 (1926). The passage has been preserved in Oribasius' medical encyclopaedia (3.22).

25. In early anthropological theories, the Greeks tended to attribute tenacity and stubbornness, that is to say qualities of the human will in the modern view, to the irrational part of man's personality. They are produced, according to early medical theories, by nutrition and similar factors in human life (Hippocr. *de regim.* 1.35f), very much as fortitude is (Hippocr. *de aer.* 87). Basically Plato had the same view.

26. For a collection of examples see Fränkel (above n. 3) 85ff. Comprehensively J. Böhme, *Die Seele im Epos* (1929).

27. H. W. Wolff, *Anthropologie des AT*² (1974) 57ff and 68ff.

28. In most cases the etymology of the psychological term remains obscure.

Θυμός has been explained by the phonological analogy of lat. *fumus* (Frisk, *Etym. Wörterb.* 1.694) which leads to the idea of hot or accelerated respiration as the physical medium or physical appearance of emotion, strong feelings, and drive towards action. Such a theory can be validated by the fact that respiration is frequently identified with the *vis vitalis*, the cause of motion, life, and activity, and θυμός is, in fact, also used to denote the self of man in the sense of his vitality (B. Snell, *Tyrtaios* [1969] 9ff). Still, there are some well-founded doubts as to the reliability of such an etymology (Chantraine, *Dict. étym.* II 1.446), which disregards the verb θύω "to move quickly." W. Schulze (*Quaest. epicae* 313) even postulated two etymologically different words θυμός, in order to explain the meaning "anger" which is, after all, well attested in Homer alongside "emotion, drive." On the other hand it is not difficult to assume that the first only derived from the second by way of specialization.

Yet there is no doubt about the main psychological connotation of θυμός: it does not denote, in Homeric and later Greek, the seat of emotion but emotion itself, regardless of whether or not one has to think, at least in early Greek, of an underlying substance or part of the body. Homer (like later authors) often speaks of the location of θυμός: it can be found in the φρένες (see below pp. 26) or in the breast (στῆθος/στήθεα). Being the cause of human activity, it tends to be understood as the *vis vitalis* of the living individual, which disappears at the moment of death (*Il.* 3.294), and to which moral and non-moral qualities can be attached, e.g. μεγαλήτωρ (great-hearted), ἄναλκις (ineffective), ἄγριος (savage), κακός (evil). The individual can even externalize his own θυμός in the course of self-examination: Odysseus and others speak πρὸς ὃν μεγαλήτορα θυμόν (to his great-hearted spirit, *Il.* 11.411) when they have to make up their mind.

The original meaning of ἦτορ is very likely to have been "belly, intestines" (Chantraine, *Dict. étym.* 1.418), which is regarded as the seat of temper or mood in many archaic cultures. In Homer, however, its meaning comes very near to that of θυμός and there is no indication that it is still felt as referring to a part of the human body. On the contrary, it is frequently said to be located in the heart (κραδία), in the φρένες, or in the breast (στήθεα). Sometimes impulses or emotions originate from the ἦτορ (*Il.* 21.571f ἦτορ ἄλκιμον ὡρμᾶτο; *Il.* 16.509 a.o. ὡρίνθη δὲ οἱ φίλον ἦτορ; cf. *Od.* 17.46 and 1.316 φίλον ἦτορ ἀνώγη; *Od.* 1.60 ἐντρέπεται φίλον ἦτορ [he was stirred in his strong heart]) and consequently, as in the case of θυμός, it functions as *vis vitalis*, which is absent from the dead body (*Il.* 5.250, 11.115, and 21.114). Yet more frequently ἦτορ points to temper, mood, emotional disposition rather than to emotion or impulse towards action (τεταρπομένοι φίλον ἦτορ [delighted in their hearts] *Il.* 3.705 etc.; ἀκηχεμένη φίλον ἦτορ [pained in her heart] *Il.* 5.364 etc.; μινύθει δέ μοι ἔνδοθεν ἦτορ [my heart within wastes away] *Od.* 4.467 etc.; *Il.* 16.242 θαρσύνειν . . . ἦτορ [to encourage the heart]; cf. *Il.* 3.31). The predominance of this sense in the Homeric usage of ἦτορ may be due to its having originally denoted a definite part of the body. It also occasionally became one of the Homeric terms to denote comprehensively the dominant characteristic of a man (σιδήρειον ἦτορ [iron heart], *Il.* 24.205 etc.; ἀμείλιχον ἦτορ [hard heart], *hymn.* 28.2). Sometimes θυμός and ἦτορ are synonyms (e.g. *Il.* 11.555–557 . . . ἔβη τετιηότι θυμῷ | . . . τετιημένος ἦτορ | ἦιε [he went off with sorrowful heart]), as can also be seen from adjectives like μεγαλήτωρ (great-hearted) and μεγάθυμος (great-spirited), and there is always a fairly large semantic area where both overlap. Yet what seems to be the primary meaning of θυμός, that is to say emotion, impulse towards action, occurs as the derivative cr secondary meaning of ἦτορ—and vice versa, which accounts for their overlapping as well as for a largely different usage in the language of Homer.

Φρήν, φρένες must have meant, originally, a part of the body like αὐχήν (neck), σπλήν (spleen), ἀδήν (gland). The traditional explanation, diaphragm, has been severely doubted, for the connection with φράσσω (enclose, fence in) is difficult to verify (Frisk, *Etym. Wörterb.* 2.1041f). Onians (above n. 23) tried to show that the original meaning was "lungs." The theory has been further worked out by P. N. Lockhart, who found the old sense "to breathe" for φρονεῖν still present in Homer (*Il.* 11.324f and 16.758; cf. *CPh* 61 [1966] 99ff). All this is far from certain, and the part of the body originally meant by φρήν can hardly be identified on the basis of Homeric usage alone. Yet the local connotation of the word is still recognizable, for θυμός, νόος and ἦτορ are repeatedly said to be or to rise in the φρένες. On the other hand, the meaning of φρήν seems to have been specialized in the field of intellectual activity at a comparatively early stage, as can be gathered from the use of φρονεῖν and many words ending in –φρων. Intellectual activity, however, frequently produces action without any intermediate process according to early Greek anthropology, and since moral qualities become manifest only through action, the previous intellectual activity can be qualified in an exclusively moral way: hence strange expressions like μέγα φρονεῖν (to be haughty), ἤπια or ἄγρια εἰδέναι (to be tender or brutal-minded) and so forth. Intellectual activity is even able to produce emotion that leads to action, at least according to Ho-

meric psychology, and ὀλοόφρων (baneful), κερδαλεόφρων (greedy), ἄφρων
(senseless) imply a judgement which is passed, according to modern standards,
on both intellectual and moral qualities. In the Greek view, as can be seen
already in Homer, they are inseparably linked.

The etymology of νόος is equally unknown (Frisk, *Etym. Wörterbuch* 2.323
and suppl.), all theories proposed so far being mere guesswork. It belongs very
closely to νοέω, of which the sense stretches from seeing and perceiving to
thinking and reasoning and to planning and intending. There is no trace in
Homer that νόος was formerly attached to any part of the human body, nor has
any indication been discovered so far that the intellectual connotation might
be a secondary phenomenon in the history of the word. Νόος to denote the
intellectual and thus moral quality of a man seems to go back to the Mycenean
period, as can be seen from the proper name wi-pi-no-o ('Ιφίνοος [strong-
minded]; cf. Bader, *Rev de phil* 3 sér. 43 [1969] 18). Νόος can refer to the
individual plan or intention in a given situation as well as to intellectual capacity and activity in general, and even to a man's mentality as manifested in
his behavior. Odysseus, in his travels, got to know the νόος of people in various countries, that is to say the way in which they tended to act and react (*Od.*
22.3). Consequently the νόος that may be found ἐν στήθεσσι (*Od.* 13.255 etc.)
or μετὰ φρεσί (in the breast or diaphragm), *Il.* 18.419, is particularly open to
moral evaluation, with or without reference to a special occasion—ἀφραδίῃσι
νόοιο (disorientation of mind), *Il.* 10.122, νόος θεουδής (god-fearing mind),
Od. 8.576 etc., νόος οὐδὲν ἀεικής (a not unseemly mind) *Od.* 20.366 etc.; cf.
W. Jäger, *Nus* (1967) 3ff and 172f. Since the νόος is the instrument or even the
object of planning, it can cause intention and drive or be associated with the
impulse toward action: ἕνα θυμὸν ἔχοντε νόῳ καὶ ἐπίφρονι βουλῇ: "two having
one spirit, in intent and sagacious purpose" (*Od.* 3.128); τόνδε νόον καὶ θυμόν:
"this mind and spirit" (*Il.* 4.309); νόος μενοινᾷ: "his mind strives" (*Il.* 2.92).
Νόος and βουλή are almost synonyms (*Od.* 16.373), both being subject to
change (*Il.* 15.52 μεταστρέψειε νόον, "he changes his mind").

Despite the fairly large semantic area covered by each of them and the various zones of overlapping which are due to the presence of different historical
layers in the language of the poetic tradition, the words which express Homeric psychology are terminologically well defined, most of them being unmistakable even without a context. In Homeric language the presence of
rational and irrational forces in the human soul and their interaction is beau-
tifully and most accurately portrayed. The refinement of psychological analysis and description, however, hardly depends, in either ancient or modern poetry, on the existence of such a set of unequivocal terms.

29. Fränkel (above n. 3) 84–91.

30. The earliest testimonies are Xenophanes B 7, a reference to the
Pythagorean doctrine of metempsychosis, and Anacreon fr. 360 Page. Heraclitus' philosophy, however, already presupposes the concept.

31. Μετὰ φρεσὶ σῇσι νόησον | Αἰνείαν, ἤ κέν μιν ἐρύσσεαι ἤ κεν ἐάσῃς | . . .
δαμήμεναι: "Decide whether to save Aeneas or let him be slain" (*Il.* 20.310).

Νοέω . . . φρεσὶ . . . τιμήσασθαι: "I intend to honor" (*Il.* 22.235). Οὐ θήν μιν πάλιν αὖτις ἀνήσει θυμὸς ἀγήνωρ | νεικείειν βασιλῆας: "His θυμός won't drive him again to quarrel with the princes" (*Il.* 2.276). Εἴ σ' ὀτρύνει κραδίη καὶ θυμὸς ἀγήνωρ | τοῦτον ἀλέξεσθαι: "If your heart and your θυμός drive you to fight him" (*Od.* 18.61).

32. Where an act of deliberation, intellectual perception, or irritation really affects one's feelings and, above all, determines one's decision to do something, it is performed κατὰ φρένα καὶ κατὰ θυμόν. Ὁρμαίνειν *Il.* 1.193, 11.411, 17.106, 18.15; *Od.* 4.120, 5.365 and 424, 6.118; νοεῖν *Od.* 3.264; μερμηρίζειν *Il.* 5.671, 8.169; *Od.* 4.117, 10.151, 20.10, 24.235; φράζεσθαι *Il.* 15.163; *Od.* 1.294; οἶδα *Il.* 4.163, 6.163; *Od.* 5.211; ἐρέθω *Od.* 4.813.

33. It should be noted that θυμός not only gives the impulse to act but also provides the capacity of enduring hardships: Ὀδυσσεύς . . . τλήμονα θυμὸν ἔχων (the enduring spirit of Odysseus) (*Il.* 5.670). The same can be performed by the φρήν, as can be seen from the Homeric adjectives ταλάφρων and ταλασίφρων (stout-hearted).

34. At *Il.* 13.487f concord is described as ἕνα φρεσὶ θυμὸν ἔχοντες (having a single spirit in their hearts), whereas the immutable hostility of wolf and lamb (κακὰ φρονέοντες [wishing each other mischief]), is referred to in the words οὐχ ὁμόφρονα θυμὸν ἔχοντες (not having a similar spirit) (*Il.* 22.261ff). Both θυμός and φρένες (φρονεῖν, νόος etc.) can be used separately or in combination to form the comprehensive term for a way of behaving.

35. Cf. Snell (above n. 28) 8–20.

36. Cf. H. Lloyd-Jones, *Justice of Zeus* (1970) 9.

37. E.g. ἤπια οἶδεν (he acts kindly) (*Il.* 16.73; *Od.* 18.39 etc.); οὔ τινα οἶδε θέμιστα (he does not act properly) (*Il.* 2.761); φίλα ἀλλήλοισιν εἰδότες (acting in a friendly manner toward one another) (Hom. *hymn.* 29.12).

38. *Il.* 3.63; *Od.* 13.202, 15.190, and 21.206; *Il.* 15.461 etc.

39. On the volitional aspect of human action as pointed out in Greek tragedy see J. P. Vernant and P. Vidal-Naquet, *Mythe et tragédie en Grèce ancienne* (1977) 43–74.

40. Ἀμήχανον δὲ παντὸς ἀνδρὸς ἐκμαθεῖν | ψυχήν τε καὶ φρόνημα καὶ γνώμην, πρὶν ἂν | ἀρχαῖς τε καὶ νόμοισιν ἐντρίβῃς φανῇ. (It is impossible to understand the soul, purpose and intent of any man until he is ruling in government and law.)

41. The strange dictum of Heraclitus B 85, Θυμῷ μάχεσθαι χαλεπόν· ὅ τι γὰρ ἂν θέλῃ ψυχῆς ὠνεῖται, deserves further explanation. To struggle against one's own spontaneous impulses (ὅ τι ἂν—sc. ὁ θυμός—θέλῃ) is difficult, because one's whole vital or natural existence is at stake, which becomes manifest primarily through the motion of the θυμός. At the end of Aristophanes' *Frogs* (1467) Dionysus chooses Aeschylus—against his deliberate intention which he has explained at the beginning, and also against his opinion as a literary critic. He chooses ὅνπερ ἡ ψυχὴ θέλῃ, whom his soul desires. Ψυχή in the sense of vitality as opposed to intellect is well known in fifth-century Greek (cf. Soph. *Ant.* 707 φρονεῖν . . . ψυχὴν ἔχειν; Eur. *Alc.* 108). Democritus' re-

ply to Heraclitus (B 236) sounds very traditional or even trivial: θυμῷ μάχεσθαι χαλεπόν. ἀνδρὸς δὲ τὸ κρατεῖν εὐλογίστου (it is hard to war with the spirit;
but it is for a reasonable man to conquer it).

42. Γνώμη can denote, in a legal procedure, the formal assent given by a
person: μετὰ τῆς γνώμης τῆς ἑαυτοῦ (with his own assent), which implies both
recognition and intention (Isaeus 2.8; cf. Epicur. ap. D.L. 10.20). The same
can be said of the use of γνώμη, γιγνώσκω in post-classical Greek (e.g. Jos.
bell. Jud. 1.4.9; Luc. *deor. dial.* 10.1; *de mort. Per.* 27).

43. Antiph. *or.* 6.20; Xen. *Hell.* 3.1.12; Hdt. 8.60γ etc.; cf. P. Huart,
Γνώμη *chez Thucydide* (1972) and Schneider, *Information u. Absicht bei Thuk.*
(1974) with further references.

44. Theognis speaks of worthless people (53ff and 60; cf. 831f):

λαοὶ δὲ δὴ ἄλλοι
οἳ πρόσθ' οὔτε δίκας ᾔδεσαν οὐδὲ νόμους
οὔτε κακῶν γνώμας εἰδότες οὔτ' ἀγαθῶν.

(the people are different who before knew neither justice nor law nor difference
between good and bad.)

Instead of γνώμη, διάνοια too, with the very same intellectualistic implication,
can be used in this sense: e.g. Anon. Iambl. 6; Isocr. *antid.* 7 and 69; *adv.
Soph.* 14. Isocrates also has γνώμη in the same sense (*antid.* 71) and, of course,
προαίρεσις (*antid.* 118; see n. 46).

45. Cf. ps.-Xen. *resp. Athen.* 3.10.

46. Later on, προαίρεσις was mostly used in this sense, for it had been preferred by Aristotle and the philosophical tradition. Nevertheless, γνώμη, νοῦς,
φρόνημα and the like continued to be used to refer to moral attitude in general: see Dio Pr. *or.* 72.8; Lucian, *hist. conscr.* 38f and *Alex.* 3; ps.-Call. *hist.
Alex.* 3.6.14; Inscr. Antioch. Commag. *OGI* 383 and *IstanbForschg* 23 (1963)
40ff, which represent completely different layers of language. This also applies
to the language of philosophy (Cleanth. *SVF* 1.557; Clem. *strom.* 3.9 p.
226.24 and 6.15 p. 493.24 Stählin), and it can be said, in a non-moral sense,
of the general tendency of a text (e.g. Luc. *Lexiph.* 1; cf. βούλησις in the same
meaning Gal. *de temp.* 7 p. 54 Mü.).

47. Theogn. 963f:

μήποτ' ἐπαινήσῃς πρὶν ἂν εἴδῃ ἄνδρα σαφήνεως
ὀργὴν καὶ ῥυθμὸν καὶ τρόπον ὅστις ἂν ᾖ

Don't ever praise a man before you know clearly
what sort he is in temperament, spirit and manner

and a funerary epigr. from Chios, fifth century (Friedländer, *Epigrammata* 139)
ὀργῆς δ' ἀντ' ἀγαθῆς Εἰω[. . .]ης τόδε σῆμα αὐτῇ ἐπέστησεν: (Eu[. . .]es raises
this memorial to [. . .] for her sweetness). In archaic Greek, ὀργή and θυμός
were sometimes used as synonyms: both denoted a striving that results from
irrational impulses. In post-classical Greek, however, they became synonyms
as terms for "anger" (e.g. Polyb. 3.10.5).

48. The same can be seen from the fact that πρόφρων (e.g. Eur. *Alc.* 743) and πρόθυμος (e.g. Eur. *Hcld.* 410) are synonymous, both denoting the inclination to act.

49. A change of mind because of emotional factors is mostly, but not exclusively, called μεταμέλεια (Thuc. 3.36; Plat. *Phaedr.* 230E ff) as distinguished from μετάνοια and μεταγιγνώσκω. Frequently the gods cause a man to change his intention (Aesch. *Ag.* 218ff; Soph. *Ajax* 717; Eur. *Hipp.* 240f); this is called ἄτη if the change is for the worse. Thus ἄτη, which denotes a rather archaic concept in Greek religion (see below p. 33) and is used, therefore, predominantly in poetic texts, can be said of a change of intention in ordinary prosaic Greek of the classical period (Lyc. *c. Leocr.* 92).

50. Cf. Dodds, *PCPhS* 6 (1960) 19–31 = *Wege zu Aischylos* 2 (Darmstadt 1974) 149ff.

51. Dörrie, *AAWM* 5 (1956).

52. Cf. Gärtner, *Historia* Einz. 25 (1975) 170ff who rightly observes the same concentration on the intellectual performance in the tradition of Greek historiography.

53. Latte, *PW* 16 (1933) 278–289; D. M. MacDowell, *Athenian Homicide Laws* (1963) 59ff, 110ff; R. S. Stroud, *Drakon's Law* (1968). The terms to denote intention vary according to dialect, period, and occasion (ἐκ προνοίας, ἑκών / ἑκούσιος, θέλων, γνώμῃ etc.). For parallels in Biblical law see Daube, *RIDA* 2 (1949) 189–213.

54. E. Maschke, *Willenslehre im griech. Recht* (1926); C. W. Müller, *Kurzdialoge* (1975) 132 and 154ff; K. A. Neuhausen, *De voluntarii notione* (1967).

55. See the use of ἀγνόημα, δι' ἄγνοιαν, ἀγνωμονέω Dem. 19.101 and 18.94; *UPZ* 1.501.

56. Fr. 97 Wimmer = Stob. 4.2.20 p. 127ff W.H. Cf. K. F. Hermann and Th. Thalheim, *Griech. Rechtsaltertümer* (1884) 77; F. Pringsheim, *Greek Law of Sale* (1950) 134ff.

57. This was first observed by F. Zucker, in *Studies to Robinson* (1949) 1064ff, who referred to Diod. 11.45 and 20.45 and a decree of Ptolemaeus Philometor, *ArchfPap* 6 (1920) 10ff.

58. Cf. E. R. Dodds *ad* Eur. *Bacch.* 882 (Oxford 1944) and id. *ad* Plat. *Gorg.* 456A (Oxford 1959).

59. Aesch. *Sept.* 591ff; Simonid. fr. 542, 27–30 Page; Hdt. 6.86. Euripides contrasts ἁγνὸς χείρας and ἁγνὸς φρένας (pure in hand, pure in mind) *Or.* 1602f, and Democritus frequently dwells on this topic (B 62, 68, 79, 89, and 96), which is also used by the Attic orators (Lys. 3.42; Andocid. 1.95). The whole Isocratean theory of εὐβουλία rests on this idea: since man cannot possibly acquire a both realistic and comprehensive image of his world, his intellectual capacity being too limited, and since the actual course of events is always being determined by forces stronger than man, the only achievement that seems to be praiseworthy is εὐβουλία: using rightly one's intellectual fac-

ulties. The outcome may be beyond human control (*antid.* 285; cf. Hdt. 7.1082 and Thuc. 1.140.4).

60. J. Stallmach, *Ate* (1966) and Dawe, *HSCPh* 72 (1967) 89–127. Wherever the phenomenon of ἄτη is described in archaic or classical Greek literature, attention is concentrated on the intellectual and, consequently, moral or religious blindness of the person involved. Sometimes, the gods produce that blindness by extremely drastic measures, as in the case of Ajax, or that of Xerxes before the Greek campaign. When the heart of Pharaoh is hardened or stiffened according to the Biblical account (e.g. Ex. 9:12, 10:20; cf. Hesse, *ZAW* Beih. 74 [1955] 25f), intellectual blindness is regarded as the consequence rather than the content of the process (cf. Raisänen, *Publ. Finn. Exeg. Soc.* 25 [1975], who analyzes passages from the Bible and the Koran). The concept of ἄτη in Greek thought and that of hardening in the Biblical tradition are characteristically different with regard to their intellectualistic and voluntaristic implications (see below p. 75f).

61. This view of human action does not seem to be exclusively Greek; only the vocabulary of ethical and psychological speculation which classifies that condition is particularly refined and precise at nearly all stages in the history of the Greek language. In old Indo-Iranian, however, the intellectual accomplishment and the energy which lead to human action are always denoted together by one and the same word. Cf. K. Strunk in *Monumentum Nyberg II* (1975) 283ff with further references.

62. This can still be seen in the late use of εὔνους and εὔνοια, for instance in the context of political ideology. Cf. Schubart, *APF* 12 (1937) 8ff.

63. E.g. *Il.* 5.2 and 5.3; *Od.* 16.529.

64. The classical description of the results of μένος can be found in Diomedes' ἀριστεία (*Il.* 5.1ff).

65. See above.

66. The Homeric use of μένος deserves a detailed treatment. The old numinous connotation of the word is notable also in those passages where μένος is attributed to animals (e.g. *Il.* 3.294f). On the other hand, Hesiod describes Athena having the same μένος and the same planning intelligence (βουλὴ ἐπίφρων) as her father Zeus (theog. 896).

67. L. Gierth, "Gr. Gründungsgeschichten" (diss. 1972) 133–139. Another word which seems to denote will as resulting from a numinous *vis vitalis* in the Homeric language is ἰότης. M. Leumann, however, has shown that it owes its existence only to a misunderstanding (δη–ιότητι: *Homerische Wörter* [1950] 127f).

68. In some passages (e.g. *Il.* 24.198) it has already become a synonym of θυμός, and in the Hymn to Demeter (361) the original meaning has completely disappeared: ἤπιον ἐν στήθεσσι μένος καὶ θυμὸν ἔχοντα (having a gentle disposition in his chest).

69. E.g. Soph. *Ajax* 1065.

70. Cf. Arist. *rhet.* 1406a1.

71. E.g. schol. AB to *Il.* 5.2; schol. B to *Il.* 4.66, 19.202, and 22.459; *et. Magn.* p. 579.50 Gaisford; Suid. 3 p. 363.20 Adler. Plutarch (fr. 47 Sandbach) gives an etymology of εὐμενής which clearly shows his complete ignorance of the old concept of μένος. The benevolence of the gods is called τὸ εὐμενές because of τὸ μένειν ἡμῖν τὸ εὖ ἀεὶ παρὰ τῶν θεῶν: "the good that comes from the gods remains with us always."

72. E.g. *Il.* 10.100, 13.263, and 19.62. Δυσμενής in this particular meaning of external enemy of the political community survived in the legal terminology of several cities, e.g. of Argos (*SIG* 56) and Gortyn in Crete (*Leg. Gortyn.* 6.46).

73. First attested in Pindar, who also offers εὐμενία for the first time, Aeschylus, and in a minor Homeric hymn (22.7). This numinous connotation of μένος seems to have disappeared at a very early stage in the case of μενεαίνω, μενοινάω, μέμονα, which only denote, in the language of Homer, various kinds of strong impulse towards action.

74. The word occurs again in a versified inscription of the imperial period. Hesychius explains, without further information, the form εὐμενέτειρα as εὐμενής. Sometimes, however, even εὐμένεια, "benevolence," is explained in intellectualistic terms, as can be seen from Eur. *Alc.* 210f:

> οὐ γάρ τι πάντες εὖ φρονοῦσι κοιράνοις,
> ὥστ' ἐν κακοῖσιν εὐμενεῖς παρεστάναι.

> (not all men are so well disposed to their masters that
> they stand by them loyally in times of trouble)

75. See, above all, B 1, B 2, B 45, B 50.

76. This can be seen, for instance, from the text of ancient prayers, e.g. the hymn from Palaikastro (*BSA* 15 [1908] 339; cf. K. Latte, *Kl. Schriften* [1969] 49) and the Athenian prayer M. Ant. 5.7. See M. P. Nilsson, *Gesch. d. gr. Religion* I² (1974) 157–160 and Severus, *RAC* 8 (1972) 1134–1147.

77. Lloyd-Jones's (above n. 36) assertion, "that Zeus is important as the guardian of justice in Hesiod is obvious; that it is so in the Odyssey is very nearly as obvious" seems to me slightly misleading (85). There is little doubt that a number of moral standards are already enforced by Zeus in the Iliad, and an even greater number in the Odyssey (see my *Homer-Probleme* [Köln 1970] 163f). But I cannot find, in any of the Homeric poems, the concept of Zeus' universal rule over the world of which the main principle is justice—as in Hesiod.

78. Lloyd-Jones, 33–39.

79. A. Dihle, *Goldene Regel* (1962) 24f.

80. With reference to the course of human or historical events Thucydides had already expounded the moral consequences of two contradictory concepts: the Melians, in their debate with the Athenian delegates, refer to unpredictable chance as a typical means of divine rule (τὸ θεῖον), the Athenians claim to derive their standards from ἀναγκαία φύσις, universal necessity, which is unchangeable and predictable (5.104/105). Democritus admitted chance in

moral life only as the excuse of those who had acted without due prudence (B 119).

81. Democritus remarks rather dryly that many people act viciously though knowing the better, and vice versa (B 53/53A): πολλοὶ λόγον μὴ μαθόντες ζῶσι κατὰ λόγον· πολλοὶ δρῶντες τὰ αἴσχιστα λόγους ἀρίστους ἀσκέουσιν: "Many men, though unskilled in reasoning, live in accordance with reason; many, while they do most shameful deeds, are practiced in most excellent modes of argument."

82.

> Ὧιτινι μὴ θυμοῦ κρέσσων νόος, αἰὲν ἐν ἄταις,
> Κύρνε, καὶ ἐν μεγάλαις κεῖται ἀμηχανίαις.

This is sometimes experienced in the consciousness of the acting individual. Heracles reminds Admetus that his mourning cannot alter the situation. The answer is ἔγνωκα καὐτός, ἀλλ᾽ ἔρως τις ἐξάγει: "I myself know this, but a passion impels me" (Eur. *Alc.* 1079f).

83. The term ἀκρατής (ἀκράτεια), as used in moral philosophy from the time of Plato onwards, is but a special case within the much wider use of the words. It says that a man is not in control of his emotions as he ought to be according to his knowledge of the given situation. Θυμοῦ κρατεῖν, to overcome or control one's emotions, already occurs in Democritus (B 236). Outside that terminology, a talkative person can be called ἀκρατὴς τῆς γλώσσης (Aesch. *Prom.* 864), a paralytic ἀ. τοῦ σώματος (Hippocr. *pass.*), an alcoholic ἀ. τοῦ οἴνου (Xen. *oec.* 12.11). An old man has lost control of many things he used to master previously: this leads to the poetic expression γῆρας ἀκρατές, "impotent old age" (Soph. *O.C.* 1236).

84. Later on, Aristotle was to describe in great detail what this control should be like. The intellect (φρόνησις) has to prevent man from being deceived by emotions like anger or fear, which always imply, in contrast to entirely physical affections like pain, a definite conception of an object in the world outside. Whether this conception which motivates human action is right or wrong can only be ascertained by the intellect. Thus the intellect has to guide the natural or prerational impulse which is indispensable for any kind of action, but which should be given its direction by truth rather than error. Cf. F. Ricken, *Lustbegriff in der N.E.* (1975) 96ff, esp. 101f.

85. Current opinion on this subject was analyzed very clearly by Aristotle for forensic use (*rhet.* 1373b25ff): offenders in the sense of criminal law act either knowingly and intentionally (ἑκόντες / εἰδότες) or inadvertently, without knowing what they do (ἄκοντες, ἀγνοοῦντες). The first category can be subdivided into those who execute a preconceived plan (προελόμενοι) and those whose knowledge of the better is overpowered, in the given situation, by their emotion (διὰ πάθος).

86. The concept is frequently used by Aristotle, though with some new ingredients: J. Walsh, *Aristotle's Conception of Moral Weakness* (1963); Kenny, *Phronesis* 11 (1966) 163; R. Milo, *Aristotle on Practical Knowledge* (1966); San-

tas, *Phronesis* 14 (1969) 162. Aristotle, like others, distinguishes between ἀκράτεια, which denotes the state of mind when irrational impulses from the human soul have overwhelmed reason in a given situation, and ἀκρασία, "habitual intemperance," when the intellect, being weaker than the irrational forces of the soul, has already complied with them (*E.N.* 1147b22ff etc.).

87. That someone knows the moral standards that have to be applied to the given situation, and yet cannot make up his mind accordingly, not because of either being overpowered by his own emotion or simply coerced from outside, but because of a lack of confidence in the people he has to deal with, has been described most tellingly in the Odyssey (18.228ff). Telemachus is speaking to his mother:

αὐτὰρ ἐγὼ θυμῷ νοέω καὶ οἶδα ἕκαστα,
ἐσθλά τε καὶ τὰ χέρηα· πάρος δ' ἔτι νήπιος ἦα.
ἀλλά τοι οὐ δύναμαι πεπνυμένα πάντα νοῆσαι·
ἐκ γάρ με πλήσσουσι παρήμενοι ἄλλοθεν ἄλλος
οἵδε κακὰ φρονέοντες, ἐμοὶ δ' οὐκ εἰσὶν ἀρωγοί.

(But I am wise in my heart and know each thing, whether good or less good; before I was just a little boy. But I am unable to think everything through correctly, for they intimidate me from all sides where they sit, intending injury. They are no service to me.)

Basically, he can rely on his intellectual and emotional capacities (θυμῷ νοέω καὶ οἶδα) that have to be used in moral action. But being confronted with the general hostility of the suitors (κακὰ φρονέοντες) he is incapable of seeing the right way to cope with the situation (πεπνυμένα πάντα νοῆσαι) without assistance (οὐκ εἰσὶν ἀρωγοί). It comes out most clearly that, in the last instance, everything depends on right knowledge, which also accounts for the right use of emotional forces.

88. *Philologus* 97 (1948) 125–134. The dialogue between Euripides and Socrates, however, that has been recovered in this article, seems to me rather dubious. Eur. *Med.* 1079ff may well mean, in that particular dramatic situation: my motherly feelings (θυμός) are stronger and prevent me from executing the plan (βουλεύματα) to kill the children. Cf. Dihle, *SHAW* 5 (1977).

89. Prot. 358 B/C. The whole problem has been extensively treated in modern Platonic studies. See, among others, E. R. Dodds *ad* Plat. *Gorg.* 467C ff and Gulley, *Phronesis* 10 (1965) 82ff.

90. Plato always retained this opinion. Accordingly, he used βούλησις, βούλομαι exclusively to denote intention based on rational cognition (*Gorg.* 466A; Prot. 358B/C; *Tim.* 86D ff; *Phileb.* 22B ff; *Leg.* 733A ff). In the *Cratylus* (420C) βουλή is etymologically explained from βολή, "aiming at, throw," βούλεσθαι, "to wish," and βουλεύεσθαι, "to consider, to plan." The connection of βούλησις and reason is also a well-known topic in Aristotle (*top.* 126a13; *de an.* 432b6). The monarch rules κατὰ τὴν ἑαυτοῦ βούλησιν (*pol.* 1287a10) which is, unfortunately as in every human being, subject to distortion by θυμός and ἐπιθυμία, whereas the law, having no drive towards action, can be called νοῦς

ἄνευ ὀρέξεως "reason without intention" (1287a30ff; cf. Plat. *Leg.* 714A). Since every action that has been brought about without being enforced from outside is an ἑκούσιον of the acting individual, ἑκούσιον and βουλόμενον are not necessarily identical, as such an action can have been motivated by irrational desire (*E.E.* 1223b29, *E.N.* 1111a33ff). The same applies to the use of βούλησις in later philosophy where it is defined as εὔλογος ὄρεξις (ps.-Plat. *def.* 413C, *SVF* 3.173, etc.; cf. Neuhausen [see above n. 54] 7–87). The intellectual connotation, so notable in the case of βούλησις, also applies to the term προαίρεσις in Greek moral philosophy, which points to the choice made by the intellect out of various possible aims of action. Anscombe (in *New Essays in Plato and Aristotle* [1965] 143–158, esp. 153f) has pointed out that Aristotle used the term only when the choice has been made with regard to a certain form of behavior which alone causes the moral relevance of the ensuing action. Outside the language of philosophy, βούλομαι could well be used to refer to a quite arbitrary decision (see above p. 145ff), and sometimes, when opposed to ἀνάγκη or φύσις, βούλομαι and βούλησις include the element of arbitrariness, insofar as a decision is involved which may be perfectly rational but could have been made differently. This applies, for instance, when βούλησις (βούλομαι) is called the ultimate cause of the origin of language (Galen, *plac. Plat. et Hipp.* p. 207 Müller), when contemporary writers are said to be different *naturā, non voluntate* (Cic. *de or.* 3.93), or when, according to Epicurean theory, justice comes to existence *non naturā nec voluntate sed imbecillitate hominum* (Cic. *de rep.* 3.23). Heraclitus (B 33) aligns, as possible causes of order and regularity, νόμος and βούλησις ἑνός, whereas the anonymous Sophist of ps.-Dem. 25 contrasts νόμος and the different βουλήσεις of the many (26 and 88).

91. Gulley, n. 89 above. Socrates seems to have been firmly convinced, quite contrary to current opinion (cf. Aesch. *Prom.* 266 ἑκὼν ἑκὼν ἥμαρτον: "willingly, willingly I erred"), that wrongdoing on purpose and against the knowledge of the better is simply impossible. That is why Plato (*Prot.* 345 E/F) makes him construe, against all grammatical probability, ἑκών with ἐπαίνημι (praise) and not with ἔρδῃ (do) in his interpretation of Simonides fr. 542 Page:

> πάντας δ' ἐπαίνημι καὶ φιλέω
> ἑκὼν ὅστις ἔρδῃ
> μηδὲν αἰσχρόν.

> All those I praise and love
> Willingly who do
> Nothing shameful.

92. Cf. Plato, *Gorgias*, ed. E. R. Dodds (Oxford 1959) 235ff.

93. This view, which gave considerable distinction to the meaning of the word βούλεσθαι, persisted for a very long time. A late etymologicum (*Anecdota Parisina* IV) restricts the use of βούλησις to the positive meaning (ἐπὶ ἀγαθοῦ) whereas the sense of προαίρεσις is said to be neutral (ἐπ' ἀμφοτέρων, ἀγαθοῦ τε καὶ κακοῦ p. 245.4).

94. Cf. Arist. *E.N.* 1140b22f, which is the reply to the aporia at the end of the *Minor Hippias*. Cf. J. Kube, Τέχνη *und* ἀρετή (1969).

95. Cf. J. Derbolav, *Erkenntnis u. Entscheidung* (1954) 387–403.

96. Cf. F. P. Hager, *Vernunft u. Böse im Rahmen der platonischen Ethik* (1963) 251ff; F. Solmsen, *Plato's Theology* (1942) 169f.

97. H. Görgemanns, *Beiträge z. Platons Nomoi* (1960) 135ff.

98. The vulgarized Socratic tradition, perhaps as early as Antisthenes (fr. 26/27 Decleva-Caizzi), restricted the whole problem to the simple question of how reason has to master sensuality, without much regard for the possibility that the intellect, being the dominating factor in the human soul, cannot possibly be overpowered by the senses unless it is hindered in its activities by false opinions, that is to say by the very results of intellectual endeavour. Cf. Plut. *de coh. ir.* 13.401 D/E; Diog. Laert. 2.36f. The *vis Socratica*, praised by Antisthenes (fr. 70 Decleva-Caizzi) and the Cynics as superior and more valuable than any learning, could be interpreted, in modern terms, as will (Teles fr. 3 Hense). It is, however, primarily the essence of moral knowledge (Antisth. fr. 80 Decleva-Caizzi).

99. This is the basis of the terminological use of ἐπιστήμη in Plato and later philosophy, which is absent in earlier Greek from Homer to Isocrates. Cf. J. Gould, *Plato's Ethics* (1955) 3ff. Gould erroneously attributes an exclusively "theoretical" meaning to γιγνώσκω in earlier Greek (15). The implication that cognition leads to action is particularly strong in the case of γιγνώσκω and γνώμη. See above p. 21.

100. See W. Jaeger, *Paideia* 2 (1944) 87ff.

101. According to Chrysippus a perfectly happy life (εὔροια) depends on the congruity of man's state of mind and the order of the universe: ὅταν πάντα πράττηται κατὰ τὴν συμφωνίαν τοῦ παρ' ἑκάστου δαίμονος πρὸς τὴν τοῦ τῶν ὅλων διοικητοῦ βούλησιν (when everything is done in a state of harmony between the divine element in each man and the plan of the ruler of the universe) (Diog. Laert. 7.88). Virtually the same is said by Epict. *diss.* 4.1.99f. Cf. A. A. Long, *Problems in Stoicism* (1971) 173–199 ("Freedom and Determination in the Stoic Theory of Human Action").

102. Cf. *Ethica Epicuri* fr. 22 Diano with the editor's commentary.

103. Cf. D. J. Furley, *Aristotle and Epicurus on Voluntary Actions* (1967) 161–237.

104. This applies to some of the so-called Minor Socratics and, above all, to the Sceptics.

105. Archil. fr. 130–131 West; Semonid. fr. 1; Theogn. 141f.

106. See Isocrat. *Helen* (10) 2–5, where the whole tradition of scepticism is referred to.

107. See above, n. 60.

108. See Fontenrose, *TAPhA* 102 (1971) 71–108.

109. Ὕβρις, acting outside the bounds by which all human activity should be limited, and κόρος, feeling completely satisfied, are closely connected in the archaic Greek wisdom tradition (e.g. Sol. fr. 6.3 West τίκτει κόρος ὕβριν:

"satiety begets insolence"; Orac. Bac. *ap.* Hdt. 8.77 κόρος ὕβριος υἱός: "satiety is the son of insolence"). In the state of satiety man is inclined to attribute to himself, in utter ignorance of his real position, some sort of perfection—a feeling which may lead to violence and outrage against others. An act of ὕβρις can only be settled by revenge or punishment but never by agreement (Chilon ap. Stob. 3.118 W.-H.; cf. A. Dihle, *Goldene Regel* [1962] 42). The word ὕβρις originally referred to action only, but was later on applied to the state of mind as well (e.g. Theogn. 291, 379; cf. K. Latte, *Kl. Schriften* [1969] 13).

110. For a full treatment of the topic see F. Wehrli, *Hauptrichtungen d. gr. Denkens* (1964) 69ff.

111. Aristot. fr. 1 Rose; Xen. *Mem.* 4.2.24ff.

112. H. North (*Sophrosyne*, [1966]) offers an extended collection of the material.

113. P. W. Strawson, *Freedom and Resentment* (1974) 9ff.

CHAPTER III

1. H. North, *Sophrosyne* (1966). C. R. Whitman (*Sophocles* [1951] 7ff) rightly observes that the concept of σωφροσύνη includes self-knowledge together with the activation of such a knowledge.

· 2. Plat. *Gorg.* 505C, *Apol.* 25B; Aristot. *Protr.* fr. 9 Rose.

3. Simonid. fr. 542.35 Page; Theogn. 147.

4. Critias the tyrant (B 6 and 15f), in one of his elegies, has σωφροσύνη combined with εὐσέβεια to denote comprehensively righteousness towards God and men, in the same way as piety and justice are usually put together (A. Dihle, *Kanon d. Zwei Tugenden* [1968]). Plato (*Gorg.* 507A ff) makes σωφροσύνη the foundation of εὐδαιμονία, happiness and moral perfection.

5. Nearly all scholarly work devoted to the interpretation of the *Charmides* in recent times concentrates on this problem: Wellman, *Phronesis* 9 (1964) 107–113; J. Gould, *Plato's Ethics* (1955) 36ff; Hoerber, *Phronesis* 7 (1962) 121–131; R. Dieterle, "Platons Laches und Charmides" (diss. 1966); Scheibe, *Phronesis* 12 (1967) 28–49; R. Witte, *Wissenschaft v. Guten u. Bösen* (1970); E. Martens, *Selbstbezügliches Wissen im Charmides* (1973); Oehler, *PAPhS* 118 (1974) 493–506. Cf. also Xen. *Mem.* 4.2.25.

6. Cf. H. Gauss, *Handkommentar z. d. Dialogen Platos* 1² (1954) 103, where attention is also drawn to *Theaet.* 200B.

7. The διαλανθάνων λόγος (hidden argument) of the Megarian school (Eubulides fr. 64 Döring) is about the same problem: the wise man knows everything, but he is not aware of his wisdom at the moment when he acquires it. Cf. Sedley, *PCPhS* 23 (1977) 94f.

8. Bilsen, *PhilStudien* 8 (1936/37) 190–206.

9. The motif of self-observation became important in Stoic and Neoplatonic ethics. Epictetus speaks of ἐπιστροφὴ ἐφ' αὐτὸν καὶ παρατήρησις: self-examination and observation (*diss.* 3.16.15), Marcus of παρατήρησις τοῦ ἡγεμονικοῦ: observation of the ruling element (3.4.1–2). Self-observation

leads to the awareness of one's own intellectual faculties for coping with the challenges from the outside world. Marinus (*vit. Procl.* 25) recommends ἡ εἴσω πρὸς τὸν νοῦν στροφὴ τῆς ψυχῆς: the internal direction of the soul towards the mind.

10. Cf. H. Gundert, in *Hermeneia*, Festschrift Regenbogen (1952) 87: "im lernenden Besserwerden erfüllt sich das . . . Wollen der Seele und darin liegt die platonische Form der Freiheit."

11. See, above all, Oehler (above n. 5). Oehler has shown that in Aristotle's view the activity of the divine νοῦς is exclusively self-reflective, whereas in the activity of the human intellect the awareness of its own thought only accompanies thoughts and intentions that are directed towards an objective. The self-awareness of the human mind always presupposes its being directed towards an object outside itself, whereas the divine νοῦς has no object of its thought and intention outside itself. This condition accounts for its being an unmoved mover (Brinkmann, *Aristoteles Metaphysik* [1979] 196ff). Albinus (*epit.* 10) and other Platonists after him (e.g. Procl. *elem. theol.* 168) used the Aristotelian concept of νόησις τῆς νοήσεως (*met.* 1074b35ff) to define the Platonic ideas or forms as thoughts of God (cf. Armstrong, *EntrFondHardt* 5 [1957] 403f).

12. D. Tsekourakis, *Terminology of Early Stoics* (1974).

13. Ingenkamp, *RhM* 114 (1971) 240.

14. This is, of course, different from self-control and self-observation in moral life, which were heavily stressed in Stoic education. (See above n. 9.)

15. Plotinus had to face adversaries who, as can be seen from the treatise *enn.* 5.3, simply denied the possibility of any sort of self-cognition, and whose argument, as preserved in Sext. *adv. math.* 7.310, he repeated literally (5.3.1.5). He gave a solution to the problem according to his own modification of Platonic ontology with its climax of ψυχή, νοῦς, ἕν: the Soul cannot adequately perform this particular act, since it is still dependent on sense perception, which exclusively refers to the world outside. The One transcends cognition that presupposes the split between perceiving and perceived. So only the Intellect, being the intermediate hypostasis, is likely to be able to perform the act of self-cognition. This is pointed out in great detail (5.3.7–8), since Plotinus had to surmount a large number of considerable difficulties. The closing sections of the treatise corroborate the results of the foregoing with reference to various passages from Plato and Aristotle, but without special regard to the *Charmides*.

16. *EntrFondHardt* 5 (1957) 341–390; see further Warren, *Phronesis* 9 (1964) 83–97. Marinus (*vit. Procl.* 25) describes σωφροσύνη as ἡ εἴσω πρὸς τὸν νοῦν στροφὴ τῆς ψυχῆς (cf. above n. 9), where both the element of volition and the intensified and internalized cognitive attempt are adequately pointed out.

17. Diog. Laert. 3.57; ps.-Plat. *def.* 411D.

18. Th. Gould, *Platonic Love* (1963).

19. The cosmic function of ἔρως was also discussed by Aristotle (*met.* 1072b3).

20. Cf. Hyland, *Phronesis* 13 (1968) 1–31.

21. Opstelten, *MedKonAkadWet* N. R. 22 Afd. Letterk. 1 (1959) 16f; Groningen, *ActCongressMadv* 2 (1957) 113.

22. E.g. Plat. *Symp.* 189C ff; *Phaedr.* 252B ff.

23. The *Magna Moralia* distinguish between three kinds of ὄρεξις according to the three faculties of the soul: ἐπιθυμία, θυμός, βούλησις (1187b37; cf. F. Dirlmeier *ad loc.*).

24. On the problems of bipartite psychology see W. W. Fortenbaugh, *Aristotle on Emotion* (1975).

25. For comprehensive information see W. F. R. Hardie, *Aristotle's Ethical Theory* (Oxford 1968).

26. E.g. *Charm.* 163B/E.

27. E.g. Aristot. *E.N.* 1189a26ff and 35ff, where the difference between θεωρία, ποίησις and πρᾶξις is precisely explained.

28. B 242: Πλέονες ἐξ ἀσκήσιος ἀγαθοὶ γίγνονται ἢ ἀπὸ φύσιος: "More people become virtuous by training than by nature."

29. fr. 70 and 96 Decleva-Caizzi.

30. Cf. F. Dirlmeier *ad* Aristot. *E.N.* 1095b5 (Berlin 1956, p. 273) where the material from Plato has been collected.

31. Cf. *E.N.* 1143b15.

32. Cf. *E.N.* 1152a15ff.

33. *Od.* 5.408ff and 465ff. In both cases, Homer describes in great detail what goes on in the mind of Odysseus before he makes the choice of the means and ends of the action required in the given situation—without using, of course, the word προαίρεσις.

34. A. Dihle, *Studien z. gr. Biographie*[2] (1970) 57ff.

35. Friedo Ricken, *Lustbegriff in der N.E.* (1975) 56ff.

36. Cf. the problem of just and unjust anger: Theophr. ap. Sen. *de ir.* 1.12.1; Philod. *de ir.* 41.26; Sen. *de ir.* 1.14.1 and 2.6.1.

37. Only orthodox Stoics were prepared to condemn anger altogether, along with all other affections. Seneca, on the other hand, justified it, provided it originates on the basis of the rational evaluation of one's duty to retaliate, to punish, and the like (*de ir.* 1.12.1), and Plutarch pointed to man's duty to correct his fellow man by means of anger with the ensuing acts or words, even at the expense of his own mental and emotional equilibrium (Plut. *de coh. ir.* 459c). This doctrine survived even in Christian theology. Through actions motivated by an anger that altogether disregards retaliation and exclusively aims at the sinner's education men become God's representatives on earth. This is taught by Basil (*reg. brev. tract.* 68 = *P.G.* 31.1129; cf. *Isid. Pelus. ep.* 239).

38. Alex. Aphrod. in Aristot. *met.* p. 327 Hayduck (cf. Aristot. *E.N.* 1110a9). Another way to distinguish between different kinds of intention is discussed in the *Eudemean Ethics* (1224b24ff): both the self-controlled (ἐγκρατής) and the undisciplined (ἀκρατής) act, at the same time, intentionally and non-intentionally. It depends on which part of their soul is being taken

into account. In the very act of self-control the illogical part of the soul is subject to force (βία) against its intention, whereas the act of incontinence overpowers the intellect. From the point of view of moral responsibility, however, and with regard to the whole of the soul, both acts are intentional.

39. The difference between Plato and the Socratic tradition on the one hand and Aristotle on the other can be illustrated by the following passages: Xen. *mem.* 3.9.4f; Plat. *Prot.* 358B ff, *Apol.* 25C, *Gorg.* 505C; Aristot. *E.N.* 1144b18ff, 1152a15ff, fr. 52 Rose.

40. We need not go into all the details of Aristotle's doctrine of human action, freedom, and intention (cf. K. A. Neuhausen, *De voluntarii notione* [1967] 93ff). Apparently Aristotle tried to clarify the meaning of many terms which he took over from Plato. So his distinction between ἑκούσιον—intentional but against the wishes of the acting person—and βουλόμενον greatly clarifies the formulation of a problem which had already been treated in Plato's *Gorgias* (*E.E.* 1223b29, *E.N.* 1111a33ff and 1112a14ff). Accordingly, he distinguishes between ἑκούσια κατ᾽ ὄρεξιν, κατὰ προαίρεσιν, and κατὰ διάνοιαν (voluntarily according to desire, according to choice, and according to conception, respectively: *E.E.* 1223a21ff). He observes that a man can act intentionally κατὰ διάνοιαν in the way which his reason evinces to be correct, but does not necessarily do so ἐκ or ἀπὸ διανοίας, motivated by his reasoning. The various degrees of intention, with special regard to responsibility in criminal law, can be adequately treated in Aristotelian terms (e.g. *M.M.* 1189b3ff).

41. Aristot. *E.N.* 1111b9 and 1117a17ff. Cf. J. Walsh, *Aristotle's Conception of Moral Weakness* (1963); R. Milo, *Aristotle on Practical Knowledge and Weakness of Will* (1966); Santas, *Phronesis* 14 (1969) 162ff.

42. See, for instance, G. E. M. Anscombe, *Intention*[2] (1963).

43. E.g. Stob. 2.5 p. 59.4ff Wachsm.-Hense. Chrysippus and his followers went so far as to teach that affections or emotions which impel towards action do not originate from any illogical part of the human soul but are, in fact, false judgements of the intellect (*SVF* 3.461; cf. Zeno *SVF* 1.209). So knowledge becomes the only factor in moral life altogether.

44. E.g. Diog. Laert. 10.133.

45. Cf. M. Pohlenz, *Stoa*[2] II (1949) 71. A. J. Voelke (*Volonté dans le stoicisme* [1973]) is mainly concerned with Roman Stoicism. Seneca wants to transform the gift of clemency, which his princely pupil has been given by nature, into a moral attitude from which alone conscious and responsible actions result: *ut quod nunc natura et impetus est fiat iudicium* (*de clem.* 2.2.2). The task of education has been accomplished if moral judgement and decision coincide with the order of nature.

46. See Tsekourakis (above n. 12) 75–83. The Stoics were aware, however, of the difference between moral and scientific or technical knowledge, yet they rejected, with the exception of Panaetius, the idea of Aristotle's that the difference is due to different intellectual faculties of the soul or, more precisely, to entirely different modes of intellectual activity. See Lloyd, *PBA* 56 (1970) 231.

47. E.g. Aristipp. ap. Diog. Laert. 2.93 (fr. 215 Mannebach); Euclid.

Meg. ap. Diog. Laert. 2.106f (= fr. 24 Döring); cf. Bion ap. Diog. Laert. 4.51 (= fr. 12A Kindstrand). Socratic tradition apart from Plato is repeatedly referred to in Stoic philosophy: Cic. *nat. deor.* 2.18 (cf. Xen. *mem.* 1.4.2ff); *nat. deor.* 3.27 (cf. Sext. *adv. math.* 9.98).

48. *SVF* 1.370, 3.138, 214, and 471; Sen. *ep.* 109.2. Cf. G. Scarpat, *La lettera 65 di Seneca* (1967) 213. The same topic in Epicurean doctrine is discussed by Schmid, *RAC* 5 (1962) 743ff.

49. E.g. Epict. *diss.* 1.2.33. Polybius reports repeated changes in the moral attitude (προαίρεσις) of Philip V, whereas his nature remained unchanged (7.11.1, 7.11.11, 7.13.7, 10.26.8). The change can be called μετάνοια, a term avoided in Stoic terminology. Caesar, in the view of Cicero (*ad Att.* 10.4.8), shows his notorious clemency against his nature and his *voluntas* (προαίρεσις) because of political advantage. Dionysius of Halicarnassus (*ant.* 14.6.5) wanted to make the distinction between Greeks and Barbarians not so much according to language as according to intelligence and moral attitude (σύνεσις καὶ χρηστῶν ἐπιτηδευμάτων προαίρεσις: understanding and choice of useful pursuits). In the Stoic view, προαίρεσις in that broader sense provides the basis of human freedom. A life in accordance with one's own προαίρεσις is regulated by the firm cognition of what is just and right (Epict. 1.2.33) and is not influenced by any compulsion from outside. In Middle Platonic terminology, too, προαίρεσις refers to a general attitude rather than a single decision in moral life. Προθυμία, willingness, is defined in the pseudo-Platonic *Definitions* (413E) as ἐμφανισμὸς προαιρέσεως πρακτικῆς: Manifestation of practical choice. In Aristotle, προαίρεσις frequently refers to the individual act of decision or choice, whereas the disposition to act in a certain way, that is to say according to a vice or virtue, is called ἕξις προαιρετική (see above, p. 56).

50. Cf. A. Bonhoeffer, *Epiktet u. die Stoa* (1890) 258ff.

51. On the meaning of the term πρόληψις, see also Epict. 2.17.44ff.

52. Epict. *diss.* 3.3.3f; Gell. 19.1.15; *SVF* 2.992.

53. Chrysippus, *SVF* 2.886 φαντασίαι, συγκαταθέσεις, αἰσθήσεις, ὁρμαί; cf. Iambl. *de an.* ap. Stob. 1.49.34 p. 369 W. H. φαντασία, συγκατάθεσις, ὁρμή, λόγος.

54. For further details on ἀσθενὴς συγκατάθεσις see Görler, *WürzbJahrb* 3 (1977) 83–92. The same surprising juxtaposition of elements of cognition (δόξα καὶ κρίσις: opinion and judgement) and volition (ὅλου τοῦ ἡγεμονικοῦ ῥοπή: inclination of the entire ruling part) can be found in a Stoic definition of anger and other affections, as reported by Plutarch (*SVF* 3.459).

55. *SVF* 3.278: ἰσχύς· τόνος ἱκανὸς ἐν τῷ κρίνειν καὶ πράττειν ἢ μή. "Strength: sufficient tension in judging and acting or not."

56. *SVF* 3.462; Epict. *diss.* 2.15.3.

57. E.g. *SVF* 3.173 and 3.395; Epicur. fr. 1.31 Arrighetti. The notion of ἐπιβολή became important in the philosophy of Plotinus (see below p. 115 n. 72).

58. Ἐπιβολὴ τῆς φιλοποιΐας *SVF* 3.395; cf. Diog. Laert. 7.113; Sext. *adv. math.* 7.239.

59. Ἐπιβολή 3.3.6, 3.5.7, 3.6.7, 3.8.2f; ὁρμή 3.7.3, 3.9.7, 3.15.9, 31.24.11; προαίρεσις 3.8.5, 3.8.11, 3.19.13; γνώμη 3.13.4, 3.19.11; δια-

βούλιον 3.21.1. There is no clear distribution of these terms with regard to the predominance of volitional or cognitive factors in the act of planning or deciding.

60. Ptolem. *de iudic.* 1–2.

61. Albin. didasc. 2, 24, 28, 30, etc.; ps.-Plat. *def.* 411E and 414B; Stob. 2.20 p. 137.20, 142.8, and 145.19 Wachsm.-Hense; Sext. *adv. math.* 9.167; Diog. Laert. 3.57.

62. The first Stoic to admit this distinction was Panaetius (ap. Diog. Laert. 7.92 = fr. 108 v.d. Straaten).

63. Cf. Reinhardt, *P.W.* 22 (1951) 733ff; Kidd in *Problems in Stoicism*, ed. A. A. Long (1971) 200–206; Dihle, *JHS* 93 (1973) 50–57.

64. G. Watson, *Stoic Theory of Knowledge* (1966); Sandbach in *Problems in Stoicism*, ed. A. A. Long (1971) 9–21.

65. *E.N.* 1177a16ff.

66. Dicaearchus fr. 8–9 and 25 Wehrli. Aristotle, however, gave very detailed reasons for his being in favor of theory rather than practice: perfection depends on the degree of consciousness in one's conduct of life (*E.E.* 1244b23ff).

67. The term ἐπιστήμη ἀνυπόθετος (absolute knowledge) first occurs in the pseudo-Platonic *Definitions*, being an abbreviation for the ἐπιστήμη of the ἀρχὴ ἀνυπόθετος (knowledge of the unconditioned first principle) (Plat. *Rep.* 510B; cf. Procl. *in rempubl.* 1 p. 283 and 292 Kroll).

68. Ὑπεράνω τῆς εἱμαρμένης γενέσθαι: to go beyond fate; cf. Schröder, *RAC* 7 (1969) 533ff. This conception implies that the strict regularity of the cosmic process to which man finds himself subject and the ensuing lack of freedom experienced in human life have to be taken as an indication of how imperfect the sensible world really is. The same regularity had also been interpreted, in the strict philosophical tradition, as pointing to the immutability, eternity, and perfection of the order of being. The contradictory interpretations of cosmic or natural regularity could be harmonized only by stressing, on the one hand, the irrational aspects of determination as experienced by our senses in practical life and by identifying, on the other, freedom and perfect rationality, which can be achieved through entirely spiritual activity only. The whole topic has been treated by E. Amand de Mendieta, *Fatalisme et liberté* (1945).

69. The corresponding Stoic concept of freedom in moral life, however, was difficult to accept for non-Stoics: Plut. *Stoic. repugn.* 47.1055F.

70. S. Pétrément, *Dualisme chez Platon* (1947).

CHAPTER IV

1. Theories of will have been developed, in the course of medieval and modern philosophy, for various purposes. A distinct notion of will was conceived by St. Augustine (see below Chapter VI) in order to clarify which part of the human personality is concerned with freedom, sin, and di-

vine grace, since it turned out to be difficult to describe these experiences of religious life in terms of intellect and sensuality. Medieval philosophy, in this particular field, is largely divided into Augustinian and anti-Augustinian positions; the same holds for the controversy between Luther and Erasmus and even still for Descartes' concept of *volonté dégagée*. Human freedom and all its religious and moral consequences, then, could be thought of in terms of will. Hume returned for the purposes of his ethical doctrine to the bipartite psychology of classical tradition that explained the impulse towards action by man's irrational faculties rather than his intellect, whose activity was again restricted to sheer cognition. Kant's concept was new in that he no longer regarded human will solely as a response to the utterance or impact of a suprahuman or universal will: it results, according to Kant, from the subsumption of subjective inclinations or impulses of whatever origin, as can be experienced in many ways in human life, under objective rules or standards of moral action. Freedom and responsibility thus become phenomena of an exclusively moral character. The need for a psychological explanation of what can be called will in human life was restricted to the field of ethical theory. The revived theological concept of a divine will that precedes, conditions, and indeed creates any act of human volition (e.g. Schelling, *Mythologie* 2.563f; cf. W. Beierwaltes, *Platonismus u. Idealismus* [1972] 189ff) led to the vitalistic concept of will which we find in the philosophy of Schopenhauer, Nietzsche, and their followers. Will in that particular sense is considered to permeate and determine human and non-human nature alike. Recently, existentialism, which gives priority to existence over cognition in all problems of human consciousness, makes every intellectual act depend on a preceding act of volition (J. P. Sartre, *Existentialismus ein Humanismus?* [1947] 11) which, in its turn, is considered to be entirely non-intellectual, yet to constitute human freedom. In spite of this great variety of doctrines which all demand a distinct concept of will, and despite the fact that empirical psychology apparently cannot do without the term, "knowledge rather than action, belief rather than emotion, the intellect rather than the will have been the central topics of philosophical concern"—sc. in post-medieval philosophy. This is stated in A. Kenny's brilliant study on *Action, Emotion, and Will* (1960) 1, and fully corroborated by a number of rather weak attempts to give a psychological definition of will, which can be collected from psychological and philosophical literature, such as "A conscious effort to which our intelligence has given its sanction, or at least not withheld it" (Opstelten, above Chapter III, n. 21). Kenny has contributed greatly towards clarifying by means of language analysis the various conceptual aspects of the notion of will, for no modern European language is bereft of the means to denote the act of volition, its initiation, strength, and direction, quite apart from its origin in either cognition or emotion. He tentatively ended up with a theory of volition (212ff) which comes very near to what Aristotle called προαίρεσις. Kenny's concept of will, however, is not entirely descriptive but has kept some evaluative, that is to say ethical, implications. This is elucidated by the fact, as Kenny has pointed out (91ff), that the concepts of intention (e.g. approaching the fire in order to get warm, thus improving one's state of affairs) and motive (e.g. approaching the fire because one feels cold and wants to put an end to that unwanted condition) do not suffice to cover every kind of voluntary action. Some actions are performed in order to "exemplify behavior patterns" such as gratitude, friendship, or disobedience, without being caused, in the primary act of volition leading to them, by a distinct object aimed at. Those actions, however, and the acts of volition leading to them can be described in evaluative terms only. Here we find, in a modern theory of volition, the very detail which necessitated a concept of will in the attempts to make explicit, in a coherent argument, the religious phenomenon that human action is experienced as being in accordance with or opposed to a divine commandment. Kenny has been guided, in his attempts to analyze the semantic and conceptual implications of the vocabulary of volition, to a large extent by Aristotle's theory of action (πρᾶξις), and the same applies to G. E. M. Anscombe, *Intention*[2] (1963). This has enabled them to open up for a more detailed understanding what Hegel stated in his *Grundlinien der Philosophie des Rechts* (ed. K. Löwith and M. Riedel [Frankfurt 1968] 51): Man muss sich nicht vorstellen, dass der Mensch einer Seits denkend, anderer Seits wollend sey, und dass er in der einen Tasche das Denken, in der anderen das Wollen habe . . . sondern das Wollen ist eine besondere Art des Denkens." Aristotle took great pains to show in his theory of προαίρεσις how the intellectual assessment of and decision for a certain way of acting have to be separated from the intellectual assessment of and decision for the means and end of an individual action. By distinguishing the two kinds of intellectual performance, of which only the first is open to moral judgement, Aristotle succeeded in deriving voluntary action entirely from man's intellect (see above p. 56). According to Aristotle, action can also be caused by thought only (Anscombe in *New Essays on Plato and Aristotle*, ed. R. Bambrough [1965] 155), whereas the traditional bipartite psychology has to explain human action as the result of both the choice made by the intellect and the impulse provided by the irrational faculties of the soul. This conception, however, which prevailed in many periods of Greek philosophy, caused innumerable difficulties in the attempts to solve the problems of freedom and moral responsibility and also prevented the Greeks from conceiving the notion of will.

2. There is no difficulty whatsoever in translating verbs of volition within modern European languages.

3. See for instance, Anscombe, *Intention* (above n. 1). In a recent contribution, however, A. Kenny speaks of the triad intellect-emotion-will as separate abstractions from the "observable entity" of an acting human being (*Free Will and Responsibility* [1978] 39 and 44).

4. E.g. C. G. Jung, *Psychologische Typen* (1937) 690; J. Jørgensen, *Psykologi pa biologisk Grundlag* (1946) 402ff (quoted by Løgstrup below n. 8); A. Wellek, *Polarität* (1950) passim.

5. See below Chapter VI.

6. *Wirtschaft und Gesellschaft* 4ff.

7. The plausibility of a historical account which was composed on the basis of deficient evidence is usually assessed according to these factors. See C. Schneider, *Information u. Absicht bei Thuk.* (1974) 169f, who refers to Immanuel Kant, *Mutmasslicher Anfang der Menschengeschichte* in *Werke*, ed. Weischedel Bd. 9 (Darmstadt 1968) 85f and Friedrich Schiller, *Was heisst und zu welchem Ende studiert man Universalgeschichte*, Nationalausgabe Bd. 17 (Weimar 1970) 373f.

8. K. Løgstrup in *Zeit u. Geschichte*, Festschr. Bultmann, (1964) 517–530.

9. H. Jonas in *Zeit u. Geschichte*, Festschr. Bultmann, (1964) 557–570.

10. Sherman and Curtis, *JNES* 28 (1969) 231–246.

11. Deut. 9:23; 2 Kings 17:14.

12. Hebrew *maḥš͑bōt*, rendered by "thoughts" in this passage, denotes both thoughts or considerations and intentions. The same idea occurs, for instance, in Exod. 33:19, which refers to the inexplicable choice God has made among nations and tribes by electing Israel, or Wisd. of Sol. 9:13 and Dan. 6:19ff, which illustrate how God's sovereignty surpasses by far the power of a king who rules a great empire at his pleasure.

13. Cf. 1 Kings 15:22 or Ps. 51:12 and the careful distinction between wilful and involuntary offenses in 1 Q.S. 7.3ff.

14. The root *'mn* denotes "being firm," and its derivatives in the semantic field of human behavior may refer to the firmness of the believer as well as to the object believed in.

15. E.g. Plat. *Gorg.* 454 E ff, where the restricted value of belief is stressed.

16. According to Irenaeus, Abraham acts righteously *voluntarie et sine vinculis* (ἑκουσίως καὶ ἀδέσμως) in consequence of his obedience to God (*haer.* 4.24) and the heretics sin κατὰ τὴν ἰδίαν γνώμην, by their own decision, because of their rejecting the revealed truth which they know very well (5.26.3). So obedience and disobedience rather than knowledge and ignorance constitute human freedom. The specific meaning of πίστις (faith) in the Judaeo-Christian tradition caused some interest in the question of what this term meant in the language of philosophy among educated Christians from the third century onwards. (Cf. F. Solmsen, "Early Christian Interest in the Theory of Demonstration," Festschrift Waszink [1973] 283f.) Only at a comparatively late stage of Jewish thought did faith become, occasionally, some kind of performance, comparable to almsgiving and other deeds (J. A. Ziesler, *Righteousness in Paul* [1972] 99f).

17. Sherman and Curtis (above n. 10).

18. *Apoc. Bar.* (syr.) 46.3 and 48.22–25; 4 Esdras 8.12 etc.

19. Deut. 33:20, Hos. 11:9, Ezek. 28:2; Jer. 10:23 and 17:5; Job 7:17, Ps. 94:5 and 95:6, and other passages where emphasis is laid, in various ways and contexts, on the unlimited power which God is able to exercise over mankind.

20. This applies to the New Testament as well. The man whose healing is narrated in John 9 was born blind not because of his or his parents' sin "but

that the works of God should be made manifest in him" (9:3). This is not too humane an arrangement, according to the standards of human ethics, and not too different from the glory of Zeus revealed in the fate of Hercules according to Sophocles' interpretation (*Trach.* 1278f). Owing its very existence entirely to the purposes or the pleasure of the potter, the vessel cannot possibly blame him for its specific shape and quality: this simile occurs, in the same sense, in the prophetic literature of the Old Testament (Isa. 45:9 and 64:7; Jer. 18:6) and in the theology of St. Paul (Rom. 9:21f).

21. E.g. Exod. 15:26, 18:27, 19:5, and 26:14; Deut. 11:27f and 28:1; Jer. 7:23.

22. E.g. Exod. 23:13; Mic. 6:8.

23. E.g. Gen. 20:11; Ps. 1:2, 19:8, 34:12, and 111:10; Job 28:28; Prov. 1:7. Even the Book of Wisdom, which was written under the strong influence of Greek thought, describes the progress by the sequence ἐπιθυμία παιδείας—ἀγάπη—τήρησις τῶν νόμων—ἀφθαρσία—ἐγγὺς εἶναι τοῦ θεοῦ: desire for instruction—love—observance of the law—incorruption—to be near God (Wisd. of Sol. 17 and 18).

24. E.g. Ps. 40:9 and 119:97. The will of God has to be "explored": 1 Q.S. 5.9 and 11 passim.

25. See above n. 23; Wisd. of Sol. 6:12f.

26. Strack-Billerbeck, *Kommentar zum N.T. aus Talmud und Midrasch* 3.186f and 193ff, have collected the material.

27. Gal. 3:7ff; Rom. 4:1; John 9:1ff; Matt. 3:9.

28. E.g. Plat. *Gorg.* 454E ff. Πίστις has a somewhat different meaning where it is used to render Latin *fides*. The Milesians built a temple of πίστις in 98 B.C. (A. Rehm, *Milet* I 7.295).

29. That is why obedience and faith are nearly interchangeable (Deut. 9:23; 2 Kings 17:14; Isa. 7:9; Eccles. 35 (32) 24; Jos. *ant.* 20.48).

30. H. W. Wolff, *Anthropologie des AT* (1973) 65ff and 83ff. To illustrate the absence of a fixed terminology it may suffice to note that in Ps. 16:7 the phenomenon of conscience is described and located in the kidneys, in Ps. 4:5 in the heart which, in its turn, is spoken of as the seat of all moral, intellectual, and emotional qualities in a saying from the first century A.D. ('Abōt 2.9a).

31. E.g. Ezek. 2:4 and 3:7; Isa. 6:9; Deut. 29:18; Ps. 81:13; Jer. 9:13. See above p. 00 and J. Gnilka, *Verstockung Israels* (1961).

32. Hdt. 7.12ff; Exod. 7–9 and 10:1. The Septuagint mostly uses the verbs σκληρύνω or βαρύνω to describe the process which corresponds to Hebr. *kbd* (hi.) and *hzq*.

33. 1 Q.S. 2.25–3.12 (cf. Dam. 20.9) This does not prevent the author from classifying very neatly wilful and inadvertent offenses (1 Q.S. 7.3–7).

34. Gordis, *JBL* 76 (1957) 123–138; Stern, *VT* 8 (1958) 405–418; Wolff, "Wissen um Gott bei Hosea," *Ges. Stud. z. AT* (1964) 182–205; W. Zimmerli, *Erkenntnis Gottes nach Ezechiel* (1969) 41ff; P. Bonnard et al., *Connaissance de Dieu selon le NT* (1965). The New Testament and early Christian

literature use a special term to denote religious cognition. This word, ἐπί-γνωσις, usually means cognition in general in post-classical Greek, including the Septuagint (cf. 3 Kings 7:2). Sometimes it also has the connotation of decision on purpose (*SIG.* 826D16 [117 B.C.]; Himer. *or.* 1.17). See below n. 89.

35. W. Barclay, "Turning to God," Peake Memorial Lecture (1963); *Theol. Wörterb. z. NT* 7. 722ff and 4.972ff; Heikkinen, *EcumRev* 19 (1907) 313ff.

36. Ezek. 3:20 and 18:26f.

37. H. W. Wolff, "Das Motiv der Umkehr," *Ges. Stud. z. AT* (1964) 130ff.

38. Only where Hellenistic influence became predominant was the difference between good and evil occasionally explained in terms of cognition and sensuality, for instance in 4 Macc.

39. Cf. Exod. 33:19 or Dan. 5:19–28.

40. E.g. Jer. 31:33; Jubil. 1:22f.

41. The topic has been extensively treated by G. Maier, *Mensch u. freier Wille* (1971).

42. Two πνεύματα ἐν τῷ ἀνθρώπῳ (spirits in man) *Text. Ass.* 1; two angels (*malak*) or spirits (*ruaḥ*) of cosmic relevance 1 Q.S. 3.18f and 4.15f; two διαβούλια (counsels) *XII Test. Ass.* 1; Judg. 20; two instincts of man *b. Joma* 69b; *b. Baba Bathra* 16a; *Gen. Rab.* 9.9; *Midr. Bamidb. R.* 27.8; cf. J. A. Ziesler, *Righteousness in Paul* (1972) 118. According to the beliefs of the Qumran sect everybody has been given his specific share in both spirits, so that salvation is determined by the quality of the will of each individual (cf. Maier [above n. 41] 233–259). The conception of the Two Spirits survived in some parts of early Christian literature (*Herm. mand.* 5.1; Aphraat, *Patrol. Syr.* I 1.416.17f, 744.4ff, and 848.20f; cf. Vööbus, *JbAC* 3 [1960] 152–155; Greg. Nyss. *vit. Mos.* 2 p. 45 Mus.). It is hard to believe, however, that Matt. 4:1–12, the story of Christ's temptation, alludes to the doctrine of the two spirits, as F. Dvornik is inclined to suppose (*Early Christian and Byz. Political Philosophy* I [1966] 413).

43. *Test. Jud.* 20. The text of this passage has been transmitted in two versions (α and β A S according to Charles' edition):

> Γνῶτε οὖν . . . ὅτι δύο πνεύματα σχολάζουσιν
> ἐν τῷ ἀνθρώπῳ, τὸ τῆς ἀληθείας καὶ τῆς πλάνης. Καὶ μέσον
> ἐστὶ τὸ τῆς συνέσεως τοῦ νοὸς οὗ ἐὰν θέλῃ τὸ κλῖναι. Καὶ
> τὰ τῆς ἀληθείας καὶ τὰ τῆς πλάνης γέγραπται ἐπὶ τὸ στῆθος
> 5 τοῦ ἀνθρώπου. Καὶ ἓν ἕκαστον γνωρίζει ὁ κύριος. Καὶ οὔκ
> ἐστι καιρὸς ἐν ᾧ δυνήσεται λαθεῖν ἀνθρώπων ἔργα, ὅτι ἐν
> στήθει ὀστέων αὐτῶν ἐγγέγραπται ἐνώπιον κυρίου. Καὶ τὸ
> πνεῦμα τῆς ἀληθείας κατηγορεῖ πάντων καὶ ἐμπεπύρισται ὁ
> ἁμαρτωλὸς ἐκ τῆς ἰδίας καρδίας, καὶ ἆραι πρόσωπον πρὸς τὸν
> 10 κριτὴν οὐ δύναται.
>
>   (Know therefore . . . that two spirits dwell
>   in man, that of truth and that of error. And between them

        is the understanding of the mind, inclining how it wants. And
        the deeds of truth and the deeds of error are written upon the breast
5   of man. And each of them the Lord knows. And there is no
        possibility that the works of man can escape (sc. His) notice, as
        they are graven upon the bones of his breast before the sight of the Lord. And the
        spirit of the truth weighs all things and the sinner condemns himself to the flames
        (sc. of damnation) out of his own heart, and he cannot raise his face before his
10   Judge).

Apparently the redactor to whom α ultimately belongs did not properly understand the passage on the inclination of man's intellect and dropped it, replacing, however, σύνεσις by συνείδησις, for both could mean conscience at that
time (cf. Σύνεσις, *Theol. Wörterb. z. N. T.* 7.887), although conscience is not
pointed to in this particular sentence. A. M. Dénis (*Pseudo-épigraphes grecs d'AT*
[1970] 49ff) finds no indication of Christian origin in the above passage. For
the date see J. Becker, *Entstehungsgeschichte d. Test. XII Patr.* (1970).

44. Hes. *op.* 289; *XII Test. Ass.* 1; *Didache* 1,2.

45. To avert dualistic interpretations of that doctrine, the Rabbis were eager to state that the existence of the two spirits does not testify to an independent cosmic power of evil. Both spirits are created by God, and even the bad
one is necessary in the order of creation (*b. Ioma* 69b etc.). Sometimes the two
spirits in the soul are replaced by the good and the evil angel that guide man
through his life (*Tosephta Sabb.* 17.2f). The Zoroastrian dualism, however, also
presupposes the existence of two tendencies of volition in both the cosmic
order and the soul of man (cf. Colpe, *RAC* 9 [1974] 587ff).

46. Philo (*quaest. in Ex.* 1.23–24) mentions two faculties (δυνάμεις) in
both the human soul and the cosmos. This seems to refer to Plato's doctrine of
the two souls of the cosmos (*Leg.* 10.896ff etc.) by which regular and irregular
motion are explained as resulting from spiritual activity, the latter no longer
simply attributed to matter only. Euclides the Megarian (fr. 19/20 Döring)
attached two daemons to everybody. The fragments are somewhat enigmatic.
But it seems to be certain that Euclides was thinking of Sleep and Death.
Numenius' doctrine of two souls of man reproduces the Platonic and Aristotelian bipartition into logical and illogical parts or faculties respectively. According to Numenius, only the rational part represents man's true self (fr. 44
Des Places; cf. *Corp. Herm.* 1.12ff and Philo, *de opif.* 134).

47. *XII Test. Ass.* 6 etc.

48. Ps. 1:2; 1 Q.S. 5.9 and 6.6f.

49. The exceptions are Isa. 1:19 and Job 39:9, where the will of animals is
spoken of.

50. 'Aḇōt 3.15 with the commentary by K. Marti and G. Beer (Giessen
1927).

51. E.g. 9:4; for further references to the problem of free will in Jewish
thought and in the New Testament see E. H. Merrill, *Qumran and Predestination* (1975); G. Moore, "Schicksal und freier Wille bei Josephus" (1973)
167–189.

52. Ps. 110:3; cf. Ps. 54:8; Hos. 14:5 etc.

53. Ps. 5:13, 19:15, 69:14, and 145:16; 1 Q.S. 8.6.

54. Εὐδοκία: Ps. 5:13, 18(LXX)15, 68(LXX)14, 144(LXX)16; Sir. 15:15, 29:23, etc.; θέλημα: Sir. 43:16 v. 1.; Rom. 2:15; θέλημα ἐν οὐρανοῖς: 1 Macc. 3:60; εὐδοκία: Luke 2:14; Phil. 2:13. Sometimes the words in question are unmistakably determined from the context, e.g. θέλημα (*næpæš*): Eccl. 5:3 and 12:10; 2 Kings 23:5. Their use with a determining suffix, however, certainly prevails also in post-Biblical literature. E.g. 1 Q.S. 4.32f; 18 Prec. 17; Ps. Sol. 8:39; Hen. 1.8; *XII Test. Lev.* 18; Iss. 4.3; Dan. 6:2; Napht. 3.1; Ben. 11.2. The term ἐκλογή, which denotes man's free and responsible decision in the Psalms of Solomon, may well correspond to Hebr. *raṣōn* even without a determining suffix (Maier [above n. 41] 325–340). But the word can equally well correspond to Hebr. *rᵉṣut* (see above n. 50). Εὐδοκία and θέλειν are sometimes used with the accusative, indicating a personal object, in the Septuagint and the New Testament (Ps. 21:9 and 40:12; Tob. 13:8; Matt. 12:18 and 27:43; Ign. ad Magn. 3:2). In the case of θέλειν the usage does not correspond to idiomatic Greek, which only has θέλειν τι and the like (cf. Epict. 1.4.27 and W. Bauer, *Wörterbuch zum Neuen Testament* s.v. θέλειν no. 4), whereas εὐδοκεῖν occasionally occurs with such an addition in Hellenistic Greek (*SIG*³ 672.27, dated 162 B.C.). The fact that in all these instances εὐδοκεῖν and θέλειν designate, like many corresponding verbs in Semitic and other Oriental (cf. *Ev. Thom. log.* 107) languages, both "to intend" or "to wish" and "to love" may well account for this construction.

55. Matt. 26:39; cf. Segally, *RivBibl.* 2 (1964) 257–284, and H. Riesenfeld, θέλω *im NT* (1936).

56. Campenhausen, *Kerygma u. Dogma* 23 (1977) 157–171.

57. For parallels and equivalents in Hebrew and Aramaic see Hunziger, *ZNTW* 44 (1952/53) 85ff, *ZNTW* 49 (1958) 129ff; Deichgräber, *ZNTW* 51 (1960) 132f; Feuillet, *BAGB* 4 (1974) 91f.

58. Jewish ethics of the post-Biblical period were intellectualistic in the sense that responsibility was believed to result from the knowledge of the Law of God which had been revealed to Israel; cf. H. Braun, *Spätjüd.-häretischer u. frühchr. Radikalismus* 1 (1957) 41ff. This does not contradict the firm belief that the understanding of the Law depends on the preceding act of acceptance: no one is able to understand the Law without fulfilling it (see above p. 74). But another question was occasionally discussed in Jewish literature: to what extent has God revealed the knowledge of the Adamite, Noachite, and Mosaic Laws to the gentiles? The topic is treated, for instance, in the *Revelation of Baruch* (48.38ff).

59. Syll.³ 983.4, an inscription from Lindos (second century A.D.) does not offer a parallel to Rom. 2:15 with its distinction between συνείδησις and λογισμοί (consciousness and calculation, respectively). The text—χεῖρας καὶ γνώμην καθαρούς . . . καὶ μηδὲν αὐτοῖς δεινὸν συνειδότας: "pure in hand and mind . . . conscious of nothing dreadful"—only enumerates the various aspects of purity, according to action, intention, and previous life.

60. This view, however, is held, among others, by Strack-Billerbeck *ad loc.* (p. 89) and Michel, *Römerbrief*[11] (1957) 69. The translation of ἔργα τοῦ νόμου, "die Forderung des Gesetzes," is far from convincing, since ἔργον has to refer, in the given context, to the act of performance. It is the man to be judged according to his performance rather than the Law itself that is mainly spoken of in the passage. See H. Lietzmann, *Römerbrief*[2] (1919) 40; H. Käsemann, *An die Römer* (1973) 57ff; and C. K. Barrett, *Epistle to the Romans*[2] (1962) 51. There are many passages in Biblical and post-Biblical literature where God is said to have put his commandments into the hearts of men so that they need not know the written Law in order to fulfil it (Isa. 51:7; Jubil. 1:23). This applies particularly to the Patriarchs who lived before Moses (*Apc. Bar.* [syr.] 57.2) and to the People of God in the Last Days (Jer. 31:33). According to other authors, God has written His Law into the heart of the evil spirit of the human soul (see above p. 80) to limit its activity (Strack-Billerbeck *ad* Rom. 2:15). Sometimes the image of the law code written into the heart of man is confounded with that of tables in the heart where one's good and evil deeds are registered according to the standards of the Law (Jer. 17:1; cf. Prov. 3:3; *Targ. Jerus. ad Deut.* 6:6; 2 Cor. 3:3). So both concepts, that of the law code and that of the register, can be alluded to in the same words. The first, however, is absent from Rom. 2:14f.

61. Ὅταν γὰρ ἔθνη τὰ μὴ νόμον ἔχοντα φύσει τὰ τοῦ νόμου ποιῶσιν, οὗτοι νόμον μὴ ἔχοντες ἑαυτοῖς εἰσι νόμος: "Whenever gentiles without the Law by nature perform the actions of the Law, these men without the Law are the Law unto themselves." Flückiger (*ThZ* 8 [1952] 17–42) rightly argues that Greek and modern ideas, such as φύσις as opposed to νόμος, law of nature and so forth, should be excluded from the interpretation. According to Flückiger, φύσις in this passage denotes the free or rather freed will of the reborn rather than human nature in the sense the word is used in Greek philosophy. Flückiger's interpretation implies St. Paul's belief that those among the gentiles who fulfil the Law without knowing it have already been saved through divine grace from the general corruption of mankind to become equals of Abraham or Job, as will appear on doomsday. The Pauline use of the word φύσις is difficult to assess (H. Köster, *Theolog. Wörterbuch z. NT* 9.265–268). In Rom. 2:14/15, as Köster rightly observes, stress is laid on the fact that Jews and gentiles alike have to face the judgement which is going to be passed on mankind according to the Law. The Jews have no advantage because of their knowledge of the Law, since they cannot claim to have fulfilled it, whereas at least some gentiles will turn out to be fulfillers of the Law. These simply did it on their own rather than being guided by human nature. Φύσει, in this context, means more or less "spontaneously," though certainly not "unconsciously" or "instinctively," since the actions to be judged cause religious and moral responsibility, which only applies to wilful or intentional acts. Again, a concept of will is needed to make explicit the underlying ideas. C. E. B. Cranfield (*Comm. Ep. Rom.*[6] [1975] 156) suggests taking φύσει in 2:14 along with ἔθνη τὰ μὴ νόμον ἔχοντα, for the gentiles do not have the Law by birth. Grammatically, this word

order seems possible, though not very probable. Yet the meaning of such a phrase would be more than obscure. Gentiles are undoubtedly those who have not been given the Law. They can be contrasted to the Jews by birth as well as to the proselytes, "semiproselytes," φοβούμενοι τὸν θεόν ("God-fearers"), and to many people interested in and well-informed about the Law who lived in the world of St. Paul. The latter are certainly not spoken of in our passage, for they could not possibly be called νόμον μὴ ἔχοντες ἑαυτοῖς εἰσι νόμος, "not having the Law they are the Law unto themselves." The whole argument of the passage is about the difference between those who do not know the Law but fulfil it, and those who have been told the Law but do not fulfil its order. What sense could it possibly make in this context to define the gentiles, who are ignorant of the Law, only by their not having the Law by birth?

62. Heraclit. Stoic. *alleg. Hom.* 37: Hierocl. *in carm. aur.* 14 p. 451 Mullach. See below n. 152.

63. I see no reason to understand, with R. Bultmann (*Theologie d. NT*[7] [1977] 217f) and others, the remark on the λογισμοί as epexegetic to the reference to conscience. Three witnesses are clearly spoken of in that passage. Cf. R. Jewett, *St. Paul's Anthropological Terms* (1971) 441–445, where the ἔργα τοῦ νόμου are also discussed.

64. 2 Cor. 1:12; Rom. 9:1.

65. 1 Cor. 8 passim, and 10:29.

66. Διὰ τὴν ὀργήν (on account of anger), in the same passage, refers to the ruler's intention to punish the law-breaker which, of course, everybody wants to avoid.

67. See Σύνεσις *Theolog. Wörterbuch z. NT* 7.887 (Conzelmann).

68. For a fuller treatment of the topic of conscience in Biblical and classical thought see below n. 149. For St. Paul see Armstrong, *ChurchQuartRev* 152 (1953) 438–452, where his doctrine on conscience is discussed in the wider context of his ideas about knowledge, and Thrall (*NTS* 14 [1967/68] 118ff) who duly observes (124) that St. Paul also regards conscience "as providing the stimulus to moral action."

69. Cf. Mic. 6:8: "He hath showed ye, O man, what is good, and what the Lord doth require of thee, but to do justly, to love mercy, and to walk humbly with thy God."

70. No Christian author of the first three centuries adopts or further develops St. Paul's doctrine of conscience. This applies, as is well known, to many other specific details of his theology (cf. E. Aleith, *Paulusverständnis der Alten Kirche* [1937]). Tertullian, for instance, simply identifies conscience with the inborn and natural knowledge of good and evil which the Stoics ranged among the κοιναὶ ἔννοιαι (general ideas). Cf. Spanneut, *Rech. de Théol. Anc. et Méd.* 37 (1970) 171.

71. *Apc. Bar.* (syr.) 48:38ff; cf. Strack-Billerbeck *ad* Rom. 1:20.

72. Rom. 7:15: ὃ γὰρ κατεργάζομαι οὐ γιγνώσκω· οὐ γὰρ ὃ θέλω τοῦτο πράσσω, ἀλλ' ὃ μισῶ τοῦτο: "What I do, I do not intend; what I want, this I do not do but what I hate, this I do." The parallels to this passage collected in Walter

Bauer's dictionary (Polyb. 5.82.1; Plut. *Lyc.* 3.4; Jos. *ant.* 1.195, 14.352, and 16.331) could be supplemented by Eur. *Hipp.* 380 τὰ χρήστ᾽ ἐπιστάμεσθα καὶ γιγνώσκομεν, | οὐκ ἐκπονοῦμεν δ᾽ . . . : "Good things we know | but we do not practice them," where ἐπίσταμαι primarily points to knowledge, γιγνώσκω to intention (cf. Barrett *ad loc.*).

73. Rom. 7:7ff; cf. Gal. 5:17 where the same phenomenon is spoken of and explained along the same lines.

74. Σάρξ referring only to human body and sensual life occurs, for instance, at Gal. 4:13; 2 Cor. 12:7; Col. 2:1. This is normal usage in New Testament Greek; cf. Matt. 26:41 τὸ μὲν πνεῦμα πρόθυμον, ἡ δὲ σὰρξ ἀσθενής: "the spirit is willing but the flesh is weak," where the contrast between body and spirit is meant, or John 1:13 οἳ οὐκ ἐξ αἱμάτων οὐδὲ ἐκ θελήματος σαρκὸς οὐδὲ ἐκ θελήματος ἀνδρὸς ἀλλ᾽ ἐκ θεοῦ ἐγεννήθησαν: "they who were born not from blood, neither from the will of flesh nor the will of man, but from God" which is said of those who become children of God because they have accepted the divine Logos.

75. The Pauline ideas about σάρξ and σῶμα have been extensively treated in New Testament scholarship. See, for instance, R. H. Gundry, *Soma* (1975); E. Schweizer, *Neotestamentica* (1963) 180–189; Moule, *NTS* 12 (1965/66) 106–123; W. D. Stacey, *Pauline View of Man* (1956) 198ff and, above all, R. Bultmann, *Theologie d. NT*[7] (1977) 226ff. The specifically Pauline use of σάρξ was adopted by some authors of the New Testament who wrote under the influence of his theology (e.g. 1 Pet. 4:2; Eph. 2:3 and 6:2).

76. See Jonas in *Zeit und Geschichte*, Festschr. Bultmann (1964) 557–570.

77. Cf. Phil. 2:12f: μετὰ φόβου καὶ τρόμου τὴν ἑαυτῶν σωτηρίαν κατεργάζεσθε· θεὸς γάρ ἐστιν ὁ ἐνεργῶν ἐν ὑμῖν τὸ θέλειν καὶ τὸ ἐνεργεῖν ὑπὲρ τῆς εὐδοκίας: "accomplish your own salvation with fear and trembling; for it is God who works in you both the will and the deed according to His good will." It is entirely due to the grace of God, if a man has been given the faculty to produce intention (τὸ θέλειν) according to the will of God.

78. Cf. Dihle, *RAC* 3 (1957) 748–752.

79. 2 Cor. 11:30, and 12:5ff; 1 Cor. 3:16ff.

80. Διάνοια Col. 1:21; φρόνημα Rom. 8:27 etc.; πνεῦμα Gal. 4:6; ἐπιθυμεῖν Gal. 5:17; γιγνώσκειν Rom. 7:15; νοῦς Rom. 1:28; θέλημα 1 Cor. 16:12 and 7:37; βούλομαι 2 Cor. 1:17.

81. For references see Jewett (above n. 63) 315.

82. Cf. Tit. 2:12; Gal. 5:24.

83. Νοῦς τῆς σαρκός (intelligence of the flesh) Col. 2:18; σοφὸς κατὰ σάρκα (wisdom according to the flesh) 1 Cor. 1:26; βουλεύσθαι κατὰ σάρκα (to determine according to the flesh) 2 Cor. 1:17; φρόνημα τῆς σαρκός (thought of the flesh) Rom. 8:6; γιγνώσκειν κατὰ σάρκα (understanding according to the flesh) 2 Cor. 5:16.

84. Gal. 5:17ff ἡ γὰρ σὰρξ ἐπιθυμεῖ κατὰ τοῦ πνεύματος, τὸ δὲ πνεῦμα κατὰ τῆς σαρκός· ταῦτα δὲ ἀλλήλοις ἀντίκειται, ἵνα μὴ ἃ ἐὰν θέλητε ταῦτα ποιῆτε: "flesh desires against the spirit and the spirit against the flesh: these oppose one an-

other so that you cannot do these things that you would." Cf. Rom. 8 : 6 where φρόνημα τῆς σαρκὸς is contrasted with φρόνημα τοῦ πνεύματος.

85. L.c. (above n. 63) 248f. Rom. 13 : 3 (θέλεις δὲ μὴ φοβεῖσθαι τὴν ἐξουσίαν: "you wish not to fear the authorities?") presupposes that no one is likely to provoke, on purpose, the anger of those who exercise political rule. Gal. 6 : 12 (ὅσοι θέλουσιν εὐπροσωπῆσαι ἐν σαρκὶ: those who want to be well esteemed by others in their worldly existence) has certainly not primarily been said of instinctive or unconscious behavior.

86. Cf. the famous description of that condition in 2 Cor. 6 : 4– 10.

87. Cf. Rom. 7 : 24–8 : 2.

88. Cf. Rom. 8 : 18.

89. This can be seen from the use of ἐπίγνωσις in the New Testament. The word had been used, in ordinary post-classical Greek, as a synonym of γνῶσις, sometimes even with the voluntaristic connotation of deciding (*SIG*³ 826D16). The Stoics made it a term to denote the act of cognition on the basis of foregoing sense perception. The φαντασία which the mind forms out of aesthetic impressions can be called "a signal of nature to lead to the cognition of truth" (φέγγος τῆς φύσεως πρὸς ἐπίγνωσιν ἀληθείας Sext. *adv. math.* 7.259; cf. Epict. 2.20.21; Ptolem. *de iudic.* 10). The Platonists did not use the word as a technical term. It can acquire, in their language, the meaning of knowledge, concept or theory, and indirect or secondary cognition (e.g. Plot. 3.5.1.18). The New Testament, unlike the Septuagint (1 Kings 7 : 2 etc.), restricts the use of the word to rendering cognition of God, cognition of the will of God, and, sometimes cognition of the religious and moral condition of man. This kind of cognition and knowledge derives, according to the Biblical tradition and especially in the view of St. Paul, from faith and love, that is to say from one's initial turning to God (Col. 1 : 8ff and 2 : 2ff; Eph. 4 : 11ff; Phil. 1 : 9f). It does not come out of the free use of reason, and is thus different from secular wisdom. The topic of the two kinds of knowledge is also well known from both the Synoptic and the Johanneic traditions. Through the coming and preaching of Christ which initiates or even anticipates the divine judgement (John 5 : 24 and 12 : 31), the blind, poor, and simple come to see, to know, and to be saved, since they unhesitatingly accept the mercy of God. The wise and wealthy, on the other hand, are blinded and rendered ignorant by their not accepting the salutary message (e.g. Matt. 11 : 25; John 9 : 40f). Different from that of ἐπίγνωσις is the history of ἐπίνοια. It also covers a large semantic field, including the meaning of purpose or intention, which occurs in Attic drama and in late subliterary Greek as well as in the New Testament (Acts 8 : 22). Unlike ἐπίγνωσις, ἐπίνοια never gained terminological value in the Judaeo-Christian tradition, whereas it was used, in various ways, as a philosophical term. It denotes, very much like ἔννοια, the concept or the idea which exists, on the basis of sense perception, in the human consciousness as corresponding to the objects in reality according to Epicurean (fr. 255 Us.) and Stoic (*SVF* 2 88/89 and 390) usage. But its importance was greater in the Platonic tradition (see above p. 51). If reality is to be found outside the material world, ἐπίνοια, be-

ing a means of cognition or piece of knowledge τῶν ἀσωμάτων, of incorporeal beings (Sext. *adv. math.* 1.25), loses the foundation in sense perception which it necessarily has in the view of the Stoics and Epicureans. Yet once an ἐπίνοια can be derived from a foregoing one καὶ οὕτως εἰς ἄπειρον προβαινούσης τῆς ἐπινοίας ἄναρχον γίγνεσθαι τὸ πᾶν: "and so as the process of cognition proceeds into the infinite, everything arrives at (sc. epistemological) anarchy" (Sext. *adv. phys.* 2.256). This is the most serious argument of the Sceptics against Platonic ontology. For obvious reasons, the term was of particular interest when the problem of the cognition of God was being discussed (Sext. *adv. math.* 8.56ff and 9.49ff). Since the Supreme Being transcends the area that can be covered by the ordinary or discursive use of reason, ἐπίνοια θεοῦ (the apprehension of God) is likely to be due to a specific act of cognition at the very end of intellectual progress (Dörrie, *NAWG* 2 [1967] 37). Plotinus, finally, used the term very frequently both without terminological value (e.g. 3.5.1.4 and 4.4.6.14) and also to denote a new conception of his. Ἐπίνοια accompanies human thoughts and intentions (ὁρμαὶ καὶ διανόησις), thus creating the awareness of them, whereas the divine νοῦς is, at the same time, both subject and object of its own activity, leaving no room for any additional act of becoming aware of its own being and thinking (2.9.1f and 5.9.5.1ff, etc.). Thus ἐπίνοια denotes, in the language of Plotinus, some kind of cognition together with its result, typical of intelligent beings that partake in noetic activity without being fully occupied by it. Their intentional intellectual effort enables them to grasp a piece of reality, and reality, so to speak, offers them an additional piece to perceive in consequence of that effort. The model easily applies to the problem of how to come to know something about the Supreme Being.

90. See, above all, 1 Cor. 13 : 12f.

91. 1 Cor. 13 : 1ff; 1 Thess. 1 : 4 and 5 : 8; Col. 1 : 4f. For discussion of parallels in non-Christian texts see W. Theiler, *Vorbereitung des Neuplatonismus* (1930) 148f.

92. 1 Cor. 1 : 23; Rom. 1 : 16f, etc.

93. Rom. 8 : 20ff.

94. Rom. 13 : 10; 1 Cor. 9 : 19; Phil. 2 : 1ff.

95. Rom. 4 : 16–18.

96. Rom. 11 : 32–36.

97. 1 Cor. 8 : 1–4.

98. Rom. 1 : 22; 1 Cor. 1 : 23ff; Gal. 4 : 3; Col. 1 : 9 and 4 : 8.

99. Phil. 1 : 9f; Col. 2 : 2, etc.

100. It was not until the late fourth century that Pauline epistles were, for the first time, adequately commented on as to their specific doctrines by pseudo-Ambrosius.

101. *De vir. ill.* 11. H. Chadwick has conclusively pointed out that there is no indication of any direct relation between Philo and St. Paul (*BullRylLibr* 48 [1965/66] 286ff).

102. See above p. 18.

103. The same applies to other writings of Jewish literature that betray the influence of Hellenistic philosophy, such as the Epistle of Aristeas and the Fourth Book of the Maccabeans. There is only one passage where Philo uses θέλημα (*Leg. alleg.* 3.197): ’Αβραὰμ ἀκολουθῶν θεοῦ θελήματι (Abraham following the will of God). Like Platonists and Peripatetics, the Stoics define βούλησις as εὔλογος ὄρεξις, rational appetite (*SVF* 3.173). The definition of θέλησις given in the same text (Stob. 2 p. 87.22 W.-H. ἑκούσιος βούλησις: willing intention) does not make much sense, since the meaning of ἑκούσιος is already implied in βούλησις in ordinary Greek as well as in philosophical terminology, whereas θέλησις does not necessarily have that connotation. Apparently, this definition has been put forward, like many others in comparable texts, for the sake of completeness in systematic presentation.

104. Phil. *spec. leg.* 4.187. According to *opif. dei* 3 the actions of the righteous man are always in accordance with the βούλημα τῆς φύσεως (intention of nature).

105. Proclus *in Tim.* 3 p. 209ff Diehl *ad* Plat. *Tim.* 41A/B.

106. Atticus (2nd century A.D.) argued that the change of the design of the universe or order of being could also be foreseen in the potential (δύναμις) represented by the Supreme Being (fr. IV; IX Baudry).

107. *V. Mos.* 2.61 (ἵλεως φύσις θεοῦ: gracious nature of God); *decal.* 58 (πρόνοια θεοῦ: forethought of God); *aet. mund.* 13; *res. div. her.* 246.

108. *De prov.* 1.7.

109. *Leg. alleg.* 3.78.

110. *Aet. mund.* 39–41.

111. E.g. Gen. 8:22; Ps. 74:16 and 104:14.

112. *Leg. alleg.* 3.32; cf. Aristot. fr. 12 Rose; Cic. *nat. deor.* 2.37.

113. *Leg. alleg.* 3.97–99 and 101f; *sacrif.* 55. In the view of Platonizing philosophy of the imperial period, reason is sometimes thought to be able to attain positive knowledge of God (ps.-Aristot. *de mund.* 399a32), despite his being imperceptible to the human senses. On the other hand, the method of negative theology which first occurs in Philo (see above p. 10 n. 36), seems to have been developed by Alexandrian Platonists in the first century.

114. *Leg. alleg.* 2.86 (σοφία); *Cherub.* 27 (ἀγαθότης); *fug. et inv.* 95, *plant.* 46, *v. Mos.* 2.132 (δύναμις ἵλεως); *virt.* 49 (σωτήριος δύναμις). Cf. Fascher, *RAC* 4 (1959) 432ff.

115. *Somn.* 1.185, *Leg. alleg.* 3.73; cf. *Corp. Herm.* 9.6 and 10.2.

116. *Spec. leg.* 1.45ff; cf. ps.-Aristot. *de mund.* 398a1ff.

117. Very much like his contemporary, the syncretistic author of the pseudo-Aristotelian treatise *On the universe* (399a30ff etc.), Philo uses δύναμις to denote both the power exercised and the potential represented by the Supreme Being.

118. *Deus immut.* 77.

119. *Opif.* 3, *decal.* 11, *sacr. Abr.* 18, *v. Mos.* 1.51, *Leg. alleg.* 1.5, *fig.* 10. Cf. P. Wendland, *Philos Schrift von der Vorsehung* (1892) 5.

120. That no man is able to endure direct confrontation with the divine is a

well-known motif in most religions. Cf. *Il.* 20.131 χαλεποὶ δὲ θεοὶ φαίνεσθαι ἐναργεῖς: "the gods are hard to endure when they are present in their true shape" so Elijah's vision according to 1 Kings 19.

121. *Opif.* 23.

122. *Ebr.* 145.

123. The term used is ἀπαντᾶν (to encounter) *virt.* 185; *migr. Abr.* 79.

124. *V. Mos.* 2.189f.

125. Βούλημα τῆς φύσεως (intention of nature) *opif.* 3.

126. *Leg. alleg.* 3.113 etc. Cf. Dihle, *RAC* 6 (1966) 698ff. In defining sin as πάθος (affection), Philo is followed by many Christian authors, e.g. Origen, *explan. in Ps.* 2:6 p. 268 Lo.

127. *Leg. alleg.* 2.50–52.

128. *Cherub.* 57 and 109ff, *Leg. alleg.* 2.68, *post. Cain* 35, *spec. leg.* 1.41.

129. *Migr.* 128 with reference to Gen. 12:4; *rer. div. her.* 267. This seems to be contradicted by the statement that sin results inevitably from human nature (*v. Mos.* 2.147; cf. Z. Knuth, *Sündenbegriff bei Philon* [1934]). In this context Philo has inserted the traditional Jewish doctrine of the Two Spirits (see above p. 77). He calls them δυνάμεις (powers or faculties), and locates them, the good and the bad one, in every human soul (*qu. in exod.* 1.23f). By interpreting them, at the same time, as cosmic powers through which God created the universe, Philo again finds a means to combine Jewish and Platonic (*Leg.* 10.896E ff) ideas of cosmology.

130. *Leg. alleg.* 1.64–66, 2.49 and *d. immut.* 47f; *op. mund.* 149. Cf. H. Schmidt, *Anthropologie Philons* (1933) 59f.

131. Philo's doctrine of revelation and faith is analyzed by U. Früchtel, *Kosmologische Vorstellungen bei Philo* (1968) 164ff and Mühlenberg, *ZNTW* 64 (1973) 1–18.

132. *Mut.* 81f, *conf.* 147f.

133. *Rer. div. her.* 69, 74, 85, and 265; *Leg. alleg.* 3.41.

134. *Conf.* 145f, *det.* 138f.

135. E.g. *fug. et inv.* 63 and 82.

136. *Post. Cain* 15.

137. *Post. Cain* 18–20; *sacrif.* 55.

138. In this respect Philo's ἔρως (love) differs considerably from Plato's (*spec. leg.* 1.44).

139. *Mut.* 270: The divine teacher left his pupil when he had become perfect (τέλειος) οὐχ ὅτι διεζεύχθη . . . ἀλλὰ τὸ ἑκούσιον τοῦ μαθητοῦ βουλόμενος παραστῆσαι, ἵν' ὅπερ ἔμαθε μηκέτι ἐφεστῶτος τοῦ διδασκάλου χωρὶς ἀνάγκης αὐτὸς ἐπιδεικνύμενος ἐθελουργῷ καὶ αὐτοκελεύστῳ προθυμίᾳ χρώμενος, ἐνεργῇ δι' αὐτοῦ· δίδωσι γὰρ ὁ διδάσκαλος τῷ μαθόντι τόπον πρὸς τὴν ἄνευ ὑποβολῆς ἑκούσιον μελέτην: "not intending estrangement . . . but wanting to establish his pupil's own will; so that, with the teacher no longer standing by and the pupil himself displaying his learning without compulsion and in a spirit of indefatigable and unbidden zeal, the pupil acts on his own initiative. For the (sc. divine) teacher gives his pupil opportunity for unprompted, independent action" (cf.

Plot. 2.4.11.8). Προθυμία is a favorite word of Philo's to describe the voluntaristic element of obedience, friendliness, or benevolence (*spec. leg.* 2.83, *v. Mos.* 1.63 and 2.137, *sacrif.* 57ff).

140. This is expounded in Philo's interpretation of the story of Abraham extending hospitality to the three men or angels (Gen. 18; cf. *sacrif.* 58f), who represent God himself, his δύναμις (power), and his ἀρχή (rule).

141. *Mut.* 177f, *Leg. alleg.* 3.228, *praem.* 33 etc.

142. *Leg. alleg.* 3.47f.

143. *Deus immut.* 89f, *mut.* 186, *sacrif.* 127, *Leg. alleg.* 2.83, *agric.* 17f with reference to Num. 6:9 (cf. *Leg. alleg.* 1.17). Philo explicitly distinguishes between ἀκούσιος and ἑκούσιος τροπή (voluntary and involuntary change), the former always being sudden and unexpected. Both, however, affect the human intellect.

144. *Somn.* 2.292; *Leg. alleg.* 2.60, 78, and 292, 3.211ff.

145. E.g. Lyco fr. 23 Wehrli, Polyb. 18.33.7; Epicur. fr. 522 Usener.

146. *SVF* 3.565.

147. *Decal.* 64.

148. V. Nikiprowetsky, *Elenchos chez Philon* (1967) 255–273; R. T. Wallis, "Conscience in Philo" (Center for Herm. Stud. Colloquium, Berkeley 1975).

149. The function of conscience is attributed, without a specific term, to the kidneys in Ps. 16:7, and to the heart in Ps. 4:5 (cf. *Test. Gad.* 5.1; John 3:19f). Συνείδησις means "cognition" or "awareness" in the Septuagint, not "conscience," the only exception being Wisd. of Sol. 17:11 where the influence of Greek thought and terminology is notorious (cf. *XII Test. Rub.* 4; cf. Pelletier, *REG* 80 [1967] 363–371). A term to denote "conscience" is absent also from Rabbinic literature (cf. Strack-Billerbeck *ad Rom.* 2:15). The earliest description of conscience occurs in Euripides (*Or.* 396f, cf. O. Seel in *Festschr. Dornseiff* [1953] 291ff, and M. Class, *Spudasmata* 3 [1967]), though the story of Orestes and the function of the Erinyes imply the same idea at a much earlier stage of the myth. Euripides seems to have been particularly concerned with the problem (cf. Satyr. *vit. Eur.* fr. 39 col. 2.8ff), which corroborates the attribution of Critias *TrGF* 43 F 19 to Euripides (Dihle, *Hermes* 105 [1977] 28ff). In post-classical Greek, the concept and term (συνείδησις, συνειδός, σύνεσις) of conscience seem to have been quite popular (Polyb. 18.43.13; Menand. *Monost.* 654; ps.-Isocr. *ad Demon.* 16; Jos. *c. Ap.* 2.218; Dio Cass. 52.31.6; private letter Pap. Flor. 137, etc.). Yet there is absolutely no trace of a distinct doctrine περὶ συνειδήσεως in any philosophical tradition, though the term is of some importance, for instance, in Seneca (*benef.* 4.17 and 21; ep. 25.6, 43.4, 94.55, and 106.7f; *vit. beat.* 20.4). F. Zucker (Συνείδησις– *conscientia* [1928]; cf. Snell, *Gnomon* 6 [1930] 20) attributed the terminological use of the word to the Epicureans, which cannot be sufficiently ascertained (cf. Schmid, *RAC* 5 [1962] 742), in spite of Sen. *ep.* 97.15. Marietta (*Numen* 17 [1970] 176ff) reclaims the doctrine of conscience for the Greek Stoics without offering substantial proof. Schönlein (*RhMus* 112 [1969] 289ff) tries to show that *conscientia* was coined in Latin as a forensic term, but this disregards

the priority of ethical texts in the use of the word, where it is undoubtedly a translation from the Greek. There is not much to learn from A. Cancrini, *Syneidesis* (1970). The whole topic is discussed by Chadwick, *RAC* 10 (1978) 1025ff. The most impressive description of retrospective conscience is to be found in Lucretius (3.1014ff), whereas Democritus' concept of ἑαυτὸν αἰσχύνεσθαι (feeling ashamed before oneself, B 84 and 244) seems to designate only what was called prospective conscience later on.

150. A good example of the tendency to harmonize Greek and Biblical conceptions is offered by Philo's doctrine that Isaac has received his virtue by nature (φύσει), Abraham and Jacob theirs through learning (μαθήσει) and training (ἀσκήσει; cf. *Abr.* 52; *Jos.* 1). The enumeration of the main factors through which virtue or excellence can be produced was a traditional piece of philosophical teaching from the time of Plato onwards and was handed over to nearly all philosophical systems. Philo simply applies it to the interpretation of the Bible without looking for a concept that might be more appropriate to Biblical anthropology.

151. Hes. *op.* 121ff; Phocyl. fr. 16 D. Clement of Alexandria interprets the anonymous fragment from an Attic tragedy which alludes to that idea as testifying to the Judaeo-Christian belief in the angels of God. Cf. Acts 12 : 15; Herm. *mand.* 6.2.1; Orig. *in Num. hom.* 20.3 = *PG* 12.730; Hieron. *in Eccl.* 5.428 = *PL* 23.1106f.

152. The earliest testimony is Euripides' fragment 1018 N² (ὁ νοῦς γὰρ ἡμῶν ἐστιν ἐν ἑκάστῳ θεός: "the mind is a god in each of us"), which was frequently quoted in later literature. It is likely to mean that man is determined by his own cognition and intention rather than by standards set from outside, without reference to a definite anthropological theory. Similarly, the character (ἦθος Heraclitus B 119; τρόπος Epicharm. B 17) can be spoken of as man's divine guide (δαίμων). Later on, however, Euripides' saying was used to corroborate the philosophical doctrine of human psychology, according to which the intellect (νοῦς) had to play the leading part, thus being an equivalent of the divine guide in the popular tradition: Plat. *Tim.* 90Aff; Chrysipp. *ap.* Diog. Laert. 7.88; Posidon. fr. 187 Edelstein-Kidd; ps.-Plut. *Plac.* 4.5; Cic. *nat. deor.* 2.29 and *Tusc.* 1.65; Sen. *ep.* 41.1f; Epict. *diss.* 1.14.12f; M. Ant. 5.27 and 12.26; ps.-Aristot. *de mund.* 391a12; Apul. *de deo Socr.* 16; Olymp. *in Plat. Alc.* I p. 17 Westerink. Aristotle's conception of practical intelligence (φρόνησις) as the eye of the soul to perceive ethical standards has a similar connotation (*Soph. el.* 165b35, *E.N.* 1144a29f).

153. This kind of self-examination is described by Sen. *de ir.* 3.36.3ff; Epict. *diss.* 3.10.2; Diog. Laert. 8.22; Porph. *vit. Pyth.* 40; and Hierocl. *in carm. aur.* 40ff (see above n. 62). It seems to have been cultivated, above all, in Pythagorean communities. Precise assessment of one's own shortcomings, however, had always been regarded as the basis of moral progress by Epicureans (fr. 522 Us.) and Stoics (Epict. 2.11.1).

154. Reason (νοῦς) is the guide in human life (*opif.* 30), is of divine provenance (*decal.* 134, *opif.* 77), causes human freedom (*deus immut.* 47f and 178)

and immortality (*opif.* 135, *Gig.* 14), and leads to both self-knowledge and knowledge of God (*migr. Abr.* 136 and 195, *somn.* 1.60 and 119). Philo opposes the Stoic doctrine that the human νοῦς is a scattered piece of the cosmic νοῦς, since he is not a materialist. But he agrees with the Stoic opinion according to which the physical death that dismisses the νοῦς into immortality ends, at the same time, the individual existence of man (*Cherub.* 114).

155. The most important passages are *det.* 22–27, *fug. et inv.* 117f and 131, *deus immut.* 135, *det.* 146, *rer. div. her.* 7, *praem.* 84, *Jos.* 47f, 215, and 262, *decal.* 87, *virt.* 206.

156. *Virt.* 206 τὸ συνειδός, ὃ μόνον ἐξ ἁπάντων δικαστήριον τέχναις λόγων οὐ παράγεται: "the conscience alone of all courts of judgement is not led astray by verbal skill."

157. *Fug.* 118, *deus immut.* 135 (αὐγὴ φωτὸς [ray of light] in the human soul).

158. *Det.* 22f (ἀληθὴς ἄνθρωπος ἐν τῇ ψυχῇ: the true man in the soul), *fug.* 131.

159. It prevents man from any τροπὴ ἀκούσιος: involuntary change, but if it has left the soul, κάθοδος εὐθὺς δίδοται τοῖς ἑκουσίοις σφάλμασι: an easy path is immediately given to voluntary errors (*fug.* 117; cf. 114–116), for it has been given into the διάνοια of man (*det.* 146).

160. *Det.* 146.

161. Συμπεφυκὼς καὶ συνοικῶν ἑκάστῃ ψυχῇ: con-genital and co-resident in each soul (*decal.* 87), γέρας ἐξαίρετον: a selected gift (*fug.* 118), ἐκ τῆς ἡμετέρας ψυχῆς διαζευχθείς: separated from our soul (*fug.* 117).

CHAPTER V

1. See above p. 68. The problem of how to reconcile the conceptions of divine rule and human freedom became particularly important in the post-Biblical period of Jewish thought. Jewish popular ethics in the Hellenistic environment heavily stressed the view that intention is the basis of moral evaluation rather than action and its result (e.g. *Orac. Sibyll.* 2.56ff and 123ff).

2. This argument was to prove that the belief in strict determination of every event inevitably paralyzes human activity. Cf. *SVF* 2.956/957.

3. St. Paul's doctrine of predestination in Rom. 9–11 was not properly understood and expounded until the fourth century. The Gnostics found in his writings only the arguments in favor of their determinist doctrines and against the Old Testament tradition, whereas the Orthodox largely restricted their use of his letters to the task of moral exhortation.

4. No attempt is made to give a definition of Gnosis. Cf. *Gnosis u. Gnostizismus* ed. K. Rudolph (1975) pp. xi–xviii.

5. The idea of ὑπεράνω τῶν τῆς εἱμαρμένης εἶναι, i.e. to be freed from the necessities of the created world and to return into an entirely spiritual existence, frequently occurs in Gnostic literature and denotes the very goal of sal-

vation. The road to this goal may be opened up by a ritual like that of baptism (*Exc. ex Theod.* 78), but the goal itself is reached through cognition (*Corp. Herm.* 1.27, 10.8, 12.5f; *Kore Kosmou* 15; *Corp. Herm.* fr. 20 Nock-Fest.; *Ev. Ver.* p. 30/31; cf. J. Bidez and F. Cumont, *Les mages hellénisés* [1938] 2.243).

6. See Appendix II.

7. The will of a divine being is frequently spoken of as a hypostasis or person in Gnostic systems, above all where the origin of the created universe is being described. (Book of Jeû 2.44 p. 306.19 Schmidt; *Gnost. Anonym.* p. 338.11 Schmidt; Ptolem. *ap.* Hippol. *ref.* 6.38.5f; *Corp. Herm.* 10.2–4; Asclep. 8.20; *Apocr. Iohann.* p. 31.9, 33.5, and 34.17 [*Pap.* Berol. 8502]). According to the cosmogony of *Corp. Herm.* 13, the θέλημα θεοῦ (will of God) is the father, the σοφία θεοῦ (wisdom of God) the mother of man (2). Being the result of noetic activity, the will has to be strictly separated from all irrational impulses as originating from matter. Θέλησις or θέλημα has become, in this context, the synonym of βούλησις which always denoted, at least from Plato (*Gorg.* 467) onwards, the impulse to act according to the previous cognition of the better. The same definition of θέλησις occurs in Plotinus (6.7.28), whereas the Gnostic Justin (*ap.* Hippol. *ref.* 5.24) attributes θέλησις to beings of minor dignity. Conversely, the first Hermetic treatise (1.12ff) describes the way in which a spiritual being misused for the first time its freedom to become involved with matter in terms of βούλησις. The generation of a second divine being from a superior one, which process is exclusively caused by the intellectual activity of the latter, is frequently called προβολή (προβάλλεσθαι) in Gnostic literature (e.g. Valentinus *ap.* Iren. *haer.* 1.1.1; Simon *ap.* Iren. *haer.* 1.21.1). The underlying concept also entails a component of volition, since no external cause of the act is possible. This conception, however, was not restricted to Gnostic thought. Tatian made the Logos "jump" into existence because of the will of the Father (*adv. Graec.* 5.1: θελήματι δὲ τῆς ἁπλότητος αὐτοῦ προπηδᾷ λόγος. Cf. *Ign. Magn.* 8.2; *Just. dial.* 12.8).

8. *Apocr. Joh.* p. 10.21ff (Nag Ham. Cod. III) where θέλησις is posterior to νοῦς or *Ev. Ver.* 36/37 and *Od. Sal.* 9.3 Bauer. The ἐνέργεια (activity) of the divine intellect is called θέλησις and again identified with its οὐσία (substance of being) by the Hermetics (*Corp. Herm.* 10.2). The Gnostic Ptolemaeus taught that God's will originates from his thought (*ap.* Athan. *c. Ar.* 3.59), whereas in the Hermetic treatise *Asclepius* no difference in time is admitted between God's thought, will, and action (8.12f; cf. Iren. *haer.* 1.23.2). Regardless of these variations in the Gnostic concept of divine thought and will the salvation of man always depends on cognition, which is, at the same time, cognition of both the plan or will of God and of one's own nature (*Ev. Ver.* 30; *Corp. Herm.* 1.21; *Apocr. Joh.* p. 68.13f [*Pap.*Berol. 8502]; *Ev. Thom. log.* 67; *Exc. Theod.* 78; Naassenes *ap.* Hipp. *ref.* 5.5; *Corp. Herm.* 1.12, 1.18, and 7.2 fr. 36 Festug.; Marc. *ap.* Iren. *haer.* 1.14.4; Ev. Phil. *ap.* Epiphan. Pan. 26). Turning to the Savior, repenting, love of God, or faith can easily be described in terms of cognition (*Corp. Herm.* 1.28, 4.4ff, and 5.1; cf. A. J. Festugière, *Révélation d'Hermès Trismégiste* III [1953] 109ff; Heracleon *ap.* Origen, *in Ioh.*

comm. 13.31 *GCS* 4.255), and the faculty of choice is attached to the gift of reason in man's nature (*Corp. Herm.* fr. ex Stob. XVIII Festug.) throughout Gnostic literature.

9. E.g. *Ev. Ver.* 17; Ptolem. *ap.* Athan. *c. Ar.* 3.59; Hippol. *ref.* 6.38.5ff.

10. E.g. the Gnostic myth of the fall of Sophia (*Apocr. Joh.* p. 14.9ff [Nag Ham. Cod. III]; id. p. 36.16ff [*Pap.*Berol. 8502]; Iren. *haer.* 1.2.2; *Exc. Theod.* 30). The same motive occurs in Hippol. *ref.* 6.29ff; *Epiph. Pan.* 31.11.4; *Kore Kosmou* 46; *Corp. Herm.* 1.12ff and 10.20 (cf. Festugière, *Révélation* III, 83ff). The idea of a spiritual being, such as the human self, becoming able to cause evil simply because of its preparedness to take a risk (τόλμα) and to make the wrong decision (ῥοπή) by using its freedom (ἐξουσία) is well known in the Platonic tradition, too. Cf., for instance, Max. Tyr. *or.* 41.4; *Orac. Chald.* frs. 106 and 163 des Places; Plot. 5.1.1.4 and 6.9.5.25. See below n. 65.

11. E.g. *Apocr. Joh.* pp. 51.6ff and 52.17ff (Pap. Berol. 8502). In Hermetic texts the will of God, called θέλησις or θέλημα (1.8, 4.1, 5.7, 10.2, etc.) rather than βούλησις or βουλή (9.6, 13.6; both combined: 13.4, 13.19) and *voluntas* in Latin, can be identified with his goodness (*bonitas* Asclep. 19; *benignitas* id. 26; see below n. 65). Yet the dominating aspect of the divine will seems to be its power, αὐθεντία (*Corp. Herm.* 1.2; the meaning of the word explained in *Glotta* 39 [1960] 77ff) or δύναμις (cf. Festugière, *Révélation* III, 153ff). The whole system of cosmic order and determination (εἱμαρμένη, ἀνά-γκη, τάξις) which precludes freedom of choice for inferior beings, has been brought about solely *dei nutu* (Asclep. 40). The sovereignty of the Supreme Being is extensively spoken of in Gnostic texts of different origin (e.g. *Ev. Ver.* 37; *Corp. Herm.* 13.1–7; *PGM* 4.475ff; Naassenes *ap.* Hippol. *ref.* 5.7.25 with reference to Exod. 3:14), and it is the divine will through which this power and sovereignty becomes manifest. The same applies to philosophical texts of the same period that testify to a predominantly religious interest (Numen. fr. 17 des Places; *Orac. Chald.* fr. 7 des Places). Conversely, in the view of scholarly Platonism the origin of the ordered universe is simply regarded as a natural consequence of the goodness of God (see below n. 59).

12. Θέλω μαθεῖν: "I want to learn" (*Corp. Herm.* 1.7, 1.11f, 4.6, 13.1, and 13.15; cf. Festugière, *Révélation* III, 110f; *Act. Joh.* 95). Correspondingly, religious and moral admonition is sometimes directed to the will of man: τὸ δὲ δύνασθαι γνῶναι καὶ θελῆσαι καὶ ἐλπίσαι ὁδός ἐστιν εὐθεία, "The ability to know and to wish and to hope is a straight road" (*Corp. Herm.* 11.21), or ἐπίστασαι εἰς ἑαυτόν ("pull yourself together"; cf. P*ap.* Tebt. 27.4) καὶ ἐλεύσεται or θέλη-σον καὶ γίνεται (*Corp. Herm.* 10.7). A similar admonition is formulated by the astrologer Vettius Valens (5.9 p. 220 Kroll) who wants his followers to become στρατιῶται τῆς εἱμαρμένης, "soldiers of fate." The recipient of the Hermetic revelation finds himself instructed (διδαχθείς) and endowed with power (δυνα-μωθείς 1.27). His powers, that is to say his virtues (13.7f), join his will (θέλημα) to perceive and praise the order of being (13.18f).

13. E.g. *Ev. Ver.* 17/18 and 32/33; *Corp. Herm.* 7.1, 10.8f, and 11.20f;

Iren. *haer.* 1.21.4; cf. Jonas, *TU* 81 (1962) 96ff. The stress laid on man's will which seems to contradict the dominant role of cognition can only be understood from the religious character of the Hermetic doctrine. The same applies to the emphasis laid on the power of God. Cf. above n. 9 and M. P. Nilsson, *Gesch. d. griech. Religion* II (1950) 575ff.

14. Cf. Dörrie, *NAWG* 2 (1967) 46ff. The immortality of the human soul became a topic of predominant interest from the end of the first century A.D. onwards. This can be seen from Orac. 37 of the Tübingen Theosophy (ed. Erbse, 1941), which has been shown to go back to an authentic question put to the famous oracle at Didyma in late Hellenistic times (Robert, *CRAI* [1968] 589f).

15. *SFV* 2.974–1007. Cf. Schröder, *RAC* 7 (1969) 539ff; D. Armand de Mendieta, *Fatalisme et liberté* (1945).

16. Sen. *ep.* 107.10; Cleanth. *SVF* 1.527; more drastically *SVF* 2.974.

17. The main testimony is Aulus Gellius 7.2 (*SVF* 2.1000) and Cic. *de fat.* 41.

18. Ps.-Plut. *de fat.* 9.572F–573A. Cf. Apul. *dogm. Plat.* 1.12; Calc. *in Plat. Tim.* pp. 184.10 and 206.3 Waszink; Nemes. *nat. homin.* 38 and 44, *Corp. Herm.* 12.8f. The doctrine of three gods or groups of gods was backed by Plat. *ep.* 2, 312E. The identification of divine providence (πρόνοια) and divine will seems to have been introduced by the Platonist Gaius and his school. Thus fate and its cosmic determination could be explained as a law which the Supreme Being has given to the universe (Nemes. *nat. hom.* 36 with reference to Plat. *Tim.* 39Eff). Cf. Waszink, *EntrFondHardt* 12 (1960) 64f with further references.

19. The Middle Platonic doctrine of several levels of fate corresponded to the principles of Platonic theology at that period (e.g. Numen. fr. 21/22 des Places) and could be easily reconciled with astrological determinism as accepted by the Stoics. So the Middle Platonic attitude to astrology radically differed from the doctrine of Carneades who had furnished the stock arguments for many centuries of anti-astrological polemics (cf. Schröder, *RAC* 7 [1969] 553ff). The conception of subsequent levels of determination also occurs in purely astrological texts. Ptolemaeus (*Tetrab.* 1.3.4ff) distinguishes between θεία εἱμαρμένη (divine fate) which determines the cosmic process and is therefore, ἀμετάπτωτος (unchanging), and φυσικὴ εἱμαρμένη (physical fate), which governs τὰ ἐπίγεια (earthly circumstances) and concedes ἀλλοιώσεις (alterations) in the chain of determination. The πρῶται αἰτίαι (first causes), however, always belong to the θεία εἱμαρμένη.

20. This conception originates from the interpretation of Plat. *Rep.* 617E and was generally accepted in all branches of Middle Platonism. W. Theiler (*Phyllobolia f. Von der Mühll* [1946] 35ff) has convincingly shown that Tacitus in a famous chapter (*ann.* 6.22) refers to the Epicurean doctrine of chance, the Stoic doctrine of all-embracing Heimarmene, and the Platonic conception of initial freedom of decision and subsequent determination. The Platonic view was criticized by the argument that a single chain of causation which connects

a series of events should not include different modes of causation (Nemes. *nat. hom.* 37). This kind of argument presupposes the Peripatetic distinction between the order of nature and the area of human action, where everything may happen differently (ἐνδεχόμενα καὶ ἄλλως ἔχειν).

21. The Platonist Atticus (fr. 8 *ap.* Eus. *praep. ev.* 15.12.1f) attributes to Aristotle a system of threefold causation which, however, is not to be found either in Aristotle or in Peripatetic literature of the second century. According to this conception the heavenly bodies are invariably moved by Heimarmene, in the sublunar realm everything is caused by Nature, and human affairs are governed by Reason, Prudence, and Soul. Atticus strongly opposes this opinion, primarily by the Platonic argument that the universe is animated, the whole order of nature thus resulting from a soul's activity. The terminology used in this context, however, seems to be Stoic rather than Platonic.

22. Alexander even admits, despite the anti-astrological tradition of his school, that the stars contribute to causation in the area of nature (p. 169.24 Bruns). But no Peripatetic could agree with separating, in whatever way, nature and what the Stoics called εἱμαρμένη, as apparently did some astrologers (Nemes. *nat. hom.* 36) and Bar Daiṣān of Edessa (see below n. 35).

23. A doctrine concerning freedom and fate, composed of curiously heterogeneous elements, has been preserved in an anonymous Vita Pythagorica (Phot. *bibl. cod.* 249 p. 439b36ff Bekker). The author distinguishes between four determining factors of human action: a man embarks because of his own decision (κατὰ προαίρεσιν), is driven into a tempest by chance (κατὰ τύχην), and returns safely with the aid of God (κατὰ θεοῦ πρόνοιαν). Heimarmene, the fourth factor, only provides the determining frame for the whole life of man, such as his inevitably getting older, his being subject to physical limitations, and the like. This doctrine, which has been attributed, not very convincingly, to either Agatharchides (O. Immisch, "Agatharchidea," *SHAW* [1919] 77ff) or Poseidonius (Reinhardt, *PW* 22 [1954] 764ff), supplements the Peripatetic triad of Nature, Chance, and Free Choice by God, who freely interferes with everything by his providence. Differently, perhaps Stoic, is *Aet. plac.* 1.29.7.

24. This element had already been particularly important in Aristotle's ethical theory. He defined virtues and vices as ἕξεις προαιρετικαί (choice patterns) which are brought about by exercise or training: the mind of a righteous man is inclined, in consequence of many actions according to the standards of righteousness, to decide for the righteous action in any given situation (e.g. *E.N.* 1106b36, 1140a4). The same conception became attached to the term προαίρεσις in later Stoicism, as can be seen in Epictetus. By that term he described the general inclination of the human intellect in its evaluation of the φαντασίαι (impressions) rather than the moral choice to be made in a given situation. The latter meaning of προαίρεσις clearly prevailed in earlier Greek. So προαίρεσις, at least in the language of Epictetus, came very near to our concept of good or ill will, though always pointing to a phenomenon of entirely intellectual activity (Epict. *diss.* 1.22.10, 1.22.103, and 4.6.34; *ench.* 1.5 etc.; cf. M. Pohlenz, *Stoa* II² [1949] 164).

25. Philostr. *vit. Apoll.* 5.37. The change from φιλοσοφία κατὰ φύσιν (philosophy according to nature) to φιλοσοφία θεοκλυτεῖν φάσκουσα (philosophy alleging to be God's will), as documented in that debate, was also implied in the new meaning, which the word πίστις (belief, faith) acquired in Hermetic, Jewish, and Christian literature. Cf. Lührmann, *RAC* 11 (1979) 48–122.

26. Both fragments of the Chaldean Oracles and Numenius have been recently edited by Edouard des Places (Paris 1971 and 1973), who gives an excellent description of their semi-religious character in his introductions.

27. Albinus, for instance, strictly excluded all kinds of non-rational striving for cognition from his concept of philosophy (*didasc.* 1–7), and Theon of Smyrna expects the purification of the human mind exclusively from sciences such as geometry or dialectics (*Introd. Plat.* 3.4ff; cf. Plat. *Rep.* 527D). In the period after Plotinus, however, theurgy became recognized as a part of the official Platonic tradition. Iamblichus defends the use of meaningless θεῖα ὀνόματα (sacred appellations), taken from foreign cults or magical practice, at the highest level of philosophical speculation, for the Supreme Being is not open to rational understanding (κρεῖττον ἢ ὥστε διαιρεῖσθαι εἰς γνῶσιν *de myst.* 7.4).

28. *Orac. Chald.* fr. 4, 12, and 22 des Places.

29. The same conception occurs in Gnostic doctrine (e.g. *Apocr. Joh.* 21.19ff [Pap. Berol. 8502]) and, later on, in the Neoplatonic interpretation of the Chaldean Oracles after Porphyry (e.g. Synes. *hymn.* 1.210ff and 2.90ff).

30. Cf. F. W. Cremer, *Die Chaldäischen Orakel u. Jamblich* (1969) 102ff.

31. See above n. 13.

32. The "inventor" of Gnosticism according to the Christian tradition, the Samaritan Simon Magus, was already represented as a partisan of determinism (ps.-Clem. *hom.* 10.2 and 14; *Recogn.* 5). The same argument was directed against the Stoic doctrine of Heimarmene (Just. *apol.* 2.6; cf. Albin. *epit.* 31.8).

33. E.g. Theophil. *ad Autolyc.* 2.27; Just. *dial.* 1.5; Iren. *haer.* 4.4.5. Irenaeus (5.9), interpreting 1 Cor. 15:50, holds that only by divine grace can man become able to make the right use of his freedom in order to be saved. Justin, on the other hand, is very much concerned about man's full responsibility for both his salvation and his moral conduct, because of his λογικὴ δύναμις (reasoning power) which entails the freedom of choice. The divine grace educates and instructs him to facilitate the right turn towards God (προτροπή), whereas the demons blind his intellect (*apol.* 1.10). The Son and Logos is perfect primarily with regard to his intellect (*apol.* 2.13); this can be gathered from his always being in agreement with the will of the Father (*dial.* 61). Life according to nature and according to the will of God is identical in the view of Justin (*dial.* 3.4, 8.2, and 142.3; similarly Tert. *virg. vel.* 16, *apol.* 17; cf. Otto, *MünchTheolStud* 19 [1960] 19ff), and the divine help in reaching the goal applies to man's intellect rather than to his will (*dial.* 56, *apol.* 1.61). The order of creation is open to intellectual understanding, as is nature according to philosophical cosmology (*apol.* 1.10). Conversely, Ire-

naeus blames the pagan philosophers for not having seen the will of the Creator behind the order of nature (5.29; cf. 3.3.1). Accordingly, Irenaeus stresses the volitional rather than the intellectual implication of man's obedience or disobedience to God's commandment (5.27.2; cf. 5.26.2). An interesting accentuation of the two factors occurs in ps.-Clement (*hom.* 21.27) where the significance of baptism is explained. Baptism frees from sins which have been committed ἐν ἀγνοίᾳ (in ignorance). After baptism, however, the conduct of life should be modelled on the justice of God which is described in voluntaristic terms: δίκαιον τὸ θέλημα τοῦ μὴ ἀδικεῖν, "Just is the will to do no injustice." It is the προαίρεσις in the Epictetan sense (see above n. 24) which should be changed in consequence of instruction and baptism and should lead to salvation. The same beginning of a volitional attitude, but in the opposite sense, is repeatedly referred to in early Christian demonology. The demons have been created, very much like men, with the gift of free choice and the corresponding intellectual faculty for distinguishing between good and evil. Some of them became proud of this privilege and wanted to be independent of their Creator and this persuaded them to make the wrong use of their freedom. From this fall, for which they are fully responsible, their general inclination or attitude has been changed for the worse (Just. *apol.* 2.7 and *dial.* 88; Tat. *adv. Graec.* 7 and 17.3f; Athenag. *leg.* 24.4; Tert. *adv. Marc.* 2.10; Orig. *princ.* 1.5.5, 1.8.1, etc.; Athan. *vit. Ant.* 22; Greg. Naz. *or.* 39.7; Epiph. *haer.* 66.16.1–4).

34. Clement agrees with philosophical anthropology that man's faculty to choose freely is closely linked with his intellectual equipment. So moral evil depends entirely on man's αὐτεξούσιον, his freedom of choice (*paed.* 1.62ff), obedience to God's commandment leads to life according to nature and reason (*paed.* 1.98–103), and the order of the universe is open to rational understanding (*strom.* 3.64.2f). Even the cognition of God can be supported by analogies taken from mathematics and astronomy (*strom.* 7.11.90.4). Γνώμη serves as the key word to denote both cognition and decision in moral and religious life (*paed.* 1.2; cf. Tat. *adv. Graec.* 7). Clement also stresses the cognitive implications of faith (πίστις), which he identifies with free choice (*strom.* 5.13.86.1) and with Stoic συγκατάθεσις (assent) (*strom.* 2.2.8.4; cf. 2.6.28.1), that is to say the assent which reason gives to a φαντασία (impression), built up from sensual impressions, in order to initiate action. Faith, in the view of Clement, is the basis of cognition (γνῶσις) which leads to perfection (*protr.* 9.88.1; *strom.* 2.2.8.3, 2.4.12.1, 5.86.1, 7.55.1), and there is no γνῶσις without preceding πίστις (faith); this last is said against Valentinus (*strom.* 5.1.2). Yet faith differs from other kinds of cognition: first, it always implies a decision to act, which Clement says against another Gnostic, Basilides (2.10.1–3, 11f). That is why repentance (μετάνοια), though being "slow cognition" (βραδεῖα γνῶσις) in contrast to ἀναμαρτησία (innocence) which is πρώτη γνῶσις (primary cognition) (*strom.* 2.26.5), can be understood as a species of faith which leads to the ἄφεσις ἁμαρτιῶν (deliverance from sin) (*strom.* 2.11.2). The perfect Christian, very much like the Stoic sage, does not know

of μετάνοια (cf. Didym. *in Ps. 29* p. 8.29 Kehl). Secondly, every act of cognition presupposes, in some way or other, the anticipation of its result (πρόληψις) by means of a guess (εἰκασία) about its object. Faith refers to the divine Logos, its object not being open to intellectual proof or understanding (*strom.* 2.8.4, 2.13.4, 2.16.1f). Consequently, faith itself is συγκατάθεσις (assent) and πρόληψις which precedes γνῶσις, but by no means εἰκασία, since it necessarily involves the decision to act (*paed.* 1.101.2; *strom.* 2.79.5). Being anticipation, πίστις remains inferior to γνῶσις (*strom.* 7.55.1f; cf. 6.99.1), but it is superior to normal knowledge (ἐπιστήμη), since it tends to be transformed into irrefutable perception (κατάληψις *strom.* 2.16.3–17.1). As can be seen from the preceding survey, Clement's conception of faith has important voluntaristic implications, for faith, in his view, is prior to intellectual cognition and closely linked with action and moral life (*strom.* 2.4.12.1, 5.1.3.2, 5.13.86, etc.; cf. E. F. Osborne, *Philosophy of Clement* [1957] 127; R. Mortley, *Connaissance chez Clément* [1973] 110f). Moreover, πίστις is the πρώτη πρὸς σωτηρίαν νεῦσις, first inclination toward salvation (*strom.* 2.31.3) and a function of life rather than thought (*qu. div. salv.* 10 τῆς ζωῆς ἔργον: a deed of life), and life or volition is the primary performance of the human intellect in the view of Clement (*strom.* 2.77.5). So πίστις denotes a first and non-cognitive act on the way to salvation. It is because of this particular concept of faith that Clement, though firmly rooted in the philosophical tradition, could in fact transcend the entirely intellectualistic interpretation of moral conduct and religious progress, as set out below, n. 42.

35. Bardesanes, *Liber legum regionum*, ed. Nau, *Patrol. Syr.* I 2 (1907) 450ff. *The Book of the Laws of the Countries* gives a different picture of Bar Daiṣān and his doctrine from that reported in the antiheretic literature of the Syrian church. The latter only starts in the second half of the fourth century (Ephraem), when the Bardesanites had apparently come very close to the Manicheans, whereas the *Book of the Laws*, of which the author may well be a personal disciple of Bar Daiṣān, was already quoted, in a Greek translation, by Eusebius of Caesarea early in the fourth century. In the most recent comprehensive study of Bar Daiṣān, H. J. Drijvers (*Bardaiṣān* [1966]) prefers the *Liber legum regionum* as the basis of our knowledge about him; Barbara Ehlers (*ZKG* 81 [1970] 334ff) gives greater credit to the haeresiologists. The problem is of no great importance in our context, since the *Liber legum regionum* is dated before A.D. 300 and well attested for the circle of Bar Daiṣān by its own wording. Bar Daiṣān's acquaintance with Greek philosophy is not surprising. Porphyry quoted a writing of his in Greek, and Sextus Julius Africanus knew him personally.

36. *Lib. leg. reg.* 18 refutes three different doctrines: everything is caused by fate; everything is caused by the free choice of man, except physical evil which is due to chance; everything is caused by free choice except physical evil, which is a means of divine punishment. The first opinion was held by the astrologers, the second by the Epicureans.

37. See above p. 104.

38. For the parallel from Ptolemy, *Tetrabibl.* 1.4.2–12 see above n. 21 and A. Dihle, *Kerygma u. Logos* (Festschr. Andresen, 1979).

39. Cf. Drijvers (above n. 35) 168ff.

40. See above n. 33.

41. This is a well-known topic in early Christian literature. St. Ambrose, for instance, attributes the superior wisdom of simple Christians to their faith (*fides*) which results from divine revelation and, consequently, surpasses all kinds of human knowledge (in *Hex.* 1.6.22ff; *epist* 34.2; *de bono mort.* 11.5). Thus God shapes both the wisdom and the intention of the faithful (in *Luc. comm.* 1.10; in Ps. 118 *expos.* 10.35).

42. See above n. 34. The voluntaristic connotation which Clement introduced into the concept of συγκατάθεσις (assent) exactly meets Plutarch's criticism of that specifically Stoic doctrine (*Stoic. repugn.* 47.1055F ff).

43. A surprisingly free use of philosophical terms and concepts is typical of early Christian theology. Tertullian, for instance, has derived his own psychological doctrine, as set out in *De anima*, predominantly from Stoic sources. Nevertheless he does not hesitate to refer to the Platonic tripartition of the soul or the strict distinction between spirit and soul (νοῦς / ψυχή) where he can use such details in his argument (*de resurr.* 17.5, 40.4).

44. See J. M. Rist, *Stoic Philosophy* (1969) 128ff and above n. 24.

45. Barbara Aland points out that Clement's conception of faith as voluntary assent was developed against the Gnostic doctrine of involuntary faith (*Gnosis* [1977] 205ff).

46. Origen's theory of freedom has been preserved, in the Greek original, in *de princ.* 3.1. (On Exod. 4:21ff see 3.1.8–11.) For Origen as for all his contemporaries who were accustomed to argue on Platonic lines, freedom of choice (αὐτεξούσιον) results from man's being endowed with reason, which constitutes his true self (*princ.* 1.5ff and 3.1.3) and his being the image of God (*princ.* 1.16; *in ep. ad Rom. comm.* 8.2). Accordingly, moral judgement refers to intention rather than action (*c. Cels.* 4.45). Evil which has to be understood as μὴ ὄν (non-being) exclusively comes from man's voluntary turning away from his Creator (*princ.* 2.9.3–4; *in Joh. comm.* 2.192=*GCS* 4.89). The will of God (θέλημα) is self-fulfilling, according to his boundless power (αὐθεντία *in Joh. comm.* 12.49=*GCS* 4.558), unless human activity contravenes, which only happens on earth. By adapting his will to the divine will man is able to transform his earthly existence into a heavenly one (*de orat. Dom.* 26). Yet man's voluntary turning towards evil or non-being never leads to final corruption: the divine educator constantly improves the human intellect (*in Jerem. hom.* 20.3–4=*PG* 13.530ff; *in Lev. hom.* 14.3=*GCS* 6.483ff), and even attaches conscience as a guide to supranatural cognition to man's soul (*princ.* 2.10.7; *in ep. ad Rom. comm.* 2.9 *PG* 14.892). Will, however, never becomes a factor in moral life which can be thought of independently from the act of corresponding cognition. Will originates from the intellect without being separated from its origin (*princ.* 1.2.6), very much like the verbal utterance which cannot be separated from its meaning (*in Joh. comm.* 1.38=*GCS* 4.277).

47. *SVF* 3.1175, 1177, 1181.

48. Origen mainly refers to Rom. 9.16ff and Phil. 2.12f.

49. Correspondingly, sin is explained from the cooperation of man, who misuses his freedom of choice (αὐτεξούσιον), and evil demons (*princ.* 3.3.2–5).

50. Οὐκ ἀλόγως: not without reason (*princ.* 3.3.2–5).

51. According to Origen man participates in God's eternal and spiritual substance. Consequently no human being can be excepted from salvation nor doomed to eternal damnation or annihilation (*princ.* 4.4.9ff), so that everybody will reach, after a long period of education and purification, the ultimate freedom of the entirely spiritual existence (*in Mat. comm. tom.* 17.30=*GCS* 11.671ff *in Ex. hom.* 1.16=*GCS* 8.340). God's education mainly applies to the human intellect rather than renewing the will independently from cognition. The human soul is constantly being led by exhortation and punishment to acts of cognition that reinstall its original righteousness, which has been spoiled by previous decisions resulting from error (*princ.* 2.9.5f; cf. E. Mühlenberg, in *Athanase*, ed. Kannengiesser [1973] 215–230). Thus the final goal of the education of man, individually and collectively, is the full cognition of God (see below n. 106). Origen's theory of inspiration has been formulated on the same lines. The Holy Spirit has not replaced the human intellect of the authors of the Bible, instead He has widened their intellectual capacities (H.v. Campenhausen, *Entstehung der chr. Bibel* [1968] 366f).

52. Cf. E. J. Meijering, in *Romanitas et Christianitas* (1973) 221–232.

53. *Adv. haer.* 4.37.4–6; cf. Just. *apol.* 1.43.8.

54. *Adv. haer.* 2.18.4, 4.6.5, 4.41.2, 5.27.1; cf. Matt. 9:29. Iren. *adv. haer.* 4.14, 38–39; cf. Aland (above n. 45) 168ff.

55. Iren. fr. 5 Harvey; Alex. Aphrod. *de fat.* 12; cf. Aristot. *E.N.* 1113a9.

56. *Adv. haer.* 2.1.1 and 2.18.3.

57. *Adv. haer.* 1.6.1, 2.15.3, 2.42.2, etc. Cf. Clem. Al. *paed.* 1.27.2; Firm. Mat. *err. prof. relig.* 26.3; Didym. *in Ps.* 29 p. 12.8 Kehl, and below n. 71. The identity of cognition and volition in the divine mind was also taught by the Hermetics (*Corp. Herm.* 10.2; Asclep. 8.12f), whereas most Gnostics defended the sequence cognition–intention with regard to the Supreme Being (e.g. Ptolem. ap. Athan. *c. Ar.* 3.59; see above n. 11).

58. Cf. G. May, *Schöpfung aus dem Nichts* (1978) 170ff.

59. *Adv. haer.* 2.10.2, 5.5.3, etc. Both events testify to God's sovereignty beyond the rational understanding of man, in that no object of cognition could possibly precede the act of will which, consequently, is identical with that of both cognition and action.

60. *Adv. haer.* 2.37.1, 3.23.1, 4.4.2, 5.4.2, etc.

61. In the view of most philosophers the intellect was to be called the divine guide in the human soul who leads man on his way through life (e.g. Cic. *Tusc.* 1.52ff; M. Ant. 5.10.6). Philo attributed this role to the divine πνεῦμα which is added to the natural equipment of man by divine grace and can be ascertained from the operating human conscience (see above). Similarly, Origen (*in ep. ad Rom. comm.* 2.9.3=*PG* 14.893; *princ.* 2.10.7) speaks of the

divine πνεῦμα, as do some of his followers. Didymus the Blind further developed the doctrine of the πνεῦμα τῇ ψυχῇ παρεζευγμένον (spirit yoked beside the soul), which he calls γνώμη and διάνοια and which enables the faithful to communicate with God and follow his orders (de spir. sanct. 54–57 = PL 39.1079A; in Ps. 29 p. 11.2ff Kehl, with the editor's notes pp. 162–170). But neither Origen nor Didymus mentions, in this context, the well-known topic that conscience belongs to man's natural endowment, which can be gathered from the fact that everybody, regardless of his intellectual standing, race, or religion, is able to distinguish between good and evil (Joh. Chrys. in 2 Tim. hom. 5.3; in Gen. hom. 17.1 = PG 53.153; August. lib. arb. 1.6 and 15; trin. 14.21, etc.). Origen and his followers clearly understood the gift of πνεῦμα as an additional and supranatural faculty of cognition (cf. Hieron. in Ez. comm. 1.6f = PL 25.22). The grace of God enlightens the intellect rather than transforming the will of man.

62. Dörrie, EntrFondHardt 5 (1957) 191ff.

63. For general information on Plotinus' doctrine see W. R. Inge, Philosophy of Plotinus 1, 2 (1929); Schwyzer, PW 21 (1951) 471ff; J. M. Rist, Plotinus (1965).

64. Plotinus describes the way in which the universe is constantly being structured and animated by interpreting Plato's cosmology (especially Tim. 30B and 39A), but also with the aid of Stoic concepts (Diog. Laert. 7.142; Cic. nat. deor. 2.22). Cf. P. Hadot, Porphyre et Marius Victorinus (1968) 117ff.

65. Plotinus set down a coherent doctrine of evil in the treatise 1.8 (E. Schröder, Plotinus Abhandlung πόθεν τὰ κακά [1916]; Rist, Phronesis 6 [1961] 154–166; E. Mühlenberg, Kerygma u. Dogma 15 [1969] 226–238). The inexhaustible productivity of the One constantly creates, either directly or indirectly, beings that are less perfect than the One itself (5.3.15f). They only become evil, in the strict sense of the word, if they do not turn again to their origin (5.3.15f; cf. Synes. de insomn. p. 159.15 Terzaghi; Macrob. in somn. Scip. 1.11.11; Porphyry has a somewhat different doctrine of the ἐπιστροφή, the return toward their origins, of lower beings [sent. 30.2] which has no parallel in Plotinus). That the descent of the νοῦς into beings of lower standing or the embodiment of the soul respectively has two aspects—loss of dignity / creation of the structured universe—was already taught in Middle Platonism (Albin. did. 16; Taurus ap. Iambl. ap. Stob. 1.378 W.H.; Plot. 4.8.5.1; Iambl. ap. Stob. 1.379). The descent can also be described in either intellectualistic (false judgement, ignorance: Albin ap. Stob. 1.375.10; Porph. ad Marc. 32) or voluntaristic terms (τόλμα, ῥοπή, νεῦσις: daring, inclination, respectively, Plut. ser. num. vind. 27; Plot. 1.6.5.49; Porph. antr. nymph. 11). Purely irrational volition (ὄρεξις), however, which does not originate from the cognitive faculty as does βούλησις or θέλησις (Plot. 6.8.1), is unable to create anything. In the field of ethics, it appears as love of the body which is to be shunned (Albin. did. 25; Cels. ap. Orig. c. Cels. 8.53; Plot. 1.2.4 and 1.6.7.9; Porph. ad Marc. 6). The same idea occurs in Gnostic thought. The devil has no θελήματα but only ἐπιθυμίαι, no volitions but only desires, his

faculties being exclusively destructive (Heracl. fr. 46/47 Völker). Later on, Marius Victorinus gave a Christian solution to the problem of the double aspect of the descent: descent is fall in the case of the human soul, but salutary unfolding of reality through the incarnation of the Logos (Hadot, *StudPatr* 6=*TU* 81 [1962] 419).

66. The most important topics in Plotinus' anti-Gnostic writings are the refutation of determinism and the defense of the basic goodness of the universe as the unfolding of the One. The most important treatise in this respect is 2.9, where the problem of will in particular is discussed 2.9.6.19. Cf. C. Schmidt, *TU* 20 (1901) and F. Wisse, *Hellenismus der Schriften v. N.Ham.* (1975) 60ff.

67. E.g. Iambl. *ap.* Procl. *in Plat. Tim.* I 308 Diehl; Damasc. *de princ.* 43; Procl. *in Plat. Parm.* p. 1070 Cousin; Procl. *in Plat. rep.* I 90 Kroll.

68. The sources and purpose of Porphyry's ontological system have recently been investigated by Hadot (*Entr.Fond.Hardt* 5 [1957] 108ff and *Porphyre et Marius Victorinus* [1968]). Hadot has shown that Porphyry's doctrine is based on two presuppositions, namely (1) the attribution of self-contained immobility to the One rather than to Being in general, and (2) the definition of Life as the activity of the Intellect, which conception, in turn, was based on Plat. *Soph.* 248 D/E (motion of the οὐσία, Being, in consequence of the act of cognition which indicates its δύναμις, power, of being moved) and Aristot. *met.* 1072b27 (ἡ τοῦ νοῦ ἐνέργεια ζωή: The activity of the intellect is life). Both had already been taken into account by Plotinus. But only from the time of Porphyry onwards did the triad *esse/vivere/intellegere* become largely accepted as denoting the "horizontal" unfolding of reality at the level of the Plotinian Intellect. The Porphyrian or rather Chaldean triad was set in relation to the three factors of education, the three parts of philosophy or the triad Angel/Demon/Hero (Procl. *in Plat. Tim.* III p. 165.11ff Diehl) in later speculation (cf. P. Courcelle, *Lettres grecques en occident* [1948] 179), and was further developed into many subdivisions by Proclus (*in Plat. Tim.* I p. 371f Diehl; cf. W. Beierwaltes, *Proklos* [1965] 93ff). Origen still combined the Trinitarian creed of the Christians with various triads of the philosophical tradition independently of *esse/vivere/intellegere* (*de princ.* 1.3.8): *Cum ergo primo, ut sint, habeant ex deo patre; secundo, ut rationabilia sint, habeant ex verbo; tertio, ut sint sancta, habeant ex spiritu sancto.* Here the subdivisions of physics/dialectics/ethics and nature/doctrine/training are referred to.

69. This opinion had been clearly formulated by Albinus (*epit.* 10; see above n. 27) and was shared by Plotinus and Porphyry (*sent.* 27). Only Platonists from Iamblichus onwards introduced the doctrine that the way towards the Supreme Being could be opened up, independently from intellectual endeavour, by means of prayer, incantation, and ritual, that is to say by practice taken over from popular religion, magic, and astrology. Thus theurgy, practiced only in the subculture of philosophy during the preceding centuries, became an officially recognized part of Platonic philosophy (Proclus, *The Elements of Theology,*[2] ed. E. R. Dodds [Oxford 1963] Introduction pp. xixf). Iamblichus was firmly convinced that the divine transcended all intellectual capaci-

ties of man (de myst. 1.3), and that man could be freed from the bonds of fate and matter by either cognition or theurgy (de myst. 8.6; cf. Corp. Herm. 12.6ff). This view was strictly opposed by Porphyry (ad Aneb. 2.13a; cf. Theiler, EntrFondHardt [1955] 87), despite his predilection for demonology (cf. Zintzen, RAC 9 [1976] 655ff) which was not shared by his master (2.9.9.27, 6.5 [23] 6).

70. The ethical and religious aspect of this conception, both in Platonic and Christian tradition, has been analyzed by H. Merki, Ὁμοίωσις Θεῷ (1956).

71. According to Plotinus, it is the inexhaustible wealth and the goodness of the One rather than the will to use its power to which the world owes its existence (3.2.3, 6.8.6). The will of both the Intellect and the One is always directed to what is good, especially if their noetic activity is directed towards themselves. That is why Plotinus rejects the doctrine that a superior being turns downwards to create an inferior one, though this seems to be indicated by Plato (Phaedr. 246B). In the view of Plotinus, creation of inferior beings is but the consequence of the goodness of the higher ones (3.4.15.2, 4.3.27.1 and 7; cf. H. Dörrie, Festschrift Hirschberger [1965] 119ff). Later Neoplatonists, too, defined God's goodness, his inexhaustible affluence and munificence rather than his power or will, as the cause of creation. The structured and animated universe corresponds to the divine ἀγαθότης (goodness) on a lower level of reality (Procl. in Plat. Tim. I 25f and 362ff Diehl; elem. theol. 12 and 25; Sall. de deis 7.2; August. ep. 140.4 and 57). According to Proclus the δημιουργικὴ πρόνοια (creative providence) comes from the divine βούλησις (intention) which is, in its turn, the result of the divine ἀγαθότης (in Plat. Tim. I 370f; Calcid. in Plat. Tim. pp. 204f Waszink).

72. Plotinus' vocabulary is full of words denoting kinds of volition: βούλησις, θέλησις, ἐπιβολή (τῆς διανοίας)—a Stoic term which occurs very frequently (cf. J. M. Rist, Plotinus [1965] 49ff; on Porphyry's use of the term and its voluntaristic implications see A. Smith, Porphyry's Place in the Neoplatonic Tradition [The Hague 1974] 1)—ὄρεξις, νεῦσις, ῥοπή, ἀγάπη, ἐπιστροφή, "desire," "impulse"—a Gnostic term (Valent. ap. Iren. haer. 1.4.5) which became particularly important in Plotinus' philosophy (O. Becker, Plotin u. das Problem der geistigen Aneignung [1940] 23ff; Zintzen, RhM 108 [1965] 71ff)—τόλμα, "daring," etc. Plotinus gave a more precise meaning to the traditional term προαίρεσις (Rist, EntrFondHardt 21 [1974] 106ff). He carefully distinguished between volition from irrational impulses (ὄρεξις) and intention implied in cognition (βούλησις) (6.8.13). The former, very much like sensual perception, can only get hold of an image of a piece of reality, whereas βούλησις, being a mode of noetic activity, is able to create a new hypostasis (5.3 passim; Porph. sent. 43; cf. Procl. elem. theol. 131). But intention as an intellectual phenomenon has also to be classified according to the ontological level of its performance: διάνοια corresponds to ψυχή, βούλησις to νοῦς (3.9.1.35; cf. Dodds, EntrFondHardt 5 [1957] 14). Accordingly, life as ἐνέργεια τοῦ νοῦ, activity of the intellect, is different at the various levels

(3.8.8; Porph. *sent.* 12), perfection being perfect life (1.4.3, 1.4.13). Finally, the One can be taken as pure volition (βούλησις 6.8.13), since every individual being owes its existence to a voluntary cognitive act of the antecedent hypostasis, and all these acts originate, in the last instance, from the One (cf. Procl. *elem. theol.* 7). The essentially religious idea that the Supreme Being has to be experienced and thought of primarily as creative power and intention was already widely discussed in Hermetic literature (*Corp. Herm.* 10.2; Asclep. 8.12f). But whereas in religious life the dynamistic aspect of this phenomenon undoubtedly predominates, Plotinus tried to get hold of it from the intellectualistic point of view: how is one to understand the relation between creative unity and created multiplicity? So all the voluntaristic details in Plotinus' philosophy should not be overrated (for a recent *mise au point* of the problem involved see Mortley, *AJPh* 96 [1975] 363–377). In the view of Plotinus, will or intention, insofar as it contributes to the unfolding of reality, remains the implication or result of thought and cognition. Perfect noetic activity undoubtedly is pure contemplation (θεωρεῖν) as performed by the One. This most elevated activity has no need of any preexisting object and is, therefore, entirely creative, though turned towards the contemplator. At the highest level of being the difference between thought and intention loses any significance. This concept of the ultimate unity of thought and intention, which was always present in Neoplatonic ontology, sometimes seems to be unduly neglected in Ernst Benz' study (*Marius Victorinus u. die Willensmetaphysik* [1932] 298ff). Plotinus dealt with this difficult topic, especially in 6.8.

73. The topic has been extensively treated by C. W. van Essen-Zeeman, *De plaats van de wil in Plotinus* (1946). Cf. Becker (above n. 72) 14ff and Inge (above n. 63) 1.253ff and 2.113ff.

74. Evil is due to an intentional violation of the order of being (τάξις), which is caused, in its turn, by γνώμη ἀσύμμετρος, disproportionate judgement (Porph. *ad Marc.* 32; cf. Albin. *ap.* Stob. 1.375.10 W.H.). A similar platonizing formulation has been preserved in Arnobius (see below p. 126 n. 17).

75. Cf. Theiler, *Porphyrios und Augustinus* (1933) 28f. Neither Plotinus nor Porphyry though underrated the moral importance of action (ἐπιμέλεια) which always presupposes volition, προαίρεσις, on which moral evaluation of the ensuing action entirely depends. Προαίρεσις, however, is to be found ἐν νῷ (in mind) rather than ἐν πράξει (in action) (Plot. 6.8.2; Porph. *ad Marc.* 8; cf. Simplic. *in Epict. ench.* 7 p. 44/45 Dübner: θέλησις ψυχῆς ἔνδοθεν οὖσα κίνησις: the will of the soul is an inward motion). Later Neoplatonists even tried to describe the voluntaristic aspect of what is going on in the human soul: Marinus (*vit. Procl.* 25) defines σωφροσύνη as στροφὴ τῆς ψυχῆς εἴσω εἰς τὸν νοῦν: a turning of the soul into the mind.

Porphyry, however, explained (*ad Marc.* 24) moral and spiritual progress as a performance which has an important intellectual section from which a volitional motion originates. But the whole process is initiated by the noncognitive act of faith: πιστεῦσαι δεῖ ὅτι μόνη σωτηρία ἡ πρὸς τὸν θεὸν ἐπιστροφή, καὶ πιστεύσαντα ὡς ἔνι μάλιστα σπουδάσαι τἀληθῆ γνῶναι περὶ αὐτοῦ, καὶ γνόντα ἐρασθῆναι τοῦ γνωσθέντος, ἐρασθέντα δὲ ἐλπίσιν ἀγαθαῖς τρέφειν τὴν ψυχὴν διὰ τοῦ βίου: "It is necessary to believe that to turn to God is the only salvation, and believing thus to strive exclusively to know the truth concerning Him, and knowing, to love what is so known, and loving, to nourish the soul with good hope through life." Porphyry did not restrict the voluntaristic approach to the area of asceticism, important as this factor might be in his ethical theory (*ad Marc.* 9). In a comparable way Origen explained the "Christian virtues" of 1 Cor. 13: Στοιχειώσεως μὲν ἔχειν λόγον τὴν πίστιν, προκοπῆς δὲ τὴν ἐλπίδα, τελειότητος δὲ τὴν ἀγάπην: exposition [of the Christian faith] is grounded in belief; progress [in the faith] on hope, and perfection [in the faith] on love (*in ep. ad Rom. comm.* 4.6 p. 212.4 Scherer; the Latin text *PG* 14).

76. Will remained a hypostasis in later Neoplatonic ontology, after Porphyry had introduced the Chaldean triad (e.g. Calc. *in Plat. Tim.* pp. 204f and 344f Waszink; Synes. *hymn.* 2 passim).

77. Plotinus greatly contributed to the knowledge of human psychology (H. J. Blumenthal, *Plotinus' Psychology* [1971]; G. J. P. O'Daly, *Plotinus' Philosophy of the Self* [Dublin 1973]). He discovered the difference between self-cognition and self-consciousness (Schwyzer, *EntrFondHardt* 5 [1957] 341–370), he put forward an elaborate theory of indirect cognition (2.9.1–3; cf. Dörrie, *NAWG* 2 [1967] 37), and he investigated in what way intelligence and memory constitute man's individuality (5.3.49.3, 4.3.27.25ff). But the problem of will does not seem to be one of his favorite psychological topics. The doctrine of the difference between ἐκούσιον (voluntarily) and ἐφ' ἡμῖν (in our power) which he developed from Peripatetic and Stoic sources (6.8.1; cf. Alex. Aphr. *de fat.* pp. 183f Bruns; Simplic. *in Epict. ench.* p. 14 Dübner), has not been formulated in terms of volition. So the priority of cognition became firmly established in ethical theory of late antiquity: Δῆλον . . . ὅτι προηγεῖται μὲν ἡ ὑπόληψις καὶ λογική τις οὖσα γνῶσις καὶ ἀνθρώπῳ πρέπουσα: "It is clear that perception comes first being both a logical power of thought and proper to mankind" (Simplic. *in Epict. ench.* p. 4.29 Dübner; cf. p. 33.26). Plotinus derived even the involuntary (ἄνευ διανοίας) rule or control of the soul over the body from its subconscious knowledge of a higher level of reality (2.9.1.14ff, 4.8.2).

78. The αὐτεξούσιον, freedom of choice, comes from man's capacity to grasp the ἀγαθόν (the good) by an act of cognition (6.8.5/6). In the case of the One the ἀγαθόν as the object of cognition is identical with the perceiving One (see above n. 71). That is why in the One will cannot be separated from thought. Otherwise the One's free intention would be arbitrary, since not necessarily directed towards the ἀγαθόν. For the same reason the freedom of lower beings only applies to their relationship to subordinate ones. Their relation to superior beings cannot be free for these already contain what is ἀγαθόν in the lower ones (3.9.3; Porph. *sent.* 31). The human soul, according to Plotinus, is superior to fate as determined by the stars, since it is able to perceive, in a free act of cognition, the order of being (5.1.2.1; cf. Porph. *ap.* Eus. *praep. ev.* 11.28.15). This does not entail a devaluation of the universe, as it does in

Gnostic thought (Plot. 2.9.5.6 etc.). The freedom of the Supreme Being, too, can only result from its entirely noetic nature that prevents it from suffering affection. By this argument Porphyry tried to refute theurgy, since cult, magic, or prayer is meant to influence the gods even against their cognition and intention (*ap.* Eus. *praep. ev.* 5.10.10). Iamblichus replied that a god, if called upon by such practices, always appears because of his free intention (αὐτοφανὴς καὶ αὐτοθελής *de myst.* 1.12, αὐθαίρετος id. 4.3 and 8.2; *Theosoph. Tübg.* 27 Erbse). Thus the understanding of free choice as resulting entirely from intellectual activity applies to both God and man in Neoplatonic thought (e.g. Calc. *in Plat. Tim.* p. 196 Waszink; cf. Gegenschatz, *MH* 15 [1958] 115–129).

79. Ἐγενήθη ἐκ θελήματος τοῦ πατρός, "He was born from the will of the father": *princ.* 1.2.6ff and 4.4.1. The formula, however, calls for interpretation. According to Origen, God is primarily intellect (*princ.* 1.1.6), and the procreation of the Son can also be compared with the origin of will from the intellect and of the verbal utterance from cognition or knowledge (*in Joh. comm.* 1.38 = *GCS* 4.49f). Origen did not make the clear distinction between the Son coming from and being the will of the Father (cf. also Clem. *protr.* 12.120.4). He can also call the Son εἰκὼν τοῦ πρώτου θελήματος: The image of the first will (*in Joh. comm.* 13.36 = *GCS* 234) and finds the unity of both τῇ ταὐτότητι τοῦ βουλήματος, the identity of will (*c. Cels.* 8.12; *in Joh. comm.* 4.34).

80. Already the school of Pantaenus (Clem. Alex. fr. VII = tom. III p. 224 Stählin) had tried to show that God's activity cannot possibly be described in terms of ontology, since it is only the will of God (θελήματα) which the human mind can grasp in the order of being (cf. H. Langerbeck, *Aufsätze zur Gnosis* [1967] 157–162). E. Mühlenberg kindly drew my attention to this passage.

81. Arius clearly attributed the Son to creation which originates from the will of the Father (e.g. *ap.* Athan. *de synod.* 15, *c. Ar.* 1.16 and 3.60; Jul. Hal. *comm. in Hiob.* 38.28f Hagedorn). The Son or Logos was created, according to Arius, to create, in his turn, the universe which could not have borne the direct influence of the Father (Athan. *ep.* 1 *ad Serap.* p. 134 Shapland). Arius' argument seems to have been influenced by specific doctrines of the Platonist Atticus (Stead, *JThS* 15 [1964] 16ff; Meijering, *VChr* 28 [1974] 161ff). The sovereignty and power of the divine will that is prior to all order and structure, rather than the omniscience of the divine intellect, was always regarded as the primary implication of the idea of a *creatio ex nihilo* (Iren. *adv. haer.* 2.10.2, see above nn. 58 and 59; Eus. *demonstr. ev.* 4.1.6; Basil. *hom. in hex.* 1.2, 2.2ff, and 3.2; Greg. Nyss. *opif. hom.* 32 = *PG* 44.212). That is why the formula ἦν ποτε ὅτε οὐκ ἦν, "there was when He (i.e. the Son) was not," was so heavily disputed in the Arian controversy with regard to the origin of the Son.

The orthodox doctrine of the essential unity of Father and Son as established by Athanasius draws an important argument from the Plotinian concept of the One in relation to the Intellect: the togetherness of both is described by the image of fire and light (*adv. Ar.* 3.3 etc.). Thus Athanasius defines the Son as the will of the Father having the same relation to his substance (οὐσία) as has his thought. Accordingly, Athanasius also has to reject the Gnostic— especially Valentinian—theory, according to which will results from thought as a subsequent hypostasis (*c. Ar.* 3.60). Both of them originate, in the same way and at the same time, from the substance. This again is a topic of Platonic ontology (Plot. 6.8.7) which was already used by Irenaeus (*adv. haer.* 1.6.1) and Hippolytus (*ref.* 3.38.6) in an anti-Gnostic context. In the orthodox view, the unity of Father and Son cannot be limited to their will, as was held by Arians and Apollinarists (Athan. *c. Apoll.* 2.10 and *de synod.* 23; Hilar. *de synod.* 29f; Epiphan. *haer.* 73.22.7). On the other hand, divine and human will has to be strictly separated in Christ's person (*de incarn.* 21; cf. Gesché, *RHE* 54 [1959] 403–406 and P. Gautier, *Greg.* 36 [1955] 553ff). Sharing the substance of the Father, the Son is strictly separated from creation, which originates from the will of the Creator (*de fid. orth.* 1.8). Nevertheless the Son, being generated by the Father, cannot be called ἄναρχος, without beginning. He has a beginning not in the Father's will but in His substance which is superior to will (ὑπερκείμενον τῆς βουλήσεως *c. Ar.* 1.33 and 2.2; cf. Florovsky, *StudPatr* 6 = *TU* 81 [1962] 36ff).

82. E.g. Procl. *de prov.* 44.19 and 59.1 (ἡ ἄστατος τῆς προαιρέσεως ῥοπή: "the uncertain turn of choice").

83. Rist, *EntrFondHardt* 21 (1974) 103ff. The same specific meaning had already been given to the term by Epictetus (see above n. 24). Its dominant voluntaristic connotation can be seen from passages like *ench.* 8: χάλασις σκέλους ἐμπόδιον, προαιρέσεως δ᾽ οὔ, ἐὰν μὴ αὐτὴ θέλει: ". . . limping is a hindrance of the legs, not of the faculty of choice, provided the faculty of choice itself does not admit it." Later Neoplatonists, however, did not retain the Plotinian use of the word.

84. Athan. *c. Ar.* 3.59; cf. E. P. Meijering, *Orthodoxy and Platonism*[2] (1974) 69ff. Athanasius again argued from the Neoplatonic point of view: the Intellect results neither from a decision of the One (Plot. 5.1.6.25f) nor from necessity, since the One is not subject to ἀνάγκη (6.8.7.11ff). Will or intention (βούλησις) can be defined in contrast to determination or force (ἀνάγκη). Yet God's οὐσία (substance) is identical with his ἐνέργεια (activity) or βούλησις (intention) (Athan. *Urkunde* 27.3 Opitz). The same applies to Plotinus' One (6.8.9.44ff, 6.8.13.8). On the other hand, ἀνάγκη is the law of the created world and of the inferior beings respectively, and does not apply to either God or the One. Thus the will of God cannot possibly have, as has human intention, τὴν εἰς ἑκάτερα ῥοπήν, "ambivalence" (*c. Ar.* 3.63; cf. 1.52 and 3.66), for this kind of freedom can only be defined in contrast to necessity. Virtually the same statement about God not having the choice between good and evil had already been made by Albinus (*epit.* 26.3) and Porphyry (ap. Eus. *demonstr. ev.* 4.6, *praep. ev.* 6.6.21 and 31ff). Platonists always attributed this faculty specifically to men and demons (Hierocl. Plat. ap. Phot. *bibl.* 464a3ff and 466b9ff; cf. W. Theiler, *Forschungen zum Neuplatonismus* [1966] 12f), that is to

say to ζῷα λογικά (rational animals). Animals have no προαίρεσις and, consequently, no moral responsibility (Porph. ap. Stob. 2.39 W.H.). Προαίρεσις is
the sole cause of moral evil (Athan. *adv. gent.* 2 and 5). It is realized in a chain
of individual acts of decision of which every one is free to be turned, by the
human individual in question, to either side. Conversely, the will of God (or
the One) cannot be split up into single decisions. It is inseparably linked to or
indeed identical with God's eternal and unchangeable substance (οὐσία). So
θέλειν and μὴ θέλειν (to will and not to will) and their alternation simply
do not apply to the non-intermittent will of God (Athan. *ep. ad Afr.* 8; cf.
Plot. 6.8.13ff). The ἁπλῆ οὐσία (simple substance) of God (Aristot. *met.* Z
1028a30) does not even admit a differentiation of qualities (ποιότητες). Being
and Intention, Intention and Action, Action and Procreation simply coincide
in God as they coincide in the One of Plotinus (*c. Ar.* 2.24; cf. Plot. 6.8 passim). Later in the fourth century, the same was taught by Basil (*spir. sanct.* 21
[*S.C.* 17.3]), Didymus (*de trin.* 6.4), and others, and virtually the same had
already been said, clearly without regard to specific Plotinian concepts, by the
early Alexandrians (Clem. *strom.* 6.17; Orig. *c. Cels.* 7.68).

85. Greg. Naz. *or.* 29 (*theol.* 3) 6=*PG* 36.81; cf. Meijering, *NederlTheol-
Tijdsch* 27 (1973) 224ff.

86. Cf. P. Hadot, *Porphyre et Marius Victorinus* (1969) 220ff with reference
to Plot. 6.2.8.32 and 6.7.17.25 as the basis of Porphyry's conception.

87. Orig. *princ.* 1.2.6: *Sicut voluntas procedit e mente et neque partem aliquam
mentis secat neque ab ea separatur aut dividitur*: "Thus the will proceeds from the
mind, and neither does it amputate part of the mind in any way, nor is it
separated or divided from the mind." In the second and third centuries, however, the anti-Gnostic argument of the togetherness of God's thought and will
(Iren. *haer.* 1.6.1; Hippol. *ref.* 6.38.5) did not prevent "orthodox" theologians from asserting that the Son originated from the will of the Father
(Just. *dial.* 61.1; Clem. Al. *paed.* 3.98.1; cf. H. Görgemann's note on Orig.
princ. 1.2.6).

88. Marius Victorinus' theory has been thoroughly explained by Hadot
(above n. 86), which contribution supersedes most previous studies on the
subject.

89. See above n. 7 and Theiler, *Gnomon* 10 [1934] 493ff.

90. E.g. Synes. *hymn.* 2.94ff, 3.48ff, and 4.1ff; cf. Hadot, 462ff.

91. Mar. Vict. *c. Ar.* 1.31.18–32.15 and 1.52.17–25; cf. Hadot, 300ff
and 472f. The will of the Father is directed towards His own unity rather than
towards the multiplicity which characterizes the created world. But since the
Trinity embraces, at the same time, all beings, the will of the Father is also
directed to the Son who, in his turn, wants to cause the multiplicity of creation. According to Pythagorean speculation the monad contains the potential
of all numbers and wishes (βουλήσεις) to hold them together (Moderatus of
Gadara ap. Stob. 1.21.8 W.H. and Simplic. *in Aristot. phys.* p. 231 Diels; cf.
Hadot, 312).

92. Hadot has traced the principle of predominance in philosophical theology back to Numenius (243ff).

93. However he did not overlook the ethical and soteriological implications of the new voluntarism, as can be seen from *hymn.* 2.51ff

> Miserere domine, miserere Christe!
> Velle mihi adiacet mundum et terras linquere
> Sed imbecilla pluma est velle sine subsidio tuo.
> Da fidei pennas, ut volem sursum deo.

> Have mercy, Father; have mercy, Christ!
> I would the heavens reach and earth relinquish
> But fragile is the plumage of my will without Your aid.
> Give me wings of faith to fly high to God.

The idea of perfection being defined as full cognition of God originates from the Platonic tradition, as does the firm belief that the longing for such cognition is innate in human nature (e.g. Plot. 3.5.1.8). But although this longing or will testifies to the "consanguinity" of God and man, only the intellectual act establishes the actual relationship between both of them. This condition is presupposed in Posidonius' famous interpretation of Plat. *Tim* 45B ff (fr. 85 Edelstein-Kidd ἡ τῶν ὅλων φύσις ὑπὸ συγγενοῦς ὀφείλει καταλαμβάνεσθαι τοῦ λόγου: "the nature of all beings is bound by necessity of kinship to be possessed by the Logos." Cf. *Plot* 5.3.8 and below n. 106.

94. *De opif. hom.* 4 (*PG* 44.136); *vit. Mos.* 2 p 34 Musurillo. Gregory explicitly stresses the sovereignty of man's free choice (αὐτεξούσιον . . . ἰδίοις θελήμασιν αὐτοκρατορικῶς διοικούμενον: ". . . free choice . . . [is] governed autonomously by its own individual volitions"). It was common ground of Platonic and Christian belief that this faculty belongs to man's spiritual and· intellectual self.

95. Τὸ δοκοῦν καὶ τὸ ἀρέσκον, whims and wishes (*de virg.* 12 p. 298 15 Jaeger). This doctrine again is generally accepted in Christian thought. Sin in demons and men presupposes unqualified αὐτεξούσιον (Lact. *inst.* 2.8.4).

96. *Vit. Mos.* 2 p. 34 Musurillo; cf. Albin. *did.* 31/32 and Porphyry (?) ap. Eus. *praep. ev.* 6.6.31. Plato already had restricted the meaning of βούλεσθαι to intention based on the intellectual perception of the better (*Gorg.* 467C/468E), thus excluding any kind of emotional or arbitrary decision.

97. According to Neoplatonic doctrine, demons cause evil by misleading man's judgement (Porph. *de abstin.* 2.40, *ad Marc.* 16). Conversely, beneficent demons convey to man the plans of the gods (Porph. *de regr. an.* fr.33.9ff Bidez).

98. *Vit. Mos.* 2 p. 45f and 54 Musurillo.

99. *Cat. magn.* 15.1 and 37.2. Cf. *c. Eunom.* 12 where the will of God is described as unfolding in a perfectly rational way. Basil derives the structure of the universe (ἡ τῆς φύσεως ἀκολουθία) from God's creative order (ἐκ τοῦ πρώτου προστάγματος *hom. in hexaem.* 4.2 and 5.10). He even proves the superiority of Christian faith over pagan science by the following argument: in science intel-

lectual cognition follows faith, in Christian religion cognition precedes it, since the existence of God can be ascertained in the nature of the universe, faith thus being the next step towards perfection (*ep.* 235.1).

100. Cf. A. Ritter, *Gnadenlehre Gregors* (1976) 210.

101. *Vit. Mos.* 2 p. 38 Musurillo.

102. Tert. *praescr. haer.* 7.13 and 14.5. Tertullian interprets faith as a kind of knowledge essentially different from and not necessarily combined with any other piece of conceivable knowledge. Cf. Tert. *monog.* 2.3; Just. *apol.* 1.39; Orig. *in Mt. comm. ter.* 33=*GCS* 11.61.14ff; *de princ.* 3.3.2; and Wickert, *ZThK* 62 (1965) 153ff. Platonists and orthodox Christians alike believed in the possibility of the wrong use of human freedom (αὐτεξούσιον) which inevitably causes evil and, above all, drastically restricts the further use of that gift. Priscillian, however, explicitly taught that the fall of Adam did not impair man's freedom of choice, so that all moral responsibility still stays with him (*tract.* 5 p. 63 and 8 p. 88; cf. H. Chadwick, *Priscillian* [1976] 70). The restricted freedom, however, creates or is indeed identical with ignorance and deception. That is why fallen demons can, at the same time, only ignore and deceive (Athan. *vit. Ant.* 24; Joh. Chrys. *poenit.* 1.2; Cyr. Hier. *cat.* 4.1 and 19.4). Again, the faith that restores original freedom can be defined as a kind of cognition or knowledge.

103. E. Mühlenberg, *Unendlichkeit Gottes bei Gregor* (1964). This particular doctrine of Gregory's has no close parallel in the writings of the other Cappadocians who prefer the intellectualistic approach to the problem of human perfection (e.g. Basil, *de div.* 2=*PG* 31.284A; cf. G. B. Ladner, *DOP* 12 [1958], 59–84).

104. E.g. *Vit. Mos.* 2 p. 113f Musurillo, *in cant. cant.* 5.6 p. 354ff Jaeger, *vit. Mos.* 1 p. 5 Musurillo: ἀεὶ ἐθέλειν ἐν τῷ καλῷ τὸ πλέον ἔχειν ἡ τῆς ἀνθρωπίνης φύσεως τελειότης ἐστίν: "Always to wish to have more of the good is the perfection of human nature." In the Platonic view as described, for instance, by Plotinus (5.9.1f) the philosopher who strives for perfection is to be compared to the lover always longing for the beloved.

105. This Gnostic doctrine, refuted already by Tertullian (*praescr. haer.* 7ff), has been discussed by Koschorke, *Wort u. Dienst* 14 (1977) 51ff.

106. In defining the ultimate goal of moral progress as perfect and beatifying cognition Gregory fully agrees with Platonic tradition (e.g. Plat. *Conv.* 209E ff, *Rep.* 502C ff; Plot. 1.6.7; Clem. *strom.* 2.10, 6.8, etc.; Origen, *de princ.* 3.6.3; see above n. 93), especially in the fourth century (F. Cumont, *Lux perpetua* [1949] 433; P. Courcelle, *Recherches* [1950] 107ff). Plotinus, however, distinguished between ordinary intellectual perception of the object of cognition and the cognition of the One (ἐφάψασθαι) which is but the ultimate step of progress and no longer the perception of an object (5.3.17).

107. There are, of course, a great many references to the will of man as separate from both his intellectual achievement and his emotions. But the terminology used is far from being fixed and unmistakable and does not point to a coherent theory. Gregory of Nyssa, for instance, discusses the problem of

man knowing God but turning away from his will and commandment (*vit. Mos.* p. 128f Musurillo; cf. Joh. Chrys. *in Rom. 1.26 hom. 4.2=PG* 60.417). He sees evil being brought to existence (οὐσιωθῆναι) by the voluntary act (προαίρεσις) of man who turns away from God (*or. 7 in Eccl.* p. 406f Alexander), just as darkness becomes real for any one who voluntarily closes his eyes in daylight. The phenomenon of turning is frequently described by the Neoplatonic term ἐπιστροφή in Christian texts (cf. Eus. *praep. ev.* 1.1.34 and 3.13.25). According to St. John Chrysostom, conscience, being defined as the natural or innate knowledge of God and of good and evil (*hom. in Ann.* 1.3=*PG* 53.636), leads to right decisions, independently of the intellectual standing of its owner (*hom. in Gen.* 17.1=*PG* 53.135; *expos. in Ps. 142=PG* 55.447, etc.). Man in his empirical condition has dulled this precious gift (e.g. *Doroth. Gaz. instr.* 3.40=*SC* 92.208), but it is restored to the believers by divine grace (Pallad. *hist. Laus. praef.* p. 12f Butler; cf. Cyrill. Hier. *catech.* 2.1–4 and 3.3–4). On the other hand, to man's own decision—which again is taken separately from his intellectual achievement and referred to in varying terms—has been attributed the primary part not only in moral progress but also in the process of salvation, especially by monastic authors (*Apophth. Pambo* 3=*P.G.* 65.369; Isid. Pelus. *ep.* 2.16 and 79). The inclination to act in a certain way is called ῥοπή (Greg. Naz. *de vit. sua* 4f), προθυμία (*id.* 97/110), θέλημα (Basil. *serm. ascet.* 21=PG 31.881), προαίρεσις (Isid. Pelus. *ep.* 2.16 and 79), τὸ ἐφ' ἡμῶν (Diod. Tars. fr. 21.5 Deconinck). Repentant sinners are spoken of as οἱ εἰς διάνοιαν ἐπιστροφῆς γενόμενοι in Canon 6 of the Council of Ancyra (A.D. 314), where the influence of Neoplatonic terminology is obvious. The vocabulary of will seems equally diversified in theological and non-theological and even non-literary texts (Marc. Diac. *vit. Porphyr.* 64 and 72 προαίρεσις; *id.* 75 and 89 θέλημα, βουλή). In the Greek version of the Coptic testament (θελημάτιον) of Abraham, bishop of Hermouthis in Egypt, which has been preserved on a papyrus of the eighth century, the variety of words denoting free will or intention is particularly noteworthy (F. Kenyon, *Papyri BM* [1893] no. 78). The passage where the testator corroborates his intention runs as follows: Δι' ἧς ὁμολογῶ ἑκὼν καὶ πεπεισμένος δίχα παντὸς δόλου καὶ φόβου καὶ βίας καὶ ἀπάτης καὶ ἀνάγκης τινὸς καὶ πάσης νομίμου παραγραφῆς καὶ συναρπαγῆς καὶ μηχανῆς παντοίας ἄνευ οἱασδήποτε διχονοίας καὶ κακονοίας ἀλλ' ἐξ οἰκείας *προθέσεως καὶ σκόπῳ αὐθαιρέτῳ καὶ ἐκουσίας ἐμῆς βουλήσεως* ὀρθῇ διανοίᾳ βεβαίᾳ πίστει παντὶ πληρεστάτῳ δεσποτείᾳ καὶ *αὐτοτελεῖ ἐξουσίᾳ* παρεθέμην σοι πεπεισμένος *πάσῃ προαιρέσει* ζῶν νοῶν φρονῶν ἐρρωμένην ἔχων τὴν διάνοιαν καὶ ἐπ' ἀκριβείας πολλῆς φέρων τὸν λογισμόν μου . . . .

CHAPTER VI

1. Good examples of the extended use of that Augustinian notion, which is by no means restricted to "voluntarists" like Duns Scotus or William of Occam, can be found in the writings of Rupert of Deutz (*PL* 170.437ff; cf. O. Lottin, *Psychologie* [1958] 221ff). Erich Frank (*Wissen,*

Wollen, Glauben [1955] 342ff) points out the general importance of the topic in mediaeval and modern philosophy.

2. See above p. 117.

3. The topic is exhaustively treated by H. Merki, Ὁμοίωσις θεῷ (1956).

4. E. des Places, *Syngeneia* (1964). The idea of man's having only reason in common with God was set out in great detail by Origen (*princ.* 4.4.9).

5. See above n. 4. ˝

6. Cf. Aristot. *met.* 10540a4ff.

7. *Quasi quodam partu mentis cogitatione prorumpit velle conceptum.* St. Augustine (*de trin.* 9.12.18) says the opposite; *partum mentis antecedit appetitus quidam quo id quod nosse volumus quaerendo et inveniendo nascitur proles ipsa notitia.*

8. E.g. *de trin.* 6.10.12 and 10.11.18, *conf.* 13.12. In *civ. D.* 10.23 he refutes the intermediate position of the Spirit in the Porphyrian triad, which had already been altered by Marius Victorinus (see above p. 117).

9. St. Augustine notes the incongruity between the Plotinian sequence ῞Εν / Νοῦς / Ψυχή (The One/Mind/Soul) and Porphyry's triad ῞Υπαρξις / Ζωή / Νοῦς (Existence/Life/Mind) (*civ. D.* 10.23). It is not necessary, for our purpose, to discuss the question whether St. Augustine had direct knowledge of Plotinus' writings, or whether he depended more or less exclusively on Porphyry. The extreme positions in that discussion are held by W. Theiler (*Porph. u. Aug.* [1933]) and P. Henry (*Plotin et l'occident* [1934]).

10. *Conf.* 13.11: . . . *in his igitur tribus* (sc. *esse, scire, velle*) *quam sit inseparabilis vita et una vita et una mens et una essentia, quam denique inseparabilis distinctio et tamen distinctio, videat qui potest. Certe coram se est. Adtendat in se et videat et dicat mihi. Sed cum invenerit in his aliquid et dixerit, non iam se putet invenisse illud, quod supra ista est in commutabile, quod est incommutabiliter et scit incommutabiliter et vult incommutabiliter: et utrum propter tria haec et ibi trinitas, an in singulis haec tria, ut terna singulorum sint, an utrumque miris modis simpliciter et multipliciter in se sibi fine, quo est et sibi notum est et sibi sufficit incommutabiliter id ipsum copiosa unitatis magnitudine, quis facile cogitaverit?*

11. Hadot, *StudPatr* 6 = *TU* 81 (1962) 409ff.

12. See, above all, M. Schmaus, *Psychologische Trinitätslehre d. Aug.* (1927). For further references see the bibliography attached to the most recent edition of *De trinitate* by W. J. Mountain and F. Glorie (*CorpChristserlat* 50 [1968] lxxxiiiff).

13. See above p. 113). The analogy of Trinity and soul is already referred to in the Priscillianist treatise *De trinitate* (*PL* suppl. II pp. 1487f.). Will is defined there as λόγος προφορικός. Cf. H. Chadwick, *Priscillian* (1976) 100ff.

14. The volitional aspect of the substance of the Supreme Being was discussed with varying emphasis in the history of Neoplatonic ontology, as can be seen from a comparison of Plot. 5.1.6.26 and Hierocl. Plat. ap. Phot. *bibl.* 461b9. But nowhere in Neoplatonic philosophy was the Supreme Being defined primarily as Supreme Will. Cf. also W. Beierwaltes, *Proklos* (1965) 99.

15. *De trin.* 11.2.2ff. The will (*voluntas*) which unites the faculty of perception and the perceived object in the outside world is the decisive factor in

the act of sense perception. It even works in the case of a blind or deaf man, and is strong enough to identify, in our consciousness, the real object with the mechanical impression which it causes in our corporal senses. It is also able to fit an image into the context of our memory (11.2.5) and to produce the same image from there (11.3.1). Various *voluntates* can follow each other in a coherent chain of perception. Each of them has its own goal which is subordinate to the preceding one. If, for instance, we want to see a man through a window, the perception of the window as *finis voluntatis* (the object of the will) is subordinate to the *finis voluntatis* which consists in our perception of the man. The first *finis voluntatis* on which all other *voluntates* depend is the striving for happiness. This first *voluntas*, however, is subject to corruption by the primordial sin of man (11.6.10).

16. *De trin.* 14.10.13ff. In the case of thought or entirely intellectual cognition, intention unites the object taken from memory and intellect as the cognitive faculty. That is why the *appetitus mentis* always precedes the act of thinking (*de trin.* 9.12.18; cf. above n. 7). The Augustinian theory of intellectual activity (cf. also *conf.* 8.12ff) differs from the Neoplatonic concept of νόησις τῆς νοήσεως (thought of a thought) primarily because of the role of memory (cf. *conf.* 10.8–26) and the importance attributed to will.

17. In the context of moral theory St. Augustine prefers to use the triad *esse/nosse/velle* (existence/knowledge or cognition/will) in order to denote the internal life of man (*conf.* 13.11, *civ. D.* 11.26ff, *de mor. eccl.* 20f, *de mus.* 6.13.39, *de vera rel.* 39ff). He coordinates each of these conditions or functions of the soul with a basic virtue and a basic vice: *esse* corresponds to either *humilitas* or *superbia*, *nosse* to *sapientia* or *curiositas*, *velle* to *caritas* or *concupiscentia*. Again, will as an independent factor of the governing rational part of the human soul (*mens*) has been given due emphasis. Cf. H. Kusch in *Festschrift Dornseiff* (1953) 131ff. In contrast, the traditional Greek or philosophical view of the cause of evil is formulated by Arnobius (*adv. nat.* 1.49 and 1.27; cf. Lact. *inst.* 5.14): *nos peccare non voluntatis electione sed sola iudicii caecitate*, and *id iudicamus bonum naturali caecitate quod tamen reapse malum est*. Cf. P. Krafft, *Beiträge z. Arnobius* (1966) 84ff. In his polemics against the Platonizing *viri novi* Arnobius used, for the first time, the formula *libertas voluntatis* to render Greek ἐξουσία or αὐτεξούσιον (*adv. nat.* 2.64f).

18. Will or love, which causes the only "gravitation" (*pondus: conf.* 13.9.10) in human life, has often been compared with the Platonic ἔρως—love, as described, above all, in the *Symposium*. On both sides, as stated by St. Augustine himself (*serm.* 150.4; cf. *ep.* 130.9, *de lib. arb.* 3.22f) the striving of *amor* or ἔρως is regarded as aiming at happiness or perfection (εὐδαιμονία, *beatitudo*) by means of assimilation to what is being loved (Plat. *Leg.* 10.904A–B; August. *serm.* 96.1), and disregards, in the more advanced stages on the way to perfection, the whole realm of matter and sensual life. But differently from the Platonic tradition St. Augustine does not believe that the goal is approached exclusively in a chain of cognitive acts. To him, human life and progress is to be conclusively evaluated in terms of *caritas* and *concupiscentia* or obedience and

disobedience—that is to say in terms of will—rather than in those of knowledge and error or vision and blindness (cf. E. R. Holte, *Béatitude et sagesse* [1962]). *Fruitio Dei*, the ultimate goal of human endeavor (Haussleiter, *RAC* 8 [1972] 551f), is defined by St. Augustine as continuous love of God and one's neighbor for their own sake (*ad fruendum Deo et proximo in Deo, civ. D.* 19.13.70, *de doctr. christ.* 1.4, *en. in ps.* 915, etc.), that is to say without trying to get hold or dispose of them in order to proceed towards a further goal. The perverted will (*mala voluntas*) in the empirical state of mankind, however, constantly exchanges the adequate objects of *uti* (*diligere propter aliud*, love for the sake of some other thing) and *frui* (*diligere propter se ipsum*, love for the sake of the thing itself; cf. Thraede, *JbAC* 17 [1977] 130). St. Augustine took the definitions of *uti* and *frui* from Varro (Lorenz, *ZKG* 64 [1952/53] 34–60; Pfligersdörffer, *WS* N.F. 5 [1971] 195–224).

19. Marius Victorinus interprets the Biblical doctrine of man being created after the likeness of God in terms of the special relation between the Logos, the second hypostasis of the Trinity, and human nature (*adv. Ar.* 1.20.3). St. Augustine explicitly opposes those who restrict that likeness to only one person of the Trinity. The analogy refers to the whole Trinity (*de trin.* 12.6.6f). Memory, cognition, and will, the functions of the soul, are individually attributed to the hypostases of the Trinity.

20. Cf. P. Hadot, *Porphyre et Marius Victorinus* (1968) 477ff.

21. St. Augustine was convinced that only God and the human soul are deemed worthy of philosophical investigation (*de ord.* 2.18.47; cf. E. König, *Augustinus Philosophus* [1970] 140), and that the Biblical doctrine of the creation of man after the likeness of God can be verified by the human intellect by means of introspection (*conf.* 13.11; *civ. D.* 11.26). He even ventured to speculate, from a voluntaristic point of view, about the proportion Body . Soul . . Soul : God, which indeed is hard to reconcile with the Biblical concept of creation (*in Joh. ev. comm.* 19.12). This, however, did not prevent him from duly recognizing the fundamental difference between divine and human will. Above all, God's will is unchanging and unchangeable and, therefore, identical with His substance (*conf.* 11.10.2, *civ. D.* 22.2; cf. Plot. 6.8.13.8 and 52f). That is why the question raised by Epicureans and Agnostics of whether God could have done anything before He created the universe is simply nonsensical: there is no conceivable change in the will of God and, moreover, time was only created together with the universe. The will of God is the only structuring and preserving power in the order of being (*civ. D.* 12.23, *c. Faust.* 22.30, *ep.* 140.4, etc.).

22. St. Augustine explains the priority of will to cognition in various ways. An interesting argument is to be found at *de trin.* 12.17/18: *mens notitiam suam gignit cum se novit, sed amorem suum non gignit cum se amat.* Love is the foremost appearance of will (*valentior voluntas: de trin.* 15.21.41). It is pure activity which is not performed for the sake of a result different from the activity itself, as the act of cognition is performed to produce knowledge. For further references see W. Kahl, *Primat des Willens* (1886).

23. P. Brown (*Augustine* [1969] 158ff) describes the social milieu in which St. Augustine's interest in psychology was fostered.

24. This topic has been extensively treated by H. I. Marrou, *St. Augustine et la fin de la culture antique* (1938).

25. *civ. D.* 14.6f, *de mor. eccl.* 15.25. In the traditional view of philosophy, affections were explained as either false judgements of the intellect (Stoic) or spontaneous impulses caused by the uncontrolled activity of the irrational forces of the soul (Platonic/Peripatetic). These doctrines were well known to Christian writers of the West from Latin texts such as *Cic. Tusc.* 4.14.24 or *de fin.* 3.35. Lactantius transformed the Platonic conception into straightforward dualism, very much like the Gnostics, and attributed evil directly and exclusively to the body which paralyzes the intellectual activity of man (*inst.* 7.2.8, 7.12.11 etc.; cf. Wlosok, "Laktanz," *AHAW* [1960]). St. Augustine adopted a completely different explanation by introducing the independent factor of will. He exemplifies the difference between the morally indifferent instinct or impulse which originates from the body and the affection which underlies moral judgement by the distinction of *fames* and *amor edendi* (*c. Jul. Pelag.* 4.14.67). The new concept of will basically superseded the traditional dualism of spirit and matter, which had been identified with the dualism of being and non-being or good and evil in the school of Plato, though St. Augustine still remained very much attached to the Platonic view in many areas of his doctrine.

26. *Enchir.* 28.105, *civ. D.* 14.16–26, *c. Jul. op. imp.* 6.22; cf. E. Dinkler, *Anthropologie Augustins* (1934) 113ff.

27. *Civ. D.* 22.22, where error and distorted love or will (cf. *en. in Ps.* 9.5) are explicitly listed as two different consequences of the fall of Adam. Love is led astray if it is directed to oneself instead of to one's neighbor (*en. in Ps.* 41.13, 55.9, etc.).

28. *Civ. D.* 11.23.

29. *Conf.* 8.5.10–11. The spirit represents more of the self of man than the flesh.

30. *De ver. rel.* 69ff, *conf.* 10.66; cf. Thraede, *JbAC* 17 (1977) 125. Observations made in the field of children's behavior convinced St. Augustine that *libido dominandi* precedes all experience of power and dependence in adult life (*conf.* 1.6.8).

31. Theiler (above n. 9) 187f with reference to Porph. *de abstin.* 107.20.

32. Plot. 1.6.8 and 5.1.1; Porph. *de abstin.* 107.24ff; cf. Rist, *JTS* 20 (1969) 421.

33. *De trin.* 12.14, *civ. D.* 19.12.81ff.

34. E.g. Basil, *quod deus non est auct. mali* 5 = *PG* 31.341B; Ambros. *de Isaac* 7.60.

35. Cf. Lorenz, *ThRdschau* 25 (1959) 67f.

36. *Spir. et litt.* 34.60, *Gen. ad litt.* 12.

37. *Civ. D.* 12.1–3 and 6–8, 14.1–3, 22.1; *de corrept.* 10.27, 11.32; *Gen. ad litt.* 11.16.21.

38. Cf. H. A. Deane, *Political and Social Ideas of St. Augustine* (1963) 16f.

39. *Enchir.* 18 (man is capable of doing wrong *sciens volens* because of his *mala voluntas*) in contrast to Plat. *Hipp. min.* 376B (nobody is capable of doing wrong, if he really knows the better).

40. *Civ. D.* 11.28 and 14.6/7; *conf.* 8.10ff, 19ff, 9.1, 10.37, etc.

41. *Prop. ad ep. ad Rom.* 60f, *de ver. rel.* 24.45, *serm.* 43.4f, *spir. et litt.* 31.54 and 34.60. The different view of Greek philosophy can be seen in Plat. *phaed.* 65Eff.

42. *De trin.* 8.5.8, *de lib. arb.* 1.2 and 2.2, *ep.* 120.3, *conf.* 6.5, *enchir.* 1.5. Cf. O. du Roy, *L'intelligence de la foi en la trinité* (1966). Marius Victorinus had already defined faith as the first step on the road to cognition (*in ep. ad Phil.* 1.30 = *PL* 8.1203). For him—because of his ontological approach—the content of faith (knowledge) was of greater importance than its direction or intensity (love).

43. *De util. cred.* 22, 25, 30 (against the strict separation of faith and cognition in Manichean teaching); *ep.* 120. The treatise *On patience* (*CSEL* 41) discusses the exceptional position of patience among the virtues. Patience comes into being independently of man's *liberum arbitrium*, since it is oriented, in the last instance, towards the divinely promised salvation. This, however, is the object of faith. That is why patience, as a kind of hope and very much like love (23), can only be the gift of divine grace (15).

44. *Conf.* 11.29 with the interpretation of *Phil.* 3.12–14. The relation between will and time is repeatedly discussed in the writings of St. Augustine (*conf.* 9.9–15, enchir. 9, *civ. D.* 11.11.14); cf. Brown (above n. 23) 39.

45. *Civ. D.* 14.1.8, *en. in Ps.* 64.2; cf. Brown, 321.

46. *De lib. arb.* 1.6 and 15, *de trin.* 14.21, *de doctr. christ.* 3.22, *serm.* 20.3, *conf.* 5.18, *en in Ps.* 4.11, *tract. in Joh.* 90.2.3, *en. in Ps.* 8.1 and 37.12 (where the final judgement of God on a man's conduct is said to be anticipated in his conscience). St. Augustine also believed in natural, innate standards of moral behavior which every human being shares (*ep.* 54.2–3). This was already a traditional topic of Christian theology at the time because of the attempt to identify the philosophical idea of moral life according to nature and the Judaeo-Christian conception of moral life according to the divine Law (e.g. Ambros. *serm.* 10.15, *de off.* 1.84 and 3.25, *de Abr.* 2.93, *ep.* 65.5ff). St. Augustine, however, did not simply identify the natural knowledge of moral standards with conscience though both belong to the natural equipment of man (*ep.* 157.15, *de ord.* 2.25; similarly *Joh. Chrys. in Gen. hom.* 17.1 = *PG* 53.135; Doroth. Gaz. *didasc.* 3 = *SC* 92). Later on, Johannes Climacus stated that conscience was implanted by the act of baptism (*scal. spir.* 26; cf. Chadwick, *RAC* 10 [1978] 1025ff). As discussed above (p. 97), Philo did, in fact, conceive something like the notion of will in his doctrine of conscience.

47. Schindler, *RAC* 11 (1979) 313–446.

48. The latter was called χάρισμα (grace, favor) by St. Paul (Rom. 12:6; 1 Cor. 12:4, etc.) and is, for instance, repeatedly referred to by Tertullian.

49. The complete renewal of man's personality was an important topic in early Christian mysticism; cf. H. Dörries, *Theologie d. Makarios-Symeon* (1978).

50. This idea is of particular importance in the doctrines of Origen and Gregory of Nyssa (see above pp. 116f and 119f). It is notable, however, that words like χάρις and *gratia* rarely occur in the fragments of Gnostic literature. Cf. Schindler (above n. 47) 383.

51. The synergistic view, regardless of its inherent contradiction, always prevails where a Christian text has been formulated for the purpose of moral or spiritual guidance. This can be seen, for instance, from the sermons of St. John Chrysostom, who alternately stresses divine grace and human efforts. St. Augustine's doctrine of *gratia praeveniens* also occurs in Didymus *De trinitate* (2.14): the χάρις προκατάρχουσα (grace given beforehand) is prior to all human efforts.

52. Cf. Mühlenberg, *ZNTW* 68 (1977) 95ff. The term Synergism was not coined until the sixteenth century.

53. For general information about Pelagius and Pelagianism see G. de Plinval, *Pélage* (1943) and J. Ferguson, *Pelagius* (1957).

54. The fall of men and evil angels has replaced their freedom or changeability of will by fixing them in the wrong direction (*Gen. ad litt.* 11.29.33), whereas the good angels have been given, by a special grace of God, a share in the unchangeability of the divine will (see above n. 9) which is steadily directed towards good. The only reason for evil is the perverted will of men and demons. Perversion in the case of will means being directed to what is inferior in comparison with the owner of the will. But since the will had been free before it was perverted, the *res inferior* to which the perverted will is oriented is by no means the *causa mali*. Evil has its only cause in the perverted will itself, whereas the perverted will has no cause. It results rather from a lack of cause (*causa deficiens*), since it has been provoked by what is weaker than, and hence inferior to, the origin of the will itself (*civ. D.* 12.6–9). By this argument St. Augustine reinterpreted the close interrelation between evil and non-being, as foreseen in Platonic ontology, in terms of his new voluntarism.

55. *Deus / Deus in proximo: civ. D.* 19.13.70.

56. *En. in Ps.* 33.1.4, *de serm. Dom. in monte* 1.3, *ep.* 118.22. For further references see Dihle, *RAC* 3 (1957) 771ff. On the relation between humility or pride and will in St. Augustine's doctrine see O. Schaffner, *Christliche Demut* (1939) 147ff.

57. No Christian theologian before St. Augustine, except perhaps St. Paul, had taught that any human effort in religious and moral life is completely useless unless the preceding intervention of divine grace has enabled man to go in the right direction. Even where the sinfulness of man in his empirical condition is overstressed, as is the case in many branches of monastic literature, at least a small area of human initiative is always assumed. Symeon-Macarius depicts in great detail the total sinfulness of man by which he has lost his original freedom of choice (ἐξουσία), and which prevents him from acting according

to virtue or even from recognizing his actual condition. His γνώμη and his θέλημα are paralyzed (*hom.* 3.1.1ff p. 27ff Berthold). Yet he is still able to pray, and prayer inevitably attracts the divine grace which will enter his self and renew his intention (*hom.* 3.4/5 p. 23/24 and 17.9 p. 171 Dörries-Klostermann, *hom.* 4.7.1 p. 49 Berthold). For human nature, despite the corrupting influence of sin, remains δεκτική . . . τοῦ καλοῦ τε καὶ τοῦ κακοῦ ἤτοι θείας χάριτος ἤτοι ἐναντίας δυνάμεως, ἀλλ' οὐκ ἀναγκαστική: "open to receive both the good and the evil i.e. either the divine grace or the opposite power, but never forced to receive them." (*n. hom.* 16.4/5 p. 84/85 Klostermann-Berthold; *hom.* 15.25 p. 142 and 27.10 p. 223 Dörries-Klostermann, *hom.* 6.4.1 p. 87 Berthold). An interesting theory on this topic was conceived in the school of Antioch. Repentance has two aspects. It is something to be suffered by man, but to be actively brought about by God: μεταμέλεια ἀνθρώπων μὲν πάθος, θεοῦ δὲ ἔργον [. . .], ἐπεὶ καὶ θυμὸς μὲν ἀνθρώπων ταραχὴ ψυχῆς, θεοῦ δὲ παιδεία κατὰ τῶν ἐπταικότων [. . .]. Οὕτω καὶ μεταμέλεια ἐφ' ἡμῶν μὲν μετάγνωσις . . . ἐπὶ δὲ θεοῦ μετάθεσις οἰκονομίας ". . . repentance is affection for man, but the work of God . . . since anger is a disturbance of the soul for man but is God's way of teaching sinners. So it is with us a change of heart, with God a rearranging of his order." (Diod. Tars. *in Oct. fr.* 21.5 Deconinck; cf. C. Schäublin, *Untersuchungen z. antiochenischen Exegese* [1974] 16). In this doctrine the interference of divine grace with human life is explained in ontological terms: it is the οἰκονομία (administration) which God is prepared to change because of His love for the sinner.

58. Man is aware of his moral duty, but cannot alter his will, as the lame have to be healed before they can desire effectively to walk without limping (*de perf. inst. hom.* 3.5).

59. *De virg.* 34f, *serm.* 67.2 and 188.3, *de cat. rud.* 4, etc.

60. *Tract. in Joh. ep.* 9.10 and *tract. in Joh. ad Parth.* 7.8; cf. Gallay, *RevSR* 43 (1955) 545ff.

61. *De trin.* 4.9.12, *civ. D.* 22.30. The topic *peccare nolle* / *peccare non posse* was also treated by St. Ambrose (*in Luc. comm.* 8.57) with regard to the present situation of human life. According to his interpretation of Luke 16:18, *virtus* has to be understood as *nolle peccare* rather *non posse peccare*. It is by such a *voluntas* that man is supposed to imitate consciously the *bonitas* and *simplicitas* of children who have no complete knowledge of sin and vice.

62. St. Augustine, for instance, extensively speculated on the relation between God's omnipotence and human freedom, which led to the fall of Adam. He calls the topic *res obscura* (*de vit. beat.* 1.1; cf. *civ. D.* 5.9, *ench.* 97, *de corr. et grat.* 14.45). Cf. H. Jonas, *Aug. u. das paulinische Freiheitsproblem* (1965).

63. Cf. Schindler (above n. 47) 384f.

64. *Ad Att.* 14.1.2; Plut. *Brut.* 6. Cf. Dihle, *HSCPh* 82 (1978) 179ff.

65. The term was coined by O. Regenbogen in 1936 (*Kl. Schriften* [1961] 387ff). In the view of B. Snell (*Neun Tage Latein* [1955] 20), Cat. *carm.* 72.3 for the first time testifies to the difference between *bene velle* and *amare* (cf.

75.4). This was opposed by Opstelten, "Ethisch wilsbegrip" MedKonAkad-
Wet N.R. 22 (1959) 20. Yet the explicit identification of *bene velle* with *amicitia*, and *amicitia* with *amare* is well-attested in early Latin (Plaut. *Pseud.* 233,
Trin. 438, *Truc.* 441; Lucil. fr. 1338 Marx). Undoubtedly the Romans frequently spoke of *velle* and *voluntas* where the Greeks had used a term to denote
deliberation and intention (e.g. Enn. *Med.* 269 Vahlen: *Qui volt esse quod volt
ita dat se res ut operam dabit*, or Caecil. fr. 258 Warm.: *fac velis, perficies*;
cf. Pease ad Cic. *de nat. deor.* 3.66). The tyrannical woman of Juvenal *sat.*
6.206–223 (*hoc volo, sic iubeo, sit pro ratione voluntas*) has rational insight into
the irrational way she behaves. Whether or not the Parcae whose *invida voluntas* is complained of on a tombstone (*CEL* 472) have acted deliberately, is not
indicated in the inscription and can hardly be asked.

66. Cf., for example, H. Kloesel, *Libertas* (1967) 129 where this is shown
in the case of *licentia*.

67. *Tusc.* 4.12; cf. ps.-Plat. *def.* 413C. A similar definition was given for
the term προαίρεσις in the Peripatetic tradition: ἡ ἐπὶ τὸ προκριθὲν ἐκ τῆς βου-
λῆς μετ' ὀρέξεως, impulse toward a deliberately chosen aim together with desire ὁρμή (Alex. Aphrod. *de fat.* 12; cf. Aristotl. *E.N.* 1113a9).

68. *De nat. deor.* 2.44 = Aristot. fr. 24 Rose; *de nat. deor.* 3.92, *de fin.* 2.65
(see above p. 104 n. 21). Justice exists neither *naturā* nor *voluntate*: *de rep.* 3.23
(in the speech of Furius Philus).

69. *De fat.* 9, 20, and 23. Cicero also rendered προαίρεσις, "prose style,"
by *voluntas* (*de or.* 2.22f; cf. M. Pohlenz, *Stoa*² II [1949] 139f).

70. According to Pohlenz, Cicero did, in fact, give a voluntaristic reinterpretation of Greek moral concepts in his translation of philosophical terminology. But can this conclusion really be drawn from translations like ὁμόνοια
(oneness of mind)= *voluntatum studiorum sententiarum summa consensio* (*Lael.* 15)?

71. *Tusc.* 5.5, *de nat. deor.* 3.70 (*mens voluntasque*); *Lael.* 3.40.

72. *Tusc.* 4.34 (*ex virtute proficiscuntur honestae voluntates*), and 4.82 (*pertur-
bationes—*πάθη*—ex iudiciis opinionum et voluntatibus*).

73. *Ad Att.* 10.4.8 (about Caesar) *non voluntate* (προαίρεσις) *aut natura* (φύσις) *non esse crudelem, sed quod putaret popularem esse clementiam.* Cf. Polyb.
7.11.1ff, 10,26.8.

74. On this meaning of προαίρεσις, especially in Epictetus (e.g. 2.2.36f)
and Plotinus, see above p. 60 n. 49 and A. J. Voelke, *Volonté dans le stoicisme*
(1973) 161ff.

75. *De or.* 3.56. The Catones, Scipiones etc. were wise, *non tam fortasse
docti, sed impetu mentis . . . et voluntate*. Cf. W. Görler, *Ciceros Philosophie* (1974)
165.

76. The passages are collected, *NAWG* 3 (1941) 247ff and Pohlenz (above
n. 69) 159. For more recent studies see Voelke, *RThPh* 11 (1961) 1ff and id.,
Volonté (above n. 74) p. 161ff (where, however, the interpretation of the Stoic
concept of συγκατάθεσις [assent] *de ir.* 2.1–4 is wrongly attributed to Seneca's
"voluntarism").

77. *Ep.* 20.5: *semper idem velle atque idem nolle*, which renders Zeno's καθ'ἕνα λόγον καὶ σύμφωνον ζῆν: "to live in accordance with a single harmonious principle" (*SVF* I 179).

78. *De ben.* 5.3.2.

79. *De ben.* 1.5f etc.

80. *Ep.* 81.13. The passage is directed against those who attribute the ability to act virtuously only to the wise man: *Nemo referre gratiam scit nisi sapiens. Stultus quoque, utcumque scit et quomodo potest, referat: scientia illi potius quam voluntas desit: velle non discitur. Sapiens omnia inter se comparabit, maius enim aut minus fit, quamvis idem sit, tempore, loco, causa.*

81. *SVF* III 104 etc. The virtues (φρόνησις [intelligence] etc.), being διαθέσεις (dispositions), result from intellectual instruction (ἀπὸ θεωρημάτων), their firm possession and use (φρονίμευσις [prudence] etc.), which is called ἕξις (habit, state, organization) results from exercise. This doctrine is referred to Sen. *ep.* 95.57.

82. *Ep.* 37.4–5: *Multos regis, si ratio te rexerit: ab illa disces, quid et quemadmodum adgredi debeas. Non incides in res. Neminem mihi dabis, qui sciat, quomodo quod vult coeperit velle: non consilio adductus illo, sed impetu impactus est.*

83. *Ep* 16.2: *utrum in philosophia an in ipsa vita profeceris.*

84. The stability of will (see above n. 66) is attributed to the rule of reason over emotion in *ep.* 34 or to the truth of the content of will (*si vis eadem semper velle, vera oportet velis*: *ep.* 95.58). Both agree with traditional Stoic doctrine (Guillemin, *REL* 30 [1952] 214ff), and several passages in Seneca's tragedies refer to crime or vice as resulting exclusively from the false judgement of the intellect (*Herc. fur.* 1300ff, *Herc. Oet.* 884ff, *Phoen.* 451ff and 535ff), which again is orthodox Stoic doctrine (cf. Pack, *TAPA* 71 [1940] 360ff). *Voluntas* in the tragedies often only means "wish, desire," e.g. *Herc. fur.* 313f: *Quod nimis miseri volunt / hoc facile credunt.*

85. *Donec mens sit quod bona voluntas est* (1) and, similarly, *ut habitus animi* (ἕξις) *fiat quod est impetus* (6). Here *voluntas* simply renders ὁρμή (impulse) rather than προαίρεσις (choice) in the Epictetan sense.

86. This comes out in many passages: *magna pars profectionis velle proficere* (*ep.* 71.36); or *scies esse illam* (sc. *vitam beatam*) *in excelso, sed volenti penetrabilem*; or *quid tibi opus est, ut bonus sis? Velle!* (*ep.* 80.4).

87. R. Maschke, *Willenslehre im gr. Recht* (1926).

88. The *causa Curiana* has been extensively treated in modern scholarship. For bibliographical references see W. Stroh, *Taxis u. Taktik* (1975) 85f.

89. See especially § 21: εἰ μὲν γὰρ ἀνελεῖν τὰς διαθήκας βουλόμενος μετεπέμπετο τὴν ἀρχήν, ὥσπερ ἡμεῖς φαμεν, οὐδ' εἷς ἔνεστι τούτοις λόγος· εἰ δ' οὕτω παραφρονῶν ἔτυχεν ὥσθ' ἡμᾶς περὶ ἐλαχίστου ποιεῖσθαι τοὺς γένει πρωτεύοντας καὶ χρωμένους αὐτῷ πάντων οἰκειότατα, δικαίως ἂν δήπου τὰς τοιαύτας διαθήκας ἀκύρους ποιήσαιτε. "For if he was determined to cancel the terms of his will, and as we say, sent for the authorities, then the defendants haven't the shadow of a case. But if it is the case that he was so deranged as to regard us as if we

were nothing to him, we who were closest to him by birth and treated him as his closest family, then you should render the terms of his will null and void."

90. E.g. §§ 35 and 43; cf. below n. 99.

91. For recent contributions to the interpretation of the famous proverb *summum ius summa iniuria* see Stroh (above n. 88) 89f.

92. Dihle, *RAC* 10 (1978) 254ff.

93. Latte, *PW* 16 (1933) 278ff = *Kl. Schriften* (1968) 380ff. The distinction between murder and inadvertent killing already occurs in the law of Drakon (R. S. Stroud, *Drakon's Law* [1968] 40ff). David Daube seriously questions the opinion that the distinction between liability and guilt was ever absent from archaic conceptions of law and ethics (*Roman Law* [1969] 152ff), as is widely believed in modern scholarship (e.g. A. W. H. Adkins, *Merit and Responsibility* [1960]). This is perhaps true in the sense that the standards of neither "shame culture" nor "guilt culture" (E. R. Dodds, *Greeks and the Irrational* [1966] 28ff) were ever used exclusively in the history of mankind. But the development of moral and legal thought in many archaic cultures undoubtedly testifies, with striking regularity, to an increasing assessment of the subjective factors in the evaluation of human action. Cf. A. Dihle, *Goldene Regel* (1962) 41ff.

94. In discussing problems of intentionality Aristotle easily shifts from criminal law to general standards of moral behavior (*E.N.* 1135a15–1136a9).

95. Hyper. *adv. Athenag.*, especially §13. "In der Praxis (sc. of the Athenian law courts) führte schon die Personalunion von Gesetzgeber und Richter zu einer Billigkeitsrechtsprechung," as is rightly stated by M. Fuhrmann, *SavZrom* 73 (1956) 384.

96. Cf. R. Taubenschlag, *Law of Greco-Roman Egypt* (1944) 231ff where the problem of intentionality in Hellenistic civil law is discussed. Θέλω and its derivatives denoting intention or purpose rarely occur in the legal terminology. The term for testament, for instance, is βουλημάτιον in the Greek papyri, θελημάτιον being introduced as a translation of *voluntas* only in the sixth century A.D. (*Vocabularium Jurisprudentiae Romanae* 1463).

97. This is pointed out, with special regard to Ptolemaic civil law, by E. Seidl, *Ptol. Rechtsgeschichte* (1962) 115.

98. Maschke (above n. 87) 162ff.

99. Hermag. fr. 20 Matthes; cf. Cic. *de inv.* 2.116ff. Hermagoras distinguishes between four ways of assessing the prescripts of the law in a given case ῥητὸν καὶ διάνοια, ἀντινομία (i.e. conflicting prescripts), ἀμφιβολία (ambiguity), συλλογισμός (conclusion from several prescripts). Only the first is important in our context. Hermagoras identifies ῥητὸν καὶ διάνοια with ῥητὸν καὶ ὑπεξαίρεσις (rule and exception), whereas the evaluation of *voluntas* in Roman jurisprudence is independent of that category, so that *voluntas* has to be ascertained wherever more than one meaning can be attributed to the text. The difference between wording and meaning was already referred to very frequently by the Attic orators (Lys. 10.7 οὐ περὶ τῶν ὀνομάτων διαφέρεσθαι ἀλλὰ

τῆς τούτων διανοίας: "to be concerned not with mere words, but with their intention"; Isaeus. 11.3: διάνοια, intention, of the law-giver; Isaeus. 1.35 and 43: διάνοια of the testator; Dem. 9.43; Plat. *leg.* 634E ff etc.). Aristotle (*rhet.* 1374 b11ff) recommended interpreting the διάνοια τοῦ νομοθέτου, the intention of the lawmaker, rather than the νόμος, the law, itself in order to find the ἐπιεικές (cf. Schäublin, *MH* 34 [1977] 227ff).

100. The *locus classicus* on ἐπιείκεια, equity, correcting the ἀκριβοδίκαιον, strict justice, is Aristot. *E.N.* 1137b1ff (cf. Thuc. 5.86). On ἐπιείκεια in Greek legal practice see H. Meyer-Laurin, *Gesetz u. Billigkeit* (1965) and P. Stoffels, *Billijkheit* (1954) (cf. Fuhrmann, above n. 95). In Roman law and legal science the maxim *semper in dubiis benigniora praeferenda sunt* (Gaius *Dig.* 50.17.56) is repeatedly referred to and applied to different problems (e.g. *Dig.* 1.3.25, 4.1.7, 12.1.20, 23.3.9.2, 50.17.155.2). The importance of the new idea of *aequitas* as distinct from *iustitia* during the social conflicts in the Roman republic of the second century B.C. is discussed by Badian, *ANRW* 1 (1972) 679.

101. Roman jurisprudence originated from the application of Greek popular ethics to the highly developed system of civil rather than criminal law, as has been shown by F. Schulz, *Gesch. d. röm. Rechtswissenschaft* (1961) 87f; W. Kunkel, *Röm. Recht* (1967) 179ff; Daube (above n. 93) 131ff; and others. Extreme formalism together with abstention from genuine legislation facilitated the rise of methods by which traditional formulas and procedures were continuously interpreted afresh as expressions of intentions in individual cases. This is pointed out by G. Dulckeit, *Röm. Rechtsgeschichte* (1957) 62f.

102. Wieacker, *EntrFondHardt* 13 (1966) 291–364.

103. On the developed theory of *voluntas* in Roman jurisprudence see M. Kaser, *Röm. Privatrecht* 1 (1972) 235ff and 2 (1975) 83ff.

104. Quint. *inst.* 12.2.9: *iuris quaestio omnis aut verborum proprietate aut aequi disputatione aut voluntatis coniectura continetur.* Cf. 7.5.6 and 7.6.1.

105. Cicero correctly described the virtue of justice in Peripatetic or Middle Stoic terms (*de inv.* 2.160): *iustitia est habitus animi* (ἕξις, διάθεσις: habit, disposition) *communi utilitate conservata suam cuique tribuens dignitatem* (κατ' ἀξίαν διανεμητική: distribution according to worth). Roman jurisprudence replaced *habitus animi* by *voluntas* (Ulpian. *dig.* 1.1.10 = inst. 1.1): *iustitia est constans et perpetua voluntas ius suum cuique tribuendi.*

106. *Dig.* 50.16.219 (Papinian): *in conventionibus contrahentium voluntatem potius quam verba spectari placuit*; *dig.* 35.1.101 (Papinian): *cum in condicionibus testamentorum voluntatem potius quam verba considerari oporteat.* . . . This corresponds to the general opinion as formulated by the Younger Pliny (*ep.* 2.16; similarly 4.10 and 5.7; cf. F. Schulz, *Prinzipien d. röm. Rechts* [1954] 143). The problem of how to give the juristic interpretation of the intention of an individual was particularly important in the case of a testament (H. J. Wieling, *Testamentsauslegung* [1972] 46ff where the beginnings of the interpretation according to *voluntas* are discussed). Leaving a testament, however, was re-

garded as an essential part of the dignity and almost a duty of a Roman citizen (Plut. *Cat. ma.* 9.6; cf. Schulz, 106). An edict of Constantine (*Cod. Iust.* 1.21) therefore tried to facilitate the composition of a legally valid testament: *quam ut postremae voluntatis, postquam iam aliud velle non possunt, liber sit stilus et licitum* (*liceus* v. 1.) *quod non redit arbitrium.* The special interrelation between *verba* and *voluntas* in forensic life is presupposed by an etymology which Varro offers (*De ling. Lat.* 6.69): *Spondere est dicere; spondeo a sponte, nam id valet a voluntate.* The technical term for the utterance of a legally binding formulation is explained by its assumed semantic coherence with the notion of will (cf. S. Riccobono, Festschrift Schulz [1951] 1.302ff).

107. *Dig.* 32.25.1 (Paulus): *cum in verbis nulla ambiguitas est, non debet admitti voluntatis quaestio.*

108. Children and insane persons have no will because of their lack of intelligence (*dig.* 50.17.40 Pomponius). This corresponds to the definition of health in medical literature: the healthy man *et bene valet et suae spontis est* (Cels. *de med.* 1.1). Yet slaves and persons in the *manus* of someone else have no will either, regardless of their physical and mental sanity. Because of their being *sub imperio* they are incapable of producing a legally binding will on their own (*Dig.* 50.17.4 Ulpian): *velle non creditur qui obsequitur imperio patris vel domini.* The legal notion of will has here been separated from its psychological basis to become a tool of juristic analysis.

109. A. Beck, *Röm. Recht bei Tertullian u. Cyprian* (1930).

110. Symmachus (cos. 391), a contemporary of St. Augustine, does not use the strictly terminological language of Roman law in his official reports, but prefers rhetorical or literary formulations instead (Steinwenter, *ZRG* 74 [1931] 1ff). In his famous petition concerning the altar of the goddess Victoria he refers to the fact that he is addressing the emperor both as *praefectus urbi* and as *legatus civium* (*rel.* 3.2). He stresses that this does not cause two conflicting intentions, as one could expect: *nulla est hic dissensio voluntatum. Dissensio* alone would have rendered that idea sufficiently well. But in semi-legal usage, which was familiar to every educated Roman, the decisive factor of *voluntas* could not remain unmentioned.

111. Such a transfer of concepts repeatedly happened in the history of ideas; see H. G. Gadamer, *Wahrheit u. Methode* (1975) 290–295 and 307–323.

112. From the fifth century onwards derivatives of θέλω become increasingly frequent in theological texts, e.g. καλοθελής, benevolent (Pallad. *vit. Joh. Chrys.* 65; Leont. *vit. Joh. Eleem.* 21 p. 40 Gelzer; Leont. *vit. Sym. sal.* 162.3 Rydén) perhaps under the influence of Western discussions about *voluntas*. The monotheletic doctrine of the sixth and seventh centuries created a new terminology. Maximus Confessor distinguishes between θέλημα, which determines man's moral character, and θέλησις which only denotes striving. Θέλημα is subdivided into θ. φυσικόν (natural drive towards the better) and θ. γνωμικὸν ἢ προαιρετικόν, which depends on cognition and entails the risk of acting

against nature. Christ only had the θέλημα φυσικόν (*PG* 91.12C ff; cf. H. G. Beck, *Kirche u. theol. Lit. im byz. Reich* [1969] 294f).

113. The Greek language had innumerable words to denote the intention, content, or meaning of a text: διάνοια, γνώμη, βούλησις, δύναμις, θέλημα, προαίρεσις, etc.

BIBLIOGRAPHY

Periodicals and series listed in the Année Philologique have been
quoted accordingly; all other abbreviations are self-explanatory.

Adkins, A. W. H. *Merit and Responsibility*. Oxford 1960.

Aland, B. "Gnosis und Kirchenväter. Ihre Auseinandersetzung um die Interpretation des Evangeliums." *Gnosis* (Festschrift Jonas). Göttingen 1977, 158–215.

———. *Erwählungstheologie und Menschklassenlehre. Die Theologie des Herakleon als Schlüssel der christlichen Gnosis?* Nag Hammadi Stud. 8. Leiden 1977.

Aleith, E. *Das Paulusverständnis der Alten Kirche*. ZNTW Beiheft 18. 1937.

Amand de Mendieta, D. *Fatalisme et liberté dans l'antiquité grecque*. Louvain 1945. Reprinted 1973.

Anscombe, G. E. M. *Intention.*[2] Oxford 1963.

———. "Thought and Action in Aristotle." G. Bambrough (ed.), *New Essays in Plato and Aristotle*. London 1965, 143–158.

Armstrong, A. H. *The Background of the Doctrine "That the Intelligibles Are Not Outside the Intellect."* EntrFondHardt 5. 1957, 391–426.

———. Art. "Gottesschau." RAC (forthcoming).

Armstrong, C. B. "St. Paul's Theory of Knowledge." *ChurchQuartRev* 152 (1953) 438–452.

Badian, E. "Tib. Gracchus and the Roman Revolution." ANRW 1, 1972.

Bannach, K. *Die Lehre von der doppelten Macht Gottes bei Wilhelm von Ockham*. Veröffentl. d. Inst. f. Europ. Gesch. 75. Wiesbaden 1975.

Barclay, W. "Turning to God." Peake Memorial Lecture, 1963.

Barrett, C. K. *The Epistle to the Romans*. London 1957; 2nd ed. 1962.

Beck, A. *Römisches Recht bei Tertullian und Cyprian*. Halle 1930.

Beck, H. G. *Kirche und theologische Literatur im byzantinischen Reich*. Hdb. d. Altertumswiss. 12.2.1. München 1969.

Becker, J. *Untersuchungen zur Entstehungsgeschichte der Testamente der XII Patriarchen*. Leiden 1970.

Becker, O. *Plotin und das Problem der geistigen Aneignung*. Berlin 1940.

Beierwaltes, W. *Proklos*. Frankfurt 1965.

———. *Platonismus und Idealismus*. Frankfurt 1972.

Benz, E. *Marius Victorinus und die Entstehung der abendländischen Willensmetaphysik*. Stuttgart 1932.

Bidez, J., and Cumont, F. *Les mages hellénisés*. Paris 1938.

Bilsen, A. van. "Platos *Charmides* en de Sophrosyne." *PhilStud* 8 (1936/37) 190–206.

Blumenthal, H. J. *Plotinus' Psychology*. Amsterdam 1971.

Böhme, J. *Die Seele und das Ich im homerischen Epos*. Leipzig 1929.

Bonhoeffer, A. *Epiktet und die Stoa*. Stuttgart 1890.

Bonnard, P. *La connaissance de Dieu selon le Nouveau Testament et son milieu*. Cahiers Bibliques 3. 1965.

Botterweck, G. J. *"Gott erkennen" im Sprachgebrauch des Alten Testaments*. Bonn. Bibl. Beiträge 2. 1951.

Braun, H. *Spätjüdisch-häretischer und frühchristlicher Radikalismus* 1. Tübingen 1957.

Braunert, H. "Jüdische Diaspora und Judenfeindschaft im Altertum." *Geschichte in Wissenschaft und Unterricht* 24 (1975) 531–547.

Brinkmann, K. *Aristoteles' allgemeine und spezielle Metaphysik*. Berlin 1979.

Brown, P. *Augustine of Hippo*. London 1967.

Bultmann, R. *Theologie des Neuen Testaments*.[7] Tübingen 1977.

Burkert, W. "Zur geistesgeschichtlichen Einordnung einiger Pseudopythagorica." *EntrFondHardt* 18 (1971) 23–102.

Campenhausen, H. von. "Gebetserhörung in den überlieferten Jesusworten und in der Reflexion des Johannes." *Kerygma und Dogma* 23 (1977) 157–171.

————. *Die Entstehung der christlichen Bibel*. Stuttgart 1968.

Cancrini, A. *Syneidesis—il tema semantico della conscientia nella Grecia antica*. Roma 1970.

Catanzaro, C. J. de. "Fear, Knowledge, and Love: A Study in Old Testament Piety." *CanadJournTheol*. 9 (1963) 166–173.

Chadwick, H. Art. "Gewissen." *RAC* 10 (1978) 1025–1107.

————. *Priscillian of Avila*. Oxford 1976.

Cherniss, H. *Aristotle's Criticism of Plato and the Academy*.[2] Baltimore 1946.

Clarke, G. W. "The Date of the Oration of Tatian." *HThR* 60 (1967) 123–126.

Class, M. "Gewissensanregungen in der griechischen Tragödie." *Spudasmata* 3 (1967).

Colpe, C. "Heidnische, jüdische und christliche Überlieferung in den Schriften von Nag Hammadi 5." *JbAC* 19 (1976) 120–138.

————. Art. "Geister." *RAC* 9 (1974) 587ff.

Coulon, V. "Kritische und exegetische Bemerkungen zu Sophokles und Aristophanes." *RhM* 103 (1960) 110ff.

Courcelle, P. *Recherches sur les confessions de St. Augustin*. Paris 1950.

————. *Les lettres grecques en occident*.[2] Paris 1948.

Cranfield, C. E. B. *Critical and Exegetical Commentary on the Epistle to the Romans*.[6] Edinburgh 1975.

Cremer, F. W. *Die Chaldäischen Orakel und Jamblich de mysteriis*. Meisenheim 1969.

Cumont, F. *Lux perpetua*. Roma 1949.

O'Daly, G. J. P. *Plotinus' Philosophy of the Self*. Dublin 1973.

Daube, D. *Roman Law*. Edinburgh 1969.

————. "Error and Accident in the Bible." *RIDA* 2 (1949) 189–213.

Dawe, R. D. "Some Reflections on Ate and Hamartia." *HSCPh* 72 (1967) 89–124.

Deane, H. A. *The Political and Social Ideas of St. Augustine.* New York 1963.

Deichgräber, R. "ἄνθρωποι εὐδοκίας." *ZNTW* 51 (1960) 132f.

Dénis, A. M. *Introduction aux pseudo-épigraphes grecs d'Ancien Testament.* Leiden 1970.

Derbolav, J. *Erkenntnis und Entscheidung.* Wien/Stuttgart 1954.

Dieterle, R. "Platons Laches und Charmides." Diss. Freiburg 1966.

Dihle, A. "Gerechtigkeit." *RAC* 10 (1978) 254ff.

―――. "Zur Schicksalslehre des Bardesanes." *Kerygma und Logos* (Festschrift Andresen). Göttingen 1979.

―――. "Demut." *RAC* 3 (1957) 735–778.

―――. *Der Kanon der Zwei Tugenden.* Köln 1968.

―――. *Studien zur griechischen Biographie.*[2] Göttingen 1970.

―――. "Posidonius' System of Moral Philosophy." *JHS* 93 (1973) 50–57.

―――. "Das Satyrspiel 'Sisyphos.'" *Hermes* 105 (1977).

―――. "Ethik." *RAC* 6 (1966) 646–796.

―――. "Euripides' Medea." *SHAW* 1977, 5.

―――. "Cicero, *ad Att.* 14.1.2." *HSCPh* 82 (1978) 179ff.

―――. *Die goldene Regel.* Göttingen 1962.

Dillon, J. "The Transcendence of God in Philo." Center for Hermeneutical Studies, Berkeley. Protocol of the 16th colloquy 1975.

Dinkler, E. *Die Anthropologie Augustins.* Stuttgart 1934.

Dirlmeier, F. *Aristoteles, Nikomachische Ethik übersetzt und kommentiert von F.D.* Berlin 1956.

Dodds, E. R. "The Parmenides of Plato and the Origin of the Neoplatonic 'One.'" *CQ* 22 (1928) 129–143.

―――. "Numenius and Ammonius." *EntrFondHardt* 5 (1957) 1–62.

―――. *The Greeks and the Irrational.*[5] Berkeley 1966.

―――. "Die Rolle des Ethischen und des Politischen in der 'Orestie.'" *Wege zu Aischylos* 2. Darmstadt 1974, 149ff.

Dörrie, H. "Die Frage nach dem Transzendenten im Mittelplatonismus." *EntrFondHardt* 5 (1957) 191ff.

―――. *Gregor von Nyssa und die Philosophie.* Leiden 1976.

―――. "Die Erneuerung des Platonismus im 1. Jh. v.C." *Le neóplatonisme.* Actes du Colloque de Royaumont. 1969, 17ff.

―――. "Platons Reisen zu fernen Völkern." *Romanitas et Christianitas* (Festschrift Waszink). Amsterdam 1973, 81–98.

―――. "Die Wertung der Barbaren im Urteil der Griechen." *Antike und Universalgeschichte* (Festschrift Stier). Münster 1972, 146–175.

―――. "Emanation. Ein unphilosophisches Wort im spätantiken Denken." *Parusia, Studien zur Philosophie Platons und zur Problemgeschichte des Platonismus* (Festschrift Hirschberger). Münster [1965] 119–142.

―――. "Die platonische Theologie des Kelsos in ihrer Auseinandersetzung mit der christlichen Theologie." *NAWG* 2 (1967) 371 p.

―――. "Leid und Erfahrung." *AAWM* 5 (1956).

Dörries, H. *Die Theologie des Makarios-Symeon.* Göttingen 1978.

Drijvers, H. J. *Bardaiṣān of Edessa.* Assen 1966.

Dvornik, F. *Early Christian and Byzantine Political Philosophy* I. Washington, D.C. 1966.

Dulckeit, G. *Römische Rechtsgeschichte.²* München 1957.

Edsman, C. M. "The Body and Eternal Life." *Horae Söderblomianae. Travaux publ. par Société N. Söderblom* (Mélanges J. Pedersen) Stockholm 1946. II 33–104.

Ehlers, B. "Bardesanes von Edessa, ein syrischer Gnostiker." *ZKG* 81 (1970) 334–351.

Eichrodt, W. *Theologie des Alten Testaments* I⁷. Stuttgart/Göttingen 1962.

Erffa, C. A. von. Αἰδώς. *Philologus*, Suppl. 30, 1937.

Essen-Zeeman, C. W. van. *De plaats van de wil in de philosophie van Plotinus.* Amsterdam 1946.

Ferguson, J. *Pelagius.* London 1957.

Festugière, A. J. *Personal Religion among the Greeks.* Berkeley and Los Angeles 1954.

―――. *La révélation d'Hermes Trismégiste* III. Paris 1953.

Fascher, E. Art. "Dynamis." *RAC* 4 (1959) 432ff.

Florovsky, G. "The Concept of Creation in Saint Athanasius." *StudPatr* 6 = *TU* 81 (1962) 36–57.

Flückiger, F. "Die Werke des Gesetzes bei den Heiden." *ThZ* 8 (1952) 17–42.

Fontenrose, J. "Gods and Men in the Oresteia." *TAPhA* 102 (1971) 71–108.

Fortenbaugh, W. W. *Aristotle on Emotion.* London 1975.

Fränkel, H. *Dichtung und Philosophie des frühen Griechentums.* München 1962.

Frank, E. *Wissen, Wollen, Glauben.* GesAbhZürich 1955, 1ff.

Fritz, K. von. "Νοῦς and νοεῖν in the Homeric Poems I." *CPh* 38 (1943) 79–93.

―――. "Νοῦς, νοεῖν and their Derivatives in Pre-Socratic Philosophy 1: From the Beginnings to Parmenides." *CPh* 40 (1945) 233–242.

―――. Id., 2. "The Post-Parmenidian Period." *CPh* 41 (1946) 12–34.

Früchtel, U. *Die kosmologischen Vorstellungen bei Philon von Alexandria.* Leiden 1968.

Fuhrmann, M. "Zur Entstehung des Veroneser Gaius-Textes." *ZRGrom* 73 (1956) 341–356.

Furley, D. J. *Aristotle and Epicurus on Voluntary Actions (Two studies in the Greek Atomists).* Princeton 1967, 161–237.

Gadamer, H. G. *Wahrheit und Methode.⁴* Tübingen 1975.

Gärtner, H. A. "Beobachtungen zu Bauelementen in der antiken Historiographie." *Historia* Einz. 25, 1975.

Gager, J. C. *Moses in Greco-Roman Paganism.* New York 1972.

Gaiser, K. *Platos ungeschriebene Lehre.* Stuttgart 1963.

Gallay, J. "Dilige et quod vis fac." *RecSR* 43 (1955) 545–555.

Gauss, H. *Handkommentar zu den Dialogen Platos* 1². Bern 1954.

Gegenschatz, E. "Die Freiheit der Entscheidung in der 'consolatio philosophiae' des Boethius." *MH* 15 (1958) 110–129.

Gesché, A. "L'âme humaine de Jésus dans la christologie du IVᵉ siècle." *RHE* 54 (1959) 385–425.

Gierth, L. "Griechische Gründungsgeschichten." Diss. Freiburg 1972.

Glisson, G. L. "The Will of God as Reflected in Greek Words." Diss. Southwestern Baptist Theol. Seminary 1951.

Gnilka, J. *Die Verstockung Israels. Is. 6,9/10 in der Theologie der Synoptiker*. Stud. z. At. und NT 3. München 1961.

Görgemanns, H. *Beiträge zur Interpretation von Platons Nomoi*. München 1960.

Görler, W. *Untersuchungen zu Ciceros Philosophie*. Heidelberg 1974.

―――. "Ἀσθενὴς συγκατάθεσις. Zur stoischen Erkenntnistheorie." *Würzb-Jahrb* 3 (1977) 83–92.

Gordis, R. "The Knowledge of Good and Evil in the Old Testament and the Qumran Scrolls." *JBL* 76 (1957) 123–138.

Gould, J. *The Development of Plato's Ethics*. Cambridge 1955.

Gould, Th. *Platonic Love*. London 1963.

Groningen, B. A. von. "Le Grec et ses idées morales." *ActCongressMadv* 2 (1957) 113ff.

Guillemin, A. "Sénèque directeur d'âmes, I: L'idéal." *REL* 30 (1952) 202–219.

Gulley, N. "The Interpretation of 'No one does wrong willingly' in Plato's Dialogues." *Phronesis* 10 (1965) 82–95.

Gundel, W. Art. "Astrologie." *RAC* 1 (1950) 825–830.

Gundert, H. "Die Simonides-Interpretation in Platons Protagoras." *Hermeneia* (Festschrift Regenbogen). Heidelberg 1952, 71–93.

Gundry, R. H. *Soma in Biblical Theology*. Cambridge 1975.

Hadot, P. "Être, Vie, Pensée chez Plotin et avant Plotin." *EntrFondHardt* 5 (1957) 105–158.

―――. "L'image de la Trinité dans l'âme chez Victorinus et chez Saint Augustin." *StudPatr* 6=*TU* 81 (1962) 409–442.

―――. *Porphyre et Marius Victorinus*. Paris 1968.

Hager, F. P. *Die Vernunft und das Problem des Bösen im Rahmen der platonischen Ethik und Metaphysik*. Bern 1963.

Hardie, W. F. R. "Willing and Acting." *PhilosQuart* 21 (1971) 194–206.

Haussleiter, J. Art. "Fruitio Dei." *RAC* 8 (1972) 538–555.

Heikkinen, J. W. "Notes on ἐπιστρέφω and μετανοέω." *EcumRev* 19 (1907) 313ff.

Henry, P. *Plotin et l'occident*. Paris 1934.

Hermann, K. F. and Thalheim, Th. *Griech. Rechtsaltertümer*. Tübingen 1884.

Hesse, F. "Das Verstockungsproblem im Alten Testament." *ZAW* Beiheft 74 (1955) 25f.

Hill, D. *Greek Words and Hebrew Meanings*. Cambridge 1967.

Hoerber, R. G. "Plato's Lesser Hippias." *Phronesis* 7 (1962) 121–131.

250   Bibliography

Holte, E. R. *Béatitude et sagesse. St. Augustin et le problème de la fin de l'homme dans la philosophie ancienne.* Paris 1962.

Huart, P. Γνώμη *chez Thucydide et ses contemporains.* Paris 1972.

Hunzinger, C. H. "Neues Licht auf Lc 2, 14 ἄνθρωποι εὐδοκίας." *ZNTW* 44 (1952/53) 85–90.

———. "Ein weiterer Beleg zu Lc. 2, 14: ἄνθρωποι εὐδοκίας." *ZNTW* 49 (1958) 129–130.

Hyland, D. A. "Ἔρως, Ἐπιθυμια, and Φιλια in Plato. *Phronesis* 13 (1968) 32–46.

Immisch, O. "Agatharchidea." *SHAW* 1919, 77ff.

Inge, W. R. *The Philosophy of Plotinus* ³ 1 and 2. London 1929.

Ingenkamp, H. G. "Zur stoischen Lehre vom Sehen." *RhM* 114 (1971) 240–246.

Jaeger, W. *Paideia* 2. Berlin/Leipzig 1944.

Jäger, G. *Nus in Platons Dialogen.* Göttingen 1967.

Jewett, R. *St. Paul's Anthropological Terms.* Arbeiten zur Geschichte des antiken Judentums und des Urchristentums 10. Leiden 1971.

Jørgensen, J. *Psykologi pa biologisk Grundlag.* Kopenhagen 1946.

Jonas, H. *Augustin und das paulinische Freiheitsproblem.* ² Göttingen 1965.

———. "Evangelium Veritatis and Valentinianism" *TU* 81 (1962) 96ff.

———. "Philosophische Meditation über Paulus, Römerbrief cap. 7." *Zeit und Geschichte* (Festschrift Bultmann). Tübingen 1964, 557–570.

Joüon, P. "Les verbes βούλομαι et θέλω." *RecSR* 30 (1940) 227–238.

Jung, C. G. *Psychologische Typen.* Zürich 1925.

Kahl, W. *Die Lehre vom Primat des Willens bei Augustin, Duns Scotus und Descartes.* Strassburg 1886.

Käsemann, F. *An die Römer.* Handbuch zum Neues Testamente No. 8. Tübingen 1973.

Kaser, M. *Das römische Privatrecht.* Hdb. d. Altertumswissenschaft 10.3.3.1–2. 1959.

Kenny, A. *Action, Emotion, and Will.* London 1960.

———. *Free Will and Responsibility.* London 1978.

———. "The Practical Syllogism and Incontinence." *Phronesis* 11 (1966) 163ff.

Kenyon, F. *Greek Papyri of the British Museum.* London 1893.

Kidd, J. G. "Posidonius on Emotions." A. A. Long (ed.), *Problems in Stoicism.* London 1971, 200–206.

Kloesel, H. "Libertas." *Römische Wertbegriffe.* Wege der Forschung 34. Darmstadt 1967.

Knuth, Z. *Der Sündenbegriff bei Philon von Alexandrien.* Jena 1934.

König, E. *Augustinus Philosophus.* München 1970.

Koschorke, K. "'Suchen und Finden' in der Auseinandersetzung zwischen gnostischem und kirchl.Christentum." *Wort und Dienst* 14 (1977) 51ff.

———. "Eine gnostische Pfingstpredigt. Zur Auseinandersetzung zwischen gnostischem u. kirchl.Christentum am Beispiel der 'Epistula Petri ad Philippum.'" *ZthK* 74 (1977) 323.

―――. "Der gnostische Traktat 'Testimonium Veritatis' aus dem Nag Hammadi-Codex IX. Eine Übersetzung." *ZNW* 69 (1978) 91.

Krämer, H. J. "Zu Platon Politeia 509B." *AGPh* 51 (1969) 1–30.

Krafft, P. *Beiträge zur Wirkungsgeschichte des älteren Arnobius.* Wiesbaden 1966.

Kube, J. *Ἀρετή und Τέχνη.* Berlin 1969.

Kunkel, W. *Römisches Recht.*² München 1967.

Kusch, H. "Studien über Augustinus" (Festschrift für Franz Dornseiff zum 65. Geburtstag). Leipzig 1953, 124–200.

Kuyper, L. J. "To Know Good and Evil." *Interpretation* 1 (1947) 490ff.

Langerbeck, H. *Aufsätze zur Gnosis hrg. v. H. Dörrie.* Göttingen 1967, 157–163.

Latte, K. "Mord." *PW* 16 (1933) 278/89=*Kleine Schriften.* München 1969, 380ff.

Leumann, M. *Homerische Wörter.* Basel 1950.

Lietzmann, H. *Kommentar zum Römerbrief. Handbuch zum NT* 3.1. Tübingen 1919.

Lloyd, A. C. "Activity and Description in Aristotle and the Stoa." *PBA* 56 (1970).

Lloyd-Jones, H. *The Justice of Zeus.* Berkeley 1970.

Løgstrup, K. "Wille, Wahl, Freiheit." *Zeit und Geschichte* (Festschrift Bultmann). Tübingen 1964, 517–530.

Long, A. A. *Problems in Stoicism.* London 1971.

Lorenz, R. "Augustinliteratur seit dem Jubiläum 1954." *ThRdschau* 25 (1959) 1.

―――. "Die Herkunft des augustinischen FRUI DEO." *ZKG* 64 (1952/53) 34–60.

Lottin, O. *Psychologie et morale aux XIIᵉ et XIIIᵉ siècles.* Gembloux 1958.

Lührmann, D. "Glaube." *RAC* 11 (1979) 48–122.

MacDowell, D. M. *Athenian Homicide Laws.* Manchester 1963.

Magie, D. *Roman Rule in Asia Minor* I. Princeton 1950.

Maier, G. *Mensch und freier Wille.* Tübingen 1971.

Malingrey, A. M. *Philosophia.* Paris 1961.

Marietta, Don E. Jr. "Conscience in Greek Stoicism." *Numen* 17 (1970) 176ff.

Marrou, H. J. *St. Augustin et la fin de la culture antique* 1. Paris 1938.

Martens, E. *Das selbstbezügliche Wissen in Platons Charmides.* München 1973.

Maschke, R. *Die Willenslehre im griechischen Recht.* Darmstadt 1926. 2nd edition 1968.

May, E. *Schöpfung aus dem Nichts.* Berlin 1978.

Meijering, E. P. "The Doctrine of the Will of the Trinity in the Orations of Gregor of Nazianzus." *NederlTheolTijdschr* 21 (1973) 26–33.

―――. "Wie platonisierten Christen? Zur Grenzziehung zwischen Platonismus, kirchlichem Credo und patristischer Theologie." *VChr* 28 (1974) 15–28.

————. Ἦν ποτε ὅτε οὐκ ἦν. *VChr* 28 (1974) 161–168.

————. "Die 'physische Erlösung' in der Theologie des Irenäus." *Nederl-ArchvKerkGesch* 53 (1972) 147–159.

————. *Orthodoxy and Platonism in Athanasius.*² Leiden 1974.

————. "Irenaeus' Relation to Philosophy in the Light of his Concept of Free Will." *Romanitas et Christianitas* (Festschrift Waszink). Amsterdam 1973. 221ff.

Merki, H. Ὁμοίωσις θεῷ. Bern 1956.

Merrill, E. H. *Qumran and Predestination.* Leiden 1975.

Meyer-Laurin, H. *Gesetz und Billigkeit im attischen Prozess.* Weimar 1965.

Michel, O. *Römerbrief.* Meyers kritisch-exegetischer Kommentar zum NT.¹¹ Göttingen 1957.

Milo, R. *Aristotle on Practical Knowledge and Weakness of Will.* The Hague 1966.

Moore, G. Foot. "Schicksal und freier Wille in der jüdischen Philosophie bei Josephus." *Wege der Forschung* 84 (1973) 167–189.

Moran, W. L. "The Ancient Near Eastern Background of the Love of God in Deuteronomy." *CatholBiblQuart.* 25 (1963) 77–87.

Mortley, R. "Negative Theology and Abstraction in Plotinus." *AJPh* 96 (1975) 363–377.

————. *Connaissance religieuse et herméneutique chez Clément d'Alexandrie.* Leiden 1973.

Moule, C. F. D. "St. Paul and Dualism." *NTS* 12 (1965/66) 106–123.

Mühlenberg, E. *Die Unendlichkeit Gottes bei Gregor von Nyssa.* Göttingen 1964.

————. "Das Verständnis des Bösen in neuplatonischer und frühchristlicher Sicht." *Kerygma und Dogma* 15 (1969) 226–238.

————. "Das Problem der Offenbarung bei Philo." *ZNTW* 64 (1973) 1–18.

————. "Verité et bonté de Dieu." Kannengiesser (ed.), *Politique et théologie chez Athanase.* Paris 1973.

————. "Weiviele Erlösungen kennt der Gnostiker Herakleon." *ZNTW* 66 (1975) 170–193.

————. "Synergism in Gregory of Nyssa." *ZNTW* 68 (1977) 93–122.

Müller, C. W. *Die Kurzdialoge der Appendix Platonica.* München 1975.

Neuhausen, K. A. *De voluntarii notione Platonica et Aristotelica.* Wiesbaden 1967.

Nikiprowetsky, V. *La doctrine de l'elenchos chez Philon, ses resonances philosophiques et sa portée religieuse.* Colloques nationaux du centre national de la recherche scientifique. Paris 1967.

Nilsson, M. P. *Geschichte der griechischen Religion.*³ München 1974.

North, H. *Sophrosyne, Self-Knowledge and Self-Restraint in Greek Literature.* Ithaca 1966.

Oehler, K. "Aristotle on Self-Knowledge." *PAPhS* 118 (1974) 493–506.

Onians, R. B. *The Origins of European Thought.* Cambridge 1951.

Opstelten, J. C. "Beschouwingen naar aanleiding van het outbreken van ons ethisch wilsbegrip in de oud-griekse ethiek." *MedKonAkadWet* N. R. 22 Afd. Letterk. 1 (1959) 16ff.

Osborne, E. F. *The Philosophy of Clement of Alexandria*. Cambridge 1957.

Otto, S. "Natura und Dispositio. Untersuchung zum Naturbegriff und zur Denkform Tertullians." *MünchTheolStud* 19 (1960) 19ff.

Pack, R. A. "On Guilt and Error in Senecan Tragedy." *TAPhA* 71 (1940) 360–371.

Pagels, E. A. "The Valentinian Claim to Esoteric Exegesis of Romans as Basis for Anthropological Theory." *VChr* 26 (1972) 241ff.

Pelletier, A. "Deux expressions de la notion de conscience dans le judaïsme hellenistique et le christianisme naissant." *REG* 80 (1967) 363–371.

Pétrément, S. *Le dualisme chez Platon, des gnostiques et les manichéens*. Paris 1947.

Pfligersdörfer, G. "Zu den Grundlagen des augustinischen Begriffspaares uti-frui." *WS* N.F. 5 (1971) 195–224.

Places, E. des. *Syngeneia. La Parenté de l'homme avec dieu d'Homère à la patristique*. Paris 1964.

Plinval, G. de. *Pélage*. Lausanne 1943.

Pohlenz, M. "Philosophie und Erlebnis in Senecas Dialogen." *NAWG* (1941) 247ff.

———. *Die Stoa*² II. Göttingen 1949.

Pringsheim, F. *The Greek Law of Sale*. Weimar 1950.

Rad, G. von. *Theologie des Alten Testaments*⁶ 1. München 1969.

———. *Weisheit in Israel*. Neukirchen 1970.

Raisänen, H. "The Idea of Divine Hardening." *PublFinnExegSoc* 25 (1975).

Regenbogen, O. *Kleine Schriften*. München 1961.

Reinhardt, K. "Poseidonios." *PW* 22 (1954) 764ff.

Riccobono, S. "La volontà nella prassi guidiziaria guidata dai pontifici" (Festschrift Fritz Schulz) 1. Weimar 1951, 302–309.

Ricken, F. *Der Lustbegriff in der Nikomachischen Ethik des Aristoteles*. Göttingen 1975.

Riesenfeld, H. *Zum Gebrauch von θελῶ (sic) im NT*. Uppsala 1936.

Rist, J. M. "Plotinus on Matter and Evil." *Phronesis* 6 (1961) 154–166.

———. *Plotinus: The Road to Reality*. Cambridge 1965.

———. "Augustine on Free Will and Predestination." *JThS* 20 (1969) 420–447.

———. *Stoic Philosophy*. Cambridge 1969.

———. "Prohairesis: Proclus, Plotinus et alii." *EntrFondHardt* 21 (1974) 103–122.

Ritter, A. *Die Gnadenlehre Gregors von Nyssa: Gregor von Nyssa und die Philosophie*, hrg. von H. Dörrie. Leiden 1976, 195–236.

Robert, L. "Trois oracles de la Théosophie et un prophète d'Apollon." *CRAI* (1968) 586–599.

Roy, O. du. *L'intelligence de la foi en la trinité chez St. Augustin. Genèse de sa théologie trinitaire jusqu'en 391*. Paris 1966.

Rudolph, K. (ed.). *Gnosis und Gnostizismus*. Darmstadt 1975.

Rydbeck, L. *Fachprosa, vermeintliche Volkssprache und Neues Testament*. Uppsala 1967.

Sandbach, F. H. "Phantasia Kataleptike." A. A. Long (ed.), *Problems in Stoicism.* London 1971, 9–21.

Santas, G. "Aristotle on Practical Inference, the Explanation of Action and Akrasia." *Phronesis* 14 (1969) 162ff.

Sartre, J.-P. *Ist der Existentialismus ein Humanismus?* Zürich 1947.

Scarpat, G. *La lettera 65 di Seneca.* Brescia 1967.

Schäublin, C. *Untersuchungen zur Methode und Herkunft der antiochenischen Exegese.* Köln 1974.

————. "Homerum ex Homero." *MH* 34 (1977) 221–227.

Schaffner, O. *Christliche Demut.* Würzburg 1939.

Scheibe, E. "Über Relativbegriffe in der Philosophie Platons." *Phronesis* 12 (1967) 28–49.

Schindler, A. "Gnade." *RAC* 11 (1979).

Schmaus, M. *Die psychologische Trinitätslehre des hl. Augustinus.* Münster 1927.

Schmid, W. "Epikur." *RAC* 5 (1962) 682–819.

Schmidt, C. "Plotins Stellung zum Gnostizismus und zum kirchlichen Christentum." *TU* 20 (1901).

Schmidt, H. *Die Anthropologie Philons von Alexandrien.* Würzburg 1933.

Schneider, C. *Information und Absicht bei Thukydides.* Göttingen 1974.

Schönlein, P. W. "Zur Entstehung eines Gewissensbegriffs bei Griechen und Römern." *RhM* 112 (1969) 289–305.

Schottroff, L. "Der Glaube und die feindliche Welt." *ZNTW* Beih. 37 (1969) 63ff.

Schröder, E. *Plotins Abhandlung πόθεν τὰ κακά.* Borna-Leipzig 1916.

Schröder, H. O. "Fatum (Heimarmene)." *RAC* 7 (1969) 525–636.

Schubart, W. "Das hellenistische Königsideal nach Inschriften und Papyri." *APF* 12 (1937) 1ff.

Schulz, F. *Geschichte der römischen Rechtswissenschaft.* Weimar 1961.

————. *Prinzipien des römischen Rechts.* Berlin 1954.

Schulze, W. *Quaestiones Epicae.* Gütersloh 1892.

Schweizer, E. "Rm. 1,3 und der Gegensatz von Fleisch und Geist vor und bei Paulus." *Neotestamentica.* Zürich 1963, 180–189.

Schwyzer, H.-R. "'Bewusst' und 'unbewusst' bei Plotin." *EntrFondHardt* 5 (1957) 341–390.

Schwyzer, R. "Plotinos." *PW* 21 (1951) 471ff.

Seel, O. "Zur Vorgeschichte des Gewissensbegriffs im altgriechischen Denken." (Festschrift Dornseiff). Leipzig 1957, 291–319.

Sedley, D. "Diodorus Cronus and Hellenistic Philosophy." *PCPhS* 23 (1977) 74–120.

Segally, G. "La volontà del Figlio e del Padre nella tradizione sinottica." *RivBibl* 2 (1964) 257–284.

Seidl, E. *Ptolemäische Rechtsgeschichte.* Glückstadt-Hamburg² 1962.

Severus, E. von. "Gebet." *RAC* 8 (1972) 1134–1258.

Sherman, S. L. and Curtis, J. B. "Divine-human Conflicts in the Old Testament." *JNES* 28 (1969) 231–246.

Snell, B. "Die Ausdrücke für den Begriff des Wissens." *Phil. Untersuchungen* 29 (1924).

――――. Review of Zucker, *Syneidesis-Conscientia*. *Gnomon* 6 (1930) 21–30.

――――. "Das frühste Zeugnis über Sokrates." *Philologus* 97 (1948) 125–134.

――――. *Neun Tage Latein*. Göttingen 1955.

――――. *Tyrtaios und die Sprache des Epos*. Göttingen 1969.

Solmsen, F. *Plato's Theology*. Ithaca, N.Y. 1942.

――――. "Bad Shame and Related Problems in Phaedra's Speech." *Hermes* 101 (1973) 420–441.

――――. "Early Christian Interest in the Theory of Demonstration. *Romanitas et Christianitas*" (Festschrift Waszink). Amsterdam 1973. 283ff.

Spanneut, M. "La notion de nature des Stoiciens aux Pères de l'Église." *Rech. de Théol. Anc. et Méd.* 37 (1970) 165–173.

Spoerri, W. *Späthellenistische Berichte über Welt, Kultur und Götter*. Basel 1959.

Stacey, W. D. *The Pauline View of Man in Relation to its Judaic and Hellenistic Background*. London 1956.

Stallmach, J. *Ate*. Meisenheim 1966.

Stead, G. C. "The Platonism of Arius." *JThS* 15 (1964) 16–31.

Steinwenter, A. "Die Briefe des Qu. Aur. Symmachus als Rechtsquelle." *ZRG* 74 (1957) 1–25.

Stern, H. S. "The Knowledge of Good and Evil." *VT* 8 (1958) 405–418.

Stern, M. *Greek and Latin Authors on Jews and Judaism* I. Jerusalem 1974.

Stoffels, P. *Billijkheit in het Oud-Griekse Recht*. Amsterdam 1954.

Stroh, W. *Taxis und Taktik*. Stuttgart 1975.

Strawson, P. W. *Freedom and Resentment*. London 1974.

Stroud, R. S. *Drakon's Law on Homicide*. Berkeley 1968.

Strunk, K. *Semantisches und Formales zum Verhältnis von idg.* krátu / xratu *und griech.* κρατύς (Monumentum H. S. Nyberg II). Leiden/Teheran 1975.

Szlezák, T. A. *Pseudo-Archytas, Über die Kategorien*. Berlin 1972.

Taubenschlag, R. *The Law of Greco-Roman Egypt*. New York 1944.

Theiler, W. *Die Vorbereitung des Neuplatonismus*. Berlin 1930.

――――. *Porphyrios und Augustinus*. Halle 1933.

――――. Review of Benz, *Marius Victorinus und die Entwicklung der abendländischen Willensmetaphysik*. *Gnomon* 10 (1934) 493–499.

――――. "Tacitus und die antike Schicksalslehre." *Phyllobolia f. Peter von der Mühll*. Basel 1946, 35–90.

――――. "Gott und Seele im kaiserzeitlichen Denken." *EntrFondHardt* 3 (1955) 65–94.

――――. *Forschungen zum Neuplatonismus*. Berlin 1966.

Thraede, K. "Das antike Rom in Augustins *De civitate Dei*." *JbAC* 20 (1977) 90ff.

Thrall, M. E. "The Pauline use of συνείδησις." *NTS* 14 (1967) 118–125.

Tsekourakis, D. *Studies in the Terminology of Early Stoics*. *Hermes* Einzelschriften 32. 1974.

Unnik, W. C. van. "An Attack on the Epicureans by Flavius Josephus." *Ro-*

manitas et Christianitas (Festschrift Waszink). Amsterdam 1973.

Verdenius, W. J. "Der Logosbegriff bei Heraklit und Parmenides." *Phronesis* 12 (1967) 91–97.

Vernant, J. P. and Vidal-Naquet, P. *Mythe et tragédie en Grèce ancienne*. Paris 1977.

P. Vidal-Naquet. See P. Vernant.

Vlastos, G. "Equality and Justice in Early Greek Cosmology." *CPh* 41 (1947) 106ff.

Voelke, A. J. *RThPh* 11 (1961) 1ff.

———. *L'idée de la volonté dans le stoicisme*. Bibliothèque de philosophie contemporaine. Paris 1973.

Vööbus, A. "Aphrahat." *JbAC* 3 (1960) 152–155.

Wagner, H. *Aristoteles Physik*. Berlin 1967.

Wallis, R. T. "The Idea of Conscience in Philo of Alexandria." Center for Hermeneutical Studies, Berkeley. Colloquium 1975.

Walsh, J. *Aristotle's Concept of Moral Weakness*. New York 1963.

Walzer, R. "Galenos." *RAC* 8 (1972) 777–786.

Warren, E. W. "Consciousness in Plotinus." *Phronesis* 9 (1964) 83–97.

Wartelle, A. "Poète grec et prophète d'Israel; Eschyle et Isaie." *BAG* 13 (1967) 373–383.

Waszink, H. J. "Der Platonismus und die altchristliche Gedankenwelt." *EntrFondHardt* 3 (1955) 139–179.

———. "Porphyrios und Numenios." *EntrFondHardt* 12 (1960) 33–84.

Watson, G. *The Stoic Theory of Knowledge*. Belfast 1966.

Weber, M. *Wirtschaft und Gesellschaft*.⁴ Tübingen 1956.

Wehrli, F. *Die Schule des Aristoteles* 10. Bern 1959.

———. *Hauptrichtungen des griechischen Denkens*. Zurich 1964.

Wellek, A. *Die Polarität im Aufbau des Charakters*. Bern 1950.

Wellmann, R. R. "The Question Posed at *Charmides* 165a–166c." *Phronesis* 9 (1964) 107–113.

Wendland, P. *Philos Schrift von der Vorsehung*. Berlin 1892.

Wesel, U. *Rhetorische Statuslehre und Gesetzesauslegung der römischen Juristen*. Köln 1967.

Whitman, C. R. *Sophocles*. Cambridge, Mass. 1951.

Whittaker, J. "Moses Atticizing." *Phoenix* 21 (1967) 196–201.

———. "Neopythagoreanism and Negative Theology." *SO* 44 (1969) 109–124.

———. Ἐπέκεινα νοῦ καὶ οὐσίας. *VChr* 23 (1969) 91–104.

Wickert, U. *Studien zu den Paulus-Kommentaren Theodors von Mopsuestia*. Berlin 1963.

———. "Glauben und Denken bei Tertullian und Origenes." *ZTkH* 62 (1965) 153–177.

Wieacker, F. "Die XII Tafeln in ihrem Jahrhundert." *EntrFondHardt* 13 (1966) 291–364.

Wieling, H. J. *Testamentsauslegung im römischen Recht*. München 1972.

Wifstrand, A. "Die griechischen Verba für wollen." *Eranos* 40 (1942) 16–36.

Wilamowitz, U. von. *Griechisches Lesebuch* II². Berlin 1926.

Willink, C. W. "Some Problems of Text and Interpretation in the Hippolytus." *CQ* 62 (1968) 11ff.

Wisse, F. *Zum Hellenismus der Schriften von Nag Hammadi.* Göttinger Orientforschungen, Reihe 6, Bd. 2. Wiesbaden 1975.

Witte, R. *Die Wissenschaft vom Guten und Bösen.* Untersuchungen zur antiken Literatur und Geschichte 5. 1970.

Wlosok, A. "Laktanz und die philosophische Gnosis." *AHAW* 2 1960.

Wolff, H. W. "Wissen um Gott bei Hosea." *Gessammelte Studien zum AT.* München 1964, 182–205.

——. "Das Motiv der Umkehr in der alttestamentlichen Prophetie." *Gesammelte Studien zum AT.* München 1964.

——. *Anthropologie des Alten Testaments.* München 1974.

Wolfson, H. A. "The Knowability and Describability of God in Plato and Aristotle." *HSCPh* 56–57 (1947) 233–249.

Ziesler, J. A. *The Meaning of Righteousness in Paul.* Cambridge 1972.

Zimmerli, W. *Erkenntnis Gottes nach dem Buche Ezechiel.* Theol. Bücherei 19. 1969.

Zintzen, C. "Die Wertung von Mystik und Magie in der Neuplatonischen Philosophie." *RhM* 108 (1965) 71–100.

——. "Geister (Dämonen)." *RAC* 9 (1976) 688–797.

Zucker, F. Συνείδησις—*conscientia.* Jena 1928.

——. "Verbundenheit von Erkenntnis und Wille." *Studies Presented to D. M. Robinson* 2. 1953, 1063–1071 = *Semantica, Rhetorica, Ethica.* Berlin 1963.

Index of Greek and Latin Words

(Cross-references refer to the General Index)

Index of Passages Cited

OLD TESTAMENT
(incl. Apocryphal Texts)

TESTAMENTUM NOVUM

LATIN AUTHORS

General Index

Anger. *See* Ὀργή
Astrology, 2, 108

Body and soul, 25f, 28, 128

Causation, types of, 103, 110f
Chance, 41, 102, 104f, 109
Cognition of God: from the order of
    nature, 2f, 91 (*see also* Nature);
    through revelation, 7, 94ff
Cognition of God's imperceptibility,
    14f, 43f, 94f, 120f. *See also* The-
    ology, negative
Conscience. *See* Συνείδησις
Creation, creator, 2ff, 71f, 91f, 112f,
    116f, 126

Evil, origin of, 60f, 99, 128f

Faith, 75ff, 129. *See also* Πίστις
Fate, 44, 103ff
Flesh and spirit, 128f. *See also* Σάρξ,
    Πνεῦμα
Freedom of choice, 41, 46, 59, 68f,
    95f, 104f, 107, 111f, 114, 119,
    126f, 132, Appendix II

Grace of God, 75f, 87, 91ff, 101, 111,
    129ff

Humility, 85f, 129ff

Intellect: and emotion, 38, 54, 69,
    83, 93f, 97, 101, 104, 119, 128,
    142; and intention, 21, 26ff, 36ff,
    69ff, 101, 108, 110ff, 115, 119,
    124, 142

Judgement, final, 79ff, 89, 109

Knowledge, types of, 46, 50ff, 56,
    59f, 88, 94f, 119f

Law, divine, 15f, 72f, 78f, 80f, 112
Love, 52ff, 75, 87f, 130ff

Matter and spirit, 53, 66f, 84, 90,
    100f, 103f, 124f, 128

Nature, rational order of, 1ff, 18, 36f,
    40, 55, 106, 142

Obedience, 13ff, 71ff, 93, 97, 111f

Philosophy, types of, 11ff, 106
"Philosophy of the Barbarians," 7
Power of God, 3f, 92f, 101, 112
Prayer, 3f
Predetermination, 41, 46, 59f, 71, 99,
    101, 107f, 126, Appendix II
Pride, 84ff, 111, 128
Progress, moral, 96, 111, 115, 120f,
    135
Providence, 99, 103

Salvation, 79, 89, 100f, 106f, 126,
    132. *See also* Σωτηρία
Self-cognition, 44ff, 52f, 110f
Stiffheartedness, 75f, 110f, 119
Synergism, 129f

Theology, negative, 10f, 120
Theory and practice, 59, 65f
Triad, Chaldean, 107, 114, 116, 124
Triad, Neoplatonic, 113f, 117, 123f, 127

267

Designer: William Snyder
Compositor: G & S Typesetters, Inc.
Text: Linotron 202 Garamond
Display: Phototypositor Weiss
Printer: Braun-Brumfield, Inc.
Binder: Braun-Brumfield, Inc.